3D Online Multimedia & Games

Processing, Transmission and Visualization

3D Online Multimedia & Games

Processing, Transmission and Visualization

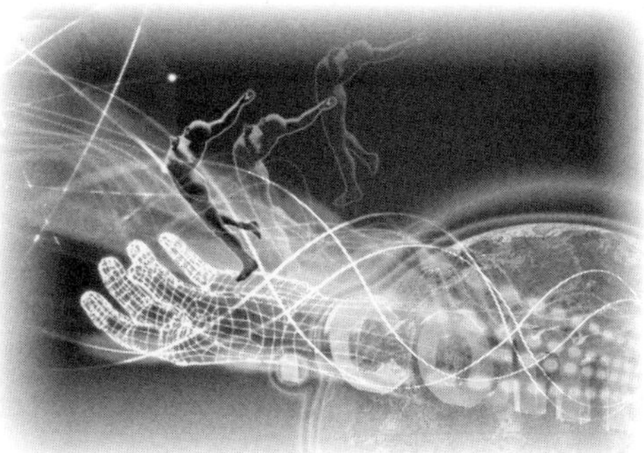

Irene Cheng
University of Alberta, Canada
University of Pennsylvania, USA

Guido M. Cortelazzo
University of Padova, Italy

Anup Basu
University of Alberta, Canada

Satish K Tripathi
SUNY Buffalo, USA

World Scientific

NEW JERSEY • LONDON • SINGAPORE • BEIJING • SHANGHAI • HONG KONG • TAIPEI • CHENNAI

Published by

World Scientific Publishing Co. Pte. Ltd.
5 Toh Tuck Link, Singapore 596224
USA office: 27 Warren Street, Suite 401-402, Hackensack, NJ 07601
UK office: 57 Shelton Street, Covent Garden, London WC2H 9HE

British Library Cataloguing-in-Publication Data
A catalogue record for this book is available from the British Library.

3D ONLINE MULTIMEDIA AND GAMES
Processing, Transmission and Visualization

ISBN-13 978-981-270-587-7
ISBN-10 981-270-587-2

Printed in Singapore by World Scientific Printers

Contents

List of Contributors

Prof. David Taubman,
University of New South Wales,
Sydney, Australia

Prof. Lindsay MacDonald,
London College of Communications, UK

Dr. Pietro Zanuttig,
University of Padova, Italy

Nilcola Brusco,
University of Padova, Italy

Luca Ballan,
University of Padova, Italy

Yinzhi Yu,
Microsoft Research, Washington, USA

Asheq Khan,
University of Buffalo, USA

Other contributors,
Computing Science Department,
University of Alberta, USA

Chapter 1

Introduction

1.1 Overview

Over the years the word "Multimedia" has meant a variety of things to different people. In this book we will use multimedia to cover image, video and 3D (image and three-dimensional model) content; as well as consider the network transmission related to these types of content.

Our focus will be on "Online" multimedia applications and related technologies. The requirements and challenges for online applications differ significantly from offline or standalone applications. For example, in a standalone computer gaming environment the size of the images and 3D models being used may not be an issue of major concern as long as there is sufficient memory on the computer being used, while the time taken to display 3D objects would be a primary concern to enhance the speed of interactivity. For online gaming, however, the speed of communication among a collection of players located remotely from one another is an important factor in the design.

A standalone imaging system, that is designed to record diagnostic information for doctors, only needs to record data with a high enough quality to detect abnormal conditions. An online Tele-health application that is designed to help doctors make diagnostic decisions on patients located at a remote location would need to deal with several other issues, such as: (i) Efficient storage and representation of the multimedia information on patients so that fast retrieval and visualization is feasible; (ii) The network conditions that exist between the site recording the data (patient site) and the site visualizing the data (doctor site); (iii) Possibly allowing progressive update of a visual object through interaction with the doctor; (iv) Permitting modification or annotation on the object; (v) Supporting collaborative diagnosis among multiple doctors located at different sites.

A key difference in several approaches discussed in this book, compared to usual algorithms, is taking perceptual quality into account. Traditional methods of evaluating "quality" of multimedia objects relied on numerical measures, such as signal-to-noise ratio, which treated visual data purely as a collection of numbers and computed an estimate of the difference between the original information recorded and the data being observed. From the viewpoint of a human observer, however, the only thing that counts is the perceived quality of one object relative to another; *i.e.*, does one object look "better" than another and if so "how much better." Special attention is given to designing a metric to estimate the perceptual quality of 3D objects; in this context, setting up an environment to measure "subjective" human evaluations and statistical methods for estimating the reliability of the subjective judgments are discussed.

The topics discussed roughly cover five categories: some networking issues in online multimedia, TexMesh simplification and view independent transmission, view dependant transmission and server side rendering, content and background creation, and creating simple online games. Under networking issues we consider transmission strategies based on actively monitoring network resources, for one or more servers, and accordingly adapting or scaling the data transmitted. The objective is to provide users service quality close to a level desired by them; an area often referred to as Quality-of-Service (QoS) based delivery. A survey of strategies for wireless multimedia communication is also covered in Chapter 3. Chapters 4 to 9 cover topics related to joint texture-mesh (TexMesh) simplification, adaptive online transmission based on available bandwidth, perceptual factors and packet loss in wireless or unreliable networks. Predictive methods and rate-distortion optimization for server side rendering are discussed in Chapters 10 and 11. A brief overview of techniques for content and background creation is given in Chapters 12 and 13. Finally, some examples of simple networked online games are provided in Chapters 14 and 15.

Different strategies for 3D scene representation can be considered for online applications, including 3D TV transmission [Kang *et al.* (2000)]. Strategies can assume fixed geometry and static texture to view-dependent rendering to image based rendering with or without geometry [Magnor *et al.* (2003)]. In this book we will discuss client side rendering, with static geometry and texture, and server side view-dependant rendering, considering perceptual quality and rate-distortion optimization. Issues related to image based rendering will not be considered primarily to limit the scope of the book, but also to keep our focus more on applications with limited bandwidth.

In previous remote visualization transmission strategies, as shown by solid lines in Fig. 1.1 [Kang *et al.* (2000)], the client's request defines the processing required at the server. In contrast, the strategies described in this book involve equally important server decisions in order to generate the best possible geometry and texture rendering at the client. In Fig. 1.1 the new strategies are indicated by dotted lines, which involve both client and server policies in the remote visualization framework.

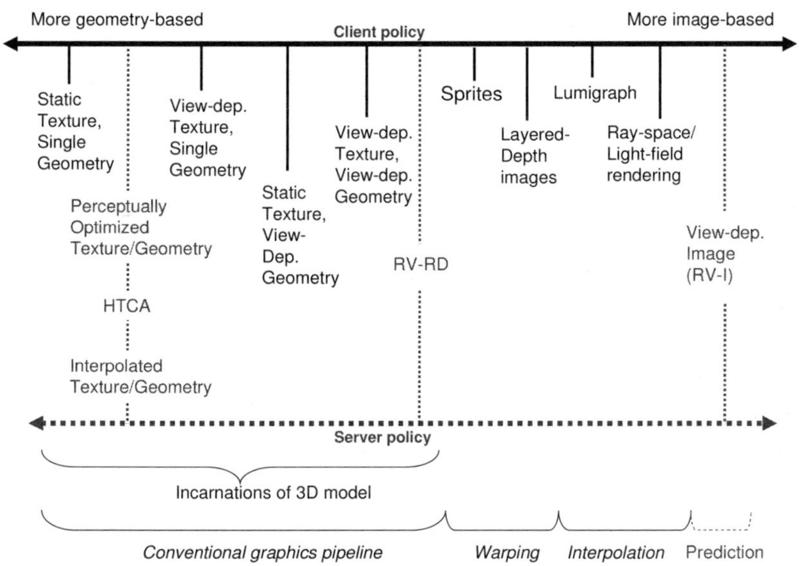

Fig. 1.1 Strategies for online 3D transmission.

The target audience for this book includes both students and researchers in multimedia, and online multimedia developers. It is expected that the readers will have a basic knowledge of JAVA or a related language, be quite familiar with the Internet, and have a keen interest in online applications. Keeping this broad group in mind several aspects of the implementations are discussed, including JAVA3D and data representations. Some of the source and object codes relating to implementations are also provided.

The implementation related discussions in this book are based on the JAVA^{TM} language. For 3D applications we will consider the JAVA3D language. An overview of the JAVA3D language is given in an online Appendix for convenience. The description of the servers relies on the open source Apache code. The primary motivation behind choosing these software platforms is that they are available to all students, researchers and practitioners free of cost; also, there are various discussion forums where development and debugging information can be obtained as and when needed.

Another topic related to a 3D multimedia environment is the representation of 3D data. We limit the scope of the current manuscript to a collection of static 3D objects which can collectively constitute a dynamic scene. 3D objects are created using surface images (texture) and a triangulated set of vertices (mesh) representing a 3D model. Other 3D representations, such as voxels, will not be discussed.

1.2 Networking Issues in Online Multimedia

Strategies for transmission of multimedia information are dependant on ongoing monitoring of network resources. Users (clients) in an online environment often have minimum requirements on the performance of an application. Performance may be measured in terms of response time for a request, jitter in video, quality of 3D models, and so on.

Providing QoS guarantees in a deterministic fashion is virtually impossible in a dynamic network, such as the Internet, where the available bandwidth can fluctuate significantly from one period of time to the next. We therefore focus on statistical approaches to bandwidth monitoring and providing QoS guarantees. In Chapter 2 an algorithm for optimal bandwidth monitoring given a single server, communicating with a client, is discussed. What is unique about this monitoring approach is that the amount of bandwidth testing is dependant on the current statistical properties of the network. Prior approaches often relied on prediction based on historical data; the problem with such methods is that the behavior of the Internet can change considerably over time, thus estimate based on data collected over the last 15 minutes, for example, may not be a good indicator of the expected characteristics in the next 15 minutes. Thus, the approach presented for bandwidth monitoring uses a starting fraction of the current time interval, in which a visual object is to be transmitted, to estimate the bandwidth.

The performance of multimedia systems can often be improved if more than one server is used in an application. For example, to retrieve a 3D object the texture component could be retrieved from one server and the mesh component from another server. Distributed retrieval, however, has many challenges, such as, distributed bandwidth monitoring, deciding how to divide a retrieval task among various servers, and combining the transmissions from various servers into one meaningful result. Some of the possible options for distributed bandwidth monitoring are presented in Chapter 2. Here again, statistical approaches are developed for the monitoring process. Two strategies for multi-server bandwidth monitoring are considered: one in which each server performs its share of a task independent of other servers, and another in which all the servers collaborate to complete a task. It is shown through statistical modeling coupled with simulation experiments that the collaborative approach is superior to the independent multi-server model.

How can we scale multimedia data based on monitored bandwidth to provide clients a statistical QoS guarantee? Some answers to this question are given in Chapter 2. It should be noted that statistical QoS guarantee is fundamentally different from traditional deterministic QoS guarantees. In a statistical approach, QoS is met with a chosen level of confidence, *e.g.*, 95% or 75% confidence. A 95% confidence level means that statistically 95 times out of 100 the approach is expected to satisfy a specified QoS requirement. Both simulations and real network tests are presented to validate the theoretical models behind single and multi-server optimal bandwidth monitoring and statistical QoS based transmission.

In Chapter 6 an alternative approach to joint texture and mesh (TexMesh) transmission considering network bandwidth and perceptual quality is presented. The strategy allows for adaptive control of remaining portion of the multimedia data to be transmitted.

1.3 Joint Texture-Mesh Simplification and View Independent Transmission

Methods for coding various types of visual information can differ significantly depending on the type of information. Images (or texture of 3D objects) can be transformed to the frequency domain for JPEG compression, or the wavelet domain for JPEG2000 compression. Video can be coded following the MPEG standard which consists of a collection of I-frames (Intra-coded static images compressed by themselves) and motion encoded frames (P-frames for Predictive coded frames & B-frames for bi-directionally coded frames); or the MPEG-4 standard which is more versatile and allows for coding of 3D meshes, background and foreground, and Regions-of-Interest (ROIs). Various strategies exist for mesh coding, with several adopting strategies for mesh simplification based on viewpoint, distance to observer, and perceptual quality.

Perceptual quality and ROI can play a key role in reducing bandwidth requirements. One of the major limitations in developing online multimedia systems is maintaining reasonably good visualization quality while communicating over links with limited and often fluctuating bandwidth. To work under these restrictions one can consider the following approach: (i) Transmit a coarse visual object quickly; (ii) Take the viewers interest into account for updating the coarse model; (iii) Use perceptual quality studies to device strategy for update of mesh vs. texture, *i.e.*, what proportion of the bandwidth should be taken for mesh transmission with the remaining bandwidth being used for texture transmission. After a brief overview of literature on 3D simplification in Chapter 4, a newer approach based on scale space filtering is discussed in Chapter 5. We consider photorealistic textured meshes, incorporating online adaptation based on available bandwidth in Chapter 6 and perceptual issues in Chapter 7. Chapter 8 accounts for tradeoffs between texture and mesh from a perceptual perspective. Strategies for 3D perceptual quality optimization under packet loss over wireless or unreliable networks are outlined in Chapter 9.

1.4 View Dependent Transmission

View independent transmission is necessary when users need to quickly interact with an object and change viewpoints fast. However, these strategies require resources at the client site for interpolation and reconstruction from partial data. When clients are slow and bandwidth is quite limited, view dependent transmission can be a better option. In Chapter 10, some alternatives for remote 3D visualization through image transmission are proposed. Predictive compression algorithms are used to reduce bandwidth requirement and overhead at the receiver. Copyright issues are also resolved because the full 3D model is not transmitted to the client. Prediction schemes can be image-based or model-based. A simple image-based prediction scheme contains redundancy between different views of the same model. To suppress redundant data, some geometry information is used to predict the new views. Pixels that cannot be predicted because of occlusion, different lighting conditions, quantization issues, etc. can exist in images. To overcome this problem, warping of two different views is combined to predict the new frame; or Layered Depth Images are taken from a single viewpoint but with multiple pixels along each line of sight are used to predict artifacts. Image-based schemes also need to handle holes filling in zooming operations. A different approach is to use model-based prediction, in which a simplified version of the mesh is stored at the client for rendering. In this case, the view rendered from the simplified mesh is subtracted from the one rendered from the complete mesh, and the difference is transmitted to the client.

Although transmitting images instead of the full model speeds up rendering time and reduces workload on the client side, little has been explored regarding how to extract the client's requested views from a 3D model effectively. In practice, video-rate is allocated for current implementations that require considerable bandwidth. Furthermore, the predictive approach can only deliver approximation and the rendered quality is significantly constrained by the network. In fact, the server has to replicate every step the client has to perform. A rate distortion theoretical approach (RV-RD) is proposed in Chapter 11, in which both server and client adopt cooperating policies in order to offer the user the best possible rendering with the available bandwidth. The client interactively determines the view of interest. Based on the client's request and available bandwidth, the server progressively transmits 3D data and texture. The received data is stored and then rendered based on the client's capacity. RV-RD is a very flexible system: at one extreme, if the server's policy ignores the viewpoint required at client side, it reduces to the transmission of a compressed representation of the whole scene. At the opposite, if the server does not transmit any 3D data, RV-RD works as a simple image transmission on demand system.

1.5 Content and Background Creation

Creating 3D content and background is a challenging problem limiting the widespread use of 3D multimedia. For 3D model creation there are active (using structured light and laser) approaches and passive approaches that do not need special lighting or other intervention. To address some of the complexities of 3D model creation, Chapter 12 reviews 3D reconstruction by passive methods. A high-level conceptual outline of the field is given, referring to the literature for technical details. The chapter discusses the framework for calibration, and first reviews major mono-modal methods: shape from silhouette, shape from shading, shape from self-shadow, shape from focus and shape from stereo. Subsequently, a general framework for multimodal methods, focusing on the deformable model techniques is outlined; in this context a specific example considering the joint use of silhouette and stereo data is presented.

Rather than constructing 3D scene geometry at considerable scanning or reconstruction cost, an alternative is to use panoramic imaging (possibly from multiple viewpoints) to create backgrounds. Chapter 13 discusses remote visualization of panoramic images following progressive compression standards. Implementations show that such an approach allows effective remote display and zoom into panoramic images for large size visualization windows. A solution is proposed following JPEG2000, which is intrinsically more efficient than JPEG and that it is scalable in image resolution and quality.

1.6 Implementing Simple Online Games

To motivate the utility of the theoretical models and associated implementations a few application scenarios are considered. In Chapter 14 we discuss how a simple two-player 3D game can be designed. This game, called "Castles," can be considered as a more complex and 3D version of the "Go" board game. The objective here is to have two players compete for space using 3D building blocks. In order to have a realistic demonstration even issues of balancing and gravitational effects of structures need to be taken into account. For an online game that does not require real-time imaging input data most of the texture and models can be pre-stored on client computers, and only the control, scene composition and interaction information needs to be transmitted and updated on an ongoing basis. The framework in Chapter 14 is extended to a networked online environment in Chapter 15, allowing multiple players to login using an online interface.

The design and implementation of a slightly more complex online game called "Siege" is discussed in Chapter 16. The idea behind Siege is to protect your tower from attacks by other players while at the same time using your own siege weapons to destroy others' towers. Siege is based on a 1983 board game called Crossbows and Catapults by Base Toys. This game gives readers an idea on how to design weapons and control their functionalities.

1.7 Online Appendices

Some of the material considered helpful in developing interactive online multimedia is supported through online appendices located at www.cs.ualberta.ca/~anup/3Dbook. At present, a review of JAVA3D and description of Remote Machine Invocation (RMI) based collaborative online 3D editing are available on this website. However, we plan to add more online implementation tutorials at this site over the next few years.

References

Kang, S. B., Szeliski, R. and Anandan, P. (2000). Geometry-image representation tradeoff for rendering, in *IEEE Int. Conference on Image Processing.*

Magnor, M., Ramanathan, P. and Girod, B. (2003). Multi-view coding for image based rendering using 3D scene geometry, *IEEE Trans. on CSVT*, pp. 1092–1106.

Chapter 2

Adaptive Bandwidth Monitoring for QoS Based Retrieval

A. Basu, I. Cheng, L. Ying and Y. Yu

2.1 Introduction

The Internet was originally designed to offer only one level of service ("best effort") to all its service users. In such an environment, all the data packets put onto the Internet has the same priority; the networks do not provide any guarantee on when the packet will be delivered or even whether it will be delivered at all. However, as new applications continue to emerge, more and more applications now need to provide some kind of quality guarantees to its users. How to provide this consistent service quality is now an active research area termed "Quality of Service" (QoS) [Vogel *et al.* (1995)], [Ferguson and Huston (1998)], [Miloucheva (1995)], [Pacifici and Stadler (1995)], [Gopalakrishna and Parulkar (1994)]. One solution to the problem is to allow the application to reserve a certain quality of network services in advance [Zhang *et al.* (1993)], [Braden *et al.* (1997)], [Ferrari *et al.* (1997)]. Once such a level of service is reserved, the underlying network will commit the corresponding resources needed and guarantee the delivery of such service. Unfortunately, some network architecture and implementations may not support reservation or only support reservation to a limited degree. One alternative approach that has generated a lot of interest in QoS based multimedia delivery application is the so-called network-aware application [Bolliger and Gross (1998)], [Bolliger and Gross (1999)], [Wang and Schulzrinne (1999)]. Several prototype systems have demonstrated this idea. In [Cheng *et al.* (2001)], the authors present a Tele-Learning system that deliver multimedia course materials (including JPEG images) to students over the Internet. The system allows the users to specify QoS parameters (time limit, resolution and quality of image) at the client side, and adapt the resolution and quality of the requested image on the server side to provide best quality image to the user while restricting transmission time within the time limit.

In related research [Bolliger and Gross (1998)] presents a framework for construction of network-aware application and gives a real example of such application, the "Chariot" image search engine. The authors concur that good bandwidth estimation is hard to achieve and need further study. [Bolliger and Gross (1999)] presents some bandwidth estimation techniques using transport and network layer metrics. Our research differs from these papers in several aspects. First, the method described in this paper uses only information obtained at the application layer to provide bandwidth estimation, so it does not assume special support from underlying layers in the network stack and is applicable to a wider group of programmers considering providing adaptive media delivery features. Second, we present the quantitative results showing how effective the bandwidth monitoring work. The previous works let the user select a time limit for object transmission, and makes the "best effort" to delivery such time limit guarantee. Our work introduces the additional parameter "Confidence goal." We let the user select this confidence goal and guarantee the time limit requirements are met by a probability set by the "Confidence goal."

Generally speaking, in order to deliver the user-requested media adaptively, the network-aware application needs to go through three phases. First, the application needs to monitor the current network condition and estimate the available bandwidth in a short future period during which the requested media will be transmitted. Second, given the specified time limit and estimated bandwidth, the application can calculate the volume of data the network is able to handle, and then adapts the media to that size. For example, if the media is a JPEG image, the application can adapt the image in terms of resolution, JPEG compression factor to produce a tailored JPEG image with a certain target size. Then in the third phase, the tailored file is transmitted to a user. Obviously, the bandwidth monitoring and estimation phase is of critical importance. Only an accurate estimation of available bandwidth allows the user request to be precisely met.

Two approaches exist to address the problem of accurate bandwidth estimation. In the first approach, the media server maintains a connection for each client currently active. The server sends testing packets periodically to the client and calculates the available bandwidth based on the time to transmit the testing packet. This maintains a history of bandwidth samples. When media delivery request is made to the server, the server estimates the available bandwidth of the future period by using a type of average of the history bandwidth samples. This method is used in [Cheng *et al.* (2001)]. However, there are several problems with it. Since the method uses a relatively long history of bandwidth to predict future bandwidth, the estimation result is not very accurate. And, the approach assumes the availability of history bandwidth information which sometime just not the case. More seriously, periodically sending random bits along the network for bandwidth testing purpose when no real data transmission is actually required can be a significant waste of total bandwidth of networks, since it may interfere with traffic of other users running congestion control protocol.

To address the problem mentioned above, we could measure the bandwidth "on the fly." When the client requests a multimedia object and specifies a time limit, the server first spends a fraction of the time on bandwidth testing. The remaining portion of the time limit is then used to adapt and transmit the media. Because of the congestion avoidance mechanism of various TCP protocol implementations, the throughput achieved by a connection tends to fluctuate around a range close to the maximum bandwidth available over the connection. Therefore, by taking multiple bandwidth samples at the starting fraction of a time interval, we can make a best estimation of the bandwidth available in the whole time period. A limitation of this method is that since we use the bandwidth samples at the beginning of a time interval to represent the entire duration of the time interval, the interval cannot be very long; otherwise the overall traffic over the entire path may change significantly and unpredictably influence the available bandwidth. As we shall see later, in our experiments, 10-30 second time-intervals seem to be appropriate for our experimental environment.

A problem associated with the proposed approach is that the fraction of time limit used for bandwidth testing is a pure overhead, reducing the portion of user specified time that really used for actual data transmission. The challenge is one of balancing the benefits of more accurate estimation of bandwidth (at the cost of more bandwidth testing time) and more transmission time (at the cost of less accurate estimation).

Online applications often require retrieval from several servers. Thus, extending the work on a single server, we discuss two strategies for monitoring the bandwidth at several servers. The first approach assumes that the servers work independently and do not (or cannot) cooperate; in this case the most reliable links are chosen to transmit the scalable multimedia information. The assumption behind this approach is that each server retrieves a fixed part of a multimedia object, and this part is determined after the bandwidth monitoring process and cannot be changed during the retrieval process. In the second approach, we consider a retrieval strategy where the different servers collaborate in the retrieval process; *i.e.*, if a server finishes its share of the retrieval task it helps with the retrieval task of other servers. Given this "collaborative" retrieval scenario, a new distributed monitoring algorithm is proposed. Simulation results show that the second algorithm, where applicable, is more effective than the algorithm for independent distributed retrieval. It is important to note that it is easier to develop applications using an independent retrieval model, since there is no need to dynamically adjust the retrieval tasks among the various servers.

In this chapter, we discuss a mathematical model to quantify the benefit and loss of bandwidth estimation spending and use it to achieve an optimal proportion of bandwidth testing. Bandwidth testing is treated as sampling from a population, and providing estimates based on "probabilistic confidence levels." When each new sample is taken, we calculate how much new knowledge of the population has been gained. We then compare this benefit with the cost of one sample (the time spent). We continue the sampling until the marginal benefit is less than the cost. For distributed retrieval from multiple servers, the single server model is generalized considering independent retrieval and then a collaborative retrieval model.

We implement the method in a Java program and test it on two typical network environments, campus network and dial-up network. To the best of our knowledge, [Yu *et al.* (2003)] is the first research that provides quantitative results as to how effective the bandwidth monitoring part is in a network-aware application. For the case of multiple servers, we test the validity of our models through simulations.

The remainder of this chapter is organized as follows: Section 2.2 describes the architecture, algorithm and simulation results for retrieval from a single or distributed independent servers. The approach in Section 2.2 is extended in Section 2.3 to address the problem when the servers can dynamically collaborate to complete a retrieval task. A summary is given in Section 2.4.

2.2 Probabilistic QoS Based Retrieval from a Single or Distributed Independent Servers

Mathematical Model

We assume a server and a client need to make a one-off transmission of a multimedia object (from server to client). No previous bandwidth information is available for the connection between the server and client. The user on the client side has specified a time limit T for the transmission. Neither exceeding the time limit T nor under-utilizing the time T is desirable. The first fraction t of T will be used for bandwidth testing to obtain the bandwidth estimation B for the future period $(T - t)$. The server then adapts the multimedia object to be exactly of the size $(T - t) \cdot B$ and then transmits it to the client. An over-estimation of bandwidth will make the transmission exceed the time limit, while under-estimation will under-utilize the time limit, thus actually delivering a media object that could have had better quality (with a larger size). Our problem is how to determine the appropriate t, and deliver as much data as possible to the client within the time limit specified. To simplify the model, we ignore the time needed for adaptation of a media object, since objects can be stored with multiple resolution levels or be dynamically adapted in a short time given a fast processor.

To estimate the bandwidth, we use slices of equal length. Suppose each time slice has length t_s, we then have T/t_s, time slices. Each time slice has a bandwidth value $x_i = \frac{C_i}{t_s}$ $(i = 1, 2 \ldots T/t_s)$, where C_i is a count of bytes received during the ith time slice. These bandwidth values can be viewed as random variables. We obtain the bandwidth value of the first t/t_s slices, and then use the average of these samples to estimate the average of the T/t_s population.

We first define the following variables for further discussion.

Definition 2.1: Notation

- T is the time limit for the multimedia object transmission specified by a user.
- t is the time used for bandwidth testing.
- t_s is the length of each time slice used for obtaining bandwidth samples.
- $N = \frac{T}{t_s}$, N is the number of time slices in period T, which generates our bandwidth population, $X_1, X_2, \ldots, X_N$.
- $n = \frac{t}{t_s}$, n is the number of time slices in period t, which generates

our bandwidth samples, $x_1, x_2, \ldots, x_n$.

- $\mu = \frac{\sum_N X_i}{N}$, μ is the average of N bandwidth population, the actual average bandwidth we are trying to calculate.
- $\sigma^2 = \frac{\sum_N (x_i-\mu)^2}{N}$, σ^2 is the variance of N bandwidth population.
- $\bar{x} = \frac{\sum_n x_i}{n}$, $\bar{x}$ is the average of the n bandwidth samples, $x_1, x_2, \ldots, x_n$.
- $s^2 = \frac{\sum_n (x_i-\bar{x})^2}{n-1}$, s^2 is the variance of the n bandwidth samples.

With the notation defined above, our problem can be stated as "given n, N, $\bar{x}$, s^2, estimate μ."

In statistics, $\bar{x}$ is commonly used as an estimate of μ. Given n, N, $\bar{x}$ and s^2, the random variable μ has a probability distribution centered at $\bar{x}$. If we assume the random variable X (the bandwidth in one slice) is a normal variable (*i.e.*, follows the normal distribution), then

$$d = \frac{\mu - \bar{x}}{\frac{s}{\sqrt{n}} \cdot \sqrt{\frac{N-n}{N-1}}} \tag{2.1}$$

is a continuous random variable following the "Student's t-Distribution" with degree of freedom n (number of samples) [Harnett (1982)].[1] We use character d instead of t to specify the t-Distribution random variable to avoid name confliction with the time t we have already defined.

We believe that the assumption of normality of variable X is reasonable, since within a short period the available bandwidth tends to approach a constant. Moreover, the t-distribution is said to be quite "robust", which means that the assumption of normality of X can be relaxed without significantly changing the sampling distribution of the t-distribution (Equation (8.1)).

Thus given n, N, $\bar{x}$, s^2, and t-distribution, we now have the probability distribution of μ.

$$\mu = \bar{x} + d \cdot \frac{s}{\sqrt{n}} \cdot \sqrt{\frac{N-n}{N-1}} \tag{2.2}$$

[1]Mathematically, the random variable t is defined as a standardized normal variable z divided by the square root of an independently distributed chi-square variable, which has been divided by its degree of freedom; that is, $t = z/\sqrt{\chi^2/n}$.

This means that when we take n bandwidth samples, we can expect the average bandwidth within period T to be a random variable with probability distribution following Equation (8.2).

With the distribution of μ, we can infer the $100(1-\alpha)\%$ confidence interval for μ as follows,

$$\bar{x} - d_{(\alpha,n)} \cdot \frac{s}{\sqrt{n}} \cdot \sqrt{\frac{N-n}{N-1}} \leq \mu \qquad (2.3)$$

Equation (8.3) tells us that the value of μ is greater or equal to $\bar{x} - d_(\alpha, n) \cdot \frac{s}{\sqrt{n}} \cdot \sqrt{\frac{N-n}{N-1}}$ with a probability of $100(1-\alpha)\%$. With this observation we define bandwidth estimation as follows.

Definition 2.2: Safe Bandwidth Estimation

We define $\mu_{est} = \bar{x} - d_{(\alpha,n)} \cdot \frac{s}{\sqrt{n}} \cdot \sqrt{\frac{N-n}{N-1}}$ to be a safe estimation of the future bandwidth. According to the theory described above, we have a confidence of $100(1-\alpha)\%$ that the actual bandwidth will not be lower.

We mentioned that μ is a random variable centered at $\bar{x}$. From Definition 2.2, we can see that in order to provide a time limit guarantee we actually under-estimate the bandwidth. This under-estimation has its cost; if we use μ_{est} as future bandwidth estimation to determine the maximum size of the media object, the actual transmission will most likely under-utilize the remaining time $T - t$.

It can be shown that the actual time under-utilized is on the average $(T-t) - (\frac{\mu_{est} \cdot (T-t)}{\mu})$, or $(T-t)(1 - \frac{\mu_{est}}{\mu})$. So we define the under-utilized time $\widetilde{T}$ as follows:

Definition 2.3: Under-utilized Time

$\widetilde{T}(n) = (1 - \frac{\mu_{est}}{\bar{x}})(T-t) = \frac{d_{(\alpha,n)} \cdot \frac{s}{\sqrt{n}} \sqrt{\frac{N-n}{N-1}}}{\bar{x}} \cdot (T - n \cdot t_s)$. It determines the average under-utilization time with the safe estimation.

Given all the definition and analysis above, we are ready to determine how much bandwidth testing to perform in order to maximize the data delivered to a user while conforming to the time limit requirement set by the user.

From Definition 2.3, we assert $\widetilde{T}$ is decreasing as n grows and the rate of decrease diminishes (we provide an informal proof in Theorem 2.1 below) when n is relatively small compared to N. This means as we take more bandwidth samples, we can estimate the future bandwidth more accurately with the same confidence α, thus reducing the cost of time under-utilization. We can denote the benefit of each new sample as $\Delta\widetilde{T} = \widetilde{T}_n - \widetilde{T}_{n-1}$. As we said, $|\Delta\widetilde{T}|$ decreases as n grows. On the other hand, the cost of each new sample is a constant, t_s, which is a time slice. So we can compare $|\Delta\widetilde{T}|$ with t_s each time a new sample is obtained, the process of bandwidth testing continues until $|\Delta\widetilde{T}|$ is less than t_s. The pseudocode in ALGORITHM 1 below illustrates the method.

Theorem 2.1: $\widetilde{T}$ decrease as n grows, and the rate of decrease diminishes when n is relatively small compared to N.

Proof: Details of the proof can be seen in [Yu *et al.* (2003)].

Algorithm 2.1: Optimal Bandwidth Testing

```
Obtain samples x_1, x_2, x_3;
Calculate T~_2, T~_3, and ΔT~_3 = T~_3 − T~_2;
n = 3
while (|ΔT~| > t_s){
    n = n + 1;
    Obtain sample x_n,
    Calculate T~_n and ΔT~ = T~_n − T~_{n−1};
}
return μ_est;
```

Model for Distributed Monitoring

Following the notation defined earlier in this section, our problem can be stated as "Determine the value of n, so that the estimation of μ based on these n samples yields a media object with largest size being transmitted from the K servers to the client during the remaining $T - t$ time."

Assumption 2.1: The servers are assumed to adapt parts of a media object and transmit independently. That is, in the simplified model used in the analysis one server cannot assist other servers after completing its share of the retrieval task.

Definition 2.4: Bandwidth Estimate is:

$$\hat{\mu} = \bar{x} - t_{\alpha}(n-1) \cdot \frac{s}{\sqrt{n}} \cdot \sqrt{\frac{N-n}{N-1}}$$

Given n, N, $\bar{x}$ and s^2 for one channel, the random variable μ of that connection has a probability distribution centered at $\bar{x}$. If we assume the random variable x (the bandwidth in one slice) conforms to the normal distribution, then random variable $t = \frac{\mu - \bar{x}}{\frac{s}{\sqrt{n}} \cdot \sqrt{\frac{N-n}{N-1}}}$ is a continuous random variable following the "Student's t-Distribution" [Johnson *et al.* (1988)] with degree of freedom n-1. We can therefore estimate the bandwidth as $\hat{\mu} = \bar{x} - t_{\alpha}(n-1) \cdot \frac{s}{\sqrt{n}} \cdot \sqrt{\frac{N-n}{N-1}}$, so that the probability of μ being greater than $\hat{\mu}$ is $100(1-\alpha)\%$, where α is a number between 0 and 1. Therefore, the real transmission of an object on this connection will finish within time limit $100(1-\alpha)\%$ of the cases in the long term.

Definition 2.5: Expected object size

$V = \hat{\mu} \cdot (T - t) = (\bar{x} - t_{(\alpha,n)} \cdot \frac{s}{\sqrt{n}} \cdot \sqrt{\frac{N-n}{N-1}}) \cdot (N-n) \cdot t_s$

Theorem 2.2: As a function of n, the expected object size $V(n)$ has a single maximum value. Before the maximum of $V(n)$ is reached, $V(n)$ increases with n, but the rate of growth decreases. After the maximum of $V(n)$ is reached, $V(n)$ decreases as n grows, and the rate of decrease grows with n.

Proof: Follows from Theorem 2.1.

Now we consider the combination of all channels on the client. Each channel will have its own statistics on n, $\bar{x}$, s^2 and $\hat{\mu}$. We therefore have estimates $V_1(n), V_2(n) \ldots V_K(n)$ on K connections.

Theorem 2.3: The total expected object size over n connections $V(n) = \sum_{i=1}^{K} V_i(n)$ has the same property as any $V_i(n)$, which is that it has one maximum value. Before it reaches its maximum, it grows with n at a decreasing growth rate; after it reaches its maximum, it decreases as n grows, at an increasing decrease rate.

Proof:

The theorem can be proved by induction on the number K. Details can be found in [Basu *et al.* (2003)].

Based on Theorem 2.3, we propose the following algorithm:

Algorithm 2.2: Estimating Expected Object Size for Multi-server Independent Distributed Retrieval (version 1)

Obtain samples x_1, x_2 on each channel and calculate

$V(1) \leftarrow \sum_{i=1}^{K} V_i(1);$

Obtain sample $x_3$on each channel and calculate $V(2) \leftarrow \sum_{i=1}^{K} V_i(2);$

$n \leftarrow 2;$

while $(V(n) > V(n-1))\{$

$n \leftarrow n+1;$

Obtain a new sample on each of the channels;

Calculate $V(n) \leftarrow \sum_{i=1}^{K} V_i(n); \}$

return $V(n)$;

Unfortunately, the above algorithm is not always optimal. It assumes that given K channels, to maximize object size within the time limit, we will always transmit segments from all K servers. This assumption seems reasonable, but it does not always hold under Assumption 1. Consider a simple example. Suppose a user wants to transmit an object over two channels within time limit T with confidence level of $\alpha = 0.90$. When using two channels, in order to get a confidence of 0.9 that both connections will finish within the time limit, each connection must use an αvalue of around 0.95 in their calculation of V (since $0.95^2 \approx 0.90$). Now suppose connection #1 has a much larger estimated bandwidth than connection #2 so that the difference between V_1 using $\alpha = 0.90$ and $\alpha = 0.95$ is much larger than V_2. In this case, it is better to drop connection #2 and use only connection #1 for real transmission (with $\alpha = 0.90$).

To accommodate dropping channels during transmission, we propose the following method. Suppose we have K channels available, when a new sample is obtained on each channel we calculate K V values using K different $\alpha s(\alpha_1, \alpha_2 \ldots \alpha_K)$ for each connection, where each α_i is used to calculate what the V value would be on this channel if finally $i$channels are used for real transmission. We have, $\alpha_i = \alpha^{1/i}$ is the confidence level specified by the end-user. Therefore, in total we will have K^2 V values in each time slice, like in Table 2.1 below. It is obvious that the maximum value of column one of the table is the maximum V we can obtain if we use only one channel; the sum of the maximum two values of column two is the maximum V we can obtain if we use only two channels; ...; finally, the sum of all the K values of column K is the V we can obtain if we use all the K channels.

Note that given the new definition of V as the maximum described in the last paragraph, it no longer has the property of having a single maximum value (as a function of n, and the number of samples taken), as we proved previously. Nevertheless, we will show in Section 3.2.2 with simulation results that the first local maximum value is usually very close to the global maximum value of V, and therefore serves as a good enough approx-

Table 2.1 V values on K channels. Each row of the table represents K V values for one channel.

$V_1(\alpha_1)$	$V_1(\alpha_2)$	$V_1(\alpha_3)$	...	$V_1(\alpha_K)$
$V_2(\alpha_1)$	$V_2(\alpha_2)$	$V_2(\alpha_3)$	...	$V_2(\alpha_K)$
...	...	...	...	...
$V_K(\alpha_1)$	$V_K(\alpha_2)$	$V_K(\alpha_3)$	...	$V_K(\alpha_K)$

imation. Based on this, we outline a refined version of Algorithm 2.2 that accommodates dropping channel(s).

Example: Optimal retrieval from 4 servers

(1) You are considering the distributed retrieval of a video object from 4 servers, and would like to guarantee 95% overall confidence in your retrieval. Estimates of the mean bandwidth and sample standard deviation for each of the 4 servers, based on a sample size of 10, are respectively $(100, 10), (50, 30), (200, 40), (90, 50)$. (Assume **N** is large compared to **n**.)

(a) Following the concepts in the optimal distributed monitoring paper in the course notes, construct the appropriate table that helps you decide on an optimal retrieval strategy from multiple independent servers.

(b) Based on this table which servers will you use for the optimal strategy at 95% confidence level? Justify your answer.

$93351t_s$	$92073t_s$	$91242t_s$	$90816t_s$
$32554t_s$	$28718t_s$	$26226t_s$	$24948t_s$
$175405t_s$	$170291t_s$	$166968t_s$	$165265t_s$
$60856t_s$	$54463t_s$	$50310t_s$	$48180t_s$

The maximum value of column one of the table is the maximum V we can obtain if we use only one channel. V3 gives 175405.

The sum of the maximum two values of column two can be obtained using V1 & V3, which gives: 262364.

The sum of the maximum three values of column three can be obtained if we use V1, V3 & V4, which gives: 308520.

Finally, using all the channels in column four gives the maximum if all four channels are used, giving: 329209.

Since 329209 is the maximum of all the possibilities, we will have to use all four channels in this case.

Algorithm 2.3: Estimating Expected Object Size for Multi-server Independent Distributed Retrieval (refined)

Obtain samples x_1, x_2 on each channel;
Calculate $V_i(1, \alpha_j)$ for $i \in \{1, 2, ...K\}, \alpha_j \in \{\alpha_1, \alpha_2, ...\alpha_K\}$;
$V_1 = GetMax(1)$;
$n \leftarrow 1$;
while(TRUE) {
  $n \leftarrow n + 1$;
  Obtain sample x_{n+1} on each channel;
  Calculate $V_i(n, \alpha_j)$ for $i \in \{1, 2, ...K\}, \alpha_j \in \{\alpha_1, \alpha_2, ...\alpha_K\}$
  $V_n = GetMax(n)$;
  if ($V_n < V_{n-1}$) break;
}
return V_n;

The function $GetMax(n)$ takes the variable n as input and works on a 2D array $V_i(n, \alpha_j)$ (for i, $j = 1 \ldots K$, as shown in Table 2.1).

Implementation and Experiments

We answer the following questions through experiments: (a) How well does the model work in achieving our goal of performing optimal amount of bandwidth testing in bandwidth estimation? (b) How well does the model deliver the final QoS result to end-users? For example, if a user specifies its target transmission time limit associated with a confidence goal (say "meet the time limit by 95% time"), can the model really achieve this level of guarantee? Finally, we are interested in the complexity of the model. Can we implement the model efficiently so that we can make decisions based on them for retrieval applications while estimating bandwidth? In this section, we describe our implementation of the model in Java and then present the experimentation results that answer these questions.

Our implementation consists of two programs, a server and a client. The server is a background process on the server host. It listens to a known port on the server machine and waits for a connection request from a client. The client is a Java Applet embedded in an HTML page. It includes a

GUI that allows a user to specify parameters for an object transmission. There are three parameters; "Time Limit" gives the time a user wants to use for object transmission, "Confidence Goal" is the system's guarantee that with this probability the transmission will be finished within the time limit, "Time Slice" is the time used for each bandwidth sample. Figure 2.1 below is a screen capture of the Client program showing the GUI for user parameter setting.

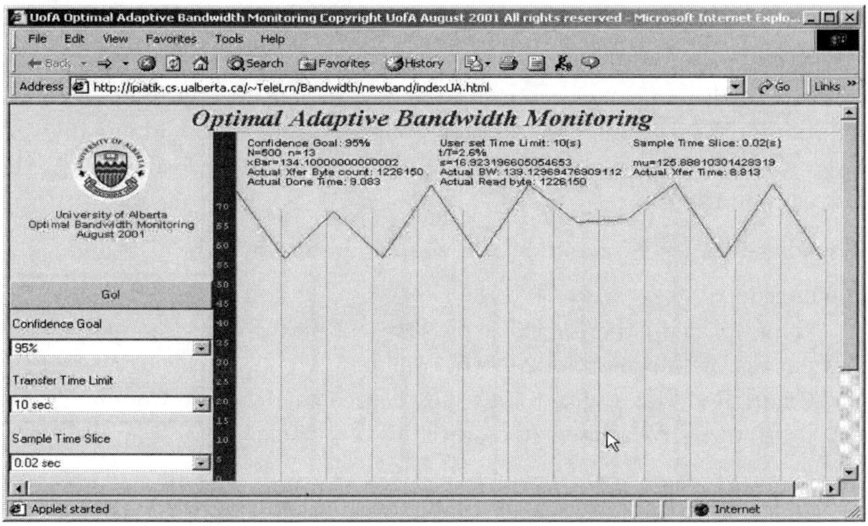

Fig. 2.1 Screen capture of the Client program.

Once the user sets the parameters and presses a "Go!" button, the following steps are executed:

1. The Client first creates a socket to the server program by connecting to the known port on the server host. It then sends a TEST command to the server. The server responds to the TEST command by sending a stream of random bytes to the client via the connection.

2. The Client receives the testing stream on the other side of the connection and at the same time counts the bytes received. For every time slice, the client divides the number of bytes received by the time slice to determine the bandwidth of this slice. This is a new bandwidth sample x_n.

3. The Client calculates $\bar{x}$, s^2, μ_{est}, and $\Delta\widetilde{T}$ as defined in Section II and compares $|\Delta\widetilde{T}|$ to t_s.

If $|\Delta\widetilde{T}| > t_s$, it repeats Step 2; otherwise it proceeds to Step 4.

4. The Client stops the testing connection, makes a new connection to server and sends a TRANSMIT command to server, along with a target size of the object which equals to $(T - t) \cdot \mu_{est}$.

5. The Server sends a byte stream of length $(T - t) \cdot \mu_{est}$ to the Client.

6. The Client receives the byte stream representing the object, records the finish time, calculates the statistics about this transmission and updates them on the right side region of the applet, as shown in Fig. 2.1.

To minimize the computation of $\widetilde{T}$ when each new sample is obtained, parts of it can be pre-computed and stored in a static array of constants. We organize the component $\frac{d_{(\alpha,n)}}{\sqrt{n}} \cdot \sqrt{\frac{N-n}{N-1}}$ into a two-dimensional array of constants, with (α, n) representing the two dimensions, so that the computation of $\widetilde{T}$ takes only two floating point multiplication and one division given $\bar{x}$ and s. Moreover, the computation s^2 can be performed using the fast computation form $s^2 = \frac{1}{n-1}(\sum_n x_i^2 - n\bar{x}^2)$. So, if we maintain the intermediate values $\sum_n x_i$and $\sum_n {x_i}^2$, the computation costs of $\bar{x}$ and s are minimized.

We performed experiments in two typical network environments. The first one is the University of Alberta campus LAN. Both the server and the client runs Red Hat Linux 6 and the client uses Netscape Communicator 4.0 as browser. We present the statistics of our experiments in Table 2.2 below.

Table 2.2 Experiment results on campus network, with Time Limit of 10s, Time Slice of 0.02s. Results are for two different confidence goals.

Confidence Goal	95%	75%
Average No. of Sample	14.6	8.7
Sample Average (kbps)	141.1	140.5
Sample Variance (kbps)	8.07	8.65
Estimation (kbps)	137.5	138.6
Actual Average (kbps)	140.9	140.7
Actual Transfer Time (s)	9.48	9.66
Actual Total Time (s)	9.79	9.85
Total No. of Exception in 100 runs	4	20

The results in Table 2.2 are based on experiments with parameters "Time Limit" = 10 seconds, "Time Slice" = 0.02 seconds. We give the results for "Confidence Goal" = 95% and 75% ($\alpha = 5$ and $\alpha = 25$). For each parameter set, we perform the transmission 100 times and report the averages.

From the results in Table 2.2, we can see that when $\alpha = 5$, it takes only 14.6 samples out of 500 ($N = 10/0.02 = 500$) to achieve the optimal amount of bandwidth testing. Only 4% of the transmissions exceed the time limit and we still utilize 94.8% of the time limit for actual application data transfer. The results for $\alpha = 25$ are similar, except that it takes fewer testing samples and thus leads to a less accurate estimate of bandwidth. This in turn produces more transmission exceeding the time limit (20%) but utilizes a larger portion of time limit for actual application data transmission (96.6%).

In the second experiment environment setting, we still use the server in University of Alberta, but use a host connected to a local broadband ISP with cable modem as client. A traceroute result shows there are 11 hops between the client and the host. The client runs Microsoft Windows 2000 Professional and Internet Explorer version 5.0. We present the same set of results in Table 2.3 below.

Table 2.3 Experiment results on home network, with time Limit of 10s, Time Slice of 0.02. Results are for two different confidence goals.

Confidence Goal	95%	75%
Average No. of Sample	21.4	15.9
Sample Average (kbps)	37.0	35.4
Sample Variance (kbps)	6.60	7.62
Estimation (kbps)	34.3	34.0
Actual Average (kbps)	37.1	35.7
Actual Transfer Time (s)	8.69	9.03
Actual Total Time (s)	9.52	9.73
Total No. of Exception in 100 runs	7	22

Comparing Table 2.3 with Table 2.2, we can see that the variance of the bandwidth is significantly larger in the home network environment. Therefore, the bandwidth testing part of the program is forced to take more samples and make more conservative estimation on future bandwidth, which in turn reduces the actual data transfer time. Nevertheless, even in this network environment, 87% of time limit is used in application data transmission when $\alpha = 5$.

We now show the effectiveness of the method by comparing the results of our method with a non-adaptive bandwidth testing method, which means the client always takes the same number of samples and use the average of these as the estimate of future bandwidth. Figure 2.2 shows the results for the campus network environment described above.

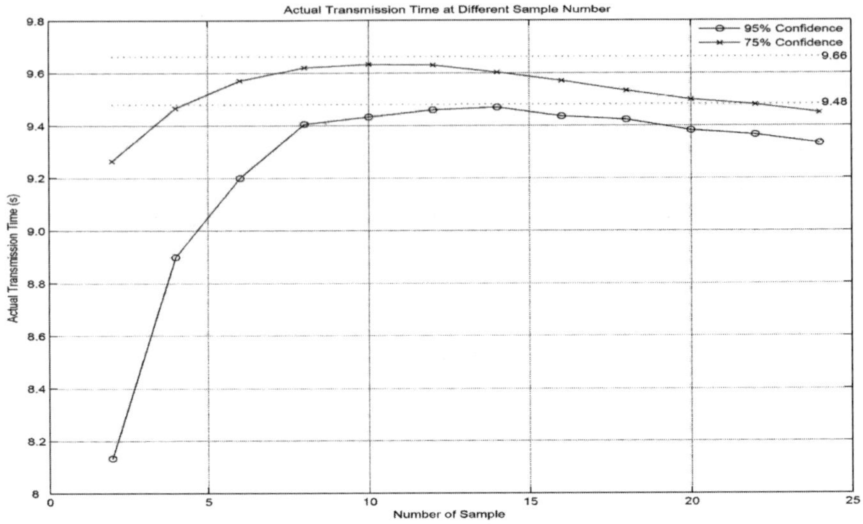

Fig. 2.2 Actual transmission time with different sample number using non-adaptive bandwidth testing.

In experiments associated with Fig. 2.2, we use the same parameters as those in Table 2.2. "Time Limit" is set to 10 seconds; "Time Slice" is 0.02 second; "Confidence Goals" are 95% and 75%. The difference is that this time we do not use the algorithm described in Section 2.2 to decide how many testing sample to take, but instead use a constant sample number. We run the transmission for different pre-set sample numbers and plot the actual transmission time (out of time limit 10 seconds) in Fig. 2.2. For easy comparison, we also plot the line $y = 9.48$ and $y = 9.66$ which is the actual transmission time using our algorithm with "Confidence Goal" of 95% and 75% respectively.

From the plot we see that our algorithm accurately arrives at the optimal number of testing samples to maximize the actual transmission time (in turn transmitting the largest possible size of an object) while guaranteeing the time limit requirement.

Simulation Results for Distributed Retrieval

Figure 2.3 is a screen capture of the simulator at work. The experimenter can change the number of channels through the "Site" menu; and the end user confidence α, total time slice number and random seeds through the "Parameters" menu. In Fig. 2.3, we have chosen two channels and $\alpha = 0.95$. We can see that there are two channel consoles in the middle,

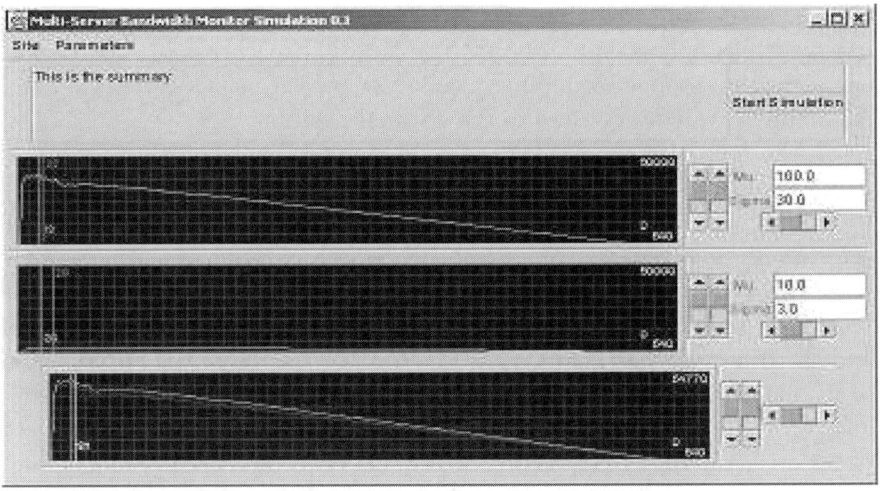

Fig. 2.3 A Screen Capture of Multi-server Bandwidth Monitor simulator.

each with text fields (labelled "Mu" and "Sigma") on the right to enter the mean and variance of the channel. After specifying the mean and variance of all the channels, the user clicks the "Start Simulation" button to start the simulation for a run (500 slices in this case). The program displays the V values at each time slice for each channel in the graph area in the channel's console. As illustrated in Fig. 2.3, the V values of both channels follow the trend of increasing rapidly at first and then decreasing gradually. For each channel, two curves are drawn, the red one represents V values if one channel is finally used, therefore it uses $\alpha_1 = 0.95$ to calculate V. The yellow one represents V values if two channels are used in real transmission, thus it uses $\alpha_2 = 0.9747$ to calculate V. Finally, the lowest component of the window in Fig. 2.3 shows the graph of the combined V values at each time slice. The red curve represents the maximum V values when one channel is used and yellow curve represent the combined V values of both channels. In this case, we can see that using both channels outperforms using only one of them, as the yellow curve is above the red one.

We stop bandwidth testing when there are three continuous occurrences of *V(n)<average(V(n), V(n-1), V(n-2), V(n-3))*. We will call this algorithm the "moving average algorithm." Going back to the combined channel component in Fig. 2.3, there are two vertical lines in the graph, one yellow and the other white. The yellow one gives the largest V value over

all time slices, and the white one is where our algorithm detects that the bandwidth sampling should finish. The largest V occurred in slice 19 and our algorithm stopped sampling at slice 21, which means it detected the maximum V value very close to the optimal position.

In the following experiment, we will compare our algorithm against a naive algorithm that always uses a fixed number of samples for the bandwidth testing. *Note that it is not possible to know the best fixed-sample size beforehand, however, to demonstrate the power of our algorithm we compare it against various fixed sample sizes.* We perform the simulation in a setting of two channels. One channel has a mean bandwidth of 100Kbps and the other 10Kbps (same as in Fig. 2.3). To measure the effectiveness of the algorithms under different network characteristics, we vary the variance on both channels. For Channel #1, we choose variance from the set {2.5, 5, 10, 15, 20, 25, 30, 35, 40, 45, 50, 55, 60}, and variance of Channel #2 is chosen from {0.25, 0.5, 1, 1.5, 2, 2.5, 3, 3.5, 4, 4.5, 5, 5.5, 6}. For each combination of channel characteristics we run both algorithms 1000 times. We exclude those runs that exceed the time limit and average the remaining on the real transmitted object size. We tested two settings for total time slice, 100 and 500. Assuming the time slice is 0.05 second, the settings correspond to 5 seconds and 25 seconds.

The results of the tests for 100 time slices are presented in Fig. 2.4 and Fig. 2.5; and the results for 500 time slices are presented in Fig. 2.6 and Fig. 2.7. Performance under small variance (where σ is less than 15% of μ) is shown in Fig. 2.4/Fig. 2.6, performance under large variance (where σ is larger than 35% of μ) is shown in Fig. 2.5/Fig. 2.7.

We point out two observations here. First, the performance of the fixed sampling algorithm depends on the number of samples used; yet the optimal number of samples varies under different total slice number and different variance of channels. By using our algorithm, we always achieve results similar to the best of the fixed sampling algorithm, no matter what the total slice number and variance are. Second, performance gain for our algorithm over fixed sampling algorithm varies for different variance ranges. Our algorithm outperforms fixed sampling by up to 17% in small variance for 100 time slices, but by only 4% in small variance for 500 time slices. This is because for small variance, the worst performing fixed sampling algorithms are those using relatively large number of fixed samples. These additional samplings constitute a larger portion of the total time for 100 total time slices than for 500 total time slices. Conversely, in the large variance case, our algorithm outperforms fixed sampling by up to 8% over 100 time slices and up to 15% over 500 time slices. This happens because of the difference when a small number of fixed samples are used, which causes aggressive under-estimation of bandwidth in the algorithms. This factor affects more when there are more remaining time slices for real transmission, 500 total time slices in this case.

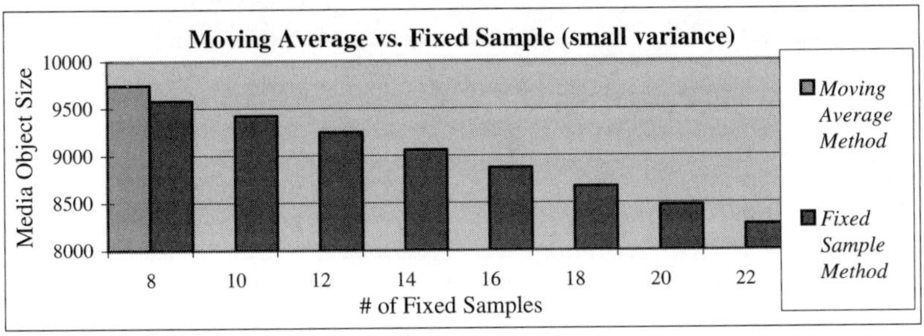

Fig. 2.4 Comparison of average size of transmitted object for two algorithms (on 100 total slices). Averaged over all small variances ($\sigma < 0.15^* \mu$) in 1000 runs.

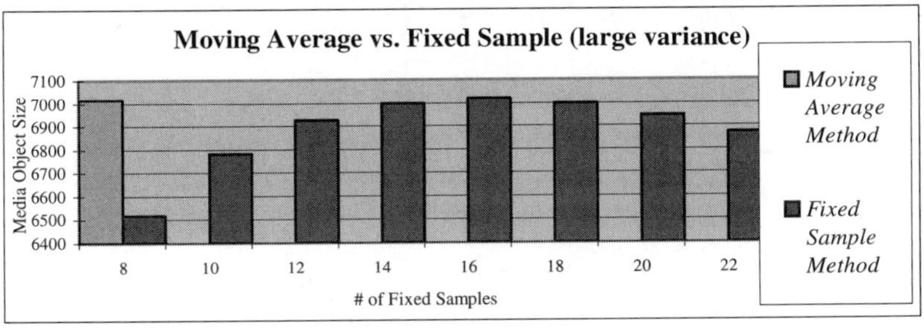

Fig. 2.5 Comparison of average size of transmitted object size for two algorithms (on 100 total slices). Averaged over all large variances ($\sigma > 0.35^* \mu$) in 1000 runs.

Another important factor in comparing the two algorithms is how well they guarantee that the real transmission will be finished within time limit. The results are shown in Fig. 2.8.

The graph compares the two algorithms for the number of runs that fails to finish the real transmission within time limit out of 1000 runs (averaged over all variances on both channels). Recall that we used $\alpha = 0.95$. We can see that our algorithm has around 95% of the runs finish transmission within the time limit. The results for the fixed sampling algorithm with different number of samples vary slightly within a 94.5–96.5% range. Thus, both algorithms deliver the guarantee of user confidence. Note that we

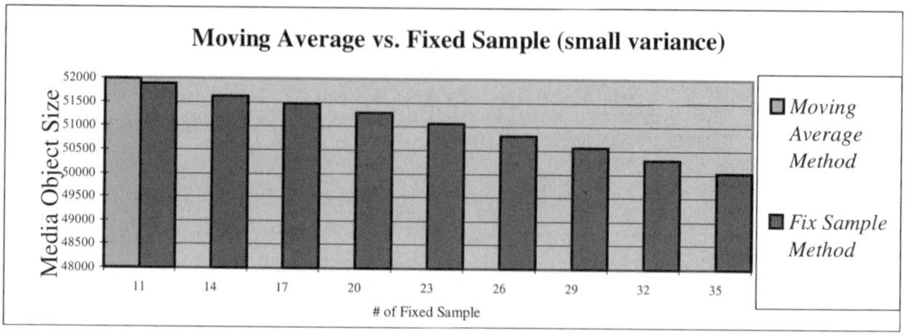

Fig. 2.6 Comparison of average size of transmitted object for two algorithms (on 500 total slices). Averaged over all small variances ($\sigma < 0.15^{*}\mu$) in 1000 runs.

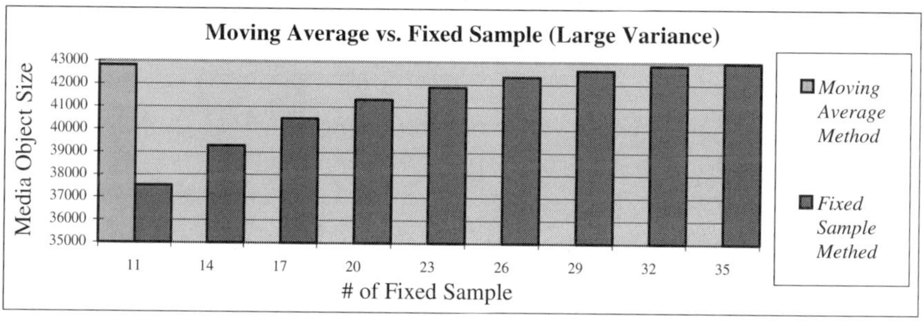

Fig. 2.7 Comparison of average size of transmitted object for two algorithms (on 500 total slices). Averaged over all large variances ($\sigma > 0.35^{*}\mu$) in 1000 runs.

calculated the values of t-distribution cut-offs using the algorithm described in [Press *et al.* (1993)] and compared these values with values provided in the t-distribution table in [Zwillinger (1996)] for verification purpose.

Finally, we present data to answer the question of "How often does our algorithm really drop a channel to achieve better performance?" We performed experiments on the two-channel case with average bandwidth of 100kbps (Channel #1) and 10kbps (Channel #2) and counted how many times the algorithm ended up using only one channel for real transmission in 1000 trials. As before, the experiments were conducted over all the variances specified in previous experiments, and the results are shown in Fig. 2.9.

It can be seen from the graph that the percentage of runs using only one channel reaches as high as 30% when variance is high on the two channels. This justifies our effort in developing an algorithm to find the optimal number of channels to use.

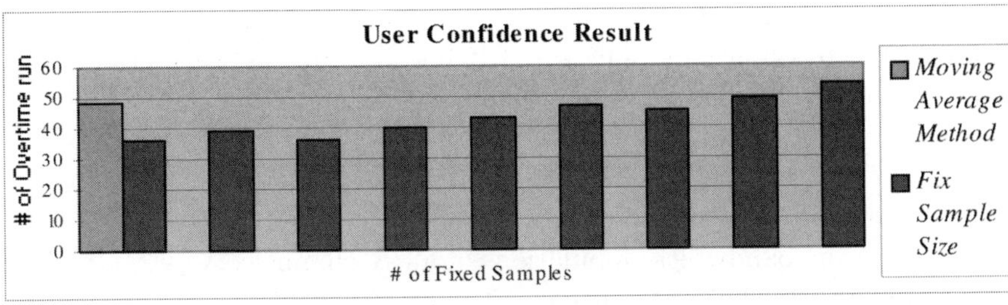

Fig. 2.8 The number of runs that fail to finish within time limit out of 1000 runs.

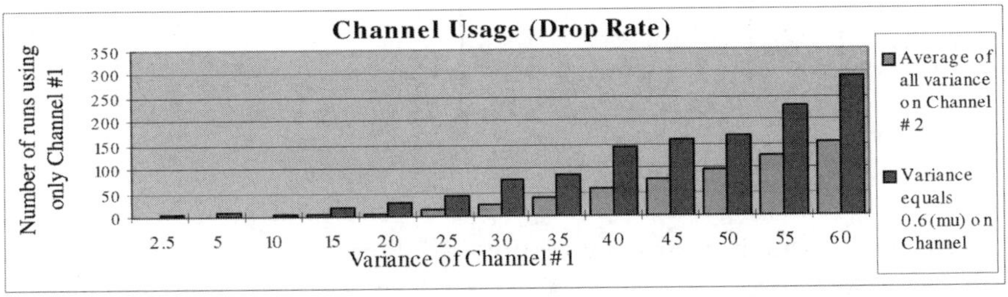

Fig. 2.9 This graph shows how many times our algorithm uses only one channel for real transmission out of 1000 runs. The x-axis is the variance of Channel #1. The dark color bar shows the number for the case where variance equals 0.6 times the mean on Channel #2, while the light color bar shows the average number for variance belonging in 0.25, 0.5, 1.0, 1.5, 2.0, 2.5, 3.0, 3.5, 4.0, 4.5, 5.0, 5.5, 6.0.

2.3 Collaborative Distributed Retrieval

Proposed Improvement

In the independent distributed retrieval architecture (Section 2.2), the client first calculates the segment sizes of objects to be delivered by selected servers, according to the relative bandwidths of all channels. Then, the client requests each selected server to deliver its segment of the object. When some servers finish delivering their own segments earlier than others they stop; although, the transmission of the whole object is not finished. The estimated object size is smaller because of this wasted bandwidth. Based on this observation, we try to improve the architecture and the statistical model by estimating and utilizing only the combined bandwidth of K channels, which is meaningful in a situation where different servers collaborate in the retrieval process.

Another problem in our previous method is that, we dropped some channels, *i.e.*, used a channel fully or dropped it altogether. To improve performance, we introduce a reliability factor that can vary between 0 and 1, compared to essentially only 0 or 1 being used in the last section. This way, unreliable channels can also participate in improving the overall performance.

Mathematical Model and Algorithm

Suppose the bandwidth populations of all K channels, $X_1, X_2, \ldots, X_K$, conform to the normal distribution, $X \sim N(\mu, \Sigma)$

Where:

$$X = \begin{pmatrix} X_1 \\ X_2 \\ \cdots \\ X_K \end{pmatrix}, \mu = \begin{pmatrix} \mu_1 \\ \mu_2 \\ \cdots \\ \mu_K \end{pmatrix}, \Sigma = \begin{pmatrix} \sigma_{11}^2 & \sigma_{12}^2 & \cdots & \sigma_{1K}^2 \\ \sigma_{21}^2 & \sigma_{22}^2 & \cdots & \sigma_{2K}^2 \\ \cdots & \cdots & \cdots & \cdots \\ \sigma_{K1}^2 & \sigma_{K2}^2 & \cdots & \sigma_{KK}^2 \end{pmatrix}$$

Instead of simply dropping the unreliable channels, as in Section 2, we introduce a reliability factor β varying between 0 and 1 for each channel. We can then form a linear combination as follows:

$Z = \beta_1 X_1 + \beta_2 X_2 + \cdots + \beta_K X_K = \beta^T X$, where, $\beta_1, \ldots, \beta_K \in [0, 1]$.

Following [Harnett (1982), Johnson *et al.* (1988)], Z has a $N(\mu_z, \sigma_z^2)$ distribution, where $\mu_z = E(Z) = \beta^T \mu$, $\sigma_z^2 = Var(Z) = \beta^T \Sigma \beta$; *i.e.*, $Z \sim N(\beta^T \mu, \beta^T \Sigma \beta)$.

Suppose $x_{k1}, xk2, \ldots, x_{kn}$are the samples for channel k. $\bar{x}_1, \bar{x}_2, \ldots, \bar{x}_K$ are the sample means for channels 1, 2, …, K (*i.e.*, $\bar{x}_k = \sum_{j=1}^{n} x_{kj}$). Let$\bar{x}$ and S be the sample mean vector and covariance matrix of the samples, respectively. The sample mean and variance of $z_1, z_2, \ldots, z_K$ are: $\bar{z} = \beta^T \bar{x}$ and $s_z^2 = \beta^T S \beta$.

For β fixed and σ_z^2 unknown, a $100(1 - \alpha)\%$ confidence interval for $\mu_z = \beta^T \mu$ is based on the student's t-distribution [Johnson *et al.* (1988)]:

$$t = \frac{\bar{z} - \mu_z}{\frac{s_z}{\sqrt{n}} \cdot \sqrt{\frac{N-n}{N-1}}} = \frac{\beta\bar{x} - \beta\mu}{\frac{\sqrt{\beta^T S \beta}}{\sqrt{n}} \cdot \sqrt{\frac{N-n}{N-1}}}. \tag{2.4}$$

Our problem is to find the estimate of μ:μ_{est}, where: $P(\mu_{est} < \beta\mu < \mu) = 1 - \alpha$, *i.e.*, $P(\beta\mu > \mu_{est}) = 1 - \alpha$. According to Equation 6.4:

$$P\left(\frac{\beta\bar{x} - \beta\mu}{\frac{\sqrt{\beta^T S \beta}}{\sqrt{n}} \cdot \sqrt{\frac{N-n}{N-1}}} < t_\alpha(n-1)\right) = 1 - \alpha$$

or,

$$P\left(\beta\mu > \beta\bar{x} - t_\alpha(n-1)\frac{\sqrt{\beta^T S\beta}}{\sqrt{n}} \cdot \sqrt{\frac{N-n}{N-1}}\right) = 1 - \alpha\,.$$

We can now define the bandwidth estimation as follows:

Definition 2.6: Bandwidth Estimate for Collaborative Retrieval is:

$$\mu_{est} = \beta\bar{x} - t_\alpha(n-1)\frac{\sqrt{\beta^T S\beta}}{\sqrt{n}} \cdot \sqrt{\frac{N-n}{N-1}} \tag{2.5}$$

When α and n are fixed, we could try to find β that maximizesμ_{est}, where $0 \leq \beta_1, \beta_2, \cdots, \beta_K \leq 1$.

Definition 2.7: Expected Object Size for Collaborative Retrieval is:

$$V = \mu_{est} \cdot (T-t) = \left(\beta\bar{x} - t_\alpha(n-1)\frac{\sqrt{\beta^T S\beta}}{\sqrt{n}} \cdot \sqrt{\frac{N-n}{N-1}}\right) \cdot (N-n) \cdot t_s$$

We now state an important theorem on the property of the function $V(n)$, which considers V as a function of n, the number of samples.

Theorem 2.4: Suppose $\beta\bar{x}$ and $\sqrt{\beta^T S\beta}$ are constants, statistically, as a function of n, the expected object size $V(n)$ has a single maximum value. Before the maximum of $V(n)$is reached, $V(n)$ increases with n, but the rate of growth decreases. After the maximum of $V(n)$ is reached, $V(n)$ decreases as n grows, and the rate of decrease grows with n.

Proof: Follows from similar theorems in [Yu *et al.* (2003)] and Section 2.2 with some of the terms and expressions changed.

Based on Theorem 2.4, we propose the following algorithm for determining the optimal Expected Object Size.

Algorithm 2.4: Estimating Expected Object Size for Multi-server Collaborative Distributed Retrieval

Obtain samples x_1, x_2 on each channel;
Compute Optimal β to calculate maximal $V(2) : V_{max}(2)$;
Obtain sample x_3 on each channel;
Compute Optimal β to calculate maximal $V(3) : V_{max}(3)$;
$n \leftarrow 3$;
while $(V_{\max}(n) > V_{\max}(n-1))\{$
    $n \leftarrow n+1$;
    Obtain a new sample on each channel;
    Compute Optimal β to calculate maximal $V(n) : V_{max}(n)$;
$\}$
return $V_{\max}(n)$;

Simulation and Experimental Results

The simulator works in a manner similar to the one in Section 2.2. In order to verify and clearly analyze the typical cases of network transmission, we first simulate with 2 servers and typical combinations of mean and standard deviation of the two channels. Then, to verify the effectiveness of random cases with multiple servers, we carry out the simulation with an arbitrary number of servers, having the mean and standard deviation of each channel also randomly generated.

Simulation with two servers

To do a 2-server simulation, as Table 2.4 shows, without loss of generality, we let the sample-generating parameters of Channel #1 be fixed and the ones of Channel #2 vary over several typical cases. For Channel #1, its bandwidth mean (μ_1) is 1000 and standard deviation (σ_1) is 10, *i.e.*, $\mu_1 = 1000$ and$\sigma_1 = 10$. For Channel #2, its mean (μ_2) varies over $\{1000, 500, 100, 50, 10, 5, 1\}$ and its standard deviation (σ_2) is chosen to be one of $\{0.1, 0.2, 0.3, 0.4, 0.5, 0.6, 0.7, 0.8\}$ times the mean. The unit of measurement of bandwidth mean is not important, and could be Kbps or Mbps. What is important are the relative sizes among the bandwidth means of various channels. We consider Channel #1 to be more reliable than Channel #2, since the mean of Channel #1 is higher and the standard deviation is lower. We do the simulation 100 times (with confidence levels 0.95 and 0.75) and compute the averages. The number of time slices is 100, *i.e.*, $N = 100$.

Table 2.4 Parameter set used in 2-server simulation.

Channel #1	μ_1	1000
	σ_1	10
Channel #2	μ_2	$\{1000, 500, 100, 50, 10, 5, 1\}$
	$\sigma_2(*\mu_2)$	$\{0.1, 0.2, 0.3, 0.4, 0.5, 0.6, 0.7, 0.8\}$

To evaluate the improved algorithm, we first verify how well it guarantees that the real transmission will be finished at the given confidence level within a time limit. We observe the percentage of overtime runs, which could not finish transmission within the time limit. We then estimate improvement over the previous algorithm, which is measured by the improved percentage of the real size of successfully transmitted media objects. In addition, we observe the behaviour of parameter β.

Guarantee of Confidence Level

When the confidence level is 95%, in most cases, the percentage of runs that fail to finish on time ranges within 4% to 8%. When the confidence level is 75%, in most cases, the percentage of runs that fail to finish on time varies between 22% to 30%. This means the confidence level of the collaborative algorithm is satisfied within a reasonable range.

Improvement over Independent Distributed Algorithm

As Fig. 2.10 shows, for 75% and confidence levels we achieve better-estimated object size. With the improved percentages varying between 0.2% to 13%. At 95% confidence level, results were similar with lower improvement rates.

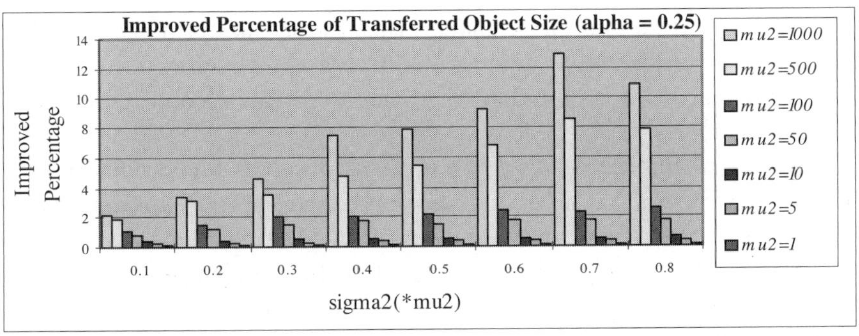

Fig. 2.10 Improved percentage of estimated object size, which finishes transmission within time limit; confidence level of 75%.

Analysis of β: When the confidence level is 95%, *i.e.*, $\alpha = 0.05$, the values of β_1 are all equal to 1, which means we fully account for the contribution of Channel #1. Table 2.5 shows the values of β_2 for different combinations of the means and standard deviations of Channel #2. As a general trend, when Channel #2 becomes more unreliable, *i.e.*, the standard deviation σ_2 becomes larger, the value of β_2 becomes smaller, which means we depend less on Channel #2 as it becomes more unreliable.

When the confidence level is 75%, *i.e.*, $\alpha = 0.25$, the values of β_1 are all equal to 1, *i.e.*, once again we fully account for the contribution of Channel #1. The values of β_2 for different combinations of the mean and standard deviation of Channel #2, are also all equal to 1. The reason is as follows: In Equation (3.2), when β_2 is less than 1, the first item,$\beta\bar{x}$, becomes smaller,

Table 2.5 The values of β_2 for different combinations of the means and standard deviations of Channel #2; confidence level is 95%, *i.e.*, $\alpha = 0.05$.

μ_2 \ $\sigma_2(*\mu_2)$	0.1	0.2	0.3	0.4	0.5	0.6	0.7	0.8
1000	1.00	1.00	1.00	1.00	0.99	0.96	0.98	0.91
500	1.00	1.00	1.00	0.99	0.99	0.93	0.94	0.95
100	1.00	1.00	1.00	1.00	0.97	0.97	0.95	0.94
50	1.00	1.00	1.00	0.99	0.97	0.97	0.97	0.95
10	1.00	1.00	1.00	1.00	0.99	0.95	0.97	0.98
5	1.00	1.00	1.00	1.00	0.99	0.97	0.97	0.96
1	1.00	1.00	1.00	0.99	1.00	0.98	0.94	0.94

and the second item, $t_\alpha(n-1)\frac{\sqrt{\beta^T S\beta}}{\sqrt{n}} \cdot \sqrt{\frac{N-n}{N-1}}$, also becomes smaller. When α increases, $t_\alpha(n-1)$ becomes smaller, thus the second term has less effect. Thus, β_2 is always equal to 1, since the decrease in the first term owing to the decrease of β_2, is larger than the decrease in the second item when α increases.

In order to further analyze the optimal β values for various network mean and variance combinations, we conducted several experiments. In most cases, if the means and variances of different channels were close to one another than β turned out to be close to 1. However, β can vary significantly from 1 when the means and variances of different channels are quite different from one another. For the 2-channel case, we set $\mu_1 = 1000$, σ_1=10. Figure 2.8 shows several typical cases of ObjectSize-β_2 curve. In Fig. 2.8(a), the estimated object size reaches maximum when $\beta_2 = 1.00$. In Fig. 2.8(b), when $\beta_2 = 0.16$, the estimated object size reaches maximum; note that the mean and the std. deviation (relative to the mean) for the second channel for this test case are significantly different from Channel 1. In Fig. 2.8(c), when $\beta_2 = 0.69$, the estimated object size reaches maximum.

For the 3-channel case, we set $\mu_1 = 1000$, σ_1=10. β_1 was always equal to 1 for the situations discussed below. Figure 2.12 shows several typical cases of the optimization function surface for varying β_2 and β_3. In most cases the surfaces are as in Fig. 2.12(a), in which the estimated object size reaches maximum when $\beta_2 = 1.00$ and $\beta_3 = 1.00$. However, in many cases such as in Fig. 2.12(b), when $\beta_2 = 0.16$ and β_3 =1.00, the estimated object size reaches maximum.

Multi-Server Simulation

To do a multi-server simulation, first we generate the number of

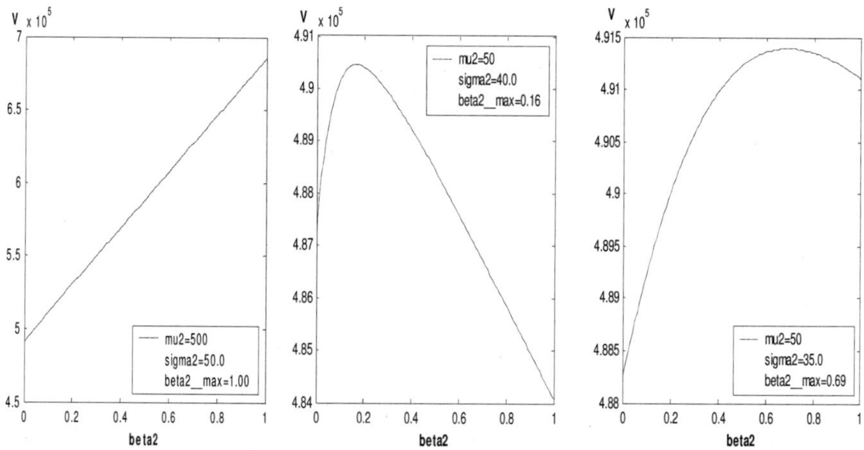

Fig. 2.11 Expected object size curves for varying β_2, 2-channel case.

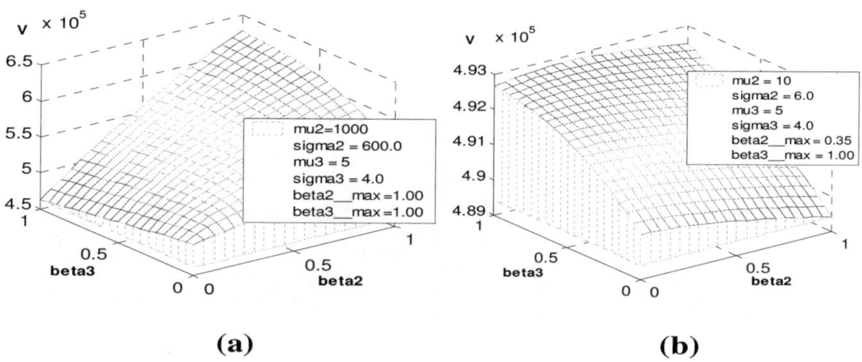

Fig. 2.12 Expected object size surfaces for varying β_2 and β_3, 3-channel case.

channels (K) randomly between 1 and 10. For each channel, its mean (μ_i) is generated randomly between 1 and 1000, and its standard deviation (σ_i) is generated randomly between 0 and μ_i. We do 30 tests. For each test, the simulation is performed 100 times (with two different confidence levels 0.95 and 0.75) and the averages are computed. The number of time slices (N) is 100.

To estimate improvement, as with the 2-server simulation, we first verify how well it guarantees that the real transmission will be finished within a time limit at the given confidence level. We observe the percentage of overtime runs, which could not finish transmission within the time limit.

Then, we measure the improved percentage of the real size of successfully transmitted media objects.

Figure 2.13 shows how well the confidence level is guaranteed. When the confidence level is 95%, in most cases, the percentage of runs that fail to finish on time ranges from 4% to 8%. When the confidence level is 75%, in most cases, the percentage of runs that fail to finish on time ranges from 20% to 27%. This means that the confidence level of the collaborative retrieval algorithm is preserved within a reasonable range.

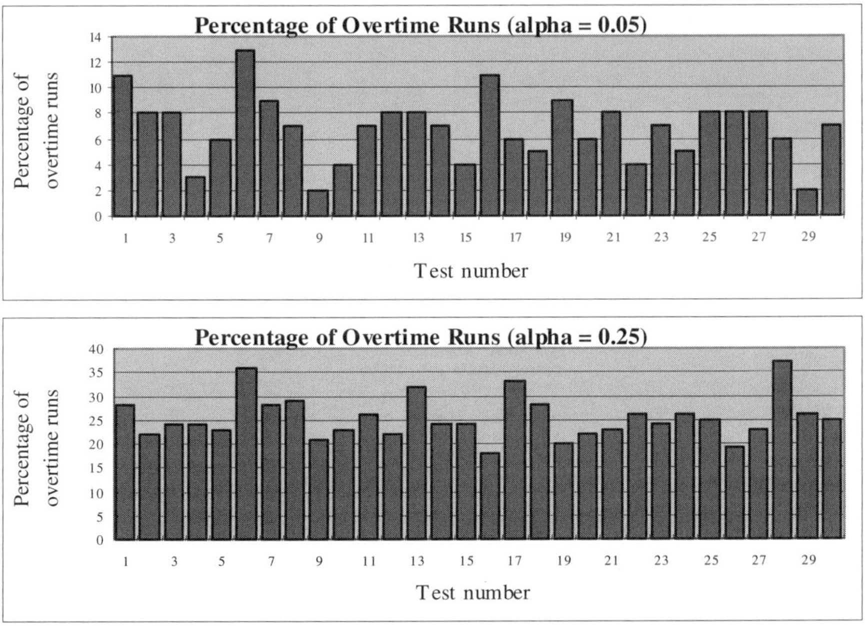

Fig. 2.13 The percentage of overtime runs, which fail to finish transmission within time limit; confidence level 95% (top) and 75% (bottom).

Figure 2.14 demonstrates how well we improve on the estimated object size. For both 95% and 75% confidence levels, we achieve better-estimated object size. The improved percentages range from 1% to 41%. We also find that the more the number of channels, the more the improvement. This is owing to the fact that with the method in Section 3.2, the more the number of channels, the higher the confidence level of each channel needs to be; because the previous method estimates each channel independently resulting in joint probabilities being the product of individual probabilities.

In other words, with the previous method the more the number of channels, the more the servers idle after finishing their independent task resulting in more bandwidth being wasted.

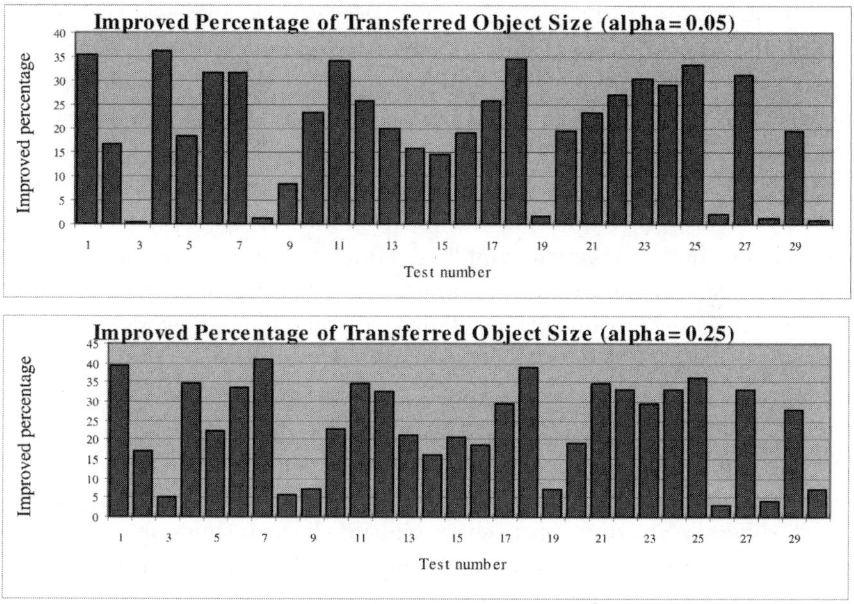

Fig. 2.14 Improved percentage of estimated object size, for transmissions completed within time limit; confidence level 95% (top) and 75% (bottom).

2.4 Summary

In this chapter, we described a model to determine the optimal amount of bandwidth testing for network-aware multimedia object retrieval applications. The model treats the bandwidth testing as sampling from an actual bandwidth population. It uses a statistical estimation method to determine the estimation confidence interval when each new bandwidth sample is obtained. This confidence interval is then used to determine whether bandwidth testing should continue. We implement the model in a pair of Java Client/Server programs and demonstrate the effectiveness and efficiency of the model. The strategy effectively determines the optimal amount of bandwidth testing to be performed in different network conditions, introduces negligible computation overhead and meets the user specified QoS requirement (time limit) with meaningful guarantee level (the confidence goal). We focus on communication between a pair of client and server in this research; in the next chapter, we will discuss extension of this model to the application of monitoring multiple servers from one client.

Following the study of single server retrieval, we analyzed the problem of optimal bandwidth monitoring for QoS based multimedia retrieval applications with distributed servers. Two approaches were proposed depending on whether or not the distributed servers complete a retrieval task independently or collaboratively. The proposed algorithms have several important features: First, it delivers a user confidence level for QoS specified by the user by accurately estimating the future bandwidth. Second, it dynamically determines how much sampling should be performed under different characteristics of the available channels so as to maximize the size of the multimedia object transmitted. Third, all the channels work together or independently to estimate the total available bandwidth. Finally, for collaborative retrieval we introduce a reliability factor between 0 and 1 for each channel, to maximize the estimated object size.

In the following chapters we will see how bandwidth monitoring can be tied to scalable multimedia, including image, video and 3D transmission. A big difference in our approach to multimedia transmission compared to traditional methods is that we will emphasize human perception, and the concept of perceptual quality, in our strategies.

References

Basu, A., Cheng, I. and Yu, Y. (2003). Multi-server optimal bandwidth monitoring for qos based multimedia delivery, in *IEEE International Symposium on Circuits and Systems* (Bangkok, Thailand).

Bolliger, J. and Gross, T. (1998). A framework-based approach to the development of network-aware applications, *IEEE Transactions on Software Engineering* **25**, 5, pp. 376–390.

Bolliger, J. and Gross, T. (1999). Bandwidth modeling for network-aware applications, in *Proceedings of Infocomm* (San Francisco, CA).

Braden, R., Zhang, L., Berson, S., Herzog and Jamin, S. (1997). *Resource ReSerVation Protocol (RSVP) Version 1 Functional Specification (RFC 2205).*

Cheng, I., Basu, A., Zhang, Y. and Tripathi, S. (2001). QoS specification and adaptive bandwidth monitoring for multimedia delivery, in *Proceeding of EUROCON* (Bratislava, Slovak Republic), pp. 485–488.

Ferguson, P. and Huston, G. (1998). *Quality of Service: Delivering QoS on the Internet and in Corporate Networks* (Wiley Computer Publishing).

Ferrari, D., Gupta, A. and Ventr, G. (1997). Distributed advance reservation of real-time connections, *ACM/Springer Verlag Journal on Multimedia Systems* **5**, 3.

Gopalakrishna, G. and Parulkar, G. (1994). Efficient quality of service in multimedia computer operating systems, Tech. rep., Dept. of CS, Washington University.

Harnett, D. (1982). *Statistical Methods*, 3rd edn. (Addison-Wesley Publishing Company, Inc.).

Miloucheva, I. (1995). Quality of service research for distributed multimedia applications, in *ACM Pacific Workshop on Distributed Multimedia Systems.*

Pacifici, G. and Stadler, R. (1995). An architecture for performance management of multimedia networks, in *IFIP/IEEE Int. Symposium on Integrated Network Management.*

Vogel, A., Kerherv'e, B., Bochmann, G. V. and Gecsei, J. (1995). Distributed multimedia and QoS: a survey, *IEEE Multimedia* **2**, 2.

Wang, X. and Schulzrinne, H. (1999). Comparison of adaptive internet multimedia applications, *IEICE Trans. on Communications* **E82-B**, 6, pp. 806–818.

Yu, Y., Cheng, I. and Basu, A. (2003). Optimal adaptive bandwidth monitoring for QoS based retrieval, *IEEE Transactions on Multimedia.*

Zhang, L., Deering, S., Estrin, D., Shenker, S. and Zappala, D. (1993). RSVP: A new resource reservation protocol, *IEEE Network* **7**, 5, pp. 8–18.

Zwillinger, D. (1996). *CRC Standard Mathematical Tables*, 30th edn. (CRC Press).

Chapter 3

Wireless Protocols

A. Khan

3.1 Introduction

Transmission Control Protocol (TCP) over Internet protocol (IP) is the de-facto protocol for reliable transmission of data over the internet. TCP is a connection-oriented transport layer protocol. It requires a TCP connection to be established between the two communicating processes before any data transmission can occur. The two main functions of TCP are to provide reliable data transfer and prevent congestion in the network. TCP employs a feedback mechanism to transmit data reliably and in-order. A congestion window is used by TCP to prevent congestion in the network.

User Datagram Protocol (UDP) is the other transport layer protocol for the Internet. Unlike TCP, UDP is a connectionless protocol that allows instantaneous communications between two processes without waiting for a connection to be established. UDP does not provide special functionalities like, reliable transmission or congestion control in the network. In the absence of congestion control, a process can send data at an unregulated rate over UDP. This favors real-time applications like streaming multimedia and Internet telephony that require a minimum data rate and can also tolerate some data losses.

TCP was designed for the wired network that incurs data losses primarily due to congestion in the network. The emergence of wireless network has introduced error-prone wireless links and mobile users or hosts. A wireless link is also sensitive to the direction of propagation, ambient noise, multi-path fading and general interference. In addition, the mobility of the hosts may cause frequent disconnections. These adverse characteristics of a wireless network can cause data losses even in the absence of congestion in the network. Since TCP attributes a loss to congestion in the network, it immediately invokes a congestion control mechanism. Upon invocation, congestion control drastically reduces the sender's transmission rate. The unnecessary invocation of congestion control makes the wired or standard TCP unsuitable for wireless networks.

Over the past ten years, Researchers have proposed numerous methods to modify the standard TCP to make it adaptable to the wireless environment. In this chapter, we present some of theses modifications or protocols. These protocols can be classified into three approaches: **link layer**, **end-to-end** or **split-connection**. The link layer approach attempts to hide the losses on a wireless link from the transport layer by performing local retransmission at the link layer. In an end-to-end approach, a TCP sender detects and recovers from losses over an error prone wireless link. Finally, the split-connection approach isolates the wireless portion of a connection from the wired portion. This allows the problems associated with the wireless link to be quarantined and solved independently.

We begin the chapter with an overview of the standard TCP in Section 3.1. In Section 3.2, a brief overview of UDP is presented. The characteristics of a wireless network that make it unsuitable for the standard TCP is discussed in Section 3.3. In Section 3.4, we categorize, describe and analyze the performance of few of the protocols that have been proposed to improve the performance of standard TCP over wireless links. In Section 3.5, the pros and cons of each of the protocols are presented and then the chapter concludes with few final thoughts.

3.2 Transmission Control Protocol

Connection Establishment

TCP is a connection-oriented protocol that requires a connection to be established between the communicating processes. The process that initiates the connection is referred to as the *client* and the process the client connects to be the *server*. The client sends a special TCP segment to request a connection with the server. Upon receiving the request, the server creates the connection and notifies the client with another special TCP segment. Finally, the client acknowledges the reception of the connection establishment segment. The first two TCP segments do not contain any application data, but data transmission can start with the third segment. Since three segments are sent between the processes, this connection establishment process is termed as a *three-way handshake.* A TCP connection is full-duplex and allows both the client and server to simultaneously transmit data to each other. Each communicating process maintains two buffers: a *send window* and a *receive window.* Data are transmitted via the send window and the received data are buffered in the receive window. A sender's *usable window* is fraction of the send window that can be used to transmit new data. The size of the usable window is limited by the available buffer space in the receiver's receive window, termed as the receiver's *advertised window.* By controlling the sender's transmission window, the receiver enforces a flow control in the network. The flow control prevents the sender from overwhelming the receiver with information. The communication between processes occurs via TCP segments. A TCP segment comprises of application data and 20 bytes of TCP header. When a process wants to transmit a stream of data (bytes) over TCP, the data are first fragmented into TCP segments and queued in the send window. The *maximum segment size* (MSS) in the header limits the maximum number of bytes that can be encapsulated per segment. Upon the completion of data transmission, the connection can be terminated by either process.

Reliable Data Transfer

One of the important functionalities of TCP is to provide a reliable and in-order transmission of data. This is achieved with the sequence (SEQ) and acknowledgement (ACK) number fields in the header of a TCP segment. The TCP sender assigns a sequence number to each segment it sends to the receiver. Each of the processes chooses its initial sequence number and notifies the other during the connection establishment phase. The sequence number of a segment reflects the byte-stream number of the first byte in the segment. As an example, if the MSS is 500 and the first segment of 500 bytes send by the sender has a SEQ# 350 then the second segment will have a SEQ# 850. The receiver acknowledges the reception of a data segment with a TCP segment, called an ACK that has a value for the ACK field. The ACK# is set to SEQ# + MSS to indicate the SEQ# of the next data segment expected by the receiver. Continuing with our example, the reception of data segment with SEQ# 350 prompts a TCP segment with ACK# 850 from the receiver. TCP uses non-decreasing cumulative acknowledgements to ensure that the transmitted data is received both reliably and in-order. This implies that an acknowledgement with ACK#

(SEQ# + MSS) will be followed by ACK# (SEQ# + 2*MSS), (SEQ# + 3*MSS) and so on, confirming the reception of MSS bytes of data each time. The TCP receiver delivers the received data in-order to the host's data in-order to the host's application layer. If a data segment other than the expected one arrives at the receiver then that segment is buffered while the receiver waits for the expected segment. Once the expected segment arrives, both the segments are acknowledged and sent in-order to the application layer.

Loss Detection and Retransmission

A transmitted segment or an acknowledgment may be lost in the network and not reach its destination. This can lead to a potential deadlock where the sender waits for an ACK segment and the receiver waits for a data segment. In such a situation, the sender is responsible for the detection of the lost segment. Upon detecting a loss, the sender retransmits the last unacknowledged data segment. A retransmission provides another opportunity for a data segment to reach the receiver and the corresponding ACK to arrive at the sender. In order to perform a retransmission, the TCP sender maintains a timer for each transmitted segment. If the timer expires before an ACK is received for the segment, the sender assumes that the segment is lost and resends it. This event is known as a *retransmission timeout* (RTO). A RTO is illustrated in Fig. 3.1 where timeout at the sender causes retransmission of segment, DATA# 2850.

The RTO value of a segment is calculated based on the round trip time (RTT) of the segment. The RTT of a segment is the time elapsed between the transmission of the segment and the arrival of an acknowledgement for the segment. The sender places a time stamp on each data segment it transmits. The receiver copies the time stamp on the ACK segment it returns for the data segment. Upon receiving the ACK, the sender subtracts the time stamp value from the current time to calculate the RTT for the segment. Due to congestion in the routers, the RTT values may fluctuate from segment to segment. In order to obtain a smooth RTT value, the sender maintains a running average of the RTT values, called the *AverageRTT*. Once the RTT of a segment is calculated, the AverageRTT is updated as follows:

$$AverageRTT = (1 - \alpha) \times AverageRTT + (\alpha \times RTT)$$

A typical value of α is 0.125 [Kurose and Ross (2001)]. The weighted AverageRTT puts more weight on recent RTT values than the old ones to

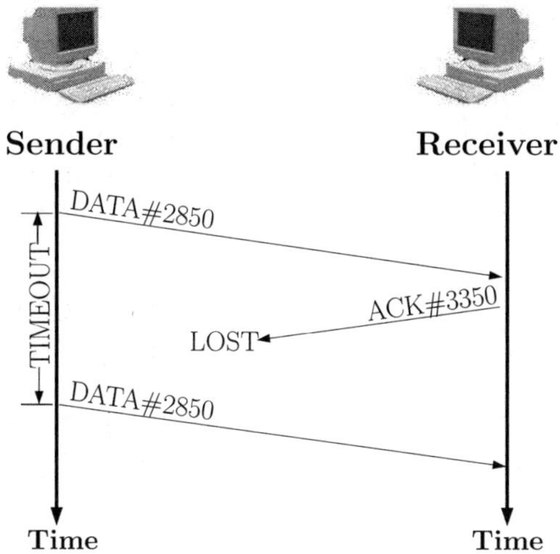

Fig. 3.1 Data retransmission based on timeout at the sender.

depict the current state of the network more accurately. From the AverageRTT, the RTO of a transmitted segment is set as follows:

$$RTO = AverageRTT + (4 \times Deviation)$$

where, Deviation is the difference between the RTT and AverageRTT and is calculated as follows:

$$Deviation = (1 - \alpha) \times Deviation + \alpha \times |RTT - AverageRTT$$

Congestion Control

In a wired network like the Internet, loss of a segment is primarily attributed to congestion in the network. The retransmission of the lost segment cannot prevent the further loss of segments in the presence of congestion. Obviously, a congestion control mechanism must be available to control the sender's transmission rate to prevent congestion in the network or minimize the losses during a congestion period. TCP Tahoe [Jacobson (1988)] was the first variation of TCP to introduce algorithms for congestion control. The proposed algorithms for congestion control were *slow start, congestion avoidance* and *fast retransmit.* Subsequent variations of TCP have introduced additional algorithms to further improve the performance of TCP in detecting and recovering from losses during congestion in the network. In this chapter, we present three such TCP variations:

Reno [Jacobson (1990)], New Reno [Hoe (1996)] and SACK [Fall and Floyd (1996)]. Reno introduces a fast recovery algorithm that follows the fast retransmit mechanism. New Reno modifies the fast recovery algorithm to recover multiple lost segments within the same transmission window. Finally, with TCP SACK, a receiver can explicitly specify the lost segments. A timeline of Tahoe, Reno, New Reno and SACK is presented in Fig. 3.2.

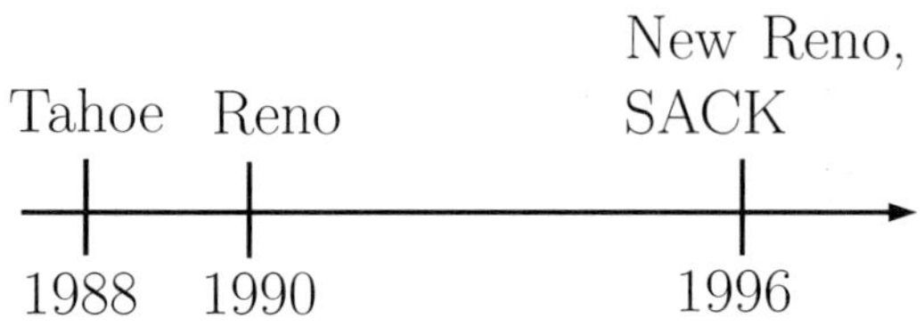

Fig. 3.2 A timeline of TCP variations with congestion control mechanism.

Tahoe

In TCP Tahoe, the sender controls congestion in the network with the aid of a *congestion window* (CWND). A CWND allows the sender to enforce flow control in the network whereas, the receiver can control the network flow with its advertised window. The sender's usable window is then set to *Minimum* (advertised window, CWND). As mentioned earlier, TCP Tahoe introduces three algorithms for congestion control: *slow start, congestion avoidance* and *fast retransmit.* The TCP sender operates in either the slow start or the congestion avoidance mode to control congestion in the network. The slow start algorithm allows the sender to quickly increase its CWND. Once equilibrium is reached, the sender switches to the congestion avoidance mode. In the congestion avoidance mode, the sender increases the CWND slowly to prevent congestion in the network.

When data transfer is initiated, the sender starts in the slow start mode with the CWND equal to one TCP segment of MSS. For each new data segment acknowledged, the sender increments the congestion window by 1 MSS. This increases the CWND exponentially per RTT until the *slow start threshold* (SSTHRESH) is reached. Upon reaching the SSTHRESH, the sender enters the congestion avoidance mode. In congestion avoidance, the sender increments its congestion window by 1/CWND for each new acknowledgement it receives. This is a linear increase of the CWND as at most one new data segment can be transmitted per RTT.

The initial value of SSTHRESH is set to an arbitrarily high value. Once a loss is detected by a timeout, the sender sets SSTHRESH to *Maximum* (CWND/2, 2) and then, the CWND to 1 to enter slow start mode. In slow start, the sender retransmits the last unacknowledged data segment. Finally, the RTO is set to a back-off interval that doubles with each consecutive timeout. The above sequence of actions reduces the traffic load in the network to control congestion. The congestion control mechanism is illustrated in Fig. 3.3. The sender starts in the slow start mode with CWND set to 1 at time zero. When an ACK arrives for the transmitted segment, the sender increases its CWND to 2 at time 1. Similarly, the acknowledgements for these two segments will increase the CWND to 4 at time 2. This is the slow start phase where the CWND doubles per RTT. Once the CWND reaches the SSTHRESH, set to 16, the sender enters the congestion avoidance mode and increases its CWND by one segment per RTT. When a timeout occurs at time 9, the sender sets SSTHRESH to 10 (half of the CWND) and then drops the CWND to 1 to invoke slow start again.

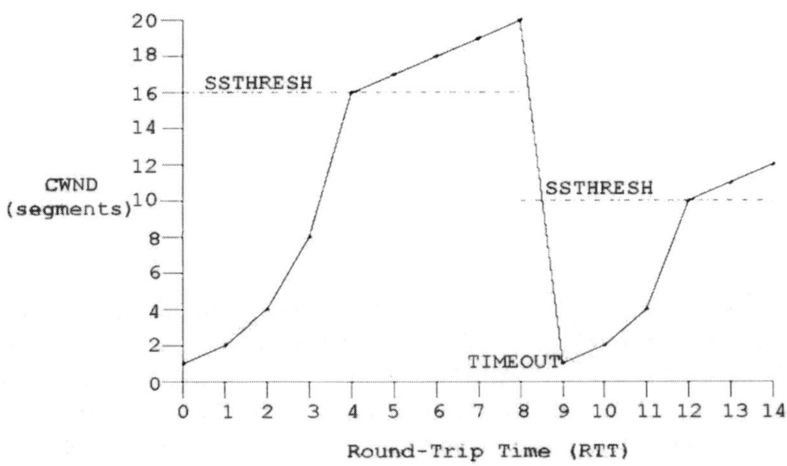

Fig. 3.3 The slow start and congestion avoidance mechanisms.

A timeout forces a TCP sender to wait for a fixed period of time before the lost segment can be retransmitted. In order to reduce the waiting period, TCP Tahoe introduces a second retransmission mechanism called the *fast retransmit*. The sender monitors the received acknowledgements to determine the states of the transmitted segments. We illustrate the

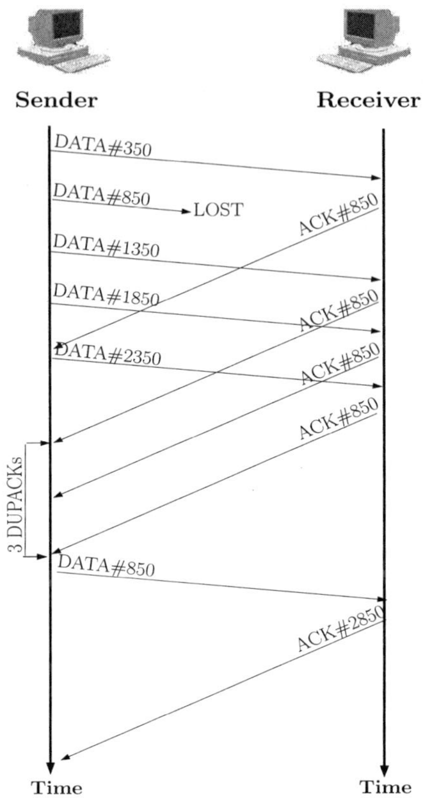

Fig. 3.4 Data retransmissions with the fast retransmit mechanism.

mechanism with an example in Fig. 3.4. Suppose at an instance, the sender has transmitted four data segments (DATA# 350, 850, 1350 and 1850) of MSS 500 to the receiver. All the segments except DATA# 850 arrive at the receiver. The arrival of the first segment DATA# 350, prompts the receiver to send an acknowledgement with ACK# 850. The loss of segment DATA# 850, allows DATA# 1350 to arrive next at the receiver. Since the receiver expected segment DATA# 850, it terms DATA# 1350 as an *out-of-order segment.* The receiver buffers an out-of-order segment but, does not acknowledge the reception of it. Instead, the receiver resends an acknowledgement requesting the lost segment. At the sender, the arrival of a new acknowledgement ACK# 850, prompts the sender to transmit a new data segment, DATA# 2350. When the sender receives two consecutives acknowledgments with the same ACK#, the latter is termed as a *duplicate acknowledgement* (DUPACK) of the first. A threshold of DUPACK (usually three) is a good indication that the transmitted data segment is lost. The sender then invokes the fast retransmit mechanism to immediately retransmit the last unacknowledged segment. The SSTHRESH is then set to *Maximum* (CWND/2, 2) and CWND is reduced to 1 to invoke the slow start mode. Upon receiving the retransmitted segment DATA# 850, the receiver acknowledges the reception of all data segments up to DATA# 2350 with ACK# 2850.

Reno

In TCP Tahoe, the sender enters the slow start mode following a fast retransmit. A slow start reduces the CWND to 1 regardless of the state of the network. However, the triple DUPACK that initiates a fast retransmit provides additional information other than just the loss of a segment. These duplicate acknowledgements are an indication that three data segments have left the network and are buffered at the receiver (DATA# 1350, 1850 and 2350 in Fig. 3.4).

TCP Reno [Jacobson (1990)] utilizes this additional information and allows the sender to enter a *fast recovery* phase following the fast retransmit. Upon receiving a triple DUPACK, the fast retransmit mechanism retransmits the last unacknowledged segment and sets the SSTHRESH to *Maximum* (CWND/2, 2) as in Tahoe. The fast recovery mechanism then sets the CWND to (SSTHRESH + 3*MSS). For each additional DUPACK received, the sender increments the CWND by 1 MSS. If allowed by the new CWND, the sender transmits a new segment. The sender exits fast recovery upon receiving a *partial acknowledgement*. A partial ACK is the first new ACK that follows the duplicate acknowledgements. The partial ACK confirms the reception of all the segments in the CWND. Before exiting fast recovery, the sender sets its CWND to SSTHRESH and enters the congestion avoidance phase.

New Reno

A partial ACK in Reno signals the end of fast recovery. However, if multiple segments from the same transmission window is lost then the sender has to wait for a RTO to retransmit the additional segments. New Reno [Hoe (1996)] avoids such an undesirable situation with a modification to the fast recovery mechanism. In New Reno, the sender only exits fast recovery when it receives a new ACK that acknowledges the reception of all the segments that were outstanding at the beginning of the fast retransmission phase. The new ACK is an acknowledgement for the highest sequence numbered segment transmitted by the sender.

In TCP with SACK, the receiver uses a SACK option in addition to the cumulative acknowledgements. A SACK option allows the receiver to notify the sender of the reception of out-of-order segments. TCP with SACK is presented in more details in Section 3.3. Among the TCP variations, TCP Reno is the most widely used version for the Internet [Kurose and Ross (2001)]. In this section, we have presented an extensive overview of TCP with a focus on the reliable data transfer and congestion control mechanism. An interested reader may refer to [Stevens (1994)] for a more elaborate description of TCP.

3.3 User Datagram Protocol

User Datagram Protocol (UDP) is a connectionless protocol that does not require a connection to be established between the communicating processes. When Process A wants to communicate with Process B over UDP, Process A stamps the port number of Process B on the data and sends it. In UDP, processes communicate via UDP datagrams. An UDP datagram comprises of application data and 8 bytes of header. Unlike TCP, UDP does not provide functionalities like reliable data transfer or congestion and flow control. The limited functionalities allow a UDP datagram to have only 8 bytes of header compared to the 20 bytes of header in a TCP segment.

A connectionless UDP is preferred over TCP when the delay in setting up a connection may be unnecessary and costly. For instance, a DNS query prefers UDP to provide a quicker service. Unlike TCP, an UDP process does not maintain connection states. This allows an UDP server to support many more active clients than a TCP server. The absence of flow and congestion control allows processes to transmit data at an unregulated rate over UDP. This characteristic of UDP suits real-time applications like Internet telephony and streaming multimedia. Both of these applications require a minimum transmission rate and are able to tolerate losses due to congestion in the network.

3.4 Limitation of TCP in Wireless Networks

TCP was developed for the wired Internet where, the end-points were fixed hosts (FH). However, the evolution of cellular and Ad hoc wireless networks has introduced mobile hosts (MH). A *cellular network* is a hierarchical-structured network where, mobile hosts reside in cells. Each cell contains a base station (BS) that acts as the communication gateway for the mobile hosts within the cell. The connection between a MH and its BS is wireless. A BS connects to the fixed network via a mobile switching center (MSC). A MSC controls multiple base stations via wired connections. On the other hand, an *Ad hoc network* is an infrastructure-less network where, the mobile hosts within the network communicate via wireless links. Each MH in an Ad hoc network has the dual responsibility of being either a sender or a receiver or a router for segments destined for other hosts. The introduction of wireless links and mobile hosts has introduced new challenges for the wired or standard TCP. The characteristics of wireless networks and their impact on TCP performance are discussed next.

Error prone links: Wireless links are prone to a high bit error rate (BER). BER is the probability of error per bit. Errors in wireless links usually occur in bursts. A wireless link toggles between two states: *good error state* and *bad error state*. In the good error state, a wireless link experiences a low BER in the range of 10^{-6}. However, in a bad error state, the BER can be as high as 10^{-2} [Bakshi *et al.* (1997)]. An error-prone link can cause frequent loss of both data and ACK segments. With the loss of ACK segments, the TCP sender may only retransmit a segment once a RTO occurs. An end-to-end retransmission incurs latency and creates traffic overload over the entire network although the loss occurred over the wireless link. The sender exponentially backs-off its RTO timer and shrinks its CWND to 1. Consecutive timeouts exponentially back-off the retransmission timer of the sender and induce an idle period of very low throughput. Hence, the error prone wireless links have falsely induced the sender to invoke congestion control when the losses were due to high BER.

Variable bandwidth: Wireless links have limited and variable bandwidth. In a cellular network, each cell has an assigned bandwidth. The bandwidth of a MH inversely varies with the number of mobile hosts in the cell. The smaller bandwidth limits the size of segments that can be transmitted over a wireless link. As a segment traverses from a wired to a wireless link, it is fragmented into smaller segments to fit the bandwidth of the wireless link. The loss of a smaller sub-segment will require retransmission of the entire segment. A retransmission may incur loses and falsely invoke congestion control to degrade the transmission throughput.

Frequent disconnections: Disconnections in a wireless network is caused due to blocked radio signals and the mobility of the nodes. In a cellular network, the migration of a MH to a new cell requires a connection to be established with a new BS. This is known as a *handoff* as the old BS hands over the communication responsibility of the MH to the new BS. A handoff induces a brief period of disconnection. A disconnection halts communication between hosts.

Disconnections are also common in an Ad hoc network. The mobility of a node causes an existing route to become stale. As a result, a new route needs to be established to the node or through the node (if it is not the destination). The creation of a new route causes disconnection and latency. In both cellular and Ad hoc networks, the segments that are in-transit as the MH moves will be lost as well and require retransmission through a RTO.

3.5 Improving Performance

Researchers over the past ten years have studied the performance of TCP over wireless networks. Several modifications or protocols have been proposed to make standard TCP adaptable to wireless links and mobile hosts. Since cellular and Ad hoc wireless networks have different architectures, specific protocols have been proposed for each. In this section, we restrict ourselves to some of the protocols that can improve the performance of TCP in a cellular network. Most of these protocols are based on the assumption that the data transfer occurs from a FH to a MH. These protocols can be categorized into three categories: link layer, end-to-end or split connection approaches as shown in Fig. 3.5.

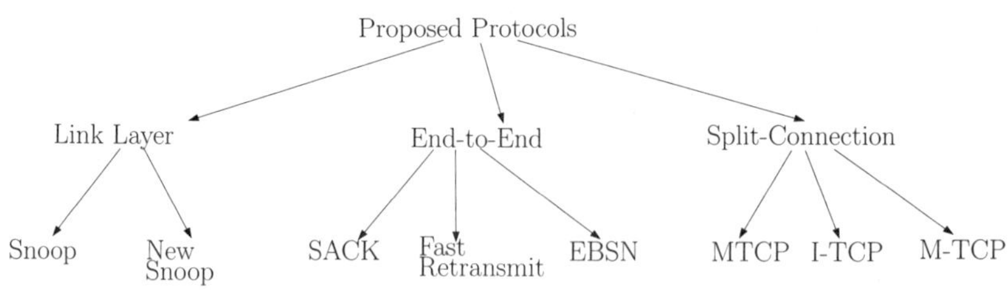

Fig. 3.5 Protocols proposed to improve TCP performance over a cellular network.

3.5.1 *Link-Layer Approach*

A link layer protocol attempts to hide the error over the wireless link from the transport layer. In this approach, a link layer proxy or agent at the BS detects a loss and performs a local recovery. In this section, we present two link layer protocols: Snoop [Balakrishnan *et al.* (1995a)], [Balakrishnan *et al.* (1995b)] and New Snoop [Hu *et al.* (2003)]

3.5.1.1 *Snoop*

The Snoop protocol addresses losses encountered over the wireless link during both data transmission and handoffs. Snoop consists of a *snoop module* and a *routing protocol*. The snoop module handles the losses during data transmission and the routing protocol minimizes losses during a handoff.

The snoop module resides at the BS and acts as a forwarding agent for the segments (both data and ACK) that pass through the BS from either direction. For every data segment received from the sender (FH), the snoop module caches a copy of the segment at the BS, if space is available, before it is forwarded to the receiver (MH). A segment in the BS buffer is removed after its reception is acknowledged by the MH. The BS also maintains a local timer to determine the average RTT for a forwarded segment over the wireless link. If the snoop module receives a DUPACK or a local RTO for a transmitted segment then it retransmits the segment from the BS buffer, if a copy of the segment is cached at the buffer. This is known as a *local retransmission*. Otherwise, the FH is notified of the failed transmission. A local retransmission by the snoop module shields the sender from the loss over the wireless link. Therefore, the sender is not forced to invoke congestion control and drop its transmission rate.

The routing protocol provides a multicast based handoff period of short duration. When the current BS, BS1 receives a handoff request from a MH, the routing protocol at BS1 starts to multicast the data destined for the MH to all the nearby base stations. The surrounding base stations only buffer the segments while BS1 still forwards the segments to the MH. Upon completion of a handoff, the new BS, BS2 starts to forward segments from its cache to the MH. Since BS2 is unaware of the segments received thus far by the MH, the initial ACK from the MH allows BS2 to synchronize with the MH. The multicast based handoff approach reduces the losses during a handoff by priming the cache at the new BS.

In [Balakrishnan *et al.* (1995a)], the performance of Snoop is measured under varying error conditions and handoff frequencies. Experiments have shown that Snoop achieves a throughput up to 20 times than that of the standard TCP under higher BER. In terms of handoff, Snoop completes a handoff within one-tenth of a time of the standard TCP. Furthermore, the mirroring of state at surrounding BS during a handoff help sustaining a throughput comparable to that achieved in the absence of a handoff.

3.5.1.2 *New Snoop*

The Snoop protocol has three potential drawbacks. First, a local retransmission of an out-of-order segment must be triggered by a local RTO at the BS. Second, the FH may timeout during a local recovery at the BS. Third, the performance of Snoop degrades in face of frequent handoffs because each handoff requires the cache to be build at the new BS. As a result, an initial period of low throughput will be observed. These shortcomings are addressed in New Snoop (NS).

In NS, like Snoop, data segments are cached at the BS if an earlier copy of the segment does not reside in the buffer and buffer space is available. A segment is removed from the cache once the MH acknowledges the reception of it. Similarly, like Snoop, an in-order segment is retransmitted by the BS if a DUPACK requesting the segment is received. In contrary to Snoop, NS maintains a DUPACK counter at the BS for the out-of-order segments in its cache. The first two DUPACKs for an out-of-order segment are relayed to the FH. However, once a third DUPACK arrives, the BS performs a local retransmission of the segment and suppresses the DUPACK. The DUPACK counter allows the BS retransmits the lost segment without waiting for a local RTO.

The second major contribution of NS is to prevent a timeout at the FH during a local recovery at the BS. This is achieved with the addition of an extra delay to the estimated RTT. The delay is calculated as the product of the RTT and BER over the wireless link. The additional delay will introduce a longer but, more stable RTT measurement at the FH. This in turn will reduce the probability of inappropriate timeouts during local recovery.

NS employs a hierarchical caching scheme where, data segments are cached both at the BS and MSC. Losses during data transmission are recovered with a local recovery from the cache at the BS. However, during a handoff, NS primes the cache of the new BS with the aid of the cache at the MSC. Once a handoff is initiated to a new base station BS2, the MSC reroutes the TCP connection to BS2 and keeps track of the segments that have been sent to BS1. During the handoff, the MSC gathers information from BS1 about the segments waiting for acknowledgements from the MH. Upon acquiring the required information, the MSC forwards the unacknowledged segments from its cache along with their RTO values to BS2.

The performance of NS is compared with Snoop under high BER and during handoffs. The results show that NS achieves about 5% more throughput than Snoop when the wireless link experiences a very high BER. However, the hierarchical caching scheme of NS recovers from losses caused by a handoff more efficiently than Snoop. In such case, the improvement in NS throughput is shown to be as much as 20% more than Snoop.

3.5.2 *End-to-End Approach*

In an end-to-end approach, the TCP sender is responsible for both the detection and end-to-end retransmission of the lost segment(s). In this section, we describe three end-to-end protocols: TCP with SACK [Fall and Floyd (1996)], Fast-retransmit [Caceres and Iftode (1995)] and EBSN [Bakshi *et al.* (1997)].

3.5.2.1 *Selective Acknowledgments*

In TCP Tahoe, Reno and New Reno, the cumulative ACK from the receiver does not include information about the out-of-order segments that may have been received and buffered at the receiver. Knowledge of the out-of-order segments buffered at the receiver may allow the sender to retransmit the missing segments in a single RTT. The concept of attaching additional information to an ACK was introduced in TCP with selective acknowledgement (SACK).

TCP with SACK provides the receiver with a SACK option in addition to the cumulative ACK. A SACK option allows the receiver to attach up to three SACK blocks to an ACK. A SACK block contains two sequence numbers. The left-hand number corresponds to the starting sequence of a contiguous block of data that has been received and buffered by the receiver. The right-hand number indicates the sequence number of the expected segment in the contiguous block. The receiver uses the first block to report the most recently received segments. Upon receiving an ACK with a SACK option, the sender retransmits the missing data segments in a single RTT without waiting for timeouts.

We illustrate TCP with SACK option with an example. Suppose at an instance, the sender transmits 5 data segments with MSS of 500 and the sequence number of the first segment being 2000. Consider the following scenarios.

Scenario 1: The first 4 segments are received but, the last one is dropped. In this case, the receiver sends a cumulative ACK with ACK# 4000 and no SACK option is specified.

Scenario 2: The 1st segment is lost but, the remaining 4 segments arrive at the receiver. Then for each of the 4 received segments, the receiver will generate ACK# 2000 to request the lost segment. Each such ACK will also include a SACK block as follows:

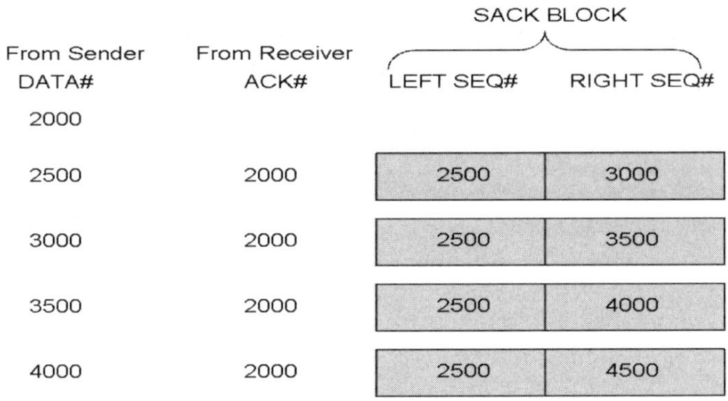

Scenario 3: The 1st and the 3rd segments are lost. In this case, the reception of the 2nd, 4th and 5th segments trigger ACK with the following SACK option:

TCP with SACK option employs the same algorithms as Reno for congestion control in the network. In [Fall and Floyd (1996)], the performance of TCP with SACK is compared with Tahoe, Reno and New Reno when multiple segments are dropped from the same transmission window. The results show that, regardless of the number of dropped segments, Tahoe is required to enter a slow start mode to recover from the losses. On the other hand, Reno waits for a RTO to recover from the loss of multiple segments. Although New Reno can recover from multiple losses without waiting for a RTO, recovery of each segment requires a single RTT. In comparison, TCP

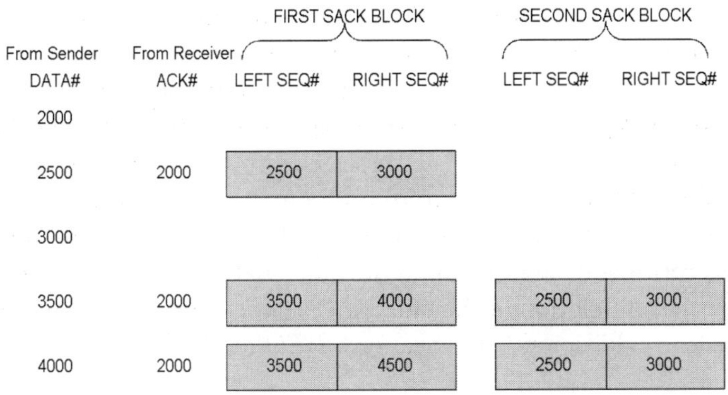

with SACK outperforms the others as it can recover from multiple losses in a single RTT. Although TCP with SACK option can improve the performance of TCP over wireless links, it is independent of any mobile wireless networking environment and is not designed to maintain performance during a handoff.

3.5.2.2 *Fast Retransmit*

In a cellular network, the migration of a MH to a new cell results in a handoff. A handoff induces an idle period of communication since the transmitted data cannot reach the MH. Upon completion of a handoff, data communication may resume once a RTO occurs at the sender. Although a handoff is usually completed within a couple of hundred milliseconds, the coarse timer used by TCP (usually 300–500 msec) enforces an idle period of few hundreds to thousands milliseconds before a RTO occurs at the FH. In order to reduce the idle period, the FH immediately invokes fast retransmit upon completion of the handoff.

The MH can notify the FH about the completion of a handoff in one of two ways. In the first approach, the MH sends a specially marked TCP ACK segment with the sequence number of the last data segment successfully received by the MH. The second approach involves sending three DUPACK to notify the FH. The first alternative requires modifications at the TCP sender whereas, the second alternative consumes more network resources. As soon as the handoff confirmation message from the MH arrives, the FH invokes the fast retransmit algorithm.

The effectiveness of the fast retransmit approach is illustrated in Fig. 3.6 when a MH undergoes a handoff from BS1 to BS2. For both Fig. 3.6(a) and 3.6(b), a MH crosses the cell boundary at time 0. Upon the arrival of a beacon from BS2, the MH and BS1 require 50 msec and 150 msec respectively, to change their routes to BS2. Additionally, it takes the FH 50 msec to invoke the fast retransmit algorithm after both the MH and BS1 have changed their routes. Two scenarios are considered. In the first scenario (Fig. 3.6(a)), the beacon from BS2 arrives instantaneously (0 msec delay) after the MH crosses into the new cell. In this case, the invocation of the fast retransmit algorithm allows the FH to start communication 50 msec after the completion of the handoff. In comparison, the standard TCP has to wait an additional 650 msec for a RTO at the FH.

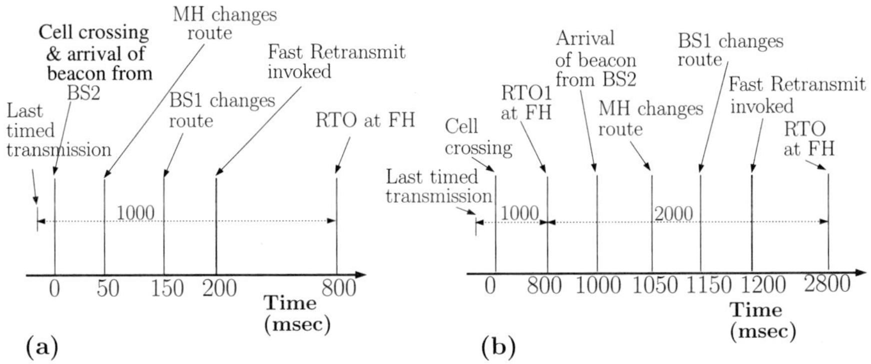

Fig. 3.6 Fast-retransmit after handoff with (a) 0 msec delay, (b) 1000 msec delay.

In the second scenario (Fig. 3.6(b)), the MH has to wait 1000 msec for the arrival of a beacon from BS2. This may force the FH to timeout before the handoff is completed and exponentially back-off its retransmission timer. As a consequence, without fast retransmit, a FH has to wait 1650 msec following the completion of a handoff to resume its transmission. The fast-retransmit procedure still allows the FH to resume communication 50 msec after the handoff. In both scenarios, the invocation of fast retransmit immediately after the completion of a handoff allows the FH to resume transmission 50 msec after the completion of a handoff.

3.5.2.3 *Explicit Bad State Notification*

As observed in Snoop, the FH may timeout while the BS performs a local recovery. Snoop avoids such a timeout largely due to the coarse granularity (~300–500 msec) of a TCP retransmission timer. A coarse timer translates to a longer RTO at the FH because the RTT between the FH and MH is much greater than the time to complete a local recovery. However, a timer of finer granularity (~100 msec) may cause the FH to timeout during local recovery at the BS. Therefore, the BS must be made aware of a local recovery

A local recovery at the BS is initiated when the wireless link resides in a bad error state and little data is able to get across to the MH as shown in Fig. 3.7(a). As a consequence, the data segments from the FH are queued at the BS. At such an instance, a notification can be sent to the FH to reduce its transmission rate. One of the possibilities is to send an *explicit congestion notification* (ECN) message. In a wired network, an ECN is used by the receiver to inform the sender of prevalent congestion in the network. Upon reception of an ECN, the sender reduces its CWND to allow the network to recover from the prevalent congestion. However, the segments already queued at the BS may require multiple local retransmissions before they reach the MH. The additional delay can cause the FH to timeout while the local recovery is in progress.

An ECN message fails to prevent a RTO at the sender because of its inability to update the RTO timer at the FH. As an alternative notification scheme, the explicit bad state notification (EBSN) mechanism is introduced. The BS sends an EBSN message to the FH after each failure to send a packet over the wireless link (Fig. 3.7(b)). Upon receiving the EBSN, the FH resets its RTO timer to its previous value. Usually, the BS continuously sends an EBSN while the wireless link resides in a bad error state. Once the FH receives an ACK, an indication that the bad error state has passed, it recalculates its RTO value. The ACK signaling the end of the bad error state can cause a large variance in the RTT calculation. However, the wireless link's exit from the bad error state will allow the smooth flow of acknowledgements to steady the RTT. Overall, the prevention of a RTO at the FH by an EBSN message avoids the unnecessary invocation of congestion control and subsequent reduction of the sender's CWND. It is shown that EBSN improves the performance of TCP by 100% in wide-area wireless networks and by 50% in local-area wireless networks.

In addition to introducing EBSN, a variation in the segment size over the wireless link is also explored in [Bakshi *et al.* (1997)]. In order to determine the optimal segment size, the performance of different segment sizes over the wireless link is empirically recorded as the BER of the link is varied. The results are then used by the BS to select the optimal segment size according to the BER of the wireless link. Experiments have shown that

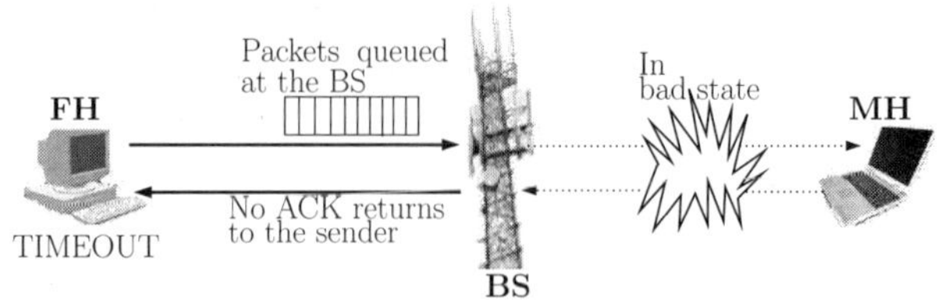

(a) Wireless link in bad state without EBSN

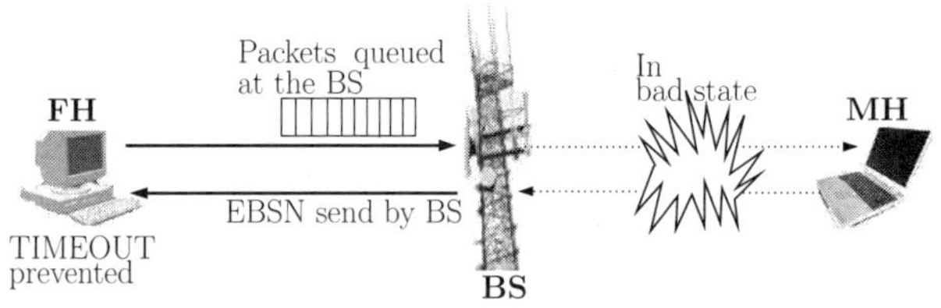

(b) Wireless link in bad state with EBSN

Fig. 3.7 The EBSN protocol.

the selection of the optimal segment size can improve the TCP throughput by 30%.

3.5.3 *Split Connection*

In the split connection approach, the connection between a FH and a MH is split into two separate connections at the BS: a wired connection between the FH and the BS and a wireless connection between the BS and the MH. The intuition behind this approach is to separate the wired and the wireless links. The isolation allows problems associated with the wireless link to be identified and solved without modification to the wired network. In this section, we discuss three split connection protocols: MTCP [Yavatkar and Bhagwat (1994)], I-TCP [Bakre and Badrinath (1995)] and M-TCP [Brown and Singh (1997)].

3.5.3.1 *Multiple TCP and Selective Repeat Protocol*

One of the first split-connection based approaches utilizes a new session layer protocol called MHP (Mobile Host Protocol). The MHP resides both at the BS and MH and serves three functions. First, it establishes a split TCP connection between a FH and a MH. Second, it recovers from losses on the wireless link during data transmission. Third, MHP transfers connection states during a handoff.

The connection setup mechanism in MTCP is depicted in Fig. 3.8. When a MH at address and port number <*MHaddr, MHport*>, intents to communicate with a FH at <*FHaddr, FHport*>, the MHP at the MH first establishes a connection with its peer at the mobile host's current BS at <*BSaddress, BSport*>. Then the peer MHP at the BS creates a proxy MHP agent that has the same address and port number (<*MHaddr, MHport*>) as the MH. Finally, the proxy MHP establishes a connection with the FH at <*FHaddr, FHport*>. A similar chain of events occur in the reverse order when a FH initiates a connection with a MH. In either case, the connection between a MH and a FH is split at the BS into two separate connections.

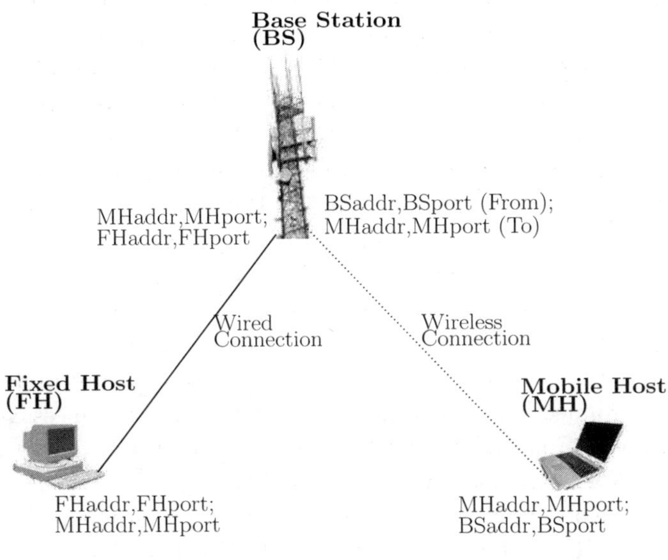

Fig. 3.8 Connection setup in a split-connection protocol.

Once a connection is established, data transfer can start between the MH and FH. When the MH sends data segments to the FH, they first arrive at the BS over the wireless link. The BS buffers the segments and immediately sends an ACK back to the sender. The buffered segments are then forwarded to the FH over the wired connection. Similarly, data segments from the FH are buffered, acknowledged and relayed to the MH. In both situations, the sender may receive an ACK before the transmitted data segment reaches the destination. Obviously, this violates the end-to-end TCP semantics. Since wireless links have a low bandwidth, the data segments sent by the MH are fragmented into smaller segments to match the smaller MTU over the wireless link. The MHP agent at the BS reassembles the smaller segments into larger segments, to utilize the greater bandwidth over the wired link, before forwarding them to the FH. Similarly, segments from the FH are fragmented into smaller segments at the BS and then forwarded to the MH .

The second functionality of MHP is to recover from losses over the wireless link. Two recovery mechanisms are proposed. In the first scheme, called *Multiple TCP* (MTCP), standard TCP is used to establish each connection. In the second scheme, a specialized protocol called *Selective Repeat Protocol* (SRP) establishes the wireless connection and the standard TCP is used to complete the second connection over the wired network. The SRP receiver uses the SACK option to report the reception of out-of-order segments. On receiving a SACK, the MHP at the BS retransmits, from its buffer, all the missing segments specified in the SACK block(s).

When a MH migrates to a new cell, the MHP is responsible for transferring the connection states. A handoff is completed in five steps. Upon receiving signals from the new base station BS2, the MHP at the MH suspends its data transfer and provides its peer at BS2 with the address of the current base station, BS1. The MHP peer at BS2 then creates a new MHP proxy for the connection. The new proxy sends a handoff message to BS1 requesting the state information for the two connections. Once the information is received, the MHP at BS2 re-creates the state information for both the connections and sends a connection resume message to the MHP of the MH. Finally, the MHP at BS1 forwards the buffered segments to BS2 and data transfer resumes with the FH.

Two notable observations can be made from a performance comparison of MTCP and SRP with a single standard TCP connection between a FH and a MH. First, SRP requires less time (better throughput) than both MTCP and the single standard TCP connection to complete the transfer because SRP can recover from multiple losses in a single RTT. Second, the performance of MTCP in the absence of both mobility and errors is better than a single TCP connection. This can be explained as follows. First, the standard TCP uses the small MTU size on the wireless link to transfer segments over the entire connection (both wired and wireless) however, reassembly at the BS allows MTCP to utilize the larger bandwidth of the wired link to send MTU of larger sizes. Second, the split-connection approach recovers faster from losses over the wireless link because the RTT between the MH and FH is reduced to the RTT between the MH and the BS.

3.5.3.2 *Indirect-TCP*

Indirect-TCP (I-TCP) is another split-connection based protocol. Like MTCP, it also requires modifications at both the BS and MH. An I-TCP daemon like MHP runs at the BS and is responsible for the creation of a split-connection between a FH and MH. In addition, the I-TCP daemon is also responsible for transferring connection states during a handoff. However, unlike MHP, it does not employ a special protocol like SRP to recover from multiple losses over the wireless link.

The I-TCP daemon creates a split-connection in a manner similar to MHP in MTCP as depicted in Fig. 3.8. Once a connection is established, data communication can be initiated between the FH and MH. In I-TCP, like MTCP, the BS buffers and immediately acknowledges a transmitted segment. As a consequence, the end-to-end TCP semantics is again violated. When the MH migrates to a new cell, the I-TCP daemon is responsible for the transfer of the connection states. A handoff is completed as follows. Upon receiving a beacon from a new base station BS2, the MH sets BS2 as its default gateway router. It then sends the address and port number of the MH and old base station BS1, to BS2. Upon receiving the connection end-points, the I-TCP daemon at BS2 creates sockets for both the wireless and wired connections to accommodate the MH. BS2 then requests the I-TCP connection states from BS1. Once the information arrives, BS2 acquires the address and port number of the FH and restarts the connection. In order to quickly resume data transmission, the timer at BS2 is reset to invoke a RTO and force BS2 to enter the slow start mode.

The performance of I-TCP is compared with a single standard TCP connection both in the absence and presence of mobility of the MH. Under both scenarios, I-TCP outperforms the single TCP connection. As mentioned in MTCP, the improved performance of I-TCP is due to the much shorter RTT between the MH and the BS. In addition, the reset of the timer at the new base station following a handoff allows I-TCP to quickly resume data transmission with the MH. On the other hand, the single TCP connection has to wait for a RTO to resume communication after a handoff.

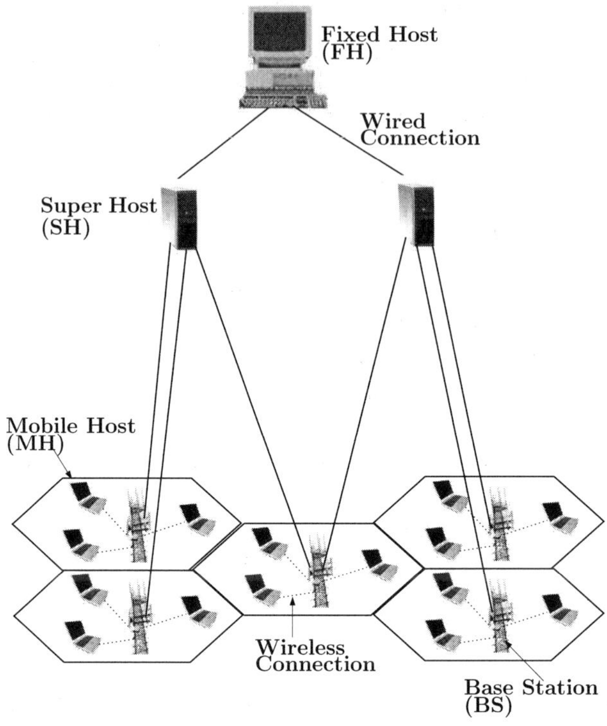

Fig. 3.9 The M-TCP architecture.

3.5.3.3 *Mobile-TCP*

Both MTCP and I-TCP have two major drawbacks. First, they violate the end-to-end TCP data transmission semantics. Second, during a handoff, a considerable amount of connection states need to be transferred to the new BS. These short comings of a split-connection based protocol have been over come with Mobile-TCP (M-TCP). The primary goal of M-TCP is to improve the performance of TCP during periods of disconnections of the MH.

M-TCP is based on a cellular architecture proposed in [Brown and Singh (1996)]. The proposed architecture is shown in Fig. 3.9. It is a three-tier hierarchical architecture akin to a standard cellular architecture. However, instead of a MSC, the new architecture includes a specialized machine termed as the *supervisor host* (SH). A SH is responsible for establishing a connection, completing a handoff and preventing unnecessary congestion control at the FH due to the disconnection of the MH. The complexity of the SH is the major drawback of the architecture.

A SH establishes a connection, split at the SH, between a FH and MH. During the connection setup, the SH dynamically assigns bandwidth to each MH based on the host's need and the condition of the wireless link. Since a wireless link is allocated the required bandwidth, data can always be transmitted at the maximum rate without congestion. Once a connection is established and the bandwidth is allocated, data communication may be initiated between the two hosts. The segments from either host is first received and buffered at the SH before being forwarded to the destination host. However, unlike MTCP and I-TCP, the received data is not instantaneously acknowledged. Instead, the SH waits for an ACK from the MH and then forwards the ACK to the FH. Clearly, M-TCP is able to preserve the end-to-end TCP semantics.

During data communication, the SH ensures that the FH does not invoke congestion control when the MH is temporarily disconnected or is in a cell with little bandwidth. In order to achieve this, the FH is forced into persist mode when the MH disconnects. A TCP sender can be forced into persist mode once the CWND is set to zero. The CWND can be set to zero when the sender receives a new ACK accompanied with a window update. To preserve a new ACK, the SH forwards to the FH all but, the last ACK it has received from the MH. However, the last ACK is also forwarded if the SH has received acknowledgements from the MH for all the transmitted data segments. In order to determine the instance at which the FH should be forced into persist mode, the SH maintains a timer to force the sender into persist mode before a RTO occurs. The FH remains in persist mode until the MH reconnects or avails itself of greater bandwidth. Upon reconnection, the MH sends an old ACK accompanied by a window update to the FH via SH. This allows the FH to exit the persist mode (a new ACK is not required to exit persist mode) and resume data transmission at full speed. The SH also maintains a timer to calculate the RTT for an ACK on the wireless link. If the MH disconnects then the SH enters persist mode at the expiration of the RTT timer without invoking congestion control. As previously, a reconnection ACK from the MH takes the SH out of persist mode.

The M-TCP architecture allows a MH to roam within the domain of the same SH (several BS are controlled by a single SH) for a longer time to avoid frequent handoffs. When a MH roams into the domain of another SH, a handoff is initiated between the two supervisor hosts. Experiments have shown that M-TCP outperforms a single standard connection when the FH and MH are placed 5 hops away. As previously mentioned, the improved performance is due to the shorter RTT over the wireless link, which allows a faster retransmission of the lost segments. However, M-TCP does not provide the same level of performance when the MH is 15 hops away from the FH. The degradation in performance is believed to be caused by the fixed network (the Internet) with a loss rate between 5.1% and 23.8% during light traffic hours. The losses over the wired network force the FH to wait for a RTO to recover.

3.6 Discussion and Final Thoughts

In this Section, we compare the pros and cons of the protocols mentioned in Section 3.4. Both the link layer protocols, Snoop and New Snoop, have three pros. First, modification is only required at the BS with the placement of a proxy or agent. Second, local retransmission by the BS hides short periods of low communication quality from the sender and prevents unnecessary invocation of congestion control by the sender. Third, the advance caching of data enables a very short handoff period (~10–20 msec) and allows the sender to resume data communication without experiencing noticeable delay.

On the other hand, the performance of Snoop degrades in face of frequent handoffs because each handoff requires the cache at the new BS to be primed, resulting in an initial period of low throughput. New Snoop avoids such problem with its hierarchical caching scheme. However, both Snoop and New Snoop will experience performance degradation if the MH is disconnected for a lengthy period of time. In such case, the FH will repeatedly timeout and retransmissions will cause the caches at the BS and MSC to overflow since no ACK from the MH arrives to clear the existing segments in the caches. In Snoop, the FH may also timeout while a local recovery is in progress at the BS. Finally, due to the limited cache space, neither Snoop nor New Snoop can always guarantee a local retransmission of a lost packet.

Among the end-to-end protocols, both TCP with SACK and the fast retransmit scheme do not require any modification to the BS. Although TCP with SACK can recover from multiple losses in a single RTT, it does not maintain performance during a handoff. On the other hand, the fast retransmit scheme is designed specifically to ensure the quick resumption of data transmission at the completion of a handoff. However, during frequent disconnections, repeated invocations of the fast retransmit algorithm will repeatedly halve the sender's CWND. Similarly, if the MH is disconnected for a lengthy period of time then a RTO at FH will invoke congestion control and shrunk the CWND. Moreover, the fast retransmit approach does not provide any special functionality beyond that of the standard TCP to quickly detect and recover from losses over the wireless links.

The major contribution of EBSN is the prevention of a RTO at the FH during a local recovery at the BS. In addition, EBSN does not require maintenance of state information at any intermediate host and is independent of the granularity of a TCP timer. On the other hand, it has three drawbacks. First, it requires modification to TCP implementation at the source. Second, bad network latency can cause the EBSN to arrive late at the sender. A delayed EBSN may not accurately depict the current state of the wireless link. Third, the bad error state period can be of a very short duration such that when the EBSN reaches the sender, the link is no longer in a bad error state. In addition, EBSN also does not consider performance degradation due to a handoff.

Among the split-connection protocols, both MTCP and I-TCP exhibit two undesirable characteristics. First, they do not maintain the end-to-end TCP data transmission semantics. Second, huge connection states need to be transferred during a handoff to recreate the connections at the new BS. M-TCP avoids such problems largely due to its specific architecture. The architecture allows M-TCP to handle frequent and lengthy disconnections more efficiently whereas, MTCP and I-TCP may run out of buffers.

On the other hand, the complexity of the supervisor host in the architecture is a major drawback of M-TCP. In addition, unlike MTCP and I-TCP, in M-TCP, the connection between a FH and MH is split at the SH and not the BS. Since the connection between a SH and BS is a wired connection, the split does not completely isolate the wireless link and its characteristics completely from the wired network. Finally, unlike I-TCP, MTCP with SRP can recover from multiple segment losses in a single RTT.

Table 3.1 summarizes the attributes of the wireless network handled by the protocols discussed in this chapter.

In this chapter, we have presented the characteristics of a wireless network that degrade the performance of standard TCP. We have then presented and analyzed the performance of few of the protocols proposed to improve the performance of TCP over wireless network. The fast emergence of both wireless networks and mobile hosts will demand an improved

Table 3.1 Summary of the proposed protocols.

	Snoop	New Snoop	SACK	FR	EBSN	MTCP	I-TCP	M-TCP
End-to-end TCP semantics	Y	Y	Y	Y	Y			Y
High BER	Y	Y	Y		Y	Y	Y	
Lengthy disconnections						Y	Y	Y
Frequent disconnections		Y				Y	Y	Y
Handoff	Y	Y		Y		Y	Y	Y

performance in the near future. Therefore, we conclude that a TCP protocol deigned for a wireless network must exhibit the following characteristics [Elaarag (2002)]:

- Erroneous triggering of congestion control mechanisms at the FH must be avoided.
- The FH should also avoid the serial timeout problem.
- Provide reliability in the face of unreliable links with high BER.
- A handoff should be completed in a smooth and efficient manner.
- The frequent and long disconnections of a MH should be handled correctly.
- The limited bandwidth and power scarcity of a MH should be taken into consideration.
- A dynamic packet size may be used depending on the dynamic bandwidth available for mobile hosts.
- End-to-end TCP data transmission semantics must be preserved.
- Finally, should provide compatibility such that, no change is required at the FH.

References

Bakre, A. and Badrinath, B. (1995). I-TCP: Indirect TCP for mobile hosts, in *Proceedings 15th Int. Conf. Distributed Computing Systems (ICDCS)*, pp. 136–143.

Brown, K. and Singh, S. (1996). A network architecture for mobile computing, in *Proceedings of IEEE INFOCOM*, pp. 1388–1396.

Brown, K. and Singh, S. (1997). M-TCP: TCP for mobile cellular networks, *Computer Communication Review*, pp. 19–43.

Bakshi, B., Krishna, P., Vaidya, N. H. and Pradhan, D. (1997). Improving performance of TCP over wireless networks, in *Int. Conf. on Distributed Computing Systems.*

Balakrishnan, H., Seshan, S. and Katz, R. (1995a). Improving reliable transport and handoff performance in cellular wireless networks, *ACM Wireless Networks* **1**, 4, pp. 469–481.

Balakrishnan, H., Seshan, S. and Katz, R. H. (1995b). Improving TCP/IP performance over wireless networks, in *presented at the 1st ACM Int. Conf. Mobile Computing and Networking (Mobicom)* (Berkeley, CA).

Caceres, R. and Iftode, L. (1995). Improving the performance of reliable transport protocols in mobile computing environments, *IEEE J. Select. Areas Comm.* **13**, pp. 850–857.

Elaarag, H. (2002). Improving TCP performance over mobile networks, *ACM Computing Surveys* **34**, 3, pp. 357–374.

Fall, K. and Floyd, S. (1996). Simulation-based comparisons of Tahoe, Reno, and SACK TCP, *Comput. Commun. Rev.*, pp. 5–21.

Hoe, J. C. (1996). Improving the start-up behavior of a congestion control scheme for TCP, in *Proc. ACM SIGCOMM* (California).

Hu, J., Feng, G. and Yeung, K. L. (2003). Hierarchical cache design for enhancing tcp over heterogeneous networks with wired and wireless links, *IEEE Trans. On Wireless Communication* **2**, 2.

Jacobson, V. (1988). Congestion avoidance and control, in *Proc. of SIGCOMM Symposium on Communications Architectures and Protocols*, pp. 314–329.

Jacobson, V. (1990). Modified TCP congestion avoidance algorithm, URL `ftp://ftp.ee.lbl.gov/email/vanj.90apr30.txt`, technical Report of end2end-interest mailing list.

Kurose, J. F. and Ross, K. W. (2001). *Computer Networking: A Top-Down Approach Featuring the Internet* (Addison & Wesley).

Stevens, R. W. (1994). *TCP/IP Illustrated, Volume 1: The Protocols* (Addison Wesley).

Yavatkar, R. and Bhagwat, N. (1994). Improving end-to-end performance of TCP over mobile internetworks, in *Proc. of Workshop on Mobile Computing Systems and Applications*, pp. 146–152.

Chapter 4

Overview of 3D Coding and Simplification

I. Cheng and L. Ying

In this book we consider texture mapped 3D meshes for representing 3D objects. There is vast literature on texture compression following the JPEG and JPEG2000 standards [JPEG (2000)], [Skodras *et al.* (2001)]. Thus we will not review these well-known and widely discussed topics here. Instead, we will briefly review the approach to texture compression adopted in many video cards, and then review existing mesh simplification strategies in this chapter.

4.1 Texture Compression for Video Cards

Even though JPEG and JPEG2000 are very useful in communication of images over bandwidth limited networks, they have some shortcomings as compression standards for texture compression in graphics video cards. One of the requirements in real-time graphics cards is the need for fast computations and access, at the rate of 30 frames per second or better. A limitation of JPEG and JPEG 2000 is that given a region in the uncompressed image it is not possible to automatically determine the corresponding region in the compressed image. The compressed image region may be image specific, since different images of the same size may compress to different sizes in the compressed domain. This makes it difficult to easily zoom into a section of a JPEG image in real time. The alternative for video cards is to use uncompressed texture files, which can be very expensive for the limited on-card memory, or use a compression method that produces the same compression ratio for all images of a given size allowing a direct mapping from a given uncompressed texture region to the corresponding compressed texture region.

r11, g11, b11	r12, g12, b12	...	
r21, g21, b21			
			r44, g44, b44

Fig. 4.1 A 4 × 4 pixels block (B) with 8 bits for each red (r), green (g) and blue (b) component, *i.e.* (r_{ij}, g_{ij}, b_{ij}) represents 24 bits, giving a total of 16x24 bits = 384 bits.

S3TC Coding

Let C_0, C_1, C_2 and C_3 be the four colors (can be in any order) in each row with C_0 and C_3 representing the lowest and highest values. C_0 and C_3 are coded by 16 bits each. The other two colors C_1 and C_2 are interpolated from C_0 and C_3 and do not need to be stored.

Each of C_0, C_1, C_2 and C_3 is denoted by a 2 bits code 00, 01, 10 and 11 respectively. 32 bits are thus used to represent the 16 colors in the 4×4 pixels block. For example, the first row can be coded as:

00 11 01 00	10 01 01 01	11 00 00 10	01 10 01 11

C_0	C_3	C_1	C_0
C_2	C_1	C_1	C_1
C_3	C_0	C_0	C_2
C_1	C_2	C_1	C_3

C_0 and C_3 are stored values while C_1 and C_2 are interpolated. For example:

Stored value: $C_0 = 5$ and $C_3 = 90$

Interpolated value: $C_1 = 33$ and $C_2 = 61$

4.2 Overview of Mesh Coding

In order to reduce the storage and transmission requirements for meshes two steps can be considered: (i) mesh simplification, *i.e.*, reducing the number of vertices used to represent an object and (ii) mesh coding, *i.e.*, reducing coding redundancies in a given mesh. We will first discuss some mesh coding algorithms followed by an overview of simplification methods.

3D meshes are widely used in visualization applications, including manufacturing, architecture, medical imaging, military, geographic information systems, and entertainment. A 3D mesh is represented by geometry and connectivity [Taubin (1999)]. An uncompressed representation, such as the VRML ASCII format [VRML (1997)], is inefficient for transmission. In general 3D mesh compression schemes handle geometry data following three steps: quantization, prediction, and statistical coding. However, they are different from each other with regard to connectivity compression.

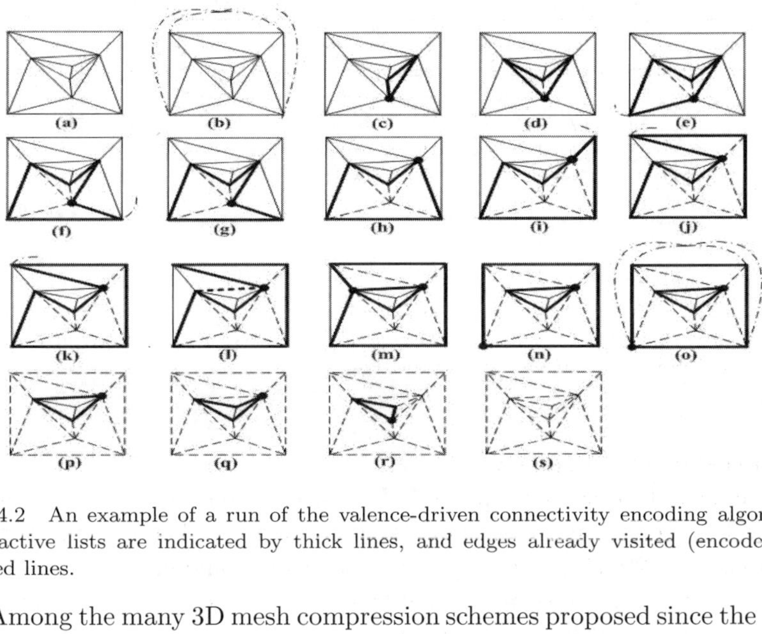

Fig. 4.2 An example of a run of the valence-driven connectivity encoding algorithm. The active lists are indicated by thick lines, and edges already visited (encoded) by dashed lines.

Among the many 3D mesh compression schemes proposed since the early 1990s [Peng *et al.* (2005)], the valence-driven approach [Touma and Gotsman (1998)] is considered to be the state-of-the-art technique for 3D mesh compression, with a compression ratio of 1.5 bits per vertex on the average to encode mesh connectivity. For mesh compression, the valence-driven approach is still among the best [Alliez and Desbrun (2001a)]. However, this approach is restricted to manifolds. Interested readers can refer to [Peng *et al.* (2005)] for more detail. A number of 3D mesh compression algorithms have been accepted as international standards. For example, Topological Surgery [Taubin and Rossignac (1998)] and Progressive Forest Split [Taubin *et al.* (1998)] have been adopted by VRML version 2 [VRML (1997)] and MPEG-4 version 2, defined as 3D Mesh Coding (3DMC) [ISO/IEC 14496-2]. Before introducing our perceptually optimized strategy in Chapter 9, we will describe how connectivity is handled in the valence-driven and 3DMC approaches, and the vulnerability of these algorithms to packet loss.

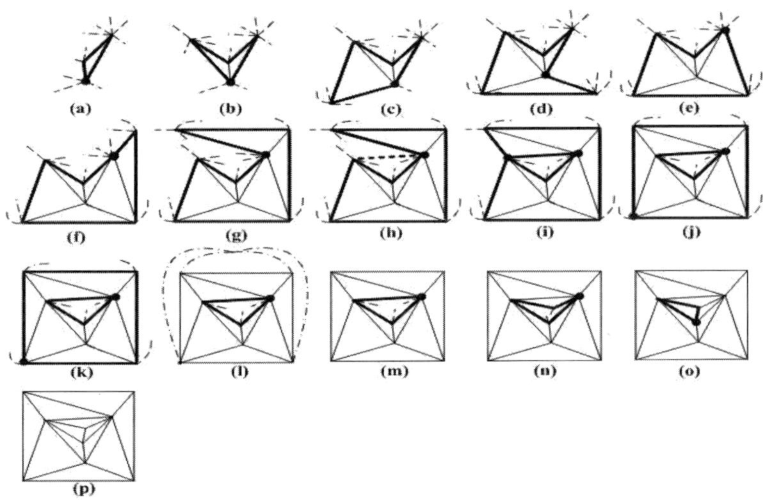

Fig. 4.3 An example of connectivity decoding (or reconstructing) from the stream of vertex valences in the valence-driven algorithm.

Valence-Driven Approach

Touma and Gotsman proposed the valence-driven algorithm to compress 3D meshes [Touma and Gotsman (1998)], which was then enhanced [Alliez and Desbrun (2001b)]. The algorithm begins by randomly selecting a triangle. Starting from a vertex of that triangle and traversing all the edges in a counter-clockwise direction (Fig. 4.2), the visited vertices are pushed into an *active list*. After visiting the associated edges, the next vertex is popped from the *active list*, and the process is repeated. The valence (or degree) of each processed vertex is output. From the stream of vertex valences, the original connectivity can be reconstructed, as shown in Fig. 4.3.

Topological Surgery

[Taubin and Rossignac (1998)] proposed a topological surgery method to compress mesh connectivity. The connectivity is represented by vertex spanning trees and triangle spanning trees. Figure 4.4 shows an example of vertex spanning tree and triangle spanning tree for a tetrahedron mesh.

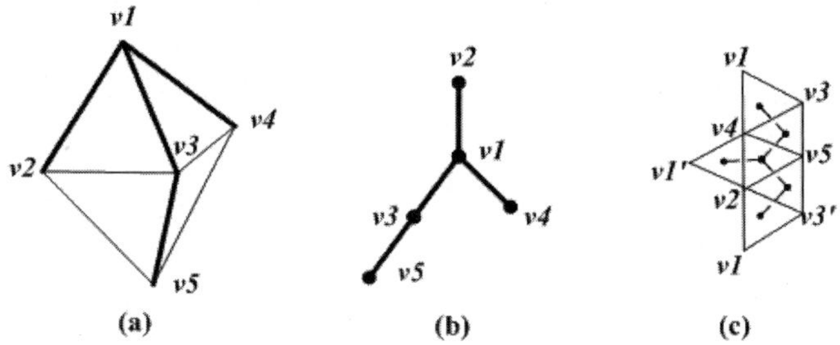

Fig. 4.4 An example of a vertex spanning tree and a triangle spanning tree for a tetrahedron mesh: (a) A tetrahedron mesh; (b) The vertex spanning tree; (c) The cut and flattened mesh with its triangle spanning tree depicted by dashed lines.

The vertex and triangle spanning trees are run-length encoded. A run is defined as a tree segment between two nodes with degrees not equal to 2. For each run of the vertex spanning tree, its length along with two additional flags are encoded. The first flag is the branching bit indicating whether a run subsequent to the current run starts at the same branching node, and the second flag is the leaf bit indicating whether the current run ends at a leaf node. Similarly, for each run of the triangle spanning tree, its length with the leaf bit is encoded. Furthermore, the marching pattern with one bit per triangle is encoded to indicate how the planar polygon is triangulated internally. The original mesh connectivity can be reconstructed from this set of information.

A run in the vertex or triangle spanning tree is a basic coding unit. The coding cost is proportional to the number of runs, which in turn depends on how the vertex spanning tree is constructed. To maximize the length of each run and minimize the number of runs generated, the vertex spanning tree is built similar to the way "we peel an orange" [Taubin and Rossignac (1998)] along a spiral path.

Experimentally, the Topological Surgery algorithm uses 2.48 7.0 bits per vertex for mesh connectivity. The time and space complexities of this algorithm are $O(N)$, where N is the maximum of the vertex number v, the edge number e, and the triangle number f in a mesh. A large memory buffer is needed to allow global random vertex access when decompressing.

Progressive Forest Split

To achieve progressive transmission of 3D meshes, [Taubin *et al.* (1998)] proposed the Progressive Forest Split method. The 3D mesh data is structured into multiple layers: one base layer and one or more enhancement layers. The base layer is encoded by the Topological Surgery algorithm. The enhancement layers use *Forest Split* operations to refine the model by cutting existing edges in the forest, creating new triangles in the crevices, and displacing the new vertices to their new positions (Fig. 4.5).

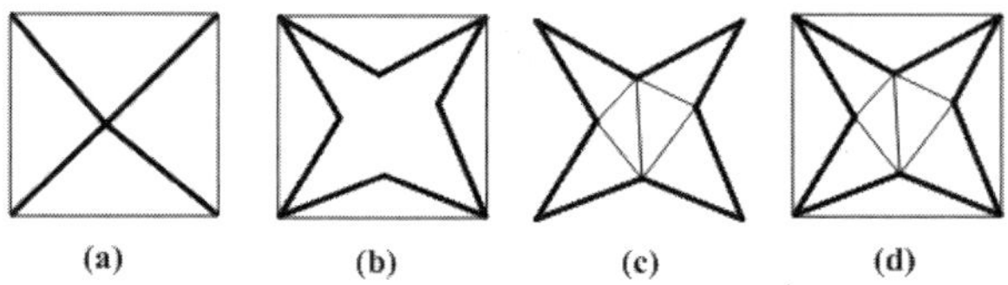

Fig. 4.5 An example of the Forest Split operation: (a) A low resolution mesh with a forest depicted by thick lines; (b) cutting the mesh along the forest edges and forming a crevice; (c) triangulation of the crevice; (d) the refined mesh.

Each forest split operation encodes the structure of the forest, triangulation of the crevices, and the vertex displacements. To encode the structure of the forest, one bit is used for each mesh edge, indicating whether or not it belongs to the forest. To encode the triangulation information of the crevices, the triangle spanning tree and the marching patterns, as in the Topological Surgery algorithm are used. To encode the vertex displacements, the difference between the original vertex position and the new position is Huffman-coded.

To progressively encode a given mesh with four or five Levels of Detail, the Progressive Forest Split algorithm uses about 7-10 bits per vertex for mesh connectivity and 20-40 bits per vertex for geometry, at 6-bit quantization resolution.

Transmission in MPEG-4 3DMC

To transmit encoded 3D meshes, characteristics including incremental rendering, error resilience, and progressive transmission are required. In the 3DMC [Pereira and Ebrahimi (2002)] bitstream, connectivity data is packed separately from the other geometry and photometry data and put into the initial part of the bitstream. This bitstream structure has two possible advantages. First, it makes incremental rendering possible. Once the decoder extracts connectivity data, it possesses the full topology. Thus, it can render part of the 3D mesh object, as it begins to decode the geometry data. Secondly, it brings error resilience. With this bitstream structure, if the connectivity data are intact, the decoder can still form the 3D mesh structure with some missing geometry or photometry data.

In order to minimize the impact of packet loss on the 3DMC decoded data in an unreliable networking environment, each 3DMC partition can be rendered independently. Without vertex graphs, reconstructing the 3D mesh is impossible. Therefore, a vertex graph, which is partitioned separately and is transmitted with higher priority, is relatively important.

Error Resilient Mesh Transmission

Current 3D mesh coding techniques mainly focus on coding efficiency, *i.e.* compression ratio, by transmitting incremental data. This approach is good without packet loss but is vulnerable to channel errors for irregular meshes. Figure 4.6 shows an example of error sensitivity of the Edgebreaker 3D mesh coding method [Lewiner *et al.* (2004)][Rossignac (1999)]. With one error character in the connectivity stream, the decoded mesh can change significantly and can be impossible to reconstruct.

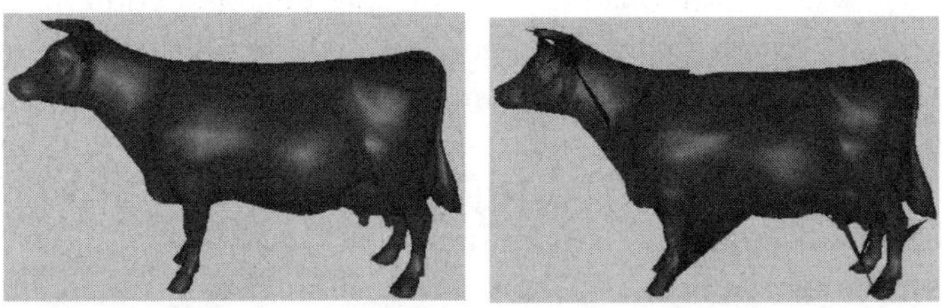

Fig. 4.6 An example of error sensitivity of the Edgebreaker 3D mesh coding method. **Left:** original 3D mesh; **Right:** Decoded 3D mesh with one error character in the decoded connectivity stream.

To transmit compressed 3D meshes over a lossy network, there are two approaches. The first approach is to compress 3D meshes in an error-resilient way. [Yan *et al.* (2001)] proposed partitioning a mesh into pieces with joint boundaries and encode each piece independently. However, if packets are lost, there are holes in the mesh resulting from missing pieces. [Jaromersky *et al.* (2005)] introduced multiple descriptions coding for 3D meshes. Each description can be independently decoded. But it assumes that the connectivity data is guaranteed to be correctly received. The second approach is to use error protection to restore lost packets [Alregib *et al.* (2005)] [Regib and Altunbasak (2002)].

Instead of transmitting duplicate packets to reduce the effect of packet loss, we adopt a perceptually optimized statistical approach in which adjacent vertices and connectivity information are transmitted in different packets so that the possibility of losing a contiguous segment of data is minimized. Furthermore, our model takes into consideration both geometry and texture data, while previous approaches discuss only geometry. Experimental results using both regular and irregular meshes show that perceptual quality is better preserved using our approach when data packets are lost over an unreliable network. In Chapter 9, we will review our statistical model, which optimizes the overall visual quality of a 3D object by allocating bandwidth appropriately between geometry and texture data.

4.3 Overview of Level of Detail (LOD) Techniques

When displaying 3D objects, the factors affecting visualization include geometric representation, texture, illumination, reflectance properties, human perception, and many others. A large number of modeling and simplification techniques were developed to focus on specific application requirements and constraints. Cartography was one of the early applications using model simplification. When 2-dimensional maps of large scale are produced, "Line generalization" is generally used to represent rivers, roads, and other features. The terrain model and height fields [Cignoni *et al.* (1997b)] [Floriani *et al.* (2000)] are useful for freight simulation applications, which require an aerial view of the scene. Many mesh simplification techniques have been proposed for more general 3-dimensional models in the last decade. Detailed surveys on mesh simplification can be found in [Heckbert and Garland (1997)] [Reddy (1997)] [Cignoni *et al.* (1997a)] [Luebke (2001)] [Pauly *et al.* (2002)]. Simplification techniques applied to parametric surfaces can be categorized as follows:

- Regular grid — This method is simple to implement. Regular range data are obtained directly from a range sensor. A simplified version can easily be generated by keeping one in every k scan-points in both the x and y directions. The sequence of simplified versions forms a pyramid hierarchy and thus level-of-detail (LOD). However, the simplified version may miss critical points or important 3D features of the object degrading visual fidelity.

- Hierarchical — In contrast to the non-adaptive property of regular grids, this method provides the adaptive counterpart of the pyramid structure. Regions are subdivided recursively forming a tree-like hierarchy such as R-Simp and BSP-Tree [Brodsky and Watson (2000)] [Shaffer and Garland (2001)]. Quadtree, k-d tree, or other divide and conquer strategies can also be used. Each branch node can only have one parent node. Hierarchical is different from other general triangulation methods such as Delaunay triangulation, where each triangle can belong to more than one parent. Hierarchical subdivision methods are fast, simple and facilitate multi-resolution modeling, but the tradeoff is a poorer visual quality than Delaunay triangulation which ensures that triangles have good aspect ratios and hence sliver (long and thin) triangles are avoided.
- Features — This approach performs triangulation based on a set of features or critical points. Edges between feature points are known as break lines. Feature detectors are usually 2×2 and 3×3 linear or nonlinear filters. Very often a weeding process is required to remove features that are too close together. An interesting research from Southard [Southard (1991)] uses the Laplacian as a measure of curvature to rank feature points, but his approach applies only to planar surface models and tends to distribute points uniformly, causing redundancy on low curvature surfaces and insufficient geometric data on high curvature surfaces.

Some other feature detection techniques found in the literature are designed for surface reconstruction, and not for model simplification. For example, an extended marching cube algorithm is used to detect feature points for surface reconstruction [Kobbelt *et al.* (2001)]. A neighborhood graph is used to extract feature lines from surface point clouds, to reconstruct a model from noisy data or under-sampled data [Gumhold *et al.* (2001)].

- Refinement — An early refinement technique can be traced back to Douglas' algorithm on 2D curve simplification [Douglas and Peucker (1973)]. Refinement methods in 3D start with a minimal approximation on a set of selected points and apply multiple passes. In each pass, the set is split and the region is re-triangulated until the final high-resolution triangulation is reached. Fowler applied a hill-climbing technique to locate a candidate point to insert into the triangulation.

A test point is initialized at the center of the triangle and it repeatedly steps up in the neighborhood until a local maximum is reached [Fowler and Little(1979)]. However, their approach may fail to find the global maximum within the triangle. Schmitt used a two-stage split-and-merge process [Schmitt and Chen (1997)]. The split process is similar to other vertex insertion algorithms. The merging process joins adjacent regions with similar face normals.

- Decimation — Opposed to the refinement methods, the idea is to start with all the range data or scan-points and recursively remove vertices from the triangulated mesh [Kalvin *et al.* (1991)] [Hinker and Hansen (1993)]. Scarlatos suggested an algorithm involving an initial triangulation and three phases: shrinking triangles with high curvature, merging adjacent coplanar triangles, and swapping edges to improve shape [Scarlatos and Pavlidis (1992)].
- Optimal — In general, optimal methods are less common than heuristic methods because they are slower and more expensive to implement. A minimum error or tolerance is defined based on some criteria. The best-effort simplification is obtained within the tolerance limit [Bronnimann and Goodrich (1994)] [Das and Goodrich (1995)]. This approach, however, is not efficient for online, especially interactive, applications.
- Perceptually driven — Different from the above techniques based on geometric metric, perceptually driven simplification methods are guided by human perception and quality preservation [Cohen *et al.* (1998)] [Lindstrom and Turk (2000)]. Vertices are removed only if they are imperceptible and do not degrade the visual quality. Most perceptually driven techniques in the literature are designed for view-dependent visualization [Luebke and Hallen (2001)] [Reddy (2001)] [Williams *et al.* (2003)].

The idea of applying LOD was discussed as early as in 1976 by Clark [Clark (1976)]. LOD can be static, dynamic or view-dependent. The traditional static approach preprocesses a number of discrete versions at different resolutions for each 3D object, corresponding to different levels of detail. At runtime, the appropriate version is chosen and rendered. This approach is simple and requires minimum runtime computation. However, only a limited number of levels are available. Instead of creating discrete versions, a dynamic approach uses a data structure to encode a continuous spectrum of detail (CLOD). The desired level can be extracted at runtime. This approach provides better granularity and uses the optimal number of polygons. The tradeoff is additional computation before rendering. The view-dependent approach is an extension of the dynamic approach. Criteria are defined to select the most appropriate level for the current view. Each approach has its advantages and disadvantages, depending on the requirements of the application. A comparison of some frequently referenced simplification techniques in the literature is given in Table 4.1.

Table 4.1 A comparison of some commonly referenced simplification techniques in the literature (To – designed for topology preservation, Vi – view-independent, Su – vertices in a coarse version is a subset of those in a finer version, Dr – allow drastic simplification, Gl – simplify taking both global and local structures into consideration, Pe – based on a perceptual metric, Co – efficient to support continuous level-of-details). The appearance preserving simplification technique provides a framework which supports both view-dependent and independent visualization. It supports both LOD and CLOD.

Simplification techniques	***To***	***Vi***	***Su***	***Dr***	***Gl***	***Pe***	***Co***
Decimation of triangle meshes 92	√	√	√	χ	χ	χ	χ
Geometric optimization 93	√	√	√	√	χ	χ	√
Voxel based object simplification 95	χ	√	χ	√	χ	χ	√
Simplification envelopes 96	√	√	√	χ	χ	χ	χ
Progressive meshes 96	χ	√	χ	√	√	χ	√
Simplification using quadric error metrics 97	χ	√	χ	√	√	χ	√
Model simplification using vertex clustering 97	χ	χ	χ	χ	√	χ	√
Adaptive real-time level-of-detail-based rendering for polygonal models 97	χ	χ	χ	√	χ	√	√
Appearance preserving simplification 98	√	√/χ	χ	χ	χ	√	√/χ
Image driven simplification 00	χ	√	χ	√	√	√	χ

4.4 Motivation

Despite the excellent research on simplification techniques in the last decade, what has not been established is an integrated simplification approach associating texture reduction with mesh simplification at multiple scales, taking human perception and network adaptation into account. The simplification techniques in the literature are inadequate in one or more of the following:

- Capability of drastic simplification — Topology preservation [Eck *et al.* (1995)] can maintain high fidelity but is not efficient when considering LOD. When viewing an object at a far distance, the HVS is insensitive to small genus embedded in the object, and therefore rendering more triangles in order to preserve these holes is not an effective way of simplification. The error minimization techniques are useful to reduce over-sampled data, or data packed too close together. However, an error metric [Schroeder *et al.* (1992)] can prevent drastic simplification to generate coarse objects to display far away from the viewpoint. The simplification envelopes algorithm [Cohen *et al.* (1996)] is based on the constraint that the simplified surface is within $\pm\varepsilon$, a user defined tolerance, from the original surface. Avoidance of self-intersection of triangles in the neighborhood prevents drastic simplification.
- Local and global consideration — Simplification can be based on ranking the importance of vertices, or feature points. For example, vertices attached to large triangles and vertices of high curvature are considered more important [Rossignac and Borrel (1993)] [Low and Tan (1997)] [Lindstrom (2000)]. The quadric error approach uses a 4×4 matrix to compute the sum of the squared distances from a vertex to the planes of neighboring triangles [Garland and Heckbert (1997)]. Limited filter window size considers the characteristics of local surfaces only; it lacks consideration of the global structure as that provided by the scale-space filtering (SSF) technique used in the TexMesh model. Simplification based only on local geometry explains why the voxel-based simplification algorithm performs poorly on models with high-frequency details such as sharp edges and squared-off corners [He *et al.* (1995)]. Many simplification methods examine local, ignoring global surface property. This may result in removing large noticeable structures from the 3D surface, instead of removing less important small details at an early stage of simplification. For example, techniques merging nearly coplanar neighboring triangles will simplify a surface from (a) to (b) (Fig. 4.7), because the faces adjacent to vertex V represent a more coplanar surface than the smaller local structures. However, simplifying from (a) to (c) is more consistent with how the human visual system perceives a change of the structure from close to far.

Simplification techniques taking both local and global 3D structures into account can thus provide better visual fidelity.

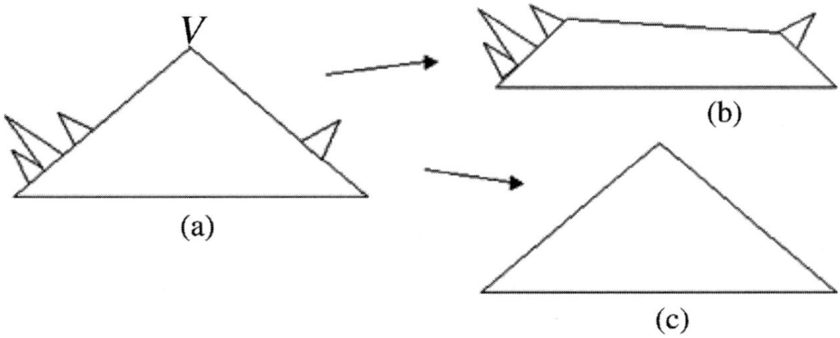

Fig. 4.7 An example of a simplification technique considering only local surface curvature, *i.e.* (a) to (b), and that taking into account of global structures *i.e.* (a) to (c).

- Efficient online performance — Error minimization or optimization techniques are often slow and expensive to implement [Nadler (1986)] [Bronnimann and Goodrich (1994)]. An efficient approach is to collect sufficient statistics during preprocessing to achieve fast online retrieval, preferably in constant time. In other words, when refining a model from a coarse level to a more detailed one, only a set of additional vertices needs to be transmitted. This incremental approach requires the coarse set to be a subset of the refined set. Many simplification techniques involve relocation of vertices and thus online transmission cannot be incremental [Brodsky and Watson (2000)] [Garland and Heckbert (1997)] [Shaffer and Garland (2001)] [Turk (1992)]. In the progressive meshes method, although the original mesh can be recovered exactly after all data are received, the edge collapse transformation creates new vertices and the *vsplit* record stream increases network workload [Hoppe (1996)]. The adaptive real-time LOD technique also involves vertex relocation [Xia *et al.* (1997)]. Some techniques are view-dependent. Although they may provide more precise visual quality for each view, the disadvantage is the increased runtime load of selecting an appropriate LOD [Luebke and Erikson (1997)]. The image-driven simplification technique compares the image after an edge collapse operation with the original image [Lindstrom and Turk (2000)]. Mean square error (MSE) is used to compute the deviation from the original image. Images are taken from multiple views in order to evaluate the quality of the entire object. The next collapsed edge is the one generating the least deviation. However, rendering the entire model for every edge in every viewpoint for different scales is expensive, even with hardware-accelerated rendering. Computational cost is a major burden for view-dependent approaches.

- Automatic selection of scale based on viewing distance — While LOD was discussed in the literature extensively, there has been no analysis regarding how a scale is selected based on viewing distance. For example, there has been no experiment showing whether scale relates to viewing distance linearly or exponentially, or by any other function. When selecting LOD, a smaller and coarser object is displayed at a farther away distance, in contrast to a bigger and finer object close to the viewpoint. A scale-distance function is therefore introduced in the TexMesh model and viewing distance is defined as the location of the 3D object relative to the viewing platform in the virtual world, which is different from the physical distance between the retina and the display device, as defined in [Luebke and Hallen (2001)]. Cohen *et al.* mentioned that the choice of LOD depends on the object's area in screen pixels, which is related to its distance from the viewpoint [Cohen *et al.* (1998)], but no discussion was presented in the paper to explain how LOD can be automatically selected based on viewing distance.
- Association of texture reduction with the mesh simplification analysis using photo-realistic texture mapping — Perception of depth and realistic texture are the main factors to achieve realism and visual fidelity in the virtual world. In recent years, researchers started to incorporate color and texture into their mesh simplification models. When texture is mentioned in the literature, it often refers to synthetic or animated texture [Turk (1991)]. Synthetic texture or per pixel color stored in each vertex [Cohen *et al.* (1998)] [Garland and Heckbert (1998)] [Soucy *et al.* (1996)] [Sander *et al.* (2001)] can be estimated or interpolated. For example, when walking through an animated scene, the next frame can be predicted based on available neighboring data [Cohen-Or *et al.* (1999)]. Using interpolated or animated texture is a compromise in applications, which require fast interactive rendering. For applications requiring real life texture, interpolating color or estimating pattern between vertices is not acceptable. The non-interpolated texture used in the TexMesh model has resolution much higher than the mesh. It was observed in perceptual experiments that the HVS is more sensitive to higher texture resolution after the mesh reaches an optimal density [Pan *et al.* (2005)]. Increased texture resolution also improves visual

fidelity for a given geometry in general. Since high-resolution texture data is large compared to mesh data, texture reduction will surely speed up 3D visualization. The TexMesh integrated approach simplifies non-interpolated photo-realistic textured mesh based on 3D feature points extracted using scale-space analysis. Photo-realistic texture maps are used in [Yu *et al.* (2000)], but their effort is on recovering geometry from texture patches retrieved from multiple photographs, and not on generating LOD. A distance-based technique is applied to photo-textured terrain [Lindstrom *et al.* (1995)]; however, color interpolation between pixels is necessary in their technique to avoid blocky appearance of terrain texture.

- Simplification based on objective perceptual evaluation — Very often the number of vertices, faces, or an error metric is used as a criterion to measure efficiency [Pauly *et al.* (2002)], when comparing simplification techniques in the literature. In fact, a geometric deviation may not cause any degradation of perception, because the HVS is insensitive to minute details below a certain limit. Experiments described later in this thesis show that perceptual quality is a more reliable and efficient measure when human perception is involved. A perceptually driven simplification technique was introduced [Luebke and Hallen (2001)], but their method applies to the rendering of a view-dependent image, while the TexMesh model applies to a view-independent 3D object. They use Gouraud-shaded meshes while photorealistic texture mapping is applied on a TexMesh object. Furthermore, their simplified models still contain redundant data, because the authors stated that their models could be reduced two to three times further in polygon count without perceptible effect. An efficient simplification technique should avoid generating redundant data, which does not improve visual quality. Watson [Watson *et al.* (2001)] compared the naming times, rating and preference techniques, but they only selected a set of views for each object, and did not apply a full 360° interactive comparison. Naming times tend to be affected by an individual's prior knowledge of the stimuli. Different LOD of an object can be recognized and named within the same response time period due to some prominent features on the 3D surface.
- Adaptation to bandwidth fluctuation — The joint geometry/texture progressive coding method applies wavelet transform to encode the mesh and texture data for transmission [Okuda and Chen (2000)]. But the method is not adaptive to fluctuating bandwidth. In order to

support online applications, geometry/texture data have to be delivered within a reasonable or user defined time. A dynamic approach, as discussed in the TexMesh model, to adjust geometry/texture resolution based on current bandwidth is more efficient. Furthermore, a perceptual metric is used in the TexMesh to determine when mesh refinement should be terminated, allocating the remaining bandwidth to texture resolution in order to enhance the overall visual fidelity.

In recent years, perceptually adaptive graphics [O'Sullivan *et al.* (2004)] has received increasing attention in the graphics and visualization community. In EUROGRAPHICS 2000, a state-of-the-art report was presented on visual perception [McNamara (2000)]. A group of researchers from computer graphics, psychology and other disciplines gathered in 2001, as a result of a joint effort between EUROGRAPHICS and SIGGRAPH, to discuss the importance of human perception when striving for realism in the virtual world [Luebke (2001)] [Reddy (2001)] [Watson *et al.* (2001)] [Williams *et al.* (2003)]. More effort has been expended on verifying geometric error estimation with perceptual evaluation experiments in order to achieve higher visual fidelity of 3D display. Most perceptually driven techniques developed so far focus on view-dependent rendering. These techniques can be applied to dynamic scenes [Reddy (2001)] [O'Sullivan *et al.* (2003)], and can be used to compute the relative resolutions between the region of interest and the periphery [Reddy (2001)] [Baudisch *et al.* (2003)]. In order to achieve visual quality, user-guided simplifications were also suggested [Pojar and Schmalstieg (2003)] [Kho and Garland (2003)]. In contrast, the TexMesh approach introduced in this thesis is view-independent, applied to relatively static 3D objects and without the need of user intervention when predicting visual quality.

Perceptual analysis is a fundamental component in the TexMesh framework. Luebke suggested that the field of polygonal simplification is getting mature [Luebke (2001)]. The simplification algorithms developed so far provide a good foundation on which other research such as perceptual evaluation of 3D quality can be built upon. As 3D scenes become commonplace in online applications, such as those on the Internet with limited and varying bandwidth, performance and efficient adaptation is an important goal. The objective of the TexMesh model is to integrate related research issues from different directions, and fix the inadequacies of previous approaches. While visual fidelity has traditionally been measured based on geometric metrics, the TexMesh model is perceptually driven, and is adaptive to fluctuating bandwidth (Fig. 4.8).

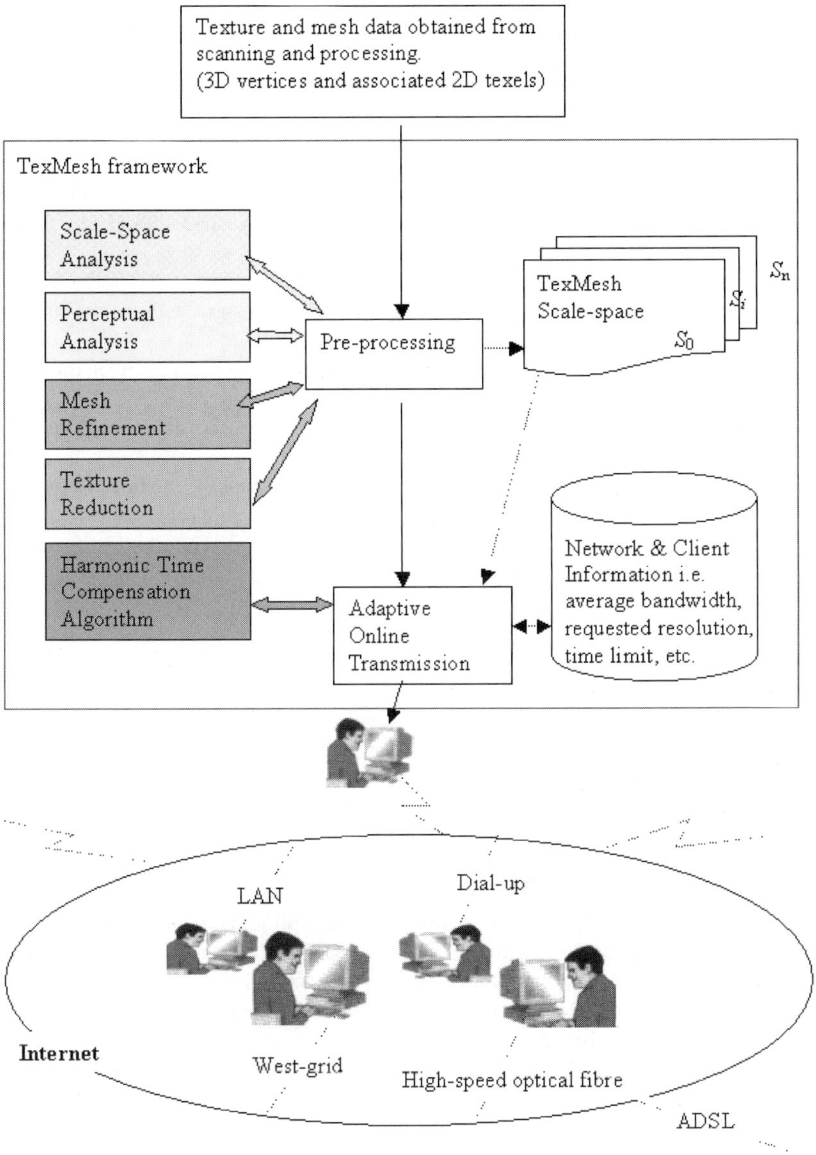

Fig. 4.8 A block diagram of the TexMesh framework and environment.

References

Alliez, P. and Desbrun, M. (2001a). Progressive encoding for lossless transmission of triangle meshes, in *SIGGRAPH*, pp. 198–205.

Alliez, P. and Desbrun, M. (2001b). Valence-driven connectivity encoding of 3D meshes, in *EUROGRAPHICS*, pp. 480–489.

Alregib, G., Altunbasak, Y. and Rossignac, J. (2005). Error-resilient transmission of 3D models, *ACM Trans. on Graphics* **24**, 2, pp. 182–208 (Early version in ICASSP 02).

Baudisch, P., DeCarlo, D., Duchowski, A. and Geisler, W. (2003). Focusing on the essential: considering attention in display design, *Communications of the ACM* **46**, 3, pp. 60–66.

Cignoni, P., Montani, C. and Scopigno, R. (1997a). A comparison of mesh simplification algorithms, *Computers & Graphics* **22**.

Cignoni, P., Puppo, E. and Scopigno, R. (1997b). Representation and visualization of terrain surfaces at variable resolution.

Clark, J. (1976). Hierarchical geometric models for visible surface algorithms, *Comm. ACM* **19**, 10, pp. 547–554.

Floriani, L. D., Magillo, P. and Puppo, E. (2000). Variant: A system for terrain modeling at variable resolution, *GeoInformatica* **4**, 3, pp. 287–315.

Gumhold, S., Wang, X. and Macleod, R. (2001). Feature extraction from point clouds, in *Proc. 10th Int'l Meshing Roundtable.*

Heckbert, P. S. and Garland, M. (1997). Survey of polygonal surface simplification algorithms, in *Multiresolution Surface Modeling Course, SIGGRAPH.*

ISO/IEC 14496-2 (2000). *Amendment 1. Coding of Audio-Visual Objects-Part 2: Visual, Version 2.*

Jaromersky, P., Wu, X. and Chiang, Y. (2005). Multiple-description geometry compression for networked interactive 3D graphics, in *International Conference on Image and Graphics.*

JPEG (2000). *JPEG 2000 Part I: Final Draft International Standard (ISO/IEC FDIS15444-1), ISO/IECJTC1 /SC29/WG1 N1855.*

Kho, Y. and Garland, M. (2003). User-guided simplification, in *Proc. ACM I3D.*

Kobbelt, L., Botsch, M., Schwanecks, U. and Seidel, H. (2001). Feature sensitive surface extraction from volume data, in *SIGGRAPH.*

Lewiner, T., Lopes, H., Rossignac, J. and Vieira, A. (2004). Efficient edgebreaker for surfaces of arbitrary topology, in *SIGGRAPH.*

Luebke, D. P. (2001). A developer's survey of polygonal simplification algorithms, *IEEE Computer Graphics and Applications*, May/June, pp. 24–35.

McNamara, A. (2000). Visual perception in realistic image synthesis, in *EUROGRAPHICS.*

O'Sullivan, C., Dingliana, J., Giang, T. and Kaiser, M. (2003). Evaluating the visual fidelity of physically based animations, *ACM Trans. on Graphics* **22**, 3.

O'Sullivan, C., Howlett, S., McDonnell, R., Morvan, Y. and O'Conor, K. (2004). Perceptually adaptive graphics, in *State of the Art Report, Eurographics.*

Pauly, M., Gross, M. and Kobbelt, L. (2002). Efficient simplification of point-sampled surfaces, in *IEEE Visualization.*

Peng, J., Kim, C.-S. and Kuo, C.-C. (2005). Technologies for 3D mesh compression: A survey, *Journal of Visual Communication and Image Representation* **16**, pp. 688–733.

Pereira, F. and Ebrahimi, T. (2002). *The MPEG-4 Book* (Prentice-Hall).

Pojar, E. and Schmalstieg, D. (2003). User-controlled creation of multiresolution mehses, in *Proc. of Symposium on Interactive 3D Graphics*, pp. 127–130.

Reddy, M. (1997). *Perceptually modulated level of detail for virtual environments*, Ph.D. thesis, University of Edinburgh.

Reddy, M. (2001). Perceptually optimized 3D graphics, *Applied Perception.*

Regib, G. and Altunbasak, Y. (2002). An unequal error protection method for packet loss resilient 3D mesh transmission, in *INFOCOM.*

Rossignac, J. (1999). Edgebreaker: Connectivity compression for triangle meshes, *IEEE Trans. on Visualization and Computer Graphics*, pp. 47–61.

Skodras, A., Christopoulos, C. and Ebrahimi, T. (2001). The JPEG2000 still image compression standard, *IEEE Signal Processing Magazine*, pp. 36–58.

Taubin, G. (1999). 3D geometry compression and progressive transmission, in *Proc. EUROGRAPHICS.*

Taubin, G., Guéziec, A., Horn, W. and Lazarus, F. (1998). Progressive forest split compression, in *SIGGRAPH.*

Taubin, G. and Rossignac, J. (1998). Geometric compression through topological surgery, in *Proc. SIGGRAPH.*

Touma, C. and Gotsman, C. (1998). Triangle mesh compression, in *Graphics Interface*, pp. 26–34.

VRML (1997). *The Virtual Reality Modeling Language (VRML)*, ISO/IEC 14772-1.

Watson, B., Friedman, A. and McGaffey, A. (2001). Measuring and predicting visual fidelity, in *SIGGRAPH*, pp. 213–220.

Williams, N., Luebke, D., Cohen, J., Kelley, M. and Schubert, B. (2003). Perceptually guided simplification of lit, textured meshes, in *ACM Symp. on Interactive 3D Graphics.*

Yan, Z., Kumar, S. and Kuo, C.-C. (2001). Error-resilient coding of 3-D graphic models via adaptive mesh segmentation, *IEEE Transactions On CSVT.*

Chapter 5

Scale-Space Filtering and LOD — The TexMesh Model

I. Cheng

5.1 Introduction

The Gaussian filter is an efficient smoothing tool in computer vision. Based on the Gaussian's kernel, Witkin [Witkin (1983)] and Koenderink formally defined the scale-space concept in 1983-84, bringing together an unrelated set of derived images at different levels of detail along the scale parameter and allowing image data to be integrated into a continuous perspective. Since then, the Gaussian kernel has often been studied in conjunction with the so called "multiple scale approach." However, scale-space filtering had mainly been applied in 2D images [Kuijper and Florack (2001)] [Bauer and Peikert (2002)] [Lindberg (1995)] [Lindberg (1998)], and only recently has this technique been used in computer graphics, with limited applications in 3D visualization. An intrinsic filter, a generalization of scale space filtering, is used to eliminate noise from image and scanned data [Boulanger *et al.* (2002)]. Relatively fewer researchers have looked into 3D model (or mesh) simplification based on feature point analysis at multiple scales. Southard applied Laplacian to rank uniformly distributed feature points on planar surfaces [Southard (1991)], and Gaussian filter is used to detect features at multiple scales [Pauly *et al.* (2003)], but their analysis is not extended to mesh integrated with real texture and adaptive on-line transmission.

5.2 LOD in Scale-Space

I propose to use scale-space filtering (SSF) to extract 3D features based on which adaptive on-line compression and transmission of 3D models can be performed. Traversal between the different scales, or levels, is achieved by varying the standard deviation parameter σ; the higher the value the more the mesh is smoothed. SSF is based on locating the zero-crossings of a signal at multiple scales. Zero-crossings can be used to detect the degree of persistence of a structure (feature) in a 3D model. Minor structures tend to diminish as σ increases, and only major structures persist at higher scales. In other words, minor features will be removed before major features in the simplification process. In contrast, major features are inserted before minor features in a refining process. The advantage of using SSF is its ability to smooth locally or globally, moderately or drastically, depending on the filter window size and the value of σ. When using a small window size, SSF eliminates signal noise in the local region. By using a bigger window size, the filtering or averaging effect covers a larger surface. Figure 5.1 is an example of global smoothing using a window size of 201 on a signal of 256 sample values. To achieve global smoothing, the window size has to be at least twice the standard deviation computed from the sample space (covering at least 97.7% of the sample data in a normal distribution). If a smaller window size is used, smoothing will be restricted and terminated before reaching the bottom scale in Fig. 5.1.

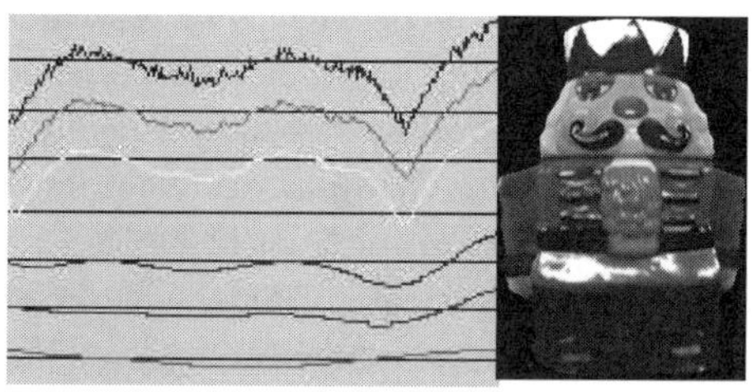

Fig. 5.1 Scale S_i increases from top to bottom. S_0 is the original signal extracted near the bottom of the Nutcracker model. Note that the local variation (fine detail) in the original signal is gradually removed and the scaled signal becomes smoother and flatter.

Theoretically, 100% global smoothing will end up with a monotonous surface losing all the surface features. However, the human visual system (HVS) is insensitive to details beyond a certain level. Thus, for a perceivable object, the filter window can be smaller than twice the standard deviation in order to save computation time. In the experiments, I applied a window size of 1.4 times the standard deviation σ (normally it should be 3σ), and found that this window size provides sufficient simplification for objects placed at a distance close to infinity in the virtual world. Further simplification beyond this point by using a bigger window is not necessary. How scale is related to viewing distance and the perceptual impact of changing scale will be discussed in Chapter 6.

The zero-crossings at different scales can be computed by applying the second derivative of the Gaussian (called Laplacian-of-Gaussian or LoG). Eighteen feature points are identified in the original signal (Fig. 5.2, right). By increasing the σ value, the number of feature points decreases from 18 to 2 as reflected by the increasing smoothness of the scaled values from the top to the bottom scales (Fig. 5.2, left).

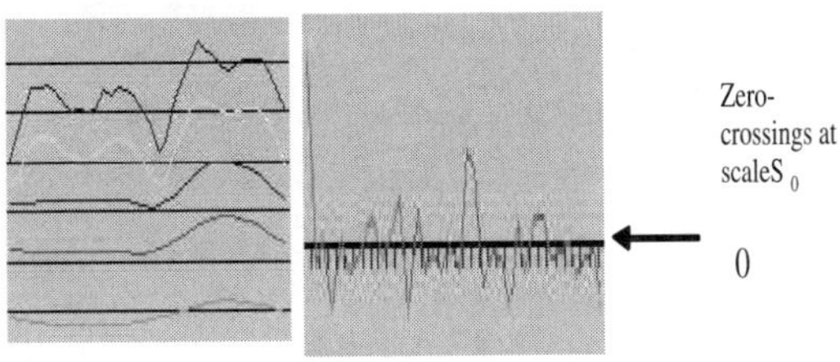

Fig. 5.2 (Left) The top is the original signal with 18 zero crossings, generated by signals extracted from the Nutcracker model. The other four smoothed scales have 8, 6, 4, and 2 zero-crossings respectively from top to bottom. (Right) 18 zero crossings detected in the original signal S_0.

SSF in 2D can be summarized by the following equations:

$$w_G(x,y) = \begin{cases} \dfrac{1}{\sigma\sqrt{2\pi}} e^{-\frac{(x^2+y^2)}{(2\sigma^2)}} & (x,y) \in W \\ 0 & elsewhere \end{cases} \tag{5.1}$$

$$w_{LoG}(x,y) = \begin{cases} -\frac{1}{\pi\sigma^4}\left[1 - \dfrac{x^2+y^2}{2\sigma^2}\right] e^{-\frac{x^2+y^2}{2\sigma^2}} & (x,y) \in W \\ 0 & elsewhere \end{cases} \tag{5.2}$$

$$f * S(x,y) = \int_{-t}^{t}\int_{-t}^{t} f(x+u, y+v)w(u,v)dudv \tag{5.3}$$

Where $w_G(x,y)$ represents the weight at pixel (x,y), f represents the original signal (image) and $f * S$ the smoothed image and the weights are assumed to be defined in a square window W of length $2t+1$. In the discrete case, *e.g.*, with a real image, summation is used instead of integrals, and the Gaussian weights are normalized so that the sum of all the weights equals 1.

5.3 Spherical Scanned Data

Modern laser scanners detect depths and generate 3D vertices in the form of point clouds. Figure 5.3 (left) shows a 6-inch dog object. The generated point cloud (Fig. 5.3 middle) is then triangulated, and mapped with the scanned texture (Fig. 5.3 right) to generate a texture mapped 3D object (Fig. 5.1).

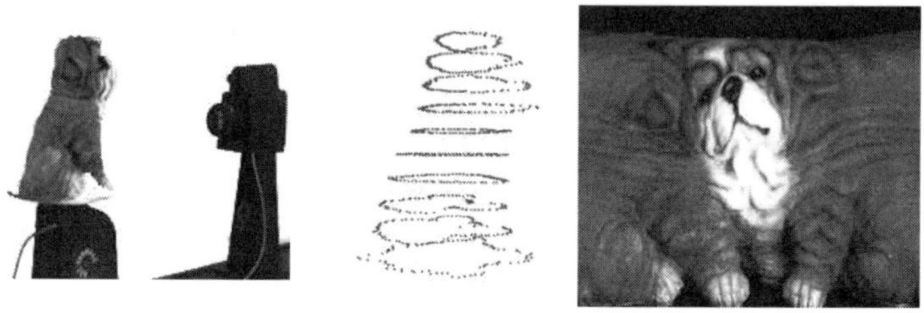

Fig. 5.3 (left) Zoomage 3D scanner and a dog object, (middle) sample of 3D scan-points, and (right) scanned texture image.

The SSF of a 3D model is achieved as follows: First note that the data acquired (Fig. 5.3 middle) can be represented as r_x (α, y); where α is the angle on a horizontal plane around the y-axis of rotation of an object, y is the vertical coordinate, and r_x denotes the perpendicular distance from the y-axis to the surface of an object for a given (α, y) pair. SSF for a 3D model is thus similar to a 2D image, for the simplified mesh representation considered here, with $f(x,y)$ replaced by r_x (α, y). Also, the appropriate scaling along the horizontal and vertical directions can be significantly different, depending on the variance of the sample points for a given region. Thus, Equations (8.1) and (8.3) need to be modified to (6.4) and (6.5):

$$w_G(\alpha, y) = \begin{cases} \dfrac{1}{\sigma\sqrt{2\pi}} e^{-\frac{\phi\alpha^2}{2\sigma^2} - \frac{\psi y^2}{2\sigma^2}} & (\alpha, y) \in W \\ 0 & elsewhere \end{cases} \tag{5.4}$$

$$Rx * S(\alpha, y) = \int_{-t}^{t}\int_{-t}^{t} Rx(\alpha + u, y + v) w(u, v) du dv \tag{5.5}$$

For uniform sample points, ϕ and ψ equal 1, but for irregular sampling, ϕ and ψ are used to accommodate the variable inter-sample distance along different axes. Note that in the actual implementation, we use two passes of 1-D filters, since all the filters discussed above are orthogonal. The vertices are first smoothed along the x-axis and then the resulting values are filtered once more along the y-axis using the filtered values. Figure 5.4 shows the face features, of a head model, changing towards a smoother spherical surface when going from low to high scales (left to right). The original mesh contains 1,872 vertices and 3,672 faces. The other five meshes are of increasing scales as described in Table 5.1.

Table 5.1 (Head model) Number of faces remaining at each scale S_i, after removing low priority vertices.

Scale S_i	# of vertices removed	# of faces in mesh
5	685	2226
7	744	2108
10	824	1948
15	985	1624
20	1196	1190

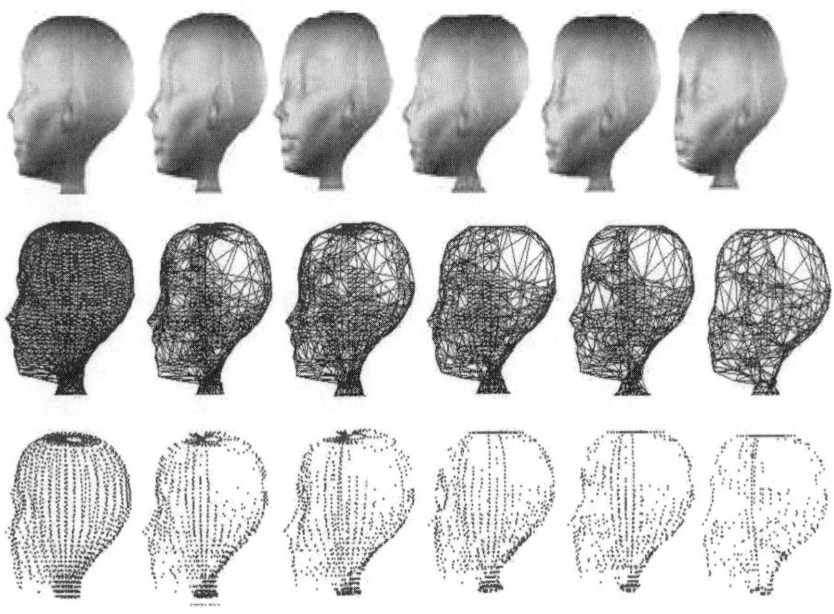

Fig. 5.4 Increasing scales from left to right of a head model: (Top) texture mapped 3D mesh, (Middle) 3D mesh and (Bottom) feature points extracted at scale S_i.

Note that in this foam head model, the surface structures of the ears and the cheeks are more prominent than that of the eyes, which are quite shallow. The back of the head is comparatively smooth. Features points are preserved longer, toward higher scales, in areas where structure are more prominent.

In the TexMesh model, statistics relating to LOD is generated during preprocessing based on feature point extraction at different scales.

The TexMesh Model

Simplification techniques developed in the past focused mainly on geometry, shaded with color per vertex or mapped with synthetic material, without integrating real life texture in a coherent manner. Many studies emphasized the importance of million of triangles in order to preserve fine details, but ignored high resolution real texture which have been shown through user evaluations to have major impact on perceptual quality in 3D visualization [Pan *et al.* (2005)]. In view of the size of texture data, compression of texture is essential for on-line transmission given limited and fluctuating bandwidth. An integrated approach combining mesh simplification and texture reduction, based on feature point extraction and distribution, is proposed in my research.

Feature points in the TexMesh model is defined as a group of vertices, which can best represent the geometry of 3D object at a given viewing distance. In Fig. 5.4, for example, the original head model contains 1872 feature points (scale S_0). After removing 1196 vertices, it is represented by 676 feature points at scale S_{20}. At any scale S_i, feature points are detected by applying *LoG*. Vertices creating zero crossings at scale S_i, are recorded as feature points and assigned the value i. Each feature point is represented by three components: $(i, (tx, ty), (gx, gy, gz))$. The second and third components are the 2D texture and 3D vertex coordinates, respectively. Vertices with stronger persistence will have higher i values (higher priority during mesh refinement), generating a priority list. During simplification, features of low priority are first removed, leaving more prominent features at higher scales. Iterative vertex removals, by integrating the removed vertex with its closest neighbor, are applied to generate each simplified version. No new vertex is generated in the process. When selecting the next edge or vertex to remove, the simplification criteria used in most methods choose the candidate which will generate the minimum deviation from the previous simplified surface. For example, in progressive meshes [Hoppe (1996)], the minimum energy cost in the neighborhood is affected by an edge collapse operation, and has to be recomputed. The simplified surface then affects the choice of the next collapse operation and the vertices to remove. In the TexMesh approach, the order of vertex removal follows the priority predetermined by applying scale-space filtering on the original 3D surface.

During refinement, features of higher priority are inserted first into the coarse model. Since real texture mapping is used in the TexMesh model, texture border has to be taken into account during the simplification process. Texel values are normalized in the range [0,1]. Vertices associated with border texels are removed only if such an operation does not distort the texture pattern. A collection of the texture border vertices of the head model (Fig. 5.4) generated from the spherical approach is shown in Fig. 5.5.

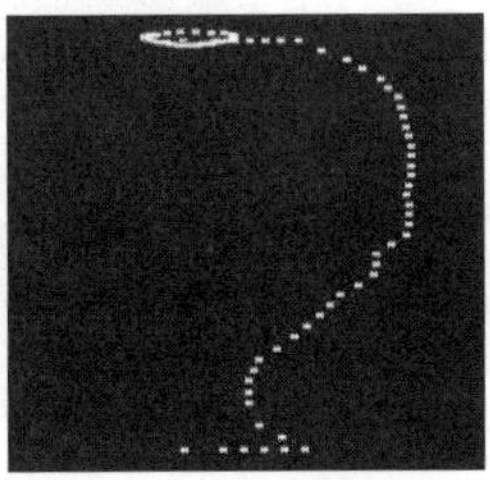

Fig. 5.5 An illustration of border vertices taken from the head model.

Preprocessing generates a scale map and a fragment map. The scale map records the feature points extracted at each scale, and the fragment map records the feature point distribution in each texture fragment.

5.4 Scale Map

Three-dimensional mesh vertices are computed from the signals captured by a 3D ranger sensor. Figure 5.6 (right) shows an example of the scanned signal, which can be processed to compute the depth information. Putting aside the depth information (z-coordinate), N vertices can be sorted and assigned unique ids L, *i.e.*, $0 \leq L < N$, based on their y then x coordinates. Note that x is derived from r_x and $\alpha \in [0,360]$ in the spherical approach, and thus is ordered for a given y value. A Scale Map is a 2D display of all 3D vertices in a matrix with rows and columns corresponding to the y and x values respectively. The default value for each vertex is 0 corresponding to scale 0 (original signal). At each scale S_i only feature points detected at that scale are updated with the value i. During preprocessing, Gaussian filters with increasing sigma (standard deviation) values σ_i are used from scale S_0 to S_{max}, *i.e.*, $0 \leq i \leq$ max scale, with S_{max} corresponding to the scale at infinity. Zero crossings are detected from the filtered space G_i where G_0 represents the set of original unfiltered range data. Starting from a coarse model, feature points not already included in the mesh can be retrieved from the scale map, in decreasing i values, to refine the model progressively. The scale map can be implemented as a priority queue, where the next required vertex is popped from the queue in constant time.

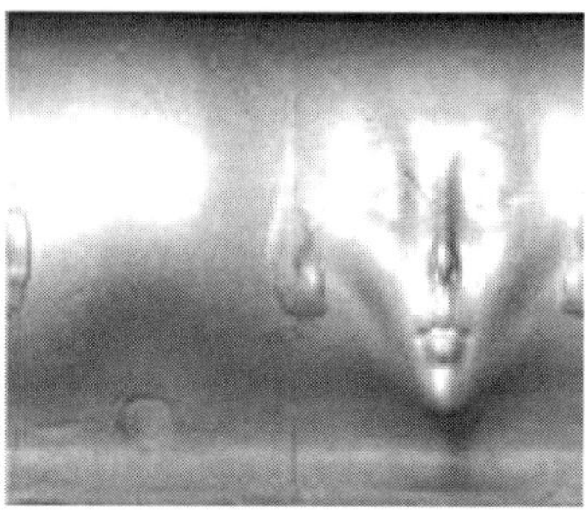

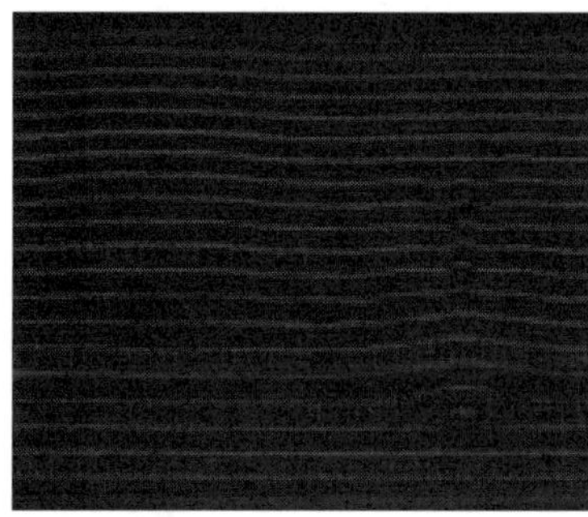

Fig. 5.6 (Left) Texture pattern and (Right) laser signal, of a head model captured by the Zoomage^R 3D scanner.

5.5 Fragmentation Approach for Texture Transmission

One characteristics of the TexMesh model is the association of texture reduction with mesh simplification. In a 3D object, with full color real texture, there are two components that can be filtered — the mesh and the texture. The texture quality $q_i(x, y)$ of a fragment (x, y) is determined based on the associated feature point density $\eta_i(x, y)$, which has a value between zero and one, and is mapped onto a compression scale. For example, in the current implementation, I use the JPEG quality scale from 0% to 100%, where 100% means no compression. While wavelet coding applies to the entire image and is geometry-independent, my approach supports variable quality determined by the density of surface structures (geometry-driven). Note that I use JPEG for convenience and wide support on the web, and in JAVA [JPEG (2006)]; however, standards such as JPEG2000 can be used as well in the future to code fragments.

The texture image of a 3D model can be transmitted as one block or a collection of sub-blocks. The advantage of dividing into sub-blocks is to make use of distributed networks and apply variable qualities to different texture blocks as explained below. The main concern is whether the additional headers information will increase the overall volume of data to be transmitted. In this section, I will show that sub-dividing into smaller blocks of optimal dimension does not increase the overall size for high resolution texture images. Instead, the sub-block approach helps to fully utilize the available bandwidth. Feature points extracted at each scale S_i are distributed onto the corresponding sub-block in a fragment map based on the 2D texture coordinates associated with each 3D feature point.

5.6 Fragment Map and Variable Texture Quality

The texture image of a 3D model is fragmented into $N_x{}^*N_y$ pieces after determining the optimal size of a fragment. To apply JPEG compression efficiently, keeping in mind the size of macroblocks, the optimal dimension of a fragment is chosen as a multiple of 16. The entire texture is also adjusted so that there is no partial fragment. For example, a texture image with dimension 4800*1600 pixels, can be divided into 7,500 fragments of size 32*32 pixels. Similar to the scale map, fragments are arranged in a matrix with N_y rows and N_x columns. Since each 3D vertex is associated with a 2D texel, it is possible to distribute the vertices into the $N_x{}^*N_y$ fragments.

Comparing fragmented and non-fragmented size

We used five texture patterns (Fig. 5.7) to compare the fragmented and non-fragmented sizes for different qualities using the Intel JPEG compression library. Each fragment has a dimension of 16*16 pixels. Experimental results show that the sum of the fragments is significantly less than the size of the non-fragmented JPEG file for images of dimension greater than 256 pixels (Table 5.2). For high resolution images, it is therefore advantageous to transmit individual fragments to the client site for recombining and rendering. The fragmented approach also facilitates image fragment retrieval from multiple repositories, parallel processing and transmission over distributed networks.

To verify the initial result, five different images of Mount Rushmore at resolution $R = 256^2, 512^2, 1024^2, 2048^2$ and 4096^2 pixels (Fig. 5.8) were

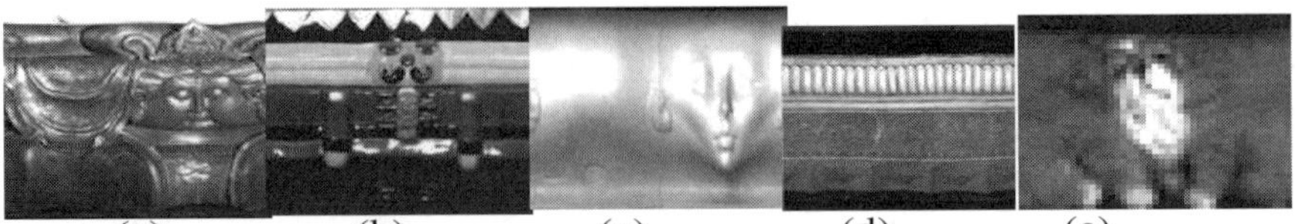

Fig. 5.7 Texture patterns used to compare the total data size required in the fragmented and non-fragmented approach.

Table 5.2 Experimental results show that the sum of sub-blocks of optimal size is significantly less than the size of a corresponding non-fragmented image for high resolution texture ($> 256^2$ pixels).

Model texture	Size (pixels)	JPEG Quality	1 file (KB)	Sum of fragments
(a)	1024^2	60%	566	293
	256^2	20%	29	44
(b)	1024^2	60%	305	222
(c)	1024^2	60%	400	253
(d)	1024^2	60%	494	269
(e)	1024^2	40%	383	226
		50%	423	237
		60%	458	249
	512^2	40%	111	62
		50%	122	66
		60%	130	70
	256^2	20%	25	42
		60%	56	47

used. The resolution is original without interpolation because the analysis on sixteen interpolated texture images showed that the fragmentation approach performed even better if interpolated images are used. Four versions of each Mt. Rushmore image containing number of fragments $n = 2^2, 4^2, 8^2$ and 16^2 respectively were generated. Each version was then tested using quality $Q = 100\%, 90\%, 80\%, 60\%, 40\%, 20\%$ and 10%. The observation is that, when $n \leq 256$ and each fragment size $\geq 128^2$ pixels, the sum of the fragment files $\Sigma f$was smaller than the single non-fragmented file F of equal JPEG quality. When $\Sigma f < F$ is true at a quality level, it is also true at lower quality levels.

In Figs. 5.9 and 5.10, it is observed that at 100% quality when fragment size ≥ 128 pixels and the number of fragments $\leq 16^2$, fragmentation does not increase the transmitted data. When increasing the number of

Fig. 5.8 Images of Mt. Rushmore at resolutions: $256^2, 512^2, 1024^2, 2048^2$ and 4096^2 pixels respectively.

fragments beyond 16^2, both the JPEG decoding time and data size are in favor of a single non-fragmented file. When restricting the number of fragments to a maximum of 16^2, the difference in decoding time is within a second for lower resolution images, and is within 2 seconds for images at a resolution of 2048^2 and 4096^2 pixels. This statistics is based on the performance of a Dell desktop computer, using Windows2000 at 1.8 GHz., with 40 GB disk space and 512MB RAM. We confirmed this finding again by using fifteen more images of different resolutions, and by applying various qualities to each image. The results are consistent. Figures 5.11 and 5.12 compare data sizes at different qualities. It can be seen that when dividing into fragments of optimal size, the sum of fragments is not bigger than the single non-fragmented file of equal JPEG quality.

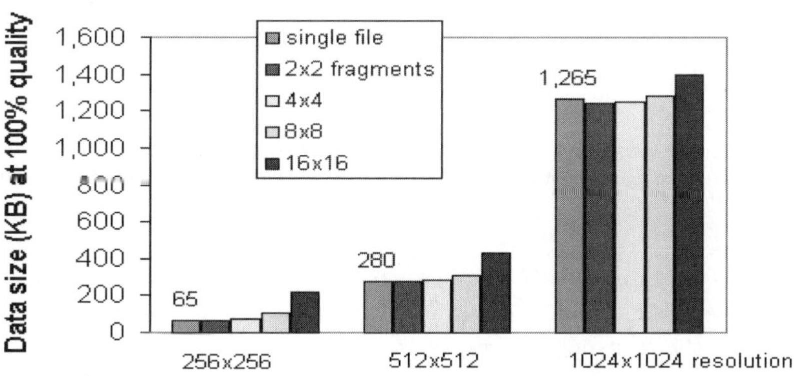

Fig. 5.9 Data size of three Mt. Rushmore images at resolution $256^2, 512^2$ and 1024^2 pixels. At each resolution, the single file size (non-fragmented) is compared with the sum of fragment with $n = 2^2, 4^2, 8^2$ and 16^2 respectively.

Based on the above finding, I keep the number of fragments n at 16^2 or less when applying the adaptive transmission strategy. Note that there is a

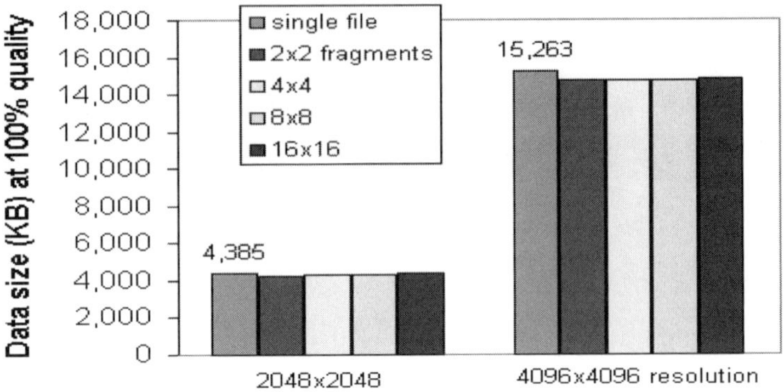

Fig. 5.10 Data size of two Mt. Rushmore images at resolution 2048^2 and 4096^2 pixels. At each resolution, the single file size (non-fragmented) is compared with the sum of fragments with $n = 2^2, 4^2, 8^2$ and 16^2 respectively.

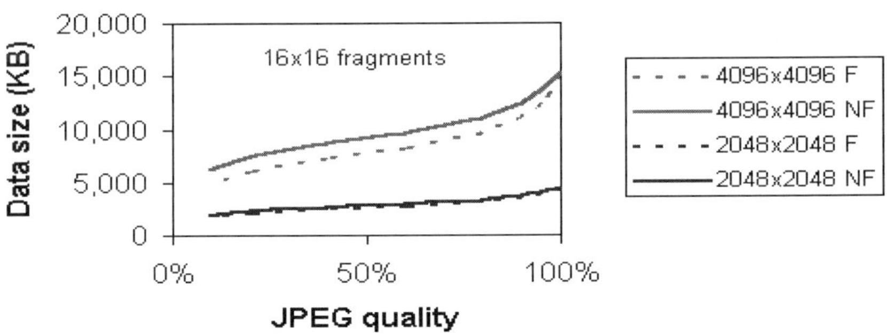

Fig. 5.11 Using images of Mt. Rushmore to compare size of non-fragmented (NF) and fragmented (F) data at resolutions 4096^2 and 2048^2 respectively. Number of fragments is 16^2.

tradeoff between using 16^2 fragments or less. The advantage of using fragments is for periodic bandwidth adaptation, so that the time deviation at the end of the transmission can be minimized. For this reason, more fragments are better. However, the JPEG coding/decoding time is proportional to the number of fragments. For example, when an image of 10.97M pixels is divided into 16^2 fragments, the additional coding/decoding time using the Dell desktop mentioned above is about 5 seconds, which is only 5% of the transmission time if we assume a network speed of 100KB/second. On the other hand, when using 8^2 fragments the deviation from a given time limit increases from 1% to 2.5%, but the coding/decoding time is reduced

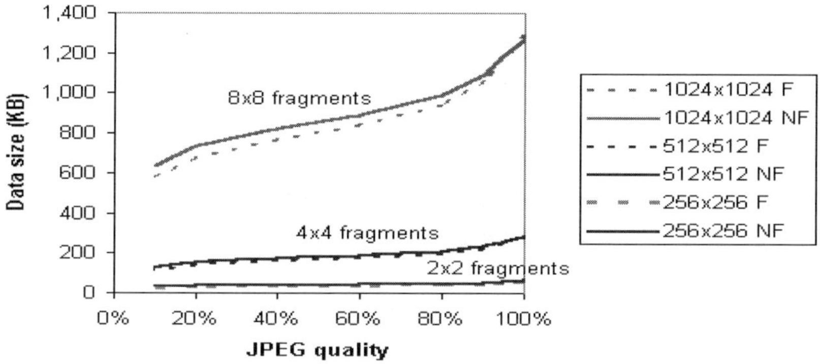

Fig. 5.12 Using images of Mt. Rushmore to compare the size of non-fragmented (NF) and fragmented (F) data at resolutions $1024^2, 512^2$ and 256^2. Number of fragments is $8^2, 4^2$ and 2^2 respectively.

to less than 2 seconds. When the number of fragments $n > 16^2$, the cost of fragmentation outweighs its benefit.

Comparing uniform and variable texture quality

By assigning variable qualities to individual fragments based on their associated feature point density, the overall perception of the 3D objects can be improved. An example is shown in Fig. 5.13 by comparing two dog objects at scale S_{25}. Variable texture qualities are applied on the left dog, while a uniform quality of 10% is applied to the right one, maintaining a total texture data size of 41 KB each. Since the eye area is associated with a higher feature point density, it is assigned a quality of 50% in the variable approach. It can be seen that the left dog has a better overall visual fidelity, contributed by the higher resolution texture around the eye area.

Since the HVS is less sensitive to details farther away, the texture quality Q_i at each scale S_i needs to increase only when i decreases towards a finer model. Given a viewing distance, the corresponding S_i and Q_i are selected. Instead of applying a uniform quality Q_i to all fragments, a variable approach is used so that texture quality of each fragment varies depending on the feature point density associated with it.

Feature point density as a visual quality predictor

I use the following grenade and nutcracker models to illustrate how different feature point densities affect the perception of 3D objects. The

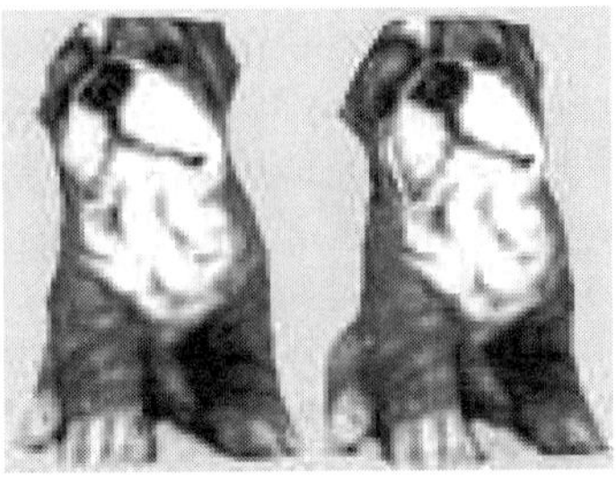

Fig. 5.13 A snapshot of 3D texture mapped dog model showing (left) variable quality and (right) uniform quality.

grenade (Figs. 5.14(c) and (d)) has vertical structures on the surface, and therefore the feature point distribution is higher than the back of the nutcracker (Figs. 5.14(a) and (b)), which is comparatively flat. Note that even if the texture quality is reduced to half, there is no significant perceptual degradation on the nutcracker (Fig. 5.14(b)). However, the grenade on the right (Fig. 5.14(d)) shows noticeably lower perceptual quality.

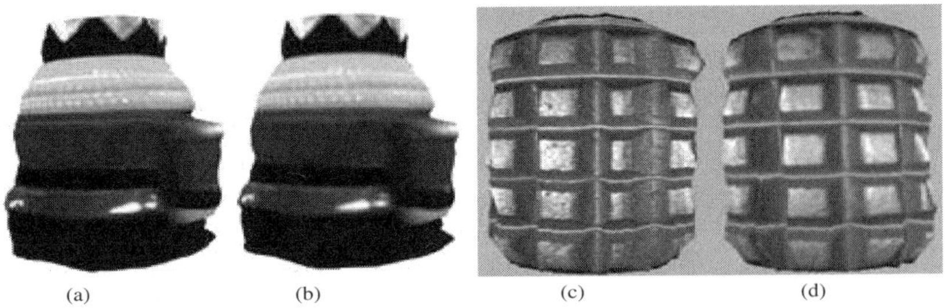

Fig. 5.14 A snapshot of the nutcracker 3D model view from the back ((a) and (b)), and the military grenade model ((c) and (d)), with original texture quality ((a) and (c)), and half of the original texture quality ((b) and (d)).

While the difference in quality of the grenades is obvious, the degraded shiny patch under the belt of the nutcracker (Fig. 5.14(b)) is less noticeable. The observation is that compression on surfaces with high feature point density is more obvious to human perception, than on surfaces with low feature point density. The perception of depth, generated by shade and contrast, makes virtual objects look realistic [Nagata (1984)]. Higher feature point density surfaces are associated with higher contrast. Thus quality reduction in these areas has more adverse effect on the perception of depth, than reducing quality in low feature point density areas. Figure 5.15, showing the Armadillo character used in appearance preserving simplification [Cohen *et al.* (1998)], is another example illustrating the perceptual impact of high and low feature point density.

Fig. 5.15 Different LOD of the Armadillo character with the number of triangles indicated at the bottom [Cohen *et al.* (1998)].

Note that the surface detail (visual quality) decreases as the feature point density decreases from left to right.

Degradation can be compensated, to a certain extent, if an appropriate texture pattern is used. This compensation phenomenon is explained by texture masking [Ferwerda *et al.* (1997)]. To simplify the initial analysis, both the nutcracker and the grenade models have simple pattern.

Based on the above analysis, we adopt a variable approach by applying different qualities on texture fragments depending on the feature point density, instead of applying a uniform quality to all fragments. Furthermore, the variable qualities are computed adaptively based on the current bandwidth. An adaptive approach is necessary when transmitting data on the Internet because bandwidth fluctuates and can adversely affect the expected quality of experience (QoE).

Before explaining how variable qualities are assigned to different fragments, the terminology used in the adaptive approach is defined below:

Notation

S_i — Scale i, *i.e.*, $0 \le i \le n$ where S_0 is the original signal and $S_n = S_{max}$ is the scale at infinity.

ΔQ — Quality tolerance limit for each scale imposing an upper and a lower bound. Analogous to the depth of field in photography, outside which an object is out of focus, ΔQ is the tolerance range when displaying 3D objects at a given distance. Given a viewing distance, the HVS finds this range of qualities satisfactory.

Q_i — Default texture quality associated with scale S_i.

(x, y) — x and y are the coordinates in the $N_x * N_y$ fragment map.

$q_i(x, y)$ — Texture quality of fragment (x, y) at S_i.

$f_i(x, y)$ — Number of feature points in fragment (x, y) at scale S_i.

$f_i^{\max}$ — The maximum number of feature points in a fragment at scale S_i.

$f_i^{\min}$ — The minimum number of feature points in a fragment at scale S_i.

$\eta_i(x, y)$ — Normalized value of $f_i(x, y)$.

$\bar{\eta}_i$ — The mean of the normalized values $\eta_i(x, y)$.

Γ — Feature point distribution threshold, *i.e.* $0 \le \Gamma \le 1$.

$d_i(x, y)$ — Data size of fragment (x, y) at S_i with quality $q_i(x, y)$.

D_i — Data size of all fragments at S_i.

At a given scale i, $f_i(x, y)$ is normalized as:

$$\eta_i(x, y) = \frac{f_i(x, y) - f_i^{\min}}{f_i^{\max} - f_i^{\min}}.$$

The texture quality $q_i(x, y)$of fragment (x, y) at scale S_i is computed as:

$$Q_i + (\eta_i(x, y) - \Gamma)\Delta Q.$$

In the current implementation, threshold $\Gamma = \bar{\eta}_i \in [0,1]$. Fragments with $\eta_i(x, y) = \Gamma$ are assigned quality Q_i. If $\eta_i(x, y) > \Gamma$, the fragment texture quality is higher than Q_i. If $\eta_i(x, y) < \Gamma$, texture quality is lower than Q_i. ΔQ controls the deviation (+/-) from Q_i Regions on the 3D model surface with higher feature point density are displayed with higher quality, and lower density regions are displayed with lower quality texture. By increasing or decreasing Γ, the overall quality of the texture image is decreased or increased accordingly, along with the data size. For each model texture, a lookup table is used to record D_i, $d_i(x, y)$ and $q_i(x, y)$ for a range of Γ. Given a time limit and the current bandwidth, the appropriate D_i, and the associated $d_i(x, y)$ are selected as the reference data size to transmit the first fragment. Details of this transmission strategy and bandwidth adaptation will be discussed in Chapter 6.

5.7 Summary

The first part of this chapter reviewed the scale-space introduced by Witkin in 1983. While scale-space analysis has been applied in image processing and computer vision extensively, its applications on 3D visualization are not fully explored. This chapter explains how SSF is used to analyze 3D surface structures and how feature points at different scales are extracted based on the detection of zero-crossing.

The second part of the chapter introduced the TexMesh model, and describes how feature points are distributed onto the texture fragments. Experiments were conducted to show that not only the fragmentation approach does not increase the total transmitted data for high resolution texture image divided into optimal fragment size, but also it improves the overall visual fidelity of the 3D object. Examples were given to illustrate how feature point density is related to shade and contrast, and how it is used as a visual quality predictor to determine texture quality assignment. In Chapter 6, the Harmonic Time Compensation Algorithm (HTCA) will be introduced.

References

Bauer, D. and Peikert, R. (2002). Vortex tracking in scale-space, in *Eurographics-IEEE TCVG Symposium on Visualization.*

Boulanger, P., Jokinen, O. and Beraldin, A. (2002). Intrinsic filtering of range images using a physically based noise model, in *Vision Interface* (Calgary, Canada).

Cohen, J., Olano, M. and Manocha, D. (1998). Appearance-preserving simplification, in *Siggraph.*

Ferwerda, J., Pattanaik, S., Shirley, P. and Greenberg, D. (1997). A model of visual masking for computer graphics, in *ACM SIGGRAPH*, pp. 143–152.

JPEG (2006). URL `http://www.jpeg.org/jpeg/`.

Kuijper, A. and Florack, L. (2001). Logical filtering in scale space, Tech. rep., Institute of Information and Computing Sciences, Utrecht Universit.

Lindberg, T. (1995). A scale selection principle for estimating image deformations, in *ICCV* (Cambridge, MA, USA), pp. 134–141.

Lindberg, T. (1998). Feature detection with automatic scale selection, *International Journal of Computer Vision*, 2.

Nagata, S. (1984). How to reinforce perception of depth in single 2D pictures — comparative study on various depth cues, *Proc. of the SID* **25**, 3, pp. 239–247.

Pan, Y., Cheng, I. and Basu, A. (2005). Quantitative metric for estimating perceptual quality of 3D objects, *IEEE Transactions on Multimedia.*

Pauly, M., Keiser, R. and Gross, M. (2003). Multi-scale feature extraction on point-sampled surfaces, in *Eurographics* (Granada, Spain).

Southard, D. A. (1991). Piecewise planar surface models from sampled data, in Patrikalakis (ed.), *Scientific Visualization of Physical Phenomena* (Springer-Verlag), pp. 667–680.

Witkin, A. (1983). Scale-space filtering, in *Int. Joint Conference on AI*, pp. 1019–1022.

Chapter 6

Adaptive Online Transmission of Photo-Realistic Textured Mesh

I. Cheng

6.1 Introduction

Efficient bandwidth utilization and optimal quality of service are among the main objectives when transmitting 3D objects. Since mesh data is usually small compared to texture data, our focus is to adapt the texture quality to the current bandwidth within a specified, or acceptable, transmission time. A historic average can be used to estimate current bandwidth [Cheng *et al.* (2001)], but this approach can cause unacceptable over or under estimation because of bandwidth fluctuations. An optimal bandwidth monitoring approach can provide a more accurate estimation by sacrificing a portion of the transmission time [Yu *et al.* (2003)]. In this chapter, an adaptive approach is proposed, which does not need to sacrifice transmission time for bandwidth estimation, while efficiently adjusting the quality of the fragments not yet transmitted.

In order to optimize bandwidth, a multi-scale incremental simplification approach is most suitable for online applications. Multi-scale allows a coarse version to be refined incrementally. However, if a simplification process involves relocation of mesh vertices or texture coordinates between scales, then an entirely new version instead of the vertices added to a coarse version, has to be transmitted [Brodsky and Watson (2000)] [Garland and Heckbert (1997)] [Shaffer and Garland (2001)] [Turk (1992)]. In the progressive meshes method, although the original mesh can be recovered exactly after all the data are received, the edge collapse transformation creates new vertices and the *vsplit* record stream increases network workload [Hoppe

(1996)]. Experimental results in Chapter 6 show that given a viewing distance two visual stimuli can be quantitatively different, but perceptually similar. For example, the two nutcracker models have similar visual quality, but the mesh resolution on the left is ten times that on the right (Fig. 6.1). Thus it is more beneficial to allocate the available computational and network resources to other related multimedia data, *e.g.* texture, instead of striving for an exact recovery of the original or denser mesh. Xia's adaptive real-time LOD technique also involves vertex relocation [Xia *et al.* (1997)]. We apply vertex removal and edge collapse without affecting the 3D point and the associated 2D texture coordinates.

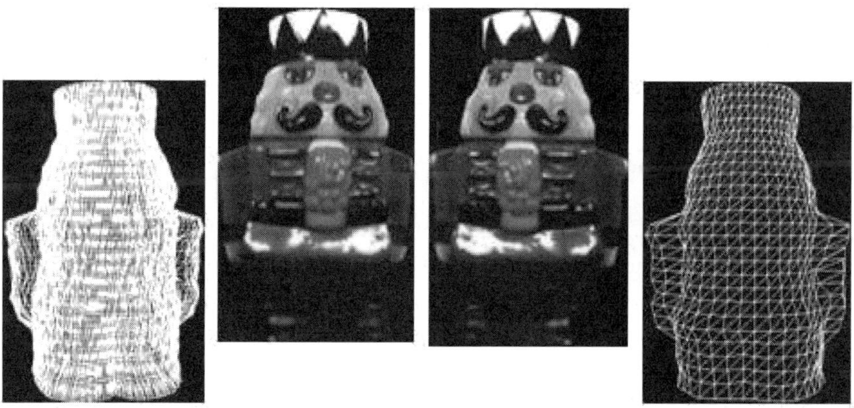

Fig. 6.1 The two nutcracker objects are perceptually similar although the mesh resolution on the left is ten times that on the right (18,720 vs. 1,872 triangles corresponding to 46 and 8 KB in .zip format).

In recent years, researchers started to incorporate color and texture into their mesh simplification models. When texture is mentioned in the literature, it often refers to synthetic or animated texture [Turk (1991)]. Synthetic texture can be estimated. For example, when walking through an animated scene, the next frame can be predicted based on available neighboring data [Cohen-Or *et al.* (1999)]. The authors demonstrated that this technique has better quality and higher compression factor than MPEG. An image-driven simplification method is used to display textures using images from multiple views [Lindstrom and Turk (2000)]. However, rendering the entire model for every edge in every viewpoint for different scales is expensive, even with hardware-accelerated rendering. The high-resolution texture used in the TexMesh model is different from the per pixel color stored in each vertex [Cohen *et al.* (1998)] [Garland and Heckbert (1998)] [Soucy *et al.* (1996)] [Heckbert and Garland (1997)], where interpolation is required when texture resolution is higher than mesh resolution. For applications requiring real-life texture, interpolating colors between vertices is not acceptable. The non-interpolated texture I use has resolution much higher than the mesh. It was observed in perceptual experiments that the human visual system is more sensitive to higher texture resolution after the mesh reaches an optimal density [Pan *et al.* (2005)]. In general, realism of virtual objects increases as texture quality increases resulting from the perception of depth [Nagata (1984)]. The TexMesh model uses photo-realistic texture images, with resolution up to millions of pixels, suitable for displaying on small monitors or high definition screens in reality centers. Phototexture is used in compressed texture maps [Yu *et al.* (2000)], but their effort is on recovering geometry from texture patches retrieved from multiple photographs. A distance-based technique is applied to photo-textured terrain [Lindstrom *et al.* (1995)]; however, color interpolation between pixels is necessary to avoid blocky appearance of terrain texture. To the best of my knowledge, the TexMesh approach is the first algorithm to introduce geometry driven texture reduction for adaptive online transmission of 3D objects, taking visual fidelity into account. My adaptive approach does not replace any image compression techniques. Instead, it enhances compression by introducing bandwidth adaptation at the application level, in addition to the reduction at the image level.

In [Okuda and Chen (2000)], the joint geometry/texture progressive coding method applies wavelet transform to encode the mesh and texture data for transmission, but the method cannot adapt to fluctuating bandwidth. Wavelets are also used to create space optimized texture maps, which did not require any hardware compression support [Balmelli *et al.* (2002)]. In my method, scale-space filtering and zero-crossing detection are applied to extract feature points. Each scale is associated with a default texture quality based on the number of feature points in it, and the quality of each fragment is allowed to deviate within a limit. The quality is later readjusted according to current bandwidth. By relating each scale to a viewing distance, automatic selection of a corresponding simplified textured mesh is possible.

Note that one major difference between wavelets and the scale-space approach is that the former scales up or down by a fixed factor of 2. In the scale-space approach, the scales at which changes occur depend on the surface features of individual objects, and are not fixed beforehand. In this chapter I extend the textured mesh (TexMesh) model to incorporate a dynamic strategy, which adapts the current bandwidth when computing texture quality of the next transmitted fragment. A Harmonic Time Compensation Algorithm (HTCA) is applied to ensure optimal use of the time limit and bandwidth. By splitting the texture into fragments, distributed transmission and parallel processing is possible.

6.2 Overview of Adaptive Strategy

The strategy for adaptive online transmission of 3D objects has several components, which are shown in Fig. 6.2.

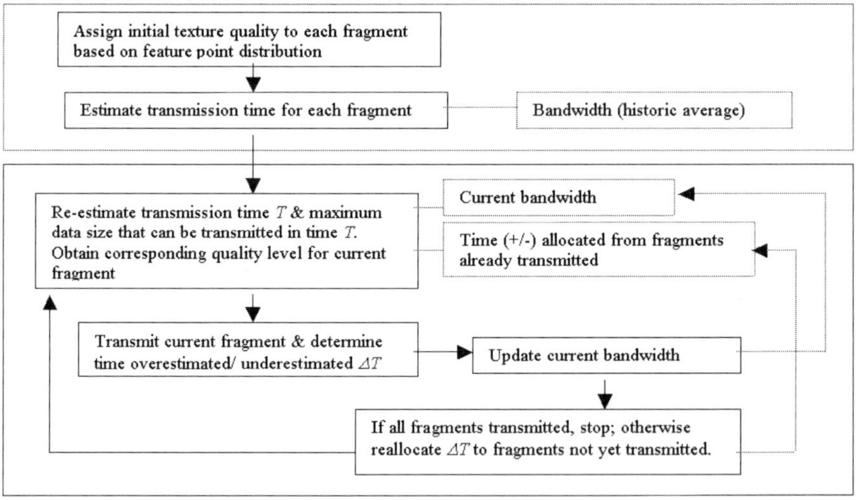

Fig. 6.2 A block diagram of the adaptive online transmission strategy.

The components are divided into two groups: preprocessing is described in the upper group, and online process is described in the lower group. The feature point density in each texture fragment is a value between zero and one, which is mapped onto a compression scale. For example, the JPEG compression scale from 0% to 100% is used in the current implementation. While wavelet coding applies to the entire image and is geometry-independent, the approach proposed here supports variable quality determined by the density of surface structures. Note that JPEG [JPEG (2006)] is currently used for convenience and wide support on the web and in JAVA; however, standards such as JPEG2000, and other efficient compression algorithms, can be used as well in the future to code fragments.

6.3 Adaptive Bandwidth Monitoring and Texture Quality Determination

Because of bandwidth fluctuation, current bandwidth has to be monitored periodically in order to maintain a good estimate of the data size that can be transmitted in a specified time T_0. To minimize the discrepancy, we reallocate the time surplus/deficit to the fragments not yet transmitted.

We adhere to the notation used in Chapter 5, where $\eta_i(x, y)$ is defined as the normalized feature point density of fragment (x, y). The $n = N_X * N_Y$ fragments are pre-sorted in decreasing $\eta_i(x, y)$ values, *i.e.*, from 1 to 0,

$$F_{list} = \{F_1, \ldots, \bar{F}, \ldots, F_n\}, \; i.e., \; \bar{F} \text{ has quality } Q_i.$$

The first fragment to be transmitted is $\bar{F}$ with quality Q_i.

Based on a time limit T_0 and a historic bandwidth average β_0, we estimate maximum data size to be transmitted as:

$$D_1 = T_0 * \beta_0$$

Where:

β_k is the current bandwidth (KB/sec.) recorded after k fragments are transmitted, *i.e.*, $0 \le k < n$. β_0 is the historic average bandwidth before transmission.

T_k is the time left after k fragments are transmitted. T_0 is the original time limit (seconds) specified, and

D_{k+1} is the maximum data size that can be transmitted given β_k and T_k.

The fragment list F_{list}, best matching D_1, is selected from a lookup table generated during preprocessing. The size of $\bar{F}$,d_1, is used to estimate the transmission time of the first fragment:

$$\vartheta_1 = T_0 * \frac{d_1}{D_1}, or \vartheta_1 = \frac{d_1}{\beta_0} \tag{6.1}$$

Where: d_k represents the data size of the kth fragment,

ϑ_k is the estimated transmission time for fragment k.

We estimate the transmission time ϑ_g for all the remaining fragments, *i.e.*, $2 \leq g \leq n$:

$$\vartheta_g = T_0 * \frac{d_g}{D_1} \tag{6.2}$$

After d_1 is transmitted, we have the updated bandwidth β_1 based on the time γ_1 recorded when transmitting d_1:

$$\beta_1 = \frac{d_1}{\gamma_1} \tag{6.3}$$

Where γ_k is the actual time needed to transmit the fragment k.

The next fragment is selected as follows:

(a) The leftmost fragment in F_{list} if $\beta_1 \leq \beta_0$, and

(b) The rightmost fragment in F_{list} if $\beta_1 > \beta_0$.

Let ΔT_k be equal to the difference between estimated and actual transmission time for k^{th} fragment; *i.e.*, $\vartheta_k - \gamma_k$

Let Δt_k be the cumulated compensation time (+/-) allocated to the kth fragment from the previous k-1 fragments (refer to Algorithm 1 below), and letwt_f be the weight applied to the fth fragment when allocating ΔT_{k-1}, *i.e.*, $k \leq f \leq n$.

The basic adaptive algorithm is as follows:

(a) If the actual bandwidth is lower than the estimated one, loss of time ΔT_1 has to be compensated when transmitting the remaining $n-1$ fragments, so that each remaining fragment has to share a portion of ΔT_1. Instead of the initial ϑ_2 computed in Equation (4.2), the 2nd fragment has $wt_2 * \Delta T_1$ seconds less, where wt_2 is the assigned weight. We regain the time by transmitting the leftmost fragment in F_{list} with reduced quality.

(b) Similarly, if the actual bandwidth is greater than the estimated one, the gained time ΔT_1 is allocated to the remaining $n-1$ fragments, so that each remaining fragment can have additional time. Instead of the initial ϑ_2, the 2nd fragment has $\vartheta_2 + wt_2 * \Delta T_1$ seconds. We adjust the time by transmitting the rightmost fragment in F_{list} with increased quality.

Based on the revised ϑ_2, we compute: $d_2 = \beta_1 * \vartheta_2$; and then obtain corresponding quality for the 2nd fragment from the lookup table using d_2. In general, after $k-1$ fragments are transmitted:

$$\Delta T_{k-1} = \vartheta_{k-1} - \gamma_{k-1} \tag{6.4}$$

$$\Delta t_k = \Delta t_k + \Delta T_{k-1} * wt_k \tag{6.5}$$

The computation of weight wt_k is explained in Algorithm 1.

$$\vartheta_k = \vartheta_g + \Delta t_k \tag{6.6}$$

$$\beta_{k-1} = \frac{d_{k-1}}{\gamma_{k-1}} \tag{6.7}$$

and,

$$d_k = \beta_{k-1} * \vartheta_k \tag{6.8}$$

The quality for the kth fragment is obtained from the lookup table based on d_k.

Bandwidth fluctuation has a larger impact on the quality if ΔT_k has to be shared by a smaller number of fragments. Therefore, fragments with quality $\cong Q_i$ are transmitted last to allow more flexibility for adjustment within the control limit ΔQ. Once the transmission is started, the quality of a fragment is self-adjusted depending on the updated bandwidth.

6.4 Harmonic Time Compensation Algorithm

Since all late fragments have to share all preceding allocations, Algorithm 4.1 assigns decreasing weights ($\frac{1}{2}, \frac{1}{3}, \frac{1}{4}, \cdots$) from $(k+1)^{th}$ to n^{th} fragments, when reallocating ΔT_k

Algorithm 6.1 — Harmonic Time Compensation

After transmitting k^{th} fragment,
let $\chi = 2$;
compute $\varsigma_k = \sum_{j=2}^{n-k+1} \frac{1}{j} = \ln(n-k+1)$;
for $(i = k+1; i \leq n; i++)\{$
    $wt_i = \frac{1}{\chi * \varsigma_k}$;
    $\Delta t_i += \Delta T_k * wt_i$; // allocate to remaining fragments
    $\chi++$;
$\}$

There are two questions we have to address:

(1) How efficient is the algorithm with respect to bandwidth optimization in a given time? and,

(2) How does the adaptive approach affect the perceptual quality?

To prove the efficiency of the algorithm, we define Π as the time surplus/deficiency with respect to the limit T_0. Π is composed of three errors: estimation error E_{est}, allocation error E_{alloc}, and compensation error E_{comp}. In Theorem 6.1, we establish the upper and lower bound of Π (Proof: See Appendix A).

Theorem 6.1: Π is bounded by:

$\Delta T_n + (\Delta T_{n-1}/2) + (1.088 + \ln|\ln(n)|)\Lambda$

Where Λ is defined as the average difference between the estimated and actual transmission time for the first $n-1$ fragments,

$$i.e.\ \Lambda = \frac{\sum_{j=1}^{n-1} \Delta T_j}{n-1}.$$

The upper and lower bounds in Theorem 6.1 are verified by experimental results in the next section. We will show that our adaptive approach does not have an adverse effect on perceptual quality for reasonable bandwidth fluctuation.

6.5 Experimental Results

Let $n = 256$, applying Theorem 6.1 and substituting 256 into Equation A.3 in Appendix A, we obtain:

$$E_{comp} \leq 2.8\Lambda \text{ if } \Lambda \geq 0, \text{ and } E_{comp} \geq 2.8\Lambda \text{ if } \Lambda < 0$$

Since Λ is the average deviation over the entire transmission period, it is expected to be small. The other two components of Π: estimation error E_{est} (Appendix A Equation A.1) and allocation error E_{alloc} (Appendix A Equation A.2), can be minimized by using sufficiently small data size for the last two fragments.

In order to see how Π responds to bandwidth fluctuation, a bandwidth monitor using JAVA and client-server architecture was implemented (Fig. 6.3). When non-adaptive mode was chosen, testing packets of fixed size were transmitted from server to client at regular intervals. The client computed the current bandwidth based on the time to transmit the packet just received. When adaptive mode was chosen, the packet size and time interval would be adjusted depending on whether the current bandwidth was below or above a predefined threshold.

Three sets of bandwidths were extracted from an Ethernet connection on different days and different times (Table 6.1). I then varied the value

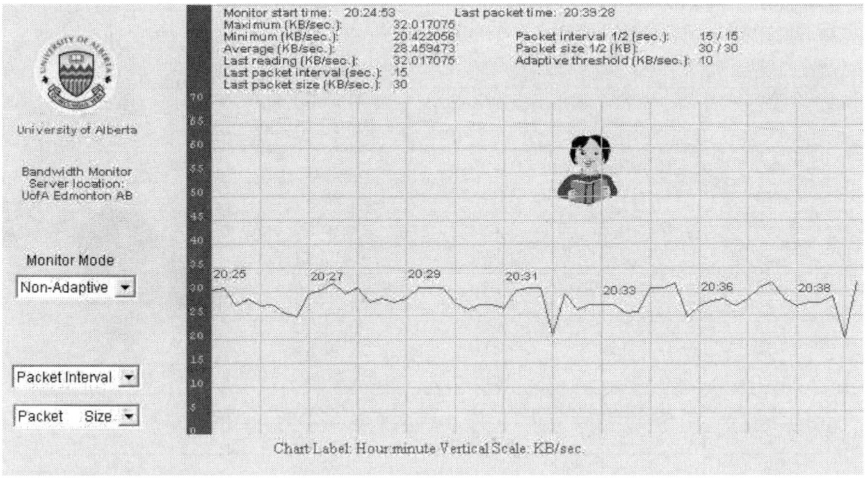

Fig. 6.3 An example of bandwidth fluctuation on an Ethernet connection.

Table 6.1 Three bandwidth sample sets were taken from an Ethernet connection on different days and different times.

Bandwidth sample set	Actual bandwidth average (KB/sec)
1	41.68
2	45.64
3	42.07

of β_0 below and above the average of the sample set within a reasonable range (Table 6.2). The test file was 418KB with 256 fragments.

One can observe that Π is minimum, when Λ is close to zero. That is when the estimated bandwidth β_0 is close to the bandwidth average (Fig. 6.4). Similar trends were obtained from samples 2 and 3. By keeping the nth and $(n-1)^{th}$ fragments sufficiently small, as in our experiments, the deviation from the time limit is within 1%. For comparison, the last column shows the discrepancy in percentage of time limit, should historic average bandwidth be used in a static approach.

To see how variable quality affects the overall visualization, we used $\beta_0 = 32$ and 50, together with a sample average of 41.68 (KB/sec), and applied to the dog texture. The original texture has quality $Q_i = 80\%$ and ΔQ_i is [40%, 100%]. Figure 6.5 shows that the perceptual quality is maintained, after applying variable qualities to fragments adaptively in

Table 6.2 Experimental results show that the Harmonic Time Compensation Algorithm had less than 1% deviation for a given time limit. β_0 was used for initial bandwidth estimation (Sample set 1).

β_0 (KB/sec)	Λ (sec)	ΠSurplus/deficit (+/−)% of limit	T_0 Time Limit (sec)	Static approach % of limit
20	0.038	0.399	20.9	52.0
23	0.031	0.346	18.17	44.8
26	0.023	0.280	16.07	37.6
29	0.015	0.195	14.41	30.4
32	0.011	0.142	13.06	23.2
35	0.003	0.010	11.94	16.0
38	−0.001	0.010	11	8.8
41	−0.004	−0.027	10.19	1.6
44	−0.008	−0.034	9.5	−5.5
47	−0.008	−0.058	8.89	−12.0
50	−0.012	−0.058	8.36	−19.8
53	−0.012	−0.090	7.88	−27.2

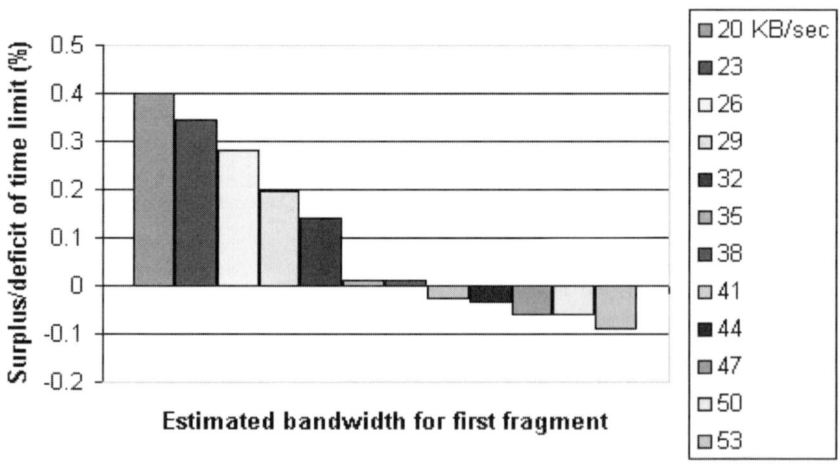

Fig. 6.4 Experimental results show that the overall time surplus/deficit Π was close to zero, when the initial estimated bandwidth β_0 was close to the bandwidth average of the transmission period (Sample set 1).

order to satisfy the time limit. Given the estimated texture in the middle, actual quality is increased in case of underestimation of actual bandwidth (left), and actual quality is decreased for overestimation (right).

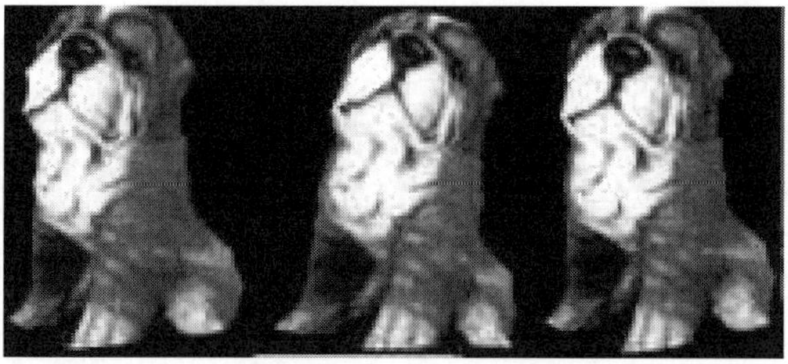

Fig. 6.5 Initial estimated texture (middle), increased quality (left) and decreased quality (right).

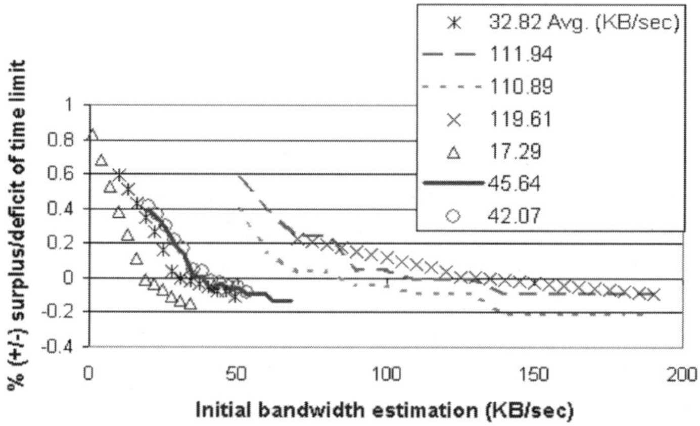

Fig. 6.6 Simulation results of seven higher speed networks — By applying different initial estimated bandwidth B_0 the final deviation from a given time limit is with 1%.

We performed fifteen more simulations using a wider range of bandwidths, including dial-up and high-speed networks. Experimental results are consistent with earlier findings. Results from seven higher speed networks are plotted in Fig. 6.6 and five from lower speed networks are plotted in Fig. 6.7. It can be seen that when the initial estimation is within a reasonable range of the bandwidth average, the overall deviation is less than 1% of the given time limit. The deviation gets smaller when the initial estimation β_0 approaches the actual average bandwidth of the entire transmission period. Since the initial estimation is based on historic average, it is not expected to be very different from the actual average for a reasonably long transmission period. Also, note that when networks have similar

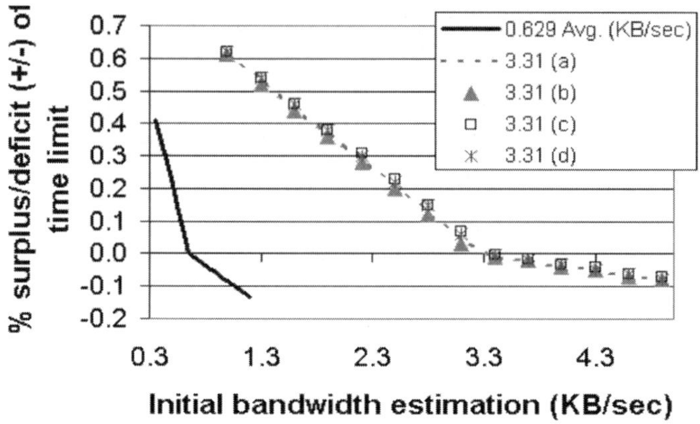

Fig. 6.7 Simulation results of five lower speed networks — By applying different initial estimated bandwidth B_0 the final deviation from a given time limit is with 1%.

average and if a network is relatively stable, *e.g.* 3.31 KB/sec. as shown by (a), (b), (c) and (d) in Fig. 6.7, the surplus/deficit curves follow a similar trend. On the other hand, although the bandwidth average of 111.94 and 110.89 KB/sec are close (Fig. 6.6), the surplus/deficit curves have different trends due to unstable bandwidth fluctuations.

The adaptive approach is most suitable for delivering best-effort QoS. It also supports distributed and parallel processing, by storing texture fragments at different sites. Texture data can be transmitted incrementally to refine the previous version. Although feature point density can be used as a visual quality predictor, geometry driven texture reduction alone is not sufficient to predict the final visual fidelity.

6.6 Summary

This chapter shows how texture fragmentation and variable quality assignment can be used to support efficient online transmission. An adaptive Harmonic Time Compensation Algorithm was introduced. Experimental results show that HTCA can adapt to bandwidth fluctuation well and thus provide better QoS. Perceptual quality is a main component in the TexMesh framework. Next, we will review the various environmental and psycho-visual factors that may affect the perception of quality.

References

Balmelli, L., Taubin, G. and Bernardini, F. (2002). Space-optimized texture maps, in *Eurographics*, pp. 411–420.

Brodsky, D. and Watson, B. (2000). Model simplification through refinement, in *Proceedings of Graphics Interface*.

Cheng, I., Basu, A., Zhang, Y. and Tripathi, S. (2001). QoS specification and adaptive bandwidth monitoring for multimedia delivery, in *Proceeding of EUROCON* (Bratislava, Slovak Republic), pp. 485–488.

Cohen, J., Olano, M. and Manocha, D. (1998). Appearance-preserving simplification, in *Siggraph*.

Cohen-Or, D., Mann, Y. and Fleishman, S. (1999). Onespacedeep compression for streaming texture intensive animations, in *Siggraph*.

Garland, M. and Heckbert, P. (1997). Simplification using quadric error metrics, in *Computer Graphics (Siggraph)*, pp. 209–216.

Garland, M. and Heckbert, P. (1998). Simplifying surfaces with color and texture using quadric error metrics, in *IEEE Visualization*.

Heckbert, P. S. and Garland, M. (1997). Survey of polygonal surface simplification algorithms, in *Multiresolution Surface Modeling Course, SIGGRAPH*.

Hoppe, H. (1996). Progressive meshes, in *Proceedings of SIGGRAPH*, pp. 99–108.

Lindstrom, P., Koller, D., Hodges, L. F., Ribarsky, W., Faust, N. and Turner, G. (1995). Level of detail management for real-time rendering of phototextured terrain, Tech. rep., GeorgiaTech, Atlanta, GA.

Lindstrom, P. and Turk, G. (2000). Image-driven simplification, *ACM Trans. on Graphics*.

Nagata, S. (1984). How to reinforce perception of depth in single 2D pictures — comparative study on various depth cues, *Proc. of the SID* **25**, 3, pp. 239–247.

Okuda, M. and Chen, T. (2000). Joint geometry/texture progressive coding of 3D models, in *IEEE Int. Conf. on Image Processing*.

Pan, Y., Cheng, I. and Basu, A. (2005). Quantitative metric for estimating perceptual quality of 3D objects, *IEEE Transactions on Multimedia*.

Shaffer, E. and Garland, M. (2001). Efficient adaptive simplification of massive meshes, in *Proc. IEEE Visualization*.

Soucy, M., Godin, G. and Rioux, M. (1996). A texture-mapping approach for the compression of colored 3D triangulations, *The Visual Computer* **12**, pp. 503–514.

Turk, G. (1991). Generating texture on arbitrary surfaces using reaction-diffusion, in *Siggraph*.

Turk, G. (1992). Re-tiling polygonal surfaces, in *Siggraph*.

Xia, J., El-Sana, J. and Varshney, A. (1997). Adaptive real-time level-of-detail-based rendering for polygonal models, *IEEE Trans. on Visualization and Computer Graphics*.

Yu, Y., Cheng, I. and Basu, A. (2003). Optimal adaptive bandwidth monitoring for QoS based retrieval, *IEEE Transactions on Multimedia.*

Yu, Y., Ferencz, A. and Malik, J. (2000). Compressing texture maps for large real environments, in *Siggraph Sketch.*

Chapter 7

Perceptual Issues in a 3D TexMesh Model

I. Cheng

7.1 Introduction

Visual fidelity is a fundamental issue in 3D visualization. Different techniques, such as illumination [Volevich *et al.* (2000)], perception of depth [Nagata (1984)] and visual masking [Ferwerda *et al.* (1997)], have been proposed to improve visual fidelity and thus enhance the realism of 3D objects in the virtual world. Many measuring criteria were suggested to compare the performance of these techniques. Comparisons were traditionally focused on geometric metrics, but in recent years, perceptual metrics have gained more attention [Luebke (2001)] [Luebke and Hallen (2001)] [Pan *et al.* (2005)] [Reitsma and Polland (2003)] [Watson *et al.* (2001)] [Williams *et al.* (2003)]. While geometric metrics provide hint leading to a decision, perceptual metrics are more reliable when making the final judgement because visual fidelity is ultimately determined by the HVS. Applying a perceptual metric is not easy because human judgement is not always unbiased. Environmental and psychological factors very often affect human judgement. Therefore successful perceptual evaluation experiments need to use a sufficiently large sample size, and sometimes preconditions have to be set. For example, in some experiments judges are divided into age groups or categorized according to academic background. Conclusion is then drawn from the experimental results. The goal is to obtain the general perceptual behavior of the population based on the statistics drawn from the sample.

7.2 Psycho-Visual Factors Affecting Visual Fidelity

Geometry and texture are two basic components of a 3D textured mesh object. Visual fidelity of the geometry and texture can be affected by various environmental and psycho-visual factors [Pan *et al.* (2005)] [Luebke and Hallen (2001)] [Nagata (1984)] [Limb (1979)]. The major factors are summarized below:

• Visual threshold [Luebke and Hallen (2001)] [Limb (1979)] — Vanishing point, at which a stimulus becomes just visible or invisible.

• Luminance of the background in contrast with the stimulus [Gonzalez and Woods (2002)] [Limb (1979)] — If the background is plain, the visual threshold will change depending on the luminance of the background in contrast to the object. This relationship is described by Weber's Law, which states that the threshold is proportional to the background luminance.

• Spatial visual masking [Limb (1979)] — A big change of luminance may be present across an edge. Such a change reduces the ability of the eye to detect distortions spatially adjacent to the changes. The detection threshold (or the contrast corresponding to the threshold of perception) of a stimulus varies inversely as a function of its distance from the edge. As a target moves across an edge, the threshold on the light side of the edge is increased.

• Temporal visual masking — Post-masking (backward masking) occurs if the perception of a stimulus is affected by a strong signal after it. A visual backward masking model suggested that, when two successive stimuli are presented within 0 to 200ms intervals, the recognition of the first stimulus (the target) can be impaired by the second (the mask) [Bugmann and Taylor (2003)]. Pre-masking occurs if it is affected by a strong signal before it.

• Spatial frequency (cycles per degree of visual arc) — Minimum detectable difference (sensitivity threshold) in luminance between a test spot on a uniform visual field, increased linearly with background luminance at daylight levels. However, virtual scenes and stimuli are not uniform, and contain complex frequency content. Outside a small frequency range, the sensitivity threshold drops off significantly. This phenomenon leads to the study on the perceptibility of contrast gratings; sinusoidal patterns that alternate between two extreme luminance values, and the following terminology:

a) Threshold contrast at a given spatial frequency is the minimum contrast that can be perceived in a grating.

b) Contrast sensitivity is the reciprocal of threshold contrast.

c) Contrast sensitivity function (CSF) plots contrast sensitivity against spatial frequency. It describes the range of perceptible contrast gratings [Luebke and Hallen (2001)].

• Feature masking — Presence of features will affect the general impression of the entire stimulus. For example, recognition of the ears of a bunny outweighs the discrimination of shape (Fig. 7.1). This concept is well understood in the cartoon industry.

Fig. 7.1 Both stimuli are recognized as a bunny based on the feature ear, although their geometric representations are very different.

• Texture masking — It can be observed that the noise added to low frequency (or plain) background is much more visible than that added to high frequency (or flowery) background. A model was developed in computer graphics which allows the choice of texture pattern to hide the effects of faceting, banding, aliasing, noise and other visual artifacts [Ferwerda *et al.* (1997)]. This technique is suitable for applications using synthetic texture. For applications displaying intrinsic photo-texture of the object, choice of another pattern is not an option.

• Short-term memory — Influence of a strong stimulus will last for a short time, which will impose a smoothing effect on the distortion measure. It is noted that people are more likely to remember bad quality than good quality.

• Visual acuity — Fovea, occupying roughly the central 1° of vision, is the region of highest sensitivity. Visual acuity, measured as the highest perceptible spatial frequency, is lower in the periphery than at the fovea.

• Visual depth — Sensation of reality occurs because of visual depth perception. Depth sensitivity, the ratio of viewing distance to depth discrimination threshold, is directly proportional to the viewing distance.

Sharp edge, clear texture, shade and gloss of the surface strengthen the sensation of depth.

• Prior knowledge or Expectation — Prior knowledge imposes on the viewer an expected geometry and texture representation. Deviation from expectation degrades visual fidelity. If a stimulus appears in an orientation different from what the viewer is familiar with, the viewer's ability to discriminate decreases.

In video applications, satisfactory frame-rate (and network latency if transmitted over the network) is an important consideration. The TexMesh model is designed for efficient 3D visualization within time and visual constraints. The focus is an optimal overall time, instead of time intervals between data packets. Spatial and temporal visual masking can have a significant effect on the continuity of a stream of video frames, but are not essential in visualizing 3D objects discussed in this thesis. The focus of the TexMesh model is on the visualization of 3D objects after a specified time is elapsed. Continuity of intermediate data stream is not important as long as the final result is satisfactory. In the next section, we will discuss the major factors that need to be taken into account when conducting perceptual evaluation experiments on 3D textured meshes.

7.3 Preparation for Visual Discrimination Experiments

The HVS is complex, and many researchers have concluded that the determination of visual fidelity cannot be replaced by simple mathematics such as the MSE (Mean Square Error). Taylor *et al.* conducted an experiment [Taylor *et al.* (1998b)] by comparing the original image with (a) a distorted image by a slight shift in luminance values, and (b) a distorted image by JPEG quantization. Although image (a) was visually similar to the original image, while image (b) was obviously degraded, MSE for image (a) is greater than that of image (b). Instead of using a geometric metric, a perceptual metric is believed to be more accurate in determining visual fidelity, because the ultimate decision is made by the HVS. As a result, many perceptually driven simplification techniques on 3D models have been suggested in the literature. A common approach to verify these techniques is to compare the evaluation generated by the algorithm with human judgement. Another approach is to apply perceptual theory to select visual difference predictors (VDP), and incorporate them in the algorithm. VDP was first introduced in 1992 [Daly (1992)]. However, previous experiments focused on static 2D images [Taylor *et al.* (1998a)] [Taylor *et al.* (1998b)], or view dependent discrimination [Luebke and Hallen (2001)]. A selected number of optimized views were used to compare stimuli [Watson *et al.* (2001)]. Only recently, a 3D view-independent technique was introduced to perform an overall quality evaluation of a 3D object [Pan *et al.* (2005)]. The following criteria are important to achieve accurate results and are taken into account in our perceptual experiments.

View-independence

In a static display or view-dependent approach, judges can only compare a limited number of silhouettes [Watson *et al.* (2001)] [Luebke and Hallen (2001)]. A viewer's gaze tends to focus at the center of the object. Thus the judgement can be affected by visual acuity, omitting details away from the fovea. A complete 360° view of the stimuli can compensate the falloff of visual acuity in the periphery of the retina, and give a more accurate comparison. 360° rotating stimuli were used in our evaluation experiments. A major difference between our experiments and those in [Pan *et al.* (2005)] is that, in our experiment we related scale with viewing distance and depth threshold, while in their experiment they did not consider viewing distance.

Luminance and highest visual sensitivity

Luminance is a crucial factor in perceptual experiments. We assume the worst case scenario, assuming visual sensitivity (ability to discriminate) is the highest when comparing stimuli. In order to enforce this assumption, the experimental environment is set to (1) normal daylight, (2) a background color, which has a reasonable contrast with the stimulus's color, and (3) a small spatial frequency just before the CSF falling off sharply [Luebke and Hallen (2001)], imposing a condition for high brightness adaptation and visual sensitivity. Furthermore, we used stimuli with plain or simple texture pattern to avoid texture masking.

Judging technique

The naming time technique [Watson *et al.* (2001)] is good to study visual latency (time between receiving a signal and taking an action), but its accuracy is not clear when evaluating visual fidelity because judgement is likely to be affected by:

- Prior knowledge of the stimulus.
- Feature masking.

In other words, the time required to recognize, and name the stimulus, does not necessarily reflect the quality of the simplified mesh.

The fact that the brain is more efficient on atomic operations can be taken into account in perceptual experiments. Expressing preference by selecting between two or more stimuli, or by rating up to five stimuli, have been used in the past and proved to produce satisfactory results [Pan *et al.* (2005)] [Taylor *et al.* (1998b)].

Short term memory

While classifying stimuli into categories, such as animal and scenery, one can divide the perceptual problem into sub-problems; presenting similar geometry and texture in consecutive tests can easily confuse judgement. The fact that strong stimulus will last for a short time will affect the next discrimination process. Stimuli should be randomly selected from different categories, and displayed in a random order.

7.4 Tradeoff Between Geometry and Texture

Texture can have the following representations:

- Color per vertex — Each 3D vertex is associated with a color value.
- Synthetic texture — Texture designed for fast interactive rendering, usually with uniform and reproducible patterns [Turk (1991)].
- Photo-realistic texture — Original texture of the object, such as that on museum exhibits and medical images, where alteration is not acceptable.

Both synthetic and realistic texture can be implemented using texture mapping. Cohen found texture mapping less restrictive than color per vertex [Cohen *et al.* (1998)]. A disadvantage of using color per vertex is the limited resolution. An initial color is stored with a vertex, but inter-vertex color has to be interpolated for higher resolution [Soucy *et al.* (1996)]. Also, the color value needs to be recomputed if a 3D vertex is shifted during simplification. Synthetic texture can be estimated or duplicated easily. For example, pattern of the next frame can be estimated based on neighboring data [Cohen-Or *et al.* (1999)]. Synthetic texture file size is usually kept small to facilitate transmission and rendering [Cohen *et al.* (1998)]. Although simple colors are often used in game applications for fast interactivity, photo-realistic texture is essential to add realism to a virtual scene. Interesting scenes are often complex and diverse, which cannot be generated by replicating a small patch of pattern. In applications where real life texture is required, every pixel value of the texture has to be recorded, without interpolation. In other words, realistic scenes are likely associated with high resolution texture files, far higher than the density of the underlying mesh. High resolution texture is emphasized in virtual realty systems, where the vertical dimension of each display panel is about a thousand pixels in resolution, but the texture image displayed is often over five thousand pixels vertically. The reason is that higher resolution texture can provide the illusion of detail.

Experiments were conducted to study under what condition, what mix of geometry and texture resolution can be used, without degrading visual fidelity [Rushmeier *et al.* (2000)]. The authors used different levels of geometry: smooth, medium and most simplified, in the experiments. They found that the perceived quality was roughly doubled, by doubling the geometry of the smooth sphere, independent of texture. Quality dropped systematically for each decrease in geometry on the medium simplified sphere, but adding texture had a significant improvement on the perceived quality. On the most simplified sphere, additional texture did little to improve the quality. There were several problems in their experiments. First, a sphere was used as the visual stimulus, which likely led to a biased judgement due to prior knowledge of the object. The scores may be different if the armadillo model [Cohen *et al.* (1998)] was used as the stimulus. Second, the objects used were of uniform color and surface finish, and therefore the result cannot be applied to 3D objects in general. The spatial frequencies generated from a uniform and a non-uniform color and surface finish, have very different impact on the HVS. Different types of objects should be used and more tests are needed to obtain a more objective and accurate conclusion.

Instead of using a sphere, three 3D objects were used as visual stimuli, and the number of judges was increased to twenty in [Pan *et al.* (2005)]. Experimental result shows that after reaching an optimal mesh density, increasing geometry has little effect on visual fidelity (Fig. 7.2). However, additional texture relates linearly to improved quality (Fig. 7.3).

For highly simplified geometry, increased texture resolution had significant impact on perceived quality. Based on these findings, visual fidelity can be improved by enhancing texture on all levels of geometry. Although a denser mesh and a higher resolution texture pattern present better fidelity in general, a trade-off between quality and bandwidth is necessary in online applications given limited network resources. It is beneficial to transmit the mesh, which is small compared to the texture, and focus on reduction of texture.

Previously, we discussed how variable texture qualities are assigned to

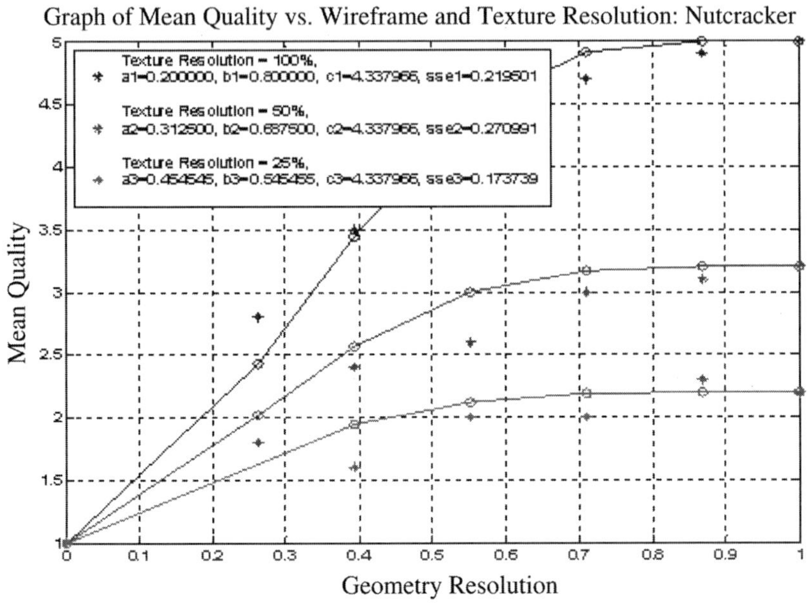

Fig. 7.2 Perceptual experiments show that visual quality relates to geometry resolution exponentially [Pan *et al.* (2005)].

fragments based on feature point density. Given a time limit, which is inadequate to transmit the full resolution object, the question is which region (fragment with high or low frequency), should be selected for quality reduction, with less impact on visual fidelity. My technique is motivated by the observation that minor variations in texture can be ignored in relatively smooth regions of a 3D surface, without significantly affecting human perception. This observation is supported by the CSF and the perception of depth, and is discussed in the next section.

7.5 Feature Point Density, Perception of Depth and Contrast Sensitivity

One of the many cues for visual depth perception is shade and sharpness [Nagata (1984)], which is represented by changing frequency, on the texture surface. On a surface with high feature point population, the texture has higher frequency due to shade, and contrast. Low frequency is less affected by quantization in the compression process, than high frequency, resulting in the more obvious degradation on the grenade model (Figs. 5.14(c) and

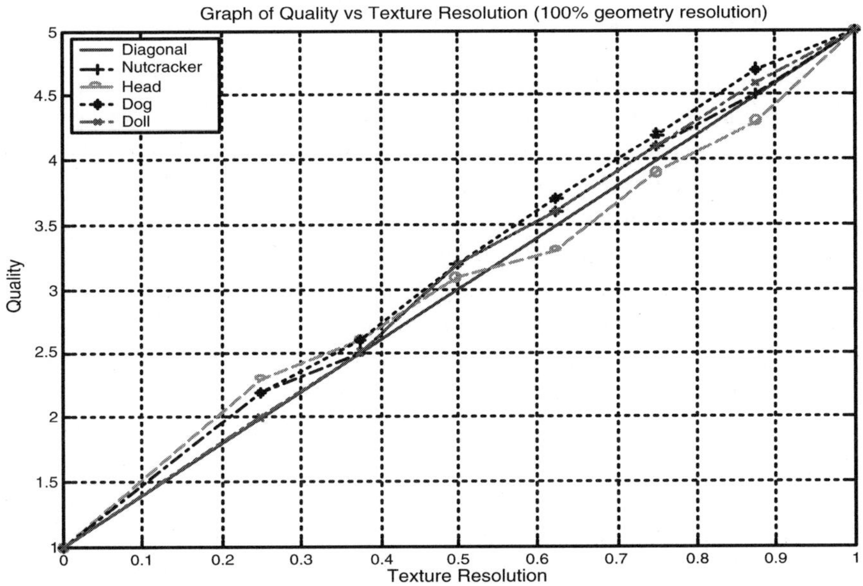

Fig. 7.3 Perceptual experiments show that visual quality relates to texture resolution linearly [Pan *et al.* (2005)].

(d)). Note that the textures of the nutcraker and grenade model are quite simple. If the objects have more complex texture, texture masking will make the degradation less obvious. To optimize the perception of depth given limited bandwidth, higher quality is assigned to higher feature density fragments. Higher qualities in these fragments also provide a cushion effect, to prevent the quality dropping too much below the default quality Q_i, causing significant visual degradation.

Brightness adaptation is good for a small value of Weber's ratio $\Delta I/I$, where ΔI is the increment of illumination discriminated 50% of the time with background illumination I. By plotting the log of Weber's ratio against log I, it is observed that brightness discrimination is poor at low levels of illumination and improves significantly as background illumination increases [Gonzalez and Woods (2002)]. The effect of illumination on vision depends not only on the light source but also the reflectance of the object. The contrast appearing on the texture is thus a predictor to visual fidelity. Under normal light source, visual discrimination is better on brighter rather than darker texture patterns. How visual sensitivity relates to contrast, and spatial frequency, is illustrated in the CSF [Luebke and Hallen (2001)].

7.6 Visual Quality Prediction (VDP)

In order to achieve visual fidelity, it is more efficient to employ a technique to determine quality while the textured mesh is generated, instead of relying on assessment and correction after it has been completed. Therefore visual quality predictors should be available to an algorithm during runtime. Since computing these predictors online is expensive, resulting in lengthy computation time which is not acceptable for interactive applications, the solution is to collect statistics during preprocessing, which can be retrieved in constant time to support online assessment.

Feature point density is a visual quality predictor in the TexMesh model. It contributes to the determination of quality for each texture fragment. Feature point density induces shade and contrast in the texture pattern. In addition to the brightness on the texture surface, as discussed above, texture complexity also contributes an important factor on perception in term of texture masking. In Chapter 9, different weights will be assigned to feature point density and texture properties, and these visual predictors will be integrated into the TexMesh model.

7.7 Two-Alternatives-Forced-Choice (2AFC)

In the two-alternative-forced-choice (2AFC) procedure, a subject is presented with two stimuli, A and B (which represent, *e.g.* x, $x + \Delta x$). The stimuli may occur in successive intervals, or they may occur in adjacent locations [Boff *et al.* (1986)]. For the purpose of this thesis, we take the latter case where A and B are placed in adjacent locations. The subject (judge)'s task is to state whether the target occurred in the left location or in the right location. In the experiments conducted for this thesis, a target was also displayed above the two stimuli so that the subject can have a reference of the original object. The subject's decision is recorded, either correct or incorrect, for each pair of stimuli. Once the judging is completed, the results are summarized. To find the visual threshold, the percentage of correct judgment is plotted as a function of Δx. To avoid response bias, sufficient evaluations, say 30, should be collected for each Δx value. The line of best fit is obtained by regression and the threshold can be located at the 75% correct performance [Weber (2006)]. When the two stimuli are clearly distinguishable, the score is 100%. If the difference is not apparent to the judge, he/she can only guess and the possibility of picking the correct stimulus is 50% after sufficient number of evaluations have been performed.

To prevent a subject from spending too much time in an evaluation, a time limit of 20 seconds was imposed in the experiments. The display is frozen after the time limit and the subject is forced to make a choice, guessing if necessary. It should not be assumed that the subject could not distinguish the stimuli because he/she may have a good idea of which one is better; but, if given unlimited time, the subject often looks for more evidence to support their decision. Forcing the subject to respond will reveal their decision. If the subject really cannot distinguish the stimuli, he/she will choose one alternative with 50% correctness (guessing).

7.8 Linear and Non-Linear Mechanism in Visual Perception

When performing prediction or statistical inference using perceptual data, we can apply either a linear or a non-linear approach. Although the visual system is demonstrably nonlinear in many circumstances [Boff *et al.* (1986)], linear models may still be applicable because some nonlinearity occurs where signals may pass through independent detection pathways. Even if each pathway is linear, the overall system may be non-linear [Boff *et al.* (1986)]. When restricting data in a particular pathway, a linear model can be applied. Nonlinearities in the visual system may be well approximated locally by a linear function.

Abbey *et al.* suggested that the linear approach is a useful starting point [Abbey and Eckstein (2002)]. In their experiments, they showed that the classification image is closely related to a linear observer. Their survey also showed that linear models have a history of use for modeling human-observer performance in noise-limited simple detection and discrimination tasks.

7.9 Summary

This chapter discusses the main environmental and psycho-visual factors that can affect the perceived quality of 3D objects. Some factors, *e.g.* temporal visual masking and velocity, are more important when dealing with dynamic than static scenes. Latency is important for video to ensure a smooth transition between frames. Since the TexMesh framework is designed for relatively static 3D textured meshes, the focus is on those factors which are likely to influence the perception of geometry and texture, appearing in a spontaneous and not sequential manner. Perceptual experiments will be discussed in the next few chapters. The goal is to understand more about biological vision, in order to integrate the knowledge with computer vision.

References

Abbey, C. and Eckstein, M. (2002). Classification image analysis: estimation and statistical inference for two-alternative forced-choice experiments, *Journal of Vision* **2**, 1, pp. 66–78.

Boff, K., Kaufman, L. and Thomas, J. (1986). Sensory processes and perception, in *Handbook of perception and human performance, Section 2*, Vol. I (A Wiley-Interscience Publication), p. 39.

Bugmann, G. and Taylor, J. (2003). A model of visual backward masking, *Submitted to Biosystems - 6.12.2003 University of Plymouth and Kings College London.*

Cohen, J., Olano, M. and Manocha, D. (1998). Appearance-preserving simplification, in *Siggraph.*

Cohen-Or, D., Mann, Y. and Fleishman, S. (1999). Onespacedeep compression for streaming texture intensive animations, in *Siggraph.*

Daly, S. (1992). Visible differences predictor: an algorithm for the assessment of image fidelity, **1616**, pp. 2–15.

Ferwerda, J., Pattanaik, S., Shirley, P. and Greenberg, D. (1997). A model of visual masking for computer graphics, in *ACM SIGGRAPH*, pp. 143–152.

Gonzalez, R. and Woods, R. (2002). *Digital Image Processing*, 2nd edn. (Prentice Hall).

Limb, J. O. (1979). Distortion criteria of the human viewer, *IEEE Trans. on Systems, Man, and Cybernetics* **9**, 12, pp. 778–793.

Luebke, D. and Hallen, B. (2001). Perceptually driven simplification for interactive rendering, in *Rendering Techniques* (Springer-Verlag).

Luebke, D. P. (2001). A developer's survey of polygonal simplification algorithms, *IEEE Computer Graphics and Applications*, May/June, pp. 24–35.

Nagata, S. (1984). How to reinforce perception of depth in single 2D pictures — comparative study on various depth cues, *Proc. of the SID* **25**, 3, pp. 239–247.

Pan, Y., Cheng, I. and Basu, A. (2005). Quantitative metric for estimating perceptual quality of 3D objects, *IEEE Transactions on Multimedia.*

Reitsma, P. and Polland, N. (2003). Perceptual metrics for character animation: sensitivity to errors in ballistic motion, *ACM Trans. on Graphics* **22**, 3, pp. 537–542.

Rushmeier, H., Rogowitz, B. and Piatko, C. (2000). Perceptual issues in substituting texture for geometry, in *Proc. SPIE Human Vision and Electronic V*, pp. 372–383.

Soucy, M., Godin, G. and Rioux, M. (1996). A texture-mapping approach for the compression of colored 3D triangulations, *The Visual Computer* **12**, pp. 503–514.

Taylor, C., Allebach, J. and Pizlo, Z. (1998a). The image fidelity asessor, in *Proc. IS&T Image Processing, Image Quality and Image Capture Systems Conference.*

Taylor, C., Pizlo, Z. and Allebach, J. (1998b). Perceptually relevant image fidelity, in *Proc. IS&T/SPIE Symposium on Electronic Imaging Science and Technology.*

Turk, G. (1991). Generating texture on arbitrary surfaces using reaction-diffusion, in *Siggraph.*

Volevich, V., Myszkowski, K., Khodulev, A. and Kopylov, E. (2000). Using the visual differences predictor to improve performance of progressive global illumination computation, *ACM Transaction On Graphics* **19**, 1, pp. 122–161.

Watson, B., Friedman, A. and McGaffey, A. (2001). Measuring and predicting visual fidelity, in *SIGGRAPH*, pp. 213–220.

Weber (2006). URL `www.usd.edu/psyc301/WebersLaw.htm`.

Williams, N., Luebke, D., Cohen, J., Kelley, M. and Schubert, B. (2003). Perceptually guided simplification of lit, textured meshes, in *ACM Symp. on Interactive 3D Graphics.*

Chapter 8

Quality Metric for Approximating Subjective Evaluation of 3D Objects

A. Basu, I. Cheng and Y. Pan

8.1 Introduction

In the previous chapters we considered the transmission of image, video and 3D data considering perceptual factors and network bandwidth. One issue that remains to be considered is: "How to estimate the perceived quality, especially for 3D objects?" Many factors, such as the number of vertices and the resolution of texture, can affect the display quality of 3D objects. When the resources of a graphics system are not sufficient to render the ideal image, degradation is inevitable. It is therefore important to study how individual factors will affect the overall quality, and how the degradation can be controlled given limited resources. In this paper, the essential factors determining the display quality are reviewed. We then integrate two important ones, resolution of texture and resolution of wireframe, and use them in our model as a perceptual metric. We assess this metric using statistical data collected from a 3D quality evaluation experiment. The statistical model and the methodology to assess the display quality metric are discussed. A preliminary study of the reliability of the estimates is also described. The contribution of this paper lies in: (a) determining the relative importance of wireframe vs. texture resolution in perceptual quality evaluation, and (b) proposing an experimental strategy for verifying and fitting a quantitative model that estimates 3D perceptual quality. The proposed quantitative method is found to fit closely to subjective ratings by human observers based on preliminary experimental results.

The constraints that can determine the display quality of a 3D image in online applications fall into two main categories. These are *Computational Constraint* and *Network Bandwidth Constraint*. An adaptive approach can be applied through compression and simplification of 3D data to make the transmitted size 10-20 times smaller than the original without noticeable distortions [Deering (1995)]. An example of geometric simplification is shown in Fig. 8.1, in which the Bunny is simplified to various resolution levels (number of triangles is 69,451 left, 1,919 middle and 462 right).

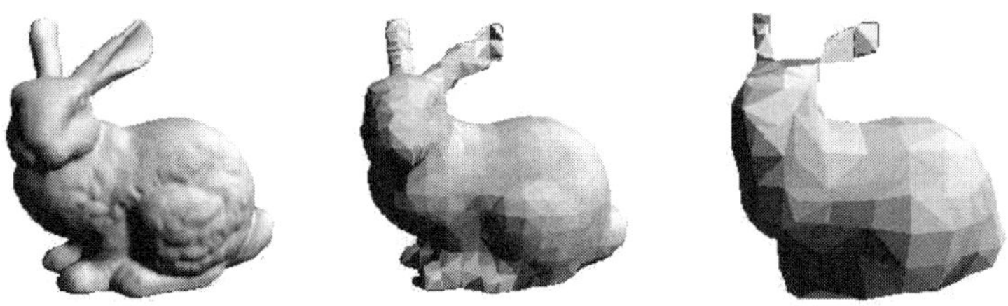

Fig. 8.1 Stanford Bunny at various resolution levels.

While most research in the literature focus on geometric compression and use only synthetic texture or color, we address both *geometry resolution* and *realistic texture resolution*, and analyze how these factors affect the overall perceptual quality and fidelity. Our analysis is based on experiments conducted on human observers. The perceptual quality metric derived from the experiments allows the appropriate level of detail (LOD) to be selected given the computation and bandwidth constraints. A detailed survey on simplification algorithms can be found in [Heckbert and Garland (1997)]. These algorithms try to control the complexity of a wireframe by developing various strategies for simplifying the level of detail (LOD) in different parts of a 3D object. In order to easily control the details on a 3D object we will follow a simple model approximation strategy based on multiresolution representation of texture and wireframe. More complex LOD models as perceived by human observers will be included in our future work. Our main contribution is in proposing and evaluating a quantitative metric that measures perceptual quality variations in a restricted online environment. For example, given limited bandwidth [Yu *et al.* (2003)] our model can give multimedia developers some insight into how to reduce the texture and wireframe details before transmission, and what is the relative importance of these two factors.

The remainder of this chapter is organized as follows: Section 8.2 reviews past work on perceptual quality evaluation. Section 8.3 examines the factors that control the fidelity of 3D images. Section 8.4 presents the user interface and environment used for conducting human evaluation experiments and proposes a quantitative metric for estimating subjective evaluations. In Section 8.5, the quantitative metric is estimated through experimental results on 3D objects; the reliability of the subjective evaluations is also discussed and measured in this section. Finally, the contents of the chapter are summarized in Section 8.6.

8.2 Review of Perceptual Quality Evaluation

In the area of image compression, Mean Square Error (MSE) is commonly used as a quality predictor. MSE is defined as:

$$MSE = \sum_{i=0}^{M-1}\sum_{j=0}^{N-1}\frac{(P_0(i,j) - P_c(i,j))^2}{MN} \tag{8.1}$$

where P_0 is the original pixel value, $P_c$is the compressed pixel value, M and N are the width and height of the image in pixels respectively. However, past research has shown that MSE does not correlate well to perceived quality based on human evaluation [Mannos and Sakrison (1974)]. Since this study, a number of new quality metrics based on the human visual system have been developed [Limb (1979)], [Stein *et al.* (1989)], [Daly (1993)], [Teo and Heeger (1994)], [Den *et al.* (1996)]. Limb originally looked at fitting an objective measure that closely estimated impairment ratings on five test pictures. Effects of distortion based on masking and filtering were considered in this work. The new models incorporate distortion criteria, psychophysical rating, spatio-temporal frequency response, color perception, contrast sensitivity and contrast masking results, achieved from different psychovisual experiments. One of the models was extended to also evaluate the distortion of digital color video [Winkler (1999)]. An error metric, to approximate perceptual video quality, was proposed by Webster *et al.* [Webster *et al.* (1993)]. Our work focuses on the 3D-display quality evaluation of geometric as well as texture data, and is different from prior work on image and video compression assessment. In the study on image synthesis, different shading and global illumination algorithms have been introduced to simulate photo-realistic effect. Since mathematical models cannot solely determine the accuracy of the display quality, human perceptual evaluation has to be taken into account. A number of perception-driven rendering algorithms were developed to incorporate the Human Visual System (HVS) as a factor to compute global illumination so as to improve perceptual accuracy [Ferwerda *et al.* (1997)], [Bolin and Meyer (2001)].

In research on 3D-model simplification, a predefined error bound is often used to measure the deviation between the original and simplified models. While such a measure can control the deviation, it does not estimate the perceptual quality of the simplified models. Most researchers leave it up to the readers to evaluate quality by showing a number of images at various simplified stages. Only recently, a few authors started to develop perceptual experiments to examine how well error metrics can reflect perceptual quality. However, their results are not encouraging.

There are many strategies available to provide smooth degradation in the fidelity of 3D images. In an early pioneering paper [Nagata (1984)], [Nagata (1991)], Nagata discussed the evaluation of subjective depth of 3D objects as a function of the variation of texture conditions between sharp and blurred images, and texture patterns of form, density, shade or polish. The evaluations were based on depth sensitivities of various cues for depth perception as a function of distance to the viewer. Three subjects two male and one female with normal stereoscopic vision were used as subjects in the experiments. Depth thresholds and viewing conditions were varied depending on a number of factors. The author extended the work [Siegel and Nagata (2000)] with M. Siegel to include studies of stereoscopy with very small inter-occular disparities, called "micro-stereopsis." Implications of the research in developing "zoneless" auto-stereoscopic displays were also discussed. Our research differs from the above study in the following aspects: (i) We do not evaluate the depth perception on 3D objects *per se*; (ii) We perform an overall quality evaluation of a 3D object based on wireframe resolution and texture resolution, wireframe resolution was not considered in the previous study; (iii) We attempt to estimate the perceptual quality depending on wireframe and texture quality using a quantitative model, in our opinion this model fitting is a new contribution.

Some of the related factors that influence perceptual quality include:

(a) Geometric Representation

The shape of a 3D object is commonly represented by a polygonal mesh, in which the vertices of the polygons provide depth information on the object surface.

(b) Texture Resolution

Construction of high quality 3D objects requires high-resolution texture images for mapping. Rushmeier *et al.* observed that covering colored geometric models with very low-resolution texture decreases the perceived quality [Rushmeier *et al.* (2000)]. Moderate resolution texture maps [Haeberli and Segal (1993)] generally provide acceptable quality. One simple way to obtain a lower resolution texture is by averaging.

(c) Shading

Rogowitz *et al.* concluded that visual quality varies significantly depending on the directions of illumination [Rogowitz and Rushmeier (2001)], and thus, comparison of different shading models should be based on the same illumination environment. Consequently, constant illumination is used in our experiments.

(d) Frame Rate

Many systems automatically decrease the frame rate to allow enough computation time to render a scene. Since the refresh rate is inversely proportional to computation time of a single frame, reducing frame rate is simple and allows smooth control of the quality of an individual frame, but will lead to the problem of flickering. It is therefore important to use the correct frame rate, and update the scene adaptively to optimize performance [Torborg and Kajiya (1996)].

(e) Distance

The impact of visual stimuli depends on the distance between the stimuli and the viewer. The contrast sensitivity function (CSF) [Mannos and Sakrison (1974)] describes how sensitive the human visual system is to various frequencies of visual stimuli. Even though distance is an important factor in perceived quality, we eliminate this factor in the current version of our proposed evaluation metric by keeping a fixed distance. However, as mentioned by Siegel and Nagata [Siegel and Nagata (2000)] we scale objects to the largest possible size on a large monitor to allow observers to have better depth perception.

(f) Visual Masking and Adaptation

Ferwerda *et al.* developed a comprehensive model of visual masking that can predict whether the presence of one visual pattern affects the perceptibility of another visual pattern when one is imposed over another [Limb (1979)], [Ferwerda *et al.* (1997)]. Visual adaptation is the phenomenon that the sensitivity of human eye changes for varying luminance, for example, we sometimes need several minutes to see well when entering a dark theatre.

(g) Other Factors

Some other important factors are discussed in psychology, such as the degree of concentration from the viewers. Fovea, the region of highest sensitivity on the retina occupies roughly a central angle of one degree of vision. Visual acuity, measured as the highest perceptible spatial frequency, is significantly lower in the visual periphery than in the fovea [Basu and Wiebe (1998)]. Thus, if within an image different objects have different resolutions, the perceived quality largely depends on the resolution of the object in focus. Since these factors vary from person to person, and from situation to situation, we will eliminate their influence in our experimental environment.

Perceptual Quality Estimation

Automatic measures based on mathematical theory were used to evaluate perceptual quality, but few studies have been performed on psycho-visual experiments to evaluate 3D object quality. There are two basic reasons: First, interactive visualization has a short history of less than ten years since the time high-performance graphics accelerators became available. Second, perceptual experiments are time-consuming and expensive. Naming time, the response time to recognize a given object, has been used in cognitive psychology research as a measure of recognition for a long time. However, naming time becomes ineffective with prior knowledge on objects. Thus, Watson *et al.* included ratings and forced choices as perceptual quality measures in their later work [Watson *et al.* (2001)]. They suggested that ratings and forced choices are better measures than naming time for a small number of participants. In addition, BMP [Bolin and Meyer (2001)], MSE and MetroMN [Cignoni *et al.* (1997b)] are excellent predictors of fidelity as measured by ratings. MetroMN is a notion and measure from the Metro tool [Cignoni *et al.* (1997b)]. Watson *et al.* used the mean of the values in BMP difference images as a measure in their experiments [Watson *et al.* (2001)]. Nevertheless, Watson *et al.* only used still images in their experiments, thus their results only apply to static scenes with a fixed viewpoint. Can their results be extended to dynamic scenes with variable viewpoints? Rogowitz *et al.* provided a negative answer in their experiments [Rogowitz and Rushmeier (2001)].

Although more experiments are needed to draw robust conclusions, our initial observation is that neither the geometry-based metric Metro nor the image-based metric MSE is a good predictor for view-independent perceptual quality of 3D objects. Nevertheless, we have learnt from previous experiments that rating is a better measure than naming time for a smaller number of participants, and illumination and animation of objects are important factors in perceptual quality. We will consider these factors in our experiments.

Incorporating Various Factors in Designing a Perceptual Metric

Since variable frame rate is expensive to implement and may be uncomfortable for viewers to experience, we do not adjust frame rates in our experiments. We choose geometric and texture resolution as our focus because they are the fundamental components of a 3D object, and their simplification can have significant impact on both computation-constrained and bandwidth-constrained graphics systems. Other factors such as shading, illumination and distance are also important in determining perceptual quality, and will be incorporated in our experiments in future work.

8.3 Experimental Environment and Derivation of a Perceptual Metric

In our interface, we start by rotating an object at a slow speed, and the users can use a scrollbar to adjust the rotation speed or stop rotation. Rotation speed is an important factor relating depth perception to motion parallax, as described in [Siegel and Nagata (2000)], Fig. 8.3]. A green grid is drawn in the background to represent the floor. Two text fields and one pull down menu are available to control the object geometry resolution in the X and Y directions, and the resolution of texture image respectively. Figure 8.2 shows the user interface and the virtual world rendering a 3D object *Nutcracker*.

3D Data Acquisition Hardware and Processing

Five 3D objects (*Doll, Nutcracker, Pot, Head and Dog*) were used as stimuli in the experiments. These objects were acquired with the *Zoomage* 3D scanner. The scanned objects were rotated and captured by the range scanner. The wireframe resolution can be up to $10,000 \times 30$ polygons for a full 360 degrees, 31 laser-lines scanned model, and texture resolution is up to 5300 pixels (vertical) $\times 40,000$ pixels (horizontal). Since all objects were lit from the front during scanning, and the viewpoint is fixed at the front of objects, the rendered scene simulates illumination from the front. Figure 8.3 illustrates the scanning process, and Fig. 8.4 shows the texture, wireframe, and the canonical view of object Nutcracker. The other objects (dog, doll, head and pot) used in the experiments are shown in Fig. 8.5.

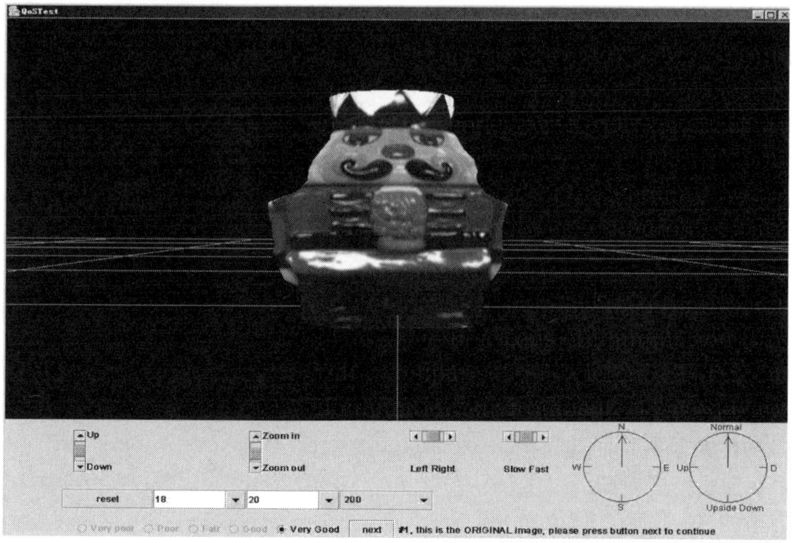

Fig. 8.2 The User Interface and the 3D Virtual World.

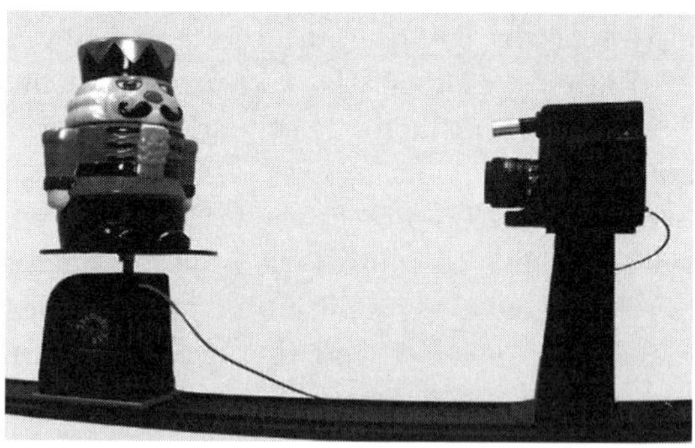

Fig. 8.3 The Zoomage 3D Scanner.

The original scanned objects were intentionally over-sampled with respect to both geometry and texture resolution. In order to study the quality degradation related to geometry and texture, we simplified the models at different stages until further simplification produced visible degradation. Details of the experimental set up can be found in [Pan *et al.* (2005)].

Experimental Process

In the experiments, there were 5 different visual objects, each object was represented by 6 levels of wireframe resolution and 3 levels of texture

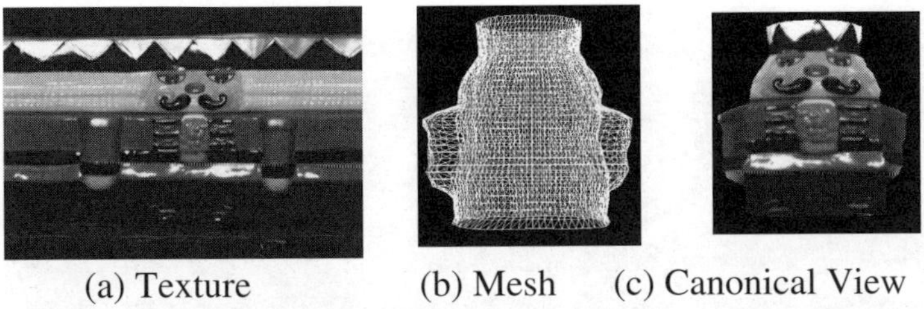

Fig. 8.4 Texture, Mesh, and the Canonical View of Nutcracker.

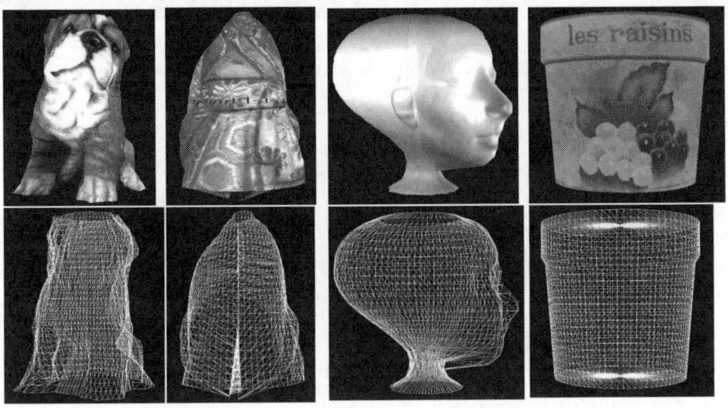

Fig. 8.5 Other objects (dog, doll, head and pot) used in qualitative experiments.

resolution, giving a total of $5 \times 6 \times 3$ rating stimuli. The highest quality referential stimulus was assigned a rating of 5 (very good), and the lowest quality one was assigned 1 (very poor). The referential stimuli were rotated at the same speed as the target stimulus to be rated, and the rotation speed of all three could be adjusted simultaneously. The participants (judges) were asked to compare the target stimulus with the two referential stimuli and assign it one of the following ratings: ***very poor (1), poor (2), fair (3), good (4), very good (5).***

8.4 Experimental Results and Analysis

Based on user evaluations we observed that, given the same texture resolution, the image quality curve of different mesh (geometry) resolutions (g) vary exponentially. This observation is represented by Equation (8.2), which is a function of g and will be tested by our experimental results.

Fig. 8.6 illustrates two referential stimuli (left and right) and one target stimulus (center) in the experiment.

$$Quality = \frac{1}{a + be^{-cg}} \tag{8.2}$$

We define g as a variable representing the level of detail of geometric data, which is implemented as the square root of the number of vertices, and a, b, c are constant coefficients. We define the minimum quality to be m, and the maximum quality to be M.

Scaling the texture and geometry between 0 and 1, and considering perceptual evaluations, we observe that:

(i) Perceived quality varies linearly with texture resolution as observed in Table 8.1 (Fig. 7.3 in Chapter 7);

(ii) Perceived quality varies following an exponential curve for geometry (Fig. 7.2).

Table 8.1 Quality vs. texture resolution for 100% geometry resolution.

Texture Object	25%	37.5%	50%	62.5%	75%	87.5%
Nutcracker	2.2	2.5	3.2	3.6	4.1	4.5
Head	2.3	2.6	3.1	3.3	3.9	4.3
Dog	2.2	2.6	3.2	3.7	4.2	4.7
Doll	2.0	2.5	3.2	3.6	4.1	4.6

It can be shown that [Pan *et al.* (2005)]:

$$Quality(g,t) = \frac{1}{\frac{1}{m+(M-m)t} + (\frac{1}{m} - \frac{1}{m+(M-m)t})(1-g)^c} \tag{8.3}$$

Reliability of the User Evaluations

It is important to discuss issues relating the reliability of our perceptual evaluations. The reliability discussions are based on studies described by Guilford [Guilford (1936)]. As stated on page 279 in [Guilford (1936)] a "reliability rating of 0.90 can be obtained with 10 to 50 judges, and a reliability rating of 0.95 can be obtained with 21 to 106 judges." It was noted that reliability "increases with the number of judges."

It was observed in the book that reliability of measurement depends on "self-correlation" where repeated sets of measurements are correlated to each other. Forming groups for self-correlation is however a difficult and time consuming task that is beyond the scope of our preliminary study. A group of judges for self-correlation needs to have comparable judging behavior. Thus extensive psychological behavior tracking over time needs to be conducted to create consistent groups of judges. Given that we do not have groups of judges to measure self-correlation, we performed the following experiments instead. In addition to the experimental results already described we conducted tests with an additional 10 judges after a time interval of about 18 months. The results obtained using the second group for the Nutcracker object are summarized in Tables 8.2 and 8.3, and the overall results for the two groups (*i.e.*, 20 judges) for the same object are shown in Tables 8.4 and 8.5. Observe in Table 8.4 that with 20 judges there are no inconsistencies in the mean evaluations; *i.e.*, the means are non-decreasing for increasing geometry resolution at each level of texture resolution.

Table 8.2 Mean Quality of Users' Evaluations for Nutcracker (Group 2).

Geometry Texture	26%	39%	55%	71%	87%	100%
100%	2.80	3.70	4.60	4.70	4.80	5.00
50%	1.70	2.30	3.00	3.20	3.10	3.10
25%	1.00	1.70	2.00	2.10	2.20	2.30

Table 8.3 Standard Deviation of Users' Evaluations for Nutcracker (Group 2).

Geometry Texture	26%	39%	55%	71%	87%	100%
100%	2.80	3.60	4.60	4.70	4.85	5.00
50%	1.75	2.35	2.80	3.10	3.10	3.15
25%	1.00	1.65	2.00	2.05	2.25	2.25

Table 8.4 Mean Quality of Users' Evaluations for Nutcracker (Combined).

Geometry Texture	26%	39%	55%	71%	87%	100%
100%	1.08	0.67	0.70	0.67	0.42	0.00
50%	0.82	0.79	0.84	0.79	0.70	0.74
25%	0.00	0.82	0.74	0.88	1.08	0.67

Table 8.5 Std. Deviation of Users' Evaluations for Nutcracker (Combined).

Geometry Texture	26%	39%	55%	71%	87%	100%
100%	1.09	0.76	0.68	0.54	0.44	0.00
50%	0.81	0.80	0.90	0.73	0.82	0.76
25%	0.00	0.82	0.76	0.84	0.87	0.72

Note that the results for the second group are very close to the first, and that the variations of the combined group are close to the individual groups. Instead of computing correlation between similar judges, we will consider correlations of the average evaluations of the two groups of judges. If we pair ratings at corresponding texture and mesh resolution levels for Nutcracker we get the (X, Y) pairs (Table 8.6) given below:

Table 8.6 Comparing average ratings at same resolution levels for Nutcracker.

X	1.0	1.6	2.0	2.0	2.3	2.2	1.8	2.4	...	4.7	4.9	5.0
Y	1.0	1.7	2.0	2.1	2.2	2.3	1.7	2.3	...	4.7	4.8	5.0

The correlation between these pairs of average evaluations is equal to 0.9938. For the dog and head objects the corresponding correlations computed to 0.9891 and 0.9947 respectively.

This study, though not strictly according to psychometric guidelines shows a strong association between repeated sets of measurements on a "similar" group of judges, leading us to believe that the reliability of our study should be fairly high, possibly higher than 0.95 (or 95%).

The number of stimuli was also noted as an important factor in [Guilford (1936)]. On page 280 of this book it was observed that: "ranking becomes difficult and irksome when there are more than 30 to 40 stimuli." In consideration of this factor it should be noted that we use only 3 stimuli at a time in our evaluation experiment, and total number of stimuli per judge is limited to 22 per object. We believe that the simplicity of our experiments resulting in fewer stimuli is much more likely to produce more reliable results than experiments trying to evaluate more factors which will obviously result in more stimuli per object.

Reducing Judging Fatigue

One of the important issues while performing perceptual experiments was judging fatigue. For example, 6 objects had to be evaluated for each model at a given texture resolution. Thus for every model $5 \times 6 = 30$ evaluations were done by a judge. Given 5 models the total number of evaluations per judge was $5 \times 30 = 150$ which can become tedious without breaks during the evaluation process. On the other hand, breaks can result in inconsistencies between one judging session and another.

We found that judges tend to get tired as the evaluation process goes on; and believe that tired judges are more likely to make errors, especially if we increase the number of objects in the future. Therefore, it would be preferable if the number of evaluations could be reduced without sacrificing the validity of the evaluation process.

An approach to solving the above problem can be found in the literature on Statistical Design of Experiments [Raghavarao 1971]. Specifically, Balanced Incomplete Block Designs (BIBD) can be adapted to address the issue of user fatigue in perceptual evaluations. BIBD works as follows in applying treatments to plots in agricultural experiments:

(a) Suppose we want to apply v treatments to b plots of land, where to each plot k (< v) treatments can be applied;

(b) Each treatment should appear at most once in each plot;

(c) Each treatment should appear in precisely r different plots;

(d) Every pair of treatments should appear together in λ different plots.

BIBDs have been shown to have statistical properties similar to complete designs, at a much smaller cost for agricultural experiments. The parameters of a BIBD are v, b, k, λ and r. BIBD can be easily related to perceptual evaluations by defining the parameters as:

v — number of models (target stimuli) to be evaluated;
b — number of judges;
k — number of models evaluated by each judge;
λ — number of different judges evaluating a given pair of models; and
r — number of different judges evaluating a given model.

These parameters of a BIBD satisfy the properties:

Property A: $vr = bk$

Property B: $\lambda(v - 1) = r(k - 1)$

In addition, the parameters of a BIBD must be positive integers considering the literal interpretations of their definitions.

Property A essentially counts the total number of evaluations. This total equals the number of judges times the number of models evaluated by each judge ($b \times k$) or the number of models times the number of times each model is judged ($v \times r$).

To verify Property B, consider a given model α. α is judged along with $(k-1)$ models by a given judge and thus in total with $r(k-1)$ models (not necessarily distinct) by various judges. Also, note that there are $(v-1)$ pairs of models in which α appears and each of these pairs is evaluated by λ different judges; giving a total of $\lambda(v-1)$ evaluation of pairs in which α appears.

Construction of BIBDs is a difficult process and often pre-constructed tables need to be used for efficiency. Also, not all designs are constructible. For example, it is not possible to have a design with 5 judges ($b = 5$), 6 models ($v = 6$) with each judge evaluating 3 models ($k = 3$); since, we cannot have an integer r satisfying Property A with these values of b, v and k. The mathematical techniques that can be used to determine solutions to arbitrary designs will be discussed in future work.

Let us consider a simple application of BIBD for reducing judging workload (and possibly fatigue) for the experimental set up in this paper. Consider the test object Nutcracker. For a given texture resolution, 6 models were evaluated by each judge. To reduce the judging workload by 50%, while ensuring that we balance the design to have same number of comparisons for all pairs of models, we can consider a BIBD with the parameters: number of judges (b) = 10, number of models (v) = 6, number of models evaluated by each judge (k) = 3, number of different judges evaluating the same model (r) = 5, and number of different judges evaluating a given pair of models (λ) = 2. It is easy to verify that the following design satisfies the parameters above, where J_i indicates the set of models evaluated by the ith judge: $J_1 = (0, 1, 2)$; $J_2 = (0, 1, 4)$; $J_3 = (0, 2, 3)$; $J_4 = (0, 3, 5)$; $J_5 = (0, 4, 5)$; $J_6 = (1, 2, 5)$; $J_7 = (1, 3, 4)$; $J_8 = (1, 3, 5)$; $J_9 = (2, 3, 4)$; $J_{10} = (2, 4, 5)$. Where 0, 1, 2, 3, 4, & 5 indicate the 6 models.

Tables 8.7 to 8.10 summarize the results of reducing the judging workload following the design just described.

It is recommended in Psychometric literature [Guilford (1936)] that correlation between repeated observations is a good measure of the reliability or similarity among test. The correlation of the average evaluations (Tables 8.1 and 8.3) between complete design and BIBD is equal to 0.991; which

Table 8.7 Mean Quality of Evaluation for Nutcracker (complete design).

Geometry Texture	26%	39%	55%	71%	87%	100%
100%	2.80	3.40	4.60	5.00	4.80	5.00
50%	1.60	3.20	3.40	3.60	3.80	4.00
25%	1.00	1.40	1.80	2.40	2.20	3.00

Table 8.8 Std. Dev. of Evaluations for Nutcracker (complete design).

Geometry Texture	26%	39%	55%	71%	87%	100%
100%	0.84	0.55	0.55	0.00	0.45	0.00
50%	0.55	0.84	0.55	0.55	0.45	0.00
25%	0.00	0.55	0.45	0.55	0.84	0.71

Table 8.9 Mean Quality of User's Evaluation for Nutcracker (BIBD).

Geometry Texture	21%	39%	55%	71%	87%	100%
100%	2.60	3.60	4.60	4.80	4.90	5.00
50%	1.60	3.20	3.50	3.60	3.90	4.00
25%	1.00	1.50	1.90	2.10	2.40	2.60

Table 8.10 Std. Deviation of User's Evaluation for Nutcracker (BIBD).

Geometry Texture	26%	39%	55%	71%	87%	100%
100%	0.70	0.52	0.52	0.42	0.32	0.00
50%	0.52	0.63	0.53	0.52	0.32	0.00
25%	0.00	0.71	0.32	0.74	0.70	0.84

is quite high based on standards suggested in [Guilford (1936)]. Also, the standard deviations (Tables 8.2 and 8.4) of the evaluation of the complete and BIBD strategies were closely correlated.

8.5 Summary

In this chapter, we first discussed factors controlling 3D image degradation and quantitative error measures approximating qualitative evaluations. A review of literature on evaluating depth perception [Nagata (1984)] was given, followed by discussion of some of the methods for evaluating visual quality of objects not considering depth estimation *per se*. In previous perceptual experiments modeling visual evaluation, the results suggest that proposed qualitative error measures are not always good indicators of perceptual quality. The correlation of qualitative measures, such as "naming time", to existing standard error measures (such as BMP, MSE, MetroMN) was also compared in prior research. However, new quantitative measures that are designed to model 3D quality have not been proposed. In order to extend prior research, we first examined the factors that determine the quality of 3D images including geometry resolution, texture resolution, shading complexity, frame rate and other psycho-visual factors. Of these factors, two (texture and geometry resolution) that affect bandwidth requirements were considered in our initial research. We designed a perceptual experiment and derived from the results a quantitative metric that approximates perceptual quality and reflects how geometry and texture resolution control the overall quality of 3D images. The strengths and limitations of this metric were also analyzed. A preliminary study suggested that the reliability of the evaluations is possibly higher than 0.95.

From the figures showing experiment results, we observe that the degradation of visual quality follows an exponential model for the geometry resolution parameter, and a linear model for the texture resolution parameter. This suggests that human viewers are far more sensitive to the distortion of texture than to that of geometry.

We plan to increase the strength of our findings by increasing the number of parameters in the model. We also want to check whether a finer-granularity rating system provides better results than the current experiments. Automatic simplification methods should be adopted to obtain the simplest ideal model, which can reduce preprocessing effort, especially if a large number of models are used as stimuli.

References

Basu, A. and Wiebe, K. J. (1998). Enhancing videoconferencing using spatially varying sensing, *IEEE Transactions on Systems, Man, and cybernetics Part A: Systems and Humans*.

Bolin, M. R. and Meyer, G. W. (2001). A perceptually based adaptive sampling algorithm, in *SIGGRAPH*, pp. 299–309.

Cignoni, P., Puppo, E. and Scopigno, R. (1997b). Representation and visualization of terrain surfaces at variable resolution.

Daly, S. (1993). The visible differences predictor: an algorithm for the assessment of image fidelity, in A. B. Watson (ed.), *Digital Images and Human Vision*

(MIT Press, Cambridge, MA), pp. 179–206.

Deering, M. (1995). Geometry compression, in *Computer Graphics Proceedings, Annual Conference Series, ACM SIGGRAPH*, pp. 13–19.

Ferwerda, J., Pattanaik, S., Shirley, P. and Greenberg, D. (1997). A model of visual masking for computer graphics, in *ACM SIGGRAPH*, pp. 143–152.

Guilford, J. (1936). *Psychometric Methods* (MacGraw-Hill Book Company Inc).

Heckbert, P. S. and Garland, M. (1997). Survey of polygonal surface simplification algorithms, in *Multiresolution Surface Modeling Course, SIGGRAPH.*

Haeberli, P. and Segal, M. (1993). Texture mapping as a fundamental drawing primitive, URL `http://www.sgi.com/grafica/texmap`.

Limb, J. O. (1979). Distortion criteria of the human viewer, *IEEE Trans. on Systems, Man, and Cybernetics* **9**, 12, pp. 778–793.

Mannos, J. L. and Sakrison, D. J. (1974). The effects of a visual fidelity criterion on the encoding of images, *IEEE Transactions on Information Theory* **20**, 4, pp. 525–535.

Nagata, S. (1984). How to reinforce perception of depth in single 2D pictures — comparative study on various depth cues, *Proc. of the SID* **25**, 3, pp. 239–247.

Nagata, S. (1991). How to reinforce perception of depth in single 2D pictures, — comparative study on various depth cues, in S. Ellis (ed.), *Pictorial Communication in Virtual and Real Environments* (Taylor and Francis, London, U.K.), pp. 527–545.

Pan, Y., Cheng, I. and Basu, A. (2005). Quantitative metric for estimating perceptual quality of 3D objects, *IEEE Transactions on Multimedia.*

Rogowitz, B. and Rushmeier, H. (2001). Are image quality metrics adequate to evaluate the quality of geometric objects, *SPIE Proceedings* **4299**.

Rushmeier, H., Rogowitz, B. and Piatko, C. (2000). Perceptual issues in substituting texture for geometry, in *Proc. SPIE Human Vision and Electronic V*, pp. 372–383.

Siegel, M. and Nagata, S. (2000). Just enough reality: Comfortable 3D viewing via micro-stereopsis, *IEEE Transactions on Circuits and Systems for Video Technology* **10**, 3, pp. 387–396.

Stein, C. S., Watson, A. B. and Hitchner, L. (1989). Psychophysical rating of image compression techniques, in *Proceedings of SPIE*, Vol. 1977, pp. 198–208.

Teo, P. and Heeger, D. (1994). Perceptual image distortion, human vision, in *Visual Processing, and Digital Display V, SPIE Proceedings*, Vol. 2179, pp. 127–141.

Torborg, J. and Kajiya, J. T. (1996). Talisman: Commodity realtime 3D graphics for the PC, in *SIGGRAPH*, pp. 353–363.

Den, C. J. V., Lambrecht, B. and Verscheure, O. (1996). Perceptual quality measure using a spatio-temporal model of the human visual system, in *Proc. of SPIE*, pp. 450–461.

Watson, B., Friedman, A. and McGaffey, A. (2001). Measuring and predicting visual fidelity, in *SIGGRAPH*, pp. 213–220.

Webster, A., Jones, C., Pinson, M., Voran, S. and Wolf, S. (1993). An objective video quality assessment system based on human perception, in *Proc. SPIE Human Vision, Visual Processing, Digital Display TV* (San Jose, USA), pp. 15–26.

Winkler, S. (1999). A perceptual distortion metric for digital color video, in *Proceedings of SPIE Human Vision and Electronic Imaging* (San Jose, CA), pp. 23–29.

Yu, Y., Cheng, I. and Basu, A. (2003). Optimal adaptive bandwidth monitoring for QoS based retrieval, *IEEE Transactions on Multimedia.*

Chapter 9

Perceptually Optimized 3D Transmission over Wireless Networks

I. Cheng and A. Basu

9.1 Introduction

Many protocols optimized to transmissions over wireless networks have been proposed. However, one issue that has not been looked into is considering human perception in deciding a transmission strategy for 3D objects. Many factors, such as the number of vertices and the resolution of texture, can affect the display quality of 3D objects. When the resources of a graphics system are not sufficient to render the ideal image, degradation is inevitable. It is therefore important to study how individual factors will affect the overall quality, and how the degradation can be controlled given limited bandwidth resources and possibility of data loss. In this paper, the essential factors determining the display quality are reviewed. We provide an overview of our research on designing a 3D perceptual quality metric integrating two important ones, resolution of texture and resolution of mesh, that control the transmission bandwidth. We then suggest alternative strategies for packet 3D transmission of both texture and mesh. These strategies are then compared with respect to preserving 3D perceptual quality under packet loss.

One of the major drawbacks with most 3D transmission algorithms is that they do not consider loss of data. Wireless communication necessitates addressing this issue. There are many wireless protocols that have been proposed in the last decade, including Transmission Control Protocol (TCP), User Datagram Protocol (UDP), Indirect-TCP (I-TCP) [Yavatkar and Bhagwat (1994)], [Bakre and Badrinath (1995)], Mobile

TCP (M-TCP) [Brown and Singh (1997)], Fast-Retransmit Approach [Caceres and Iftode (1995)], Snoop Protocol [Balakrishnan *et al.* (1995a)], [Balakrishnan *et al.* (1995b)], Explicit Bad State Notification (EBSN) [Bakshi *et al.* (1997)], Link-Level Retransmissions [Ayanoglu *et al.* (1995)], New Reno [Hoe (1996)], Selective Acknowledgments (SACK) [Fall and Floyd (1996)], Detection of Out-of-Order and Response (DOOR) [Wang and Zhang (2002)], Hierarchical Cache Design with New Snoop [Hu *et al.* (2003)], TCP with Delayed Congestion Response (TCP-DCR) [Bhandarkar *et al.* (2004)], and Wireless TCP (WTCP) [Sinha *et al.* (2002)]. Many of the proposed strategies are aimed at improving the shortcoming of TCP in invoking congestion control mechanisms for every packet loss. For wireless networks, where packet loss occurs as a result of unreliable links and route changes, the TCP strategy leads to further delays and degradation in transmission quality. Even though issues of multimedia transmission over wireless networks have received attention [Elaarag (2002)], [Fitzek and Reisslein (2001)], [Wu and Negi (2002)], relatively little work has been done addressing wireless 3D transmission. In recent research, approaches for robust transmission of mesh over wireless networks [Chen *et al.* (2003)] have been outlined. However, these methods do not take joint texture and mesh transmission into account. Also, in [Chen *et al.* (2003)] it is assumed that some parts of the mesh can be transmitted without loss over a wireless network allowing progressive mesh transmission to give good results. However, this assumption implies implementing a special standard with a combination of UDP and TCP protocols, which in general cannot be guaranteed in an arbitrary wireless environment. Special models for packet loss probability have been developed by other researchers [Lee and Chanson (2002)]. However, these models are usually associated with requirements such as retransmission. To keep our study applicable in an unrestricted wireless environment, we simply assume packet-based transmission where a certain percentage of the packets may be lost. In this scenario, we compare how various types of 3D transmission strategies fare, and how to take perceptual quality into account in designing a better strategy.

The remainder of this chapter is organized as follows: Section 9.2 examines possible strategies for 3D image transmission and analyzes which one is most suitable for optimizing perceptual quality under packet loss. Some experimental results that can be viewed from a web site are outlined in Section 9.3.

9.2 Perceptually Optimized Transmission

Scaling the texture (t) and geometry (g) between 0 and 1, it can be shown that:

$$Q(g,t) = \frac{1}{\frac{1}{m+(M-m)t} + (\frac{1}{m} - \frac{1}{m+(M-m)t})(1-g)^c} \tag{9.1}$$

Details of the perceptual evaluations and metric derivation can be found in our prior work [Pan *et al.* (2005)]. Note that the quality value varies in the range of 1 (m) to 5 (M), because of the range of values allowed in the perceptual ratings.

Consider now that b is the estimated total bandwidth for the transmission time interval, T is the texture and G is the geometry file sizes, possibly compressed, at maximum resolution. We assume that as the texture (or geometry) is scaled by a factor t (or g) in both dimensions the corresponding file sizes get reduced to t^2T (or g^2G). To utilize the bandwidth completely we must have:

$$b = t^2T + g^2G \tag{9.2}$$

Given b we can choose the relative proportion of texture and mesh to create a 3D model in many different ways, as long as Equation (9.2) is satisfied. The question is "What is the optimal choice maximizing perceptual quality?" Considering m = 1, M = 5, and c = 2.7 (approximately) for many objects based on perceptual tests, Equation (9.1) can be further simplified to:

$$Q(g,t) = \frac{1}{\frac{1}{1+4t} + (1 - \frac{1}{1+4t})(1-g)^{2.7}} \tag{9.3}$$

Maximizing Equation (9.3) is equivalent to minimizing the inverse of this equation; considering this and Equation (9.2), optimizing quality reduces to minimizing:

$$Q_{b,G,T}(t) = \frac{1}{1+4t} + \left(1 - \frac{1}{1+4t}\right)\left(1 - \sqrt{\frac{b-t^2T}{G}}\right)^{2.7} \tag{9.4}$$

where b, G and T are parameters.

Let us consider some examples of the optimization.

Example 1:

b = 100 Mbits (total bandwidth over a 10 sec. interval, say)
T = 20 Mbits

$G = 10$ Mbits

In this case t, g can both be equal to 1 and quality can be equal to 5 (the maximum) in Equation (9.3).

Example 2:

$b = 10$ Mbits, $T = 20$ Mbits, $G = 10$ Mbits

In this case t can vary in the range $[0, \sqrt{10/20}] = [0, 0.707]$ so that Equation (9.2) can be satisfied. The graph of Equation (9.4) for varying t for this case is shown in Fig. 9.1. It can be observed that the optimal t is close to 0.54 in this example.

Example 3:

$b = 12$ Mbits, $T = 20$ Mbits, $G = 10$ Mbits

In this case t can only vary in the range $[\sqrt{2/20}, \sqrt{10/20}] = [0.316, 0.707]$ so that Equation (9.2) can be satisfied. The graph of Equation (9.4) for varying t for this case is shown in Fig. 9.2. The optimal value of t is close to 0.6 for this example.

In general, given T and G for a 3D object optimum t can be pre-computed for a discrete number of b values in the range $[0, T + G]$.

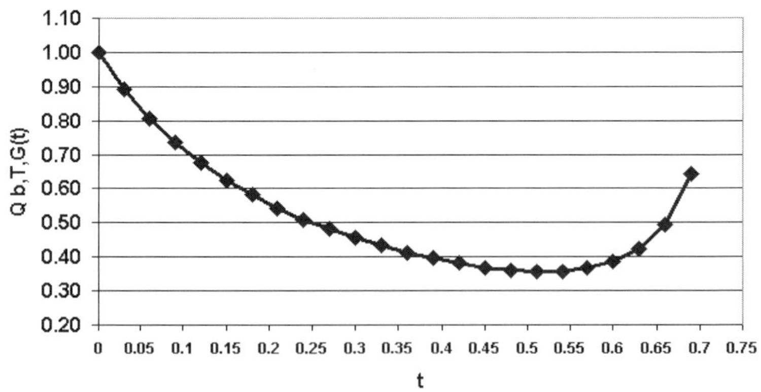

Fig. 9.1 Inverse perceptual quality curve for Example 2.

To simplify the model of wireless transmission, we assume that data is sent in packets of equal size and there is a possibility that a certain proportion of these packets may be lost. Various protocols [Ayanoglu *et al.* (1995)], [Caceres and Iftode (1995)] suggest re-transmission approaches in case of

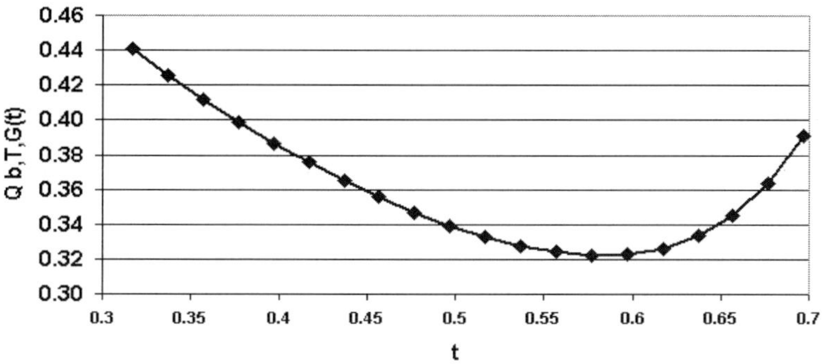

Fig. 9.2 Inverse perceptual quality curve for Example 3.

packet loss; however, re-transmission is not conducive to time bound real-time applications, such as 3D visualization for online games. We consider several possible strategies for packet construction in wireless 3D transmission, and then analyze the pros and cons of each.

Strategy A:

Packets are formed by breaking up the 3D image into fragments, where a fragment contains data from a connected (for simplicity a rectangular) region.

Limitations of Strategy A:

This strategy is simple to implement, however, missing packets can create unacceptable voids in parts of objects.

Strategy B:

Progressive transmission of 3D data in packets; *i.e.*, initial packets can store base layers (as in JPEG2000 image or Progressive Mesh [Hoppe (1996)] transmission) and later packets can contain detailed model information.

Limitations of Strategy B:

This strategy follows excellent research on simplification and can be made compatible with recent image and video coding standards. The main drawback lies in the necessity to receive packets at the base and lower levels of a hierarchy before packets at higher levels can become useful. A packet lost at the base layer, for example, would make packets received from subsequent layers of little use.

Strategy C:

Robust Progressive transmission of 3D data in packets, by transmitting multiple copies of the base layer packets.

Limitations of Strategy C:

This approach reduces the possibility of missing data in more important layers. For example, if the probability of packet loss is 10%, then if duplicate copies of all base layer packets are transmitted the chances of missing data at the base layer becomes 0.1^2, *i.e.*, 1%. The weakness of the method lies in the need to send redundant data, thereby increasing bandwidth requirements, and the lack of quality in the case where an original as well as its duplicate packet gets lost.

Strategy D:

3d Partial Information Transmission (3PIT): In this approach we break up the texture and mesh into packets by sub-sampling into overlapping but non-identical components. At the client site the overall texture and mesh are reconstructed based on interpolation from the received packets. One implementation of this approach is given by the following algorithm:

SERVER SITE:

T: original texture;

M: original mesh, in a regular form allowing easy sub-sampling;

Construct $T_1, T_2, \ldots, T_n$ *by regular, non-identical sub-sampling of* T; (**Comment**: *For example, given a* 100×100 *pixel texture* T, *we can construct* $T_1, T_2, \ldots, T_{16}$ *by defining* T_1 *as* $T(0+4i, 0+4j), i, j = 0, \ldots 24; T_2$ *as* $T(0+4i, 1+4j), i, j = 0, \ldots 24; \ldots, T_{16}$ *as* $T(3+4i, 3+4j), i, j = 0, \ldots 24.$) *Construct* $M_1, M_2, \ldots, M_n$ *by regular, non-identical sub-sampling of* M;

Form packets $P_1, P_2, \ldots, P_n$ *where* $P_i = T_i + M_i; i = 1, \ldots, n$, *with header and sub-sampling information added to each packet;*

Transmit n packets to a client on request, possibly in a randomized order;

CLIENT SITE:

Request server to transmit a 3D object;

Receive packets from server;

Uncompress mesh and texture data stored in this packet;

Set up initial display based on first packet received and interpolation information stored in header;

Update display based on next packet received;

Limitations of Strategy D:

One of the shortcomings of this approach is that the texture and mesh data receive equal importance; *i.e.*, the same fraction of each is transmitted in a packet. The perceptual quality analysis in the last section shows that for optimizing perceptual quality the relative importance of texture and mesh can vary depending on the available bandwidth; this issue is not taken into account in Strategy D.

Strategy E:

3d Perceptually Optimized Partial Information Transmission (3POPIT): This approach extends 3PIT by taking perceptual quality into account. The algorithm modifies Strategy D by a bandwidth estimation step followed by perceptually optimized packet creation. Details are described below:

SERVER SITE:

T, M: *as for Strategy D;*

Receive bandwidth estimate (B_e) *and estimated loss proportion* (L) *from requesting client;*

Compute server transmitting bandwidth: $B_s \leftarrow B_e/(1-L)$;

Compute optimum texture and geometry scaling factors $t_e \& g_e$

following procedure for minimizing Equation (4) in the last section, considering bandwidth to be B_e;

Compute scaled texture (T_s) *and mesh* (G_s), *assuming transmitting bandwidth* B_s, *based on factors* $t_e \& g_e$;

(**Comment**: *Specifically:* $Ts = \frac{t_e^2}{(1-L)}T$ *and* $Gs = \frac{g_e^2}{(1-L)}G$; *with texture and mesh possibly being interpolated to higher than the current maximum size in case the scaling factors are greater than 1.)*

Construct $T_{s1}, T_{s2}, \ldots, T_{sn}$ *by regular, non-identical sub-sampling of* T_s;

Construct $M_{s1}, M_{s2}, \ldots, M_{sn}$ *by regular, non-identical sub-sampling of* M_s;

Form packets $P_1, P_2, \ldots, P_n$ *where* $P_i = T_{si} + M_{si}; i = 1, \ldots, n$, *with header and sub-sampling information added to each packet;*

(**Comment**: *Number of packets n is chosen based on prior decision on packet size.)*

Transmit n packets to a client, possibly in a randomized order;

CLIENT SITE:

Request server to transmit a 3D object;

Receive packets from server for bandwidth estimation;

Estimate bandwidth (B_e) *based on number of packets received in a certain time interval and estimate loss proportion* (L);

Receive packets from server containing partial data on the 3D object;

Uncompress mesh and texture data stored in this packet;

Set up initial display based on first packet received and interpolation information stored in header;

Update display based on next packet received;

Comments on Strategy E:

On first observation it may appear that this strategy does not take packet loss proportion (L) into account in the transmission strategy. However, in reality this is not the case. Without any packet loss, the transmission bandwidth (B_s) would be used to compute the optimum texture and mesh scaling factors. When packets are lost the remaining packets may not be perceptually optimal for the effective bandwidth after packet loss. We thus form packets that are optimal at a lower bandwidth (B_e). Our algorithms are intentionally designed without the addition of redundant packets, since there is no way to guarantee that an original as well as its corresponding redundant packets are not lost. Also, addition of redundant packets increases bandwidth requirement thereby lowering performance with packet loss compared to lossless transmission at the effective bandwidth.

One of the drawbacks of Strategy E is the need to estimate bandwidth and packet loss ratio. This estimation based transmission may not be practical where feedback from client to a server is not reliable, or for multicasting over heterogeneous networks with varying packet loss and bandwidths. This issue needs to be addressed in future research.

9.3 Experimental Results

We show some preliminary implementations towards deploying 3POPIT over a lossy wireless network. Demonstrations can be seen at the site: www.Zoomage.com/siggraph2005.htm. Two programs are shown: (i) Combining and interpolating based on various texture and mesh sub-samples, and (ii) Comparison of perceptually optimized *vs.* non-optimized transmission. Note that our approach is consistent with recommendations in MPEG-4 [Pereira and Ebrahimi (2002)], with the novelty lying in perceptual optimization depending on available bandwidth and packet loss. Also, JAVA3D based implementation and MPEG-4 compatibility makes platform independent [Liu *et al.* (2004)] deployment possible.

Figure 9.3 shows the effect of receiving and combining 1, 2, 4 and 8 of 16 sub-samples of the standard Lena texture. The interpolation strategy used was based on weighting depending on distances of up to four of the closest neighbors of a missing pixel. We also observed that a fixed structure of packet loss, *e.g.* first boxes checked in first and third rows & fourth boxes checked in second and fourth rows on interface in Fig. 9.3 top right corner, produced noticeable distortions in image reconstructed after interpolation; by contrast, random set of packets lost often produced better results.

Figure 9.4 shows the effect of receiving and combining 2, 4 and 8 of 16 sub-samples of the nutcracker mesh. Readers can try out other combinations of texture and mesh sub-samples on the demo website. Note that results may vary from one execution to another for a random percentage of packet loss.

Figure 9.5 shows the effect of optimized *vs.* non-optimized transmission on perceptual quality. Two versions of the same model are shown, with the mesh on the left and the texture mapped on the right. Although the texture and mesh together for the top and bottom models use nearly the same bandwidth, 125 and 134 Kb respectively, the top one is favored by most viewers based on perceptual experiments.

We extended our work on regular meshes to irregular meshes as well. Current 3D mesh coding techniques mainly focus on coding efficiency, *i.e.* compression ratio, by transmitting incremental data. This approach is good without packet loss but is vulnerable to channel errors for irregular meshes. Figure 9.6 shows an example of error sensitivity of the Edgebreaker 3D mesh coding method [Lewiner *et al.* (2004)], [Rossignac (1999)]. With one error character in the connectivity stream, the decoded mesh can change significantly and can be impossible to reconstruct.

Fig. 9.3 Interpolating and reconstructing Lena image; top row shows online interface with original image (left) transmitted packets displayed with missing pixels (right) and interpolated image (middle). Bottom row when 1 (left), 4 (middle) and 8 (right) of 16 packets are received. (Readers may zoom into the pdf document to observe the small variations, near the top of the hat, between various images.)

In Fig. 9.7, 0%, 30%, 50%, 60% and 80% randomly selected packet loss was again imposed on a Queen mesh and texture. However, the lost geometry was interpolated based on neighboring vertices and valence or connectivity information, which is constant for most vertices in a regular mesh. It can be seen that smoothness on the object surface begins to deteriorate at about 60% packet loss. Visual degradation becomes more obvious at 80% packet loss.

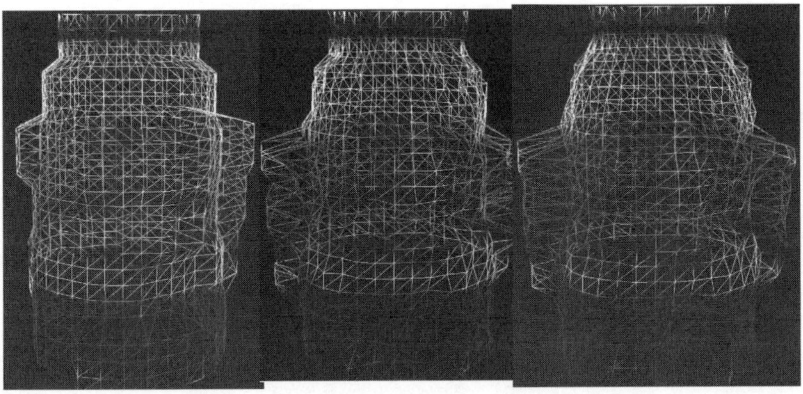

Fig. 9.4 Interpolating and reconstructing mesh of nutcracker model when 2 (left), 4 (middle) and 8 of 16 packets are received.

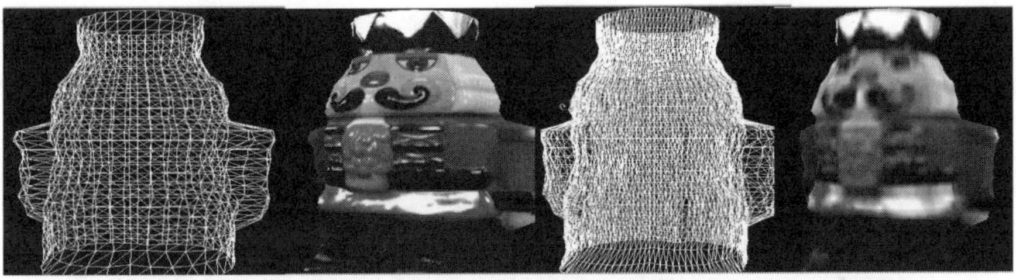

Fig. 9.5 Two representations of the Nutcracker texture+mesh models: Top has lower quality mesh, requiring 125 Kb total bandwidth, and higher perceptual quality; Bottom has higher quality mesh, resulting in lower quality texture to keep total bandwidth at 134 Kb, but has lower perceptual quality.

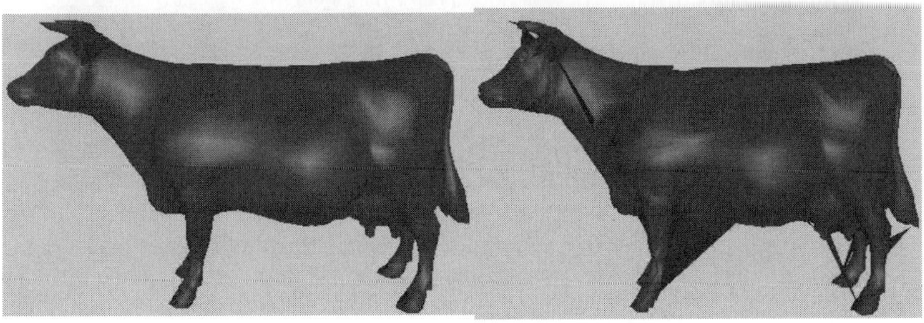

Fig. 9.6 An example of error sensitivity of the Edgebreaker 3D mesh coding method. **Left**: original 3D mesh; **Right**: Decoded 3D mesh with one error character in the decoded connectivity stream.

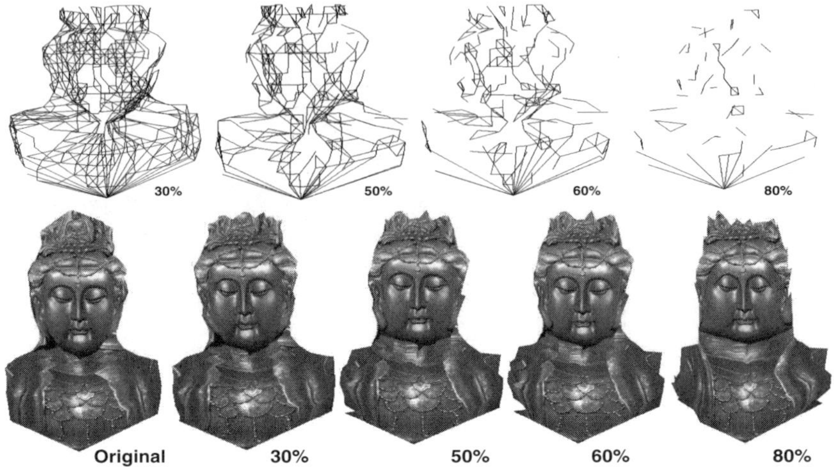

Fig. 9.7 Top row: 30%, 50%, 60% and 80% randomly selected packet loss was applied to the Queen mesh. The corresponding mesh mapped with texture is shown at the bottom.

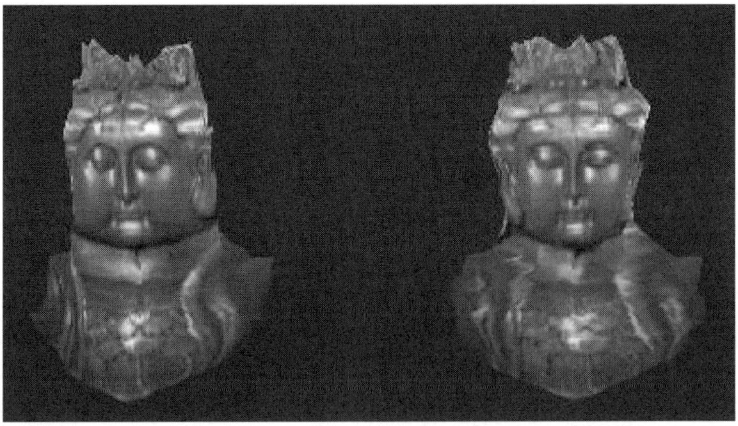

Fig. 9.8 Comparison of loss for regular vs. perceptually optimized packets.

The benefit of adding perceptual optimization during packet loss can be seen in Fig. 9.8. The model on the right is perceived to be closer to the original, though both have 80% loss.

9.4 Summary

In this chapter, we discussed factors controlling 3D image degradation and outlined an approach for estimating perceptual quality considering variations in mesh and texture resolutions. A theoretical framework for determining the relative importance of texture *vs.* mesh was presented. An approach to optimizing perceptual quality under packet loss was then outlined. Experimental results and online demos validate our approach.

We are currently working on implementing our approach on wireless handheld devices which have recently become much more powerful in processing power with much larger RAMs as well. Also, the preliminary implementation is not optimized for fast computation of interpolated values. The most computationally efficient approach for the interpolation would be to predetermine neighbors and coefficients for interpolation, given partial packet transmission, and store various look-up tables. Using lookup tables, however, requires larger RAMs for handheld devices.

Our initial approach is based on a simple multi-resolution approach to mesh and texture reduction. A more advanced and systematic method could be based on joint texture-mesh simplification following a scale-space analysis [Cheng and Boulanger (2005)]. We will investigate this direction in future research.

Acknowledgements

The support of Alberta Science and Research Authority (ASRA) and National Science and Engineering Research Council (NSERC) in making this work possible is gratefully acknowledged, as is the assistance of Matt Bates in the implementations.

References

Ayanoglu, E., Paul, S., LaPorta, T. F., Sabnani, K. K. and Gitlin, R. D. (1995). A link-layer protocol for wireless networks, *ACM/Baltzer Wireless Networks J.* **1**, pp. 47–60.

Bakre, A. and Badrinath, B. (1995). I-TCP: Indirect TCP for mobile hosts, in *Proceedings 15th Int. Conf. Distributed Computing Systems (ICDCS)*, pp. 136–143.

Balakrishnan, H., Seshan, S. and Katz, R. (1995a). Improving reliable transport and handoff performance in cellular wireless networks, *ACM Wireless Networks* **1**, 4, pp. 469–481.

Balakrishnan, H., Seshan, S. and Katz, R. H. (1995b). Improving TCP/IP performance over wireless networks, in *presented at the 1stACM Int. Conf. Mobile Computing and Networking (Mobicom)* (Berkeley, CA).

Bhandarkar, S., Sadry, N., Reddy, A. L. N. and Vaidya, N. (2004). TCP-DCR: A novel protocol for tolerating wireless channel errors, *IEEE Trans. on Mobile Computing.*

Brown, K. and Singh, S. (1997). M-TCP: TCP for mobile cellular networks, *Computer Communication Review*, pp. 19–43.

Caceres, R. and Iftode, L. (1995). Improving the performance of reliable transport protocols in mobile computing environments, *IEEE J. Select. Areas Comm.* **13**, pp. 850–857.

Chen, Z., Bodenheimer, B. and Barnes, J. (2003). Robust transmission of 3D geometry over wireless networks, in *Web3D*, pp. 161–172.

Cheng, I. and Boulanger, P. (2005). Feature extraction on 3D texmesh using scale-space analysis and perceptual evaluation, *IEEE Transactions on Circuits and Systems for Video Technology, Special Issue on Scale-space Feature Extraction.*

Elaarag, H. (2002). Improving TCP performance over mobile networks, *ACM Computing Surveys* **34**, 3, pp. 357–374.

Fall, K. and Floyd, S. (1996). Simulation-based comparisons of Tahoe, Reno, and SACK TCP, *Comput. Commun. Rev.*, pp. 5–21.

Fitzek, F. and Reisslein, M. (2001). A prefetching protocol for continuous media streaming in wireless environments, *IEEE Journal on Selected Areas in Communications* **19**, 6, pp. 2015–2028.

Hoppe, H. (1996). Progressive meshes, in *Proceedings of SIGGRAPH*, pp. 99–108.

Hoe, J. C. (1996). Improving the start-up behavior of a congestion control scheme for TCP, in *Proc. ACM SIGCOMM* (California).

Hu, J., Feng, G. and Yeung, K. L. (2003). Hierarchical cache design for enhancing tcp over heterogeneous networks with wired and wireless links, *IEEE Trans. On Wireless Communication* **2**, 2.

Lee, K. and Chanson, S. (2002). Packet loss probability for real-time wireless communication, *IEEE Trans. on Vehicular Technology* **51**, 6, pp. 1569–1575.

Lewiner, T., Lopes, H., Rossignac, J. and Vieira, A. (2004). Efficient edgebreaker for surfaces of arbitrary topology, in *SIGGRAPH.*

Liu, F., Owen, G. and Zhu, Y. (2004). Universal converter for platform independent procedural shaders in X3D, in *Siggraph.*

Pan, Y., Cheng, I. and Basu, A. (2005). Quantitative metric for estimating perceptual quality of 3D objects, *IEEE Transactions on Multimedia.*

Pereira, F. and Ebrahimi, T. (2002). *The MPEG-4 Book* (Prentice-Hall).

Rossignac, J. (1999). Edgebreaker: Connectivity compression for triangle meshes, *IEEE Trans. on Visualization and Computer Graphics*, pp. 47–61.

Sinha, P., Nandagopal, T., Venkitaraman, N., Sivakumar, R. and Bharghavan, V. (2002). WTCP: A reliable transport protocol for wireless wide-area networks, *Wireless Networks* **8**, pp. 301–316.

Wang, F. and Zhang, Y. (2002). Improving TCP performance over mobile ad-hoc networks with out-of-order detection and response, in *Proc. of ACM MOBIHOC*.

Wu, D. and Negi, R. (2002). Effective capacity: A wireless channel model for support of quality of service, *IEEE Trans. on Wireless Communications* **2**, pp. 630–643.

Yavatkar, R. and Bhagwat, N. (1994). Improving end-to-end performance of TCP over mobile internetworks, in *Proc. of Workshop on Mobile Computing Systems and Applications*, pp. 146–152.

Chapter 10

Predictive Schemes for Remote Visualization of 3D Models

P. Zanuttigh and G. M. Cortelazzo

10.1 Introduction

The most common approach for remote visualization of 3D models, used in all VRML browsers, which we will call for simplicity RV-CA (remote visualization — common approach), consists of downloading their description at the client and locally rendering them. The effectiveness of this scheme can be improved by compressing the 3D mesh descriptions and the textures [Garland and Heckbert (1997); Hoppe (1996); Schroeder *et al.* (1992); Guskov *et al.* (1999)]. This approach corresponds to an ill-conditioned telecommunication framework, since no given bandwidth and power resources can guarantee a pre-assigned quality of service (*e.g.*, starting latency less than a given time, *etc.*) since visualization at the mobile terminal is intrinsically data dependent. It may suffice to say that the visualization can only begin after the full model is received, and the transmission time of the 3D model depends on the size and characteristics of each model. Besides the just mentioned visualization latency, this approach is plagued by the following drawbacks: it ignores user interaction (it sends the whole model irrespective of the fact that the user may only want to see a small portion of it); it uses inefficiently the communication channel (the connection is never used after a burst of data sent at the beginning); the client resources are not taken into account (the model could be too large to be smoothly navigated with the limited client resources); it is difficult to protect the copyright on the 3D data (a good quality 3D model can require months of work, but when users download it, the author loses control over its distribution); network resources are used unevenly since the network has a burst of data during the 3D model transmission.

An alternative approach, which we will call RV-I (remote visualization — image-based rendering) for simplicity, avoids sending the 3D model, performs the rendering at the server side and sends the images requested by the client on an ongoing basis. In this way, the remote visualization of a virtual world at the client side is essentially turned into the framework of image transmission upon user's demand, a well-posed communication problem for which effective solutions already exist. A system for video transmission represents an upper bound with respect to the power and bandwidth resources needed for remote visualization since the rate of the user's request will be much less than 25 images per second.

This solution dramatically reduces the computational requirements at the client but the compression of the generated images becomes a crucial issue for the effectiveness of this approach. One may cope with such a problem by straightforward compression of the generated views by existing solutions derived either for still images or for image sequences, such as JPEG or MPEG, and this is certainly the natural starting point, useful also for benchmarking the performance of other possbile compression methods. However standard compression techniques would not exploit the peculiarity of the transmitted images, *i.e.*, the fact that they are synthetically generated from the same 3D model. Therefore, there is a lot of mathematical structure, *i.e.*, the 3D model's description relating the rendered views, that does not exist in other multimedia contexts, such as images or video, which in principle lends itself to be exploited for compression. How to actually exploit it is an intriguing issue still little understood and explored.

This chapter reviews the existing works in this direction in the hope of stimulating further research.

Figure 10.1 shows that there are three main possibilities for the data to be transmitted within RV-I. The first is the straightforward transmission of the views compressed by any technique. This simple approach may be motivated by various reasons. One may be limited computation and memory resources at client side [Feißt and Christ (2004)]. Another may be the desire of resorting to highly parallel compression methods in order to exploit parallel computational resources [Stegmaier *et al.* (2003)] and to achieve high data-rates over local area networks.

This approach is found in [Engel *et al.* (2000, 1999)] where the server sends a stream of images to the client which makes its requests by means of CORBA. [Tsoi and Gröller (2000)] propose an approach which dynamically

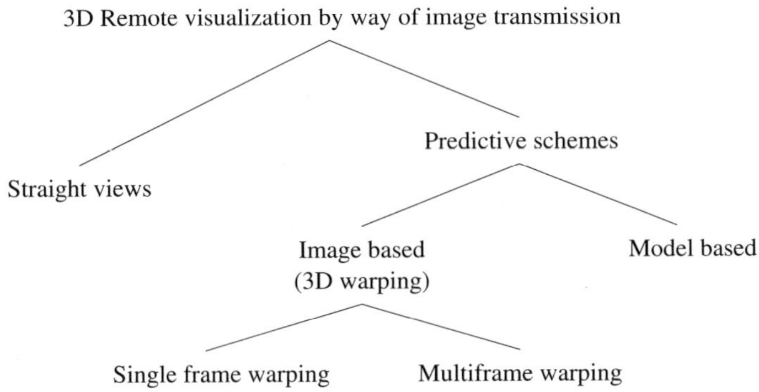

Fig. 10.1 3D remote visualization by way of image transmission.

partitions the computational duties between client and server, according to network load and client capabilities. [Engel and Ertl (1999)] introduce an approach for remotely accessing radiological data where the radiological sections are converted to VRML models and sent to the client who visualizes them with a VRML renderer. A similar approach is presented in [Bailey and Michaels (1997)]. There are also some commercial products based on the idea of moving to the server the rendering task (for example the SGI's Vizserver).

A second possibility is to predict at a client the requested view and transmit residual data between requested and predicted views. In the literature there are two major approaches to prediction. In the first [Levoy (1995); Koller *et al.* (2004)] the client has a low resolution version of the model that it uses during fast motion while the server holds the full model and sends the residual between the low and high resolution renderings when motion stops or slows down. The protection of the 3D data from unauthorized extraction, even with reconstruction techniques is considered in [Koller *et al.* (2004)].

The second predictive approach rests on 3D warping, a special case of image-based rendering (IBR). Image-based rendering is a well known concept in computer graphics [Watt (2000)] which, in a nutshell can be traced back to the idea of rendering new views by a suitable collection of images of the 3D scene (*e.g.*, previously rendered views) and depth information of some kind. It is the heart of several remote visualization techniques of 3D models since it is rather intuitive that the central issue of image based rendering is closely related to the exploitation of the redundancy among the views of the same 3D model.

Prediction by 3D warping, *i.e.*, the use of one (or several) z-buffer textured by an image in order to predict a view is first proposed in [Mark *et al.* (1997)]. Subsequently, many authors independently resorted to this rather intuitive approach.

In [Bernardini *et al.* (2002)] the predicted views, rendered by means of previous views and depth information are corrected by additional compensation data compressed in JPEG. A newer version of the system [Cortelazzo and Zanuttigh (2003)] uses JPEG2000 for better compression performance. A similar approach is described in [Yoon and Neumann (2000)], the main difference being the compression technique used in [Yoon and Neumann (2000)]. A different scheme based on the use of local projective transformations is presented in [Bernardini and Cortelazzo (2001)]. In this system each rendered view is compressed by splitting it into smaller images, which in turn are compressed by means of an MPEG-like approach, based on "generalized motion vectors" representing projective transformations between subsequent images of the sequence. In [Bao and Gourley (2004)] 3D warping is applied within a wavelet decomposition framework. In [Chang and Ger (2002)] 3D warping is based upon layered depth images [Shade *et al.* (1998)].

Image-based predictive methods for remote visualization of 3D models may differ on how to precisely predict the next view: most techniques use a single z-buffer textured by an image for the prediction and some [Mark *et al.* (1997); Yoon and Neumann (2003)] use two textured z-buffers. They may also resort to different techniques in order to compress the various types of data (z-buffer, texture, residual information) to be transmitted.

This chapter is divided in 4 sections. Section 10.2 briefly describes the general architecture of RV-I. Section 10.3 presents model-based and image-based prediction schemes. Section 10.4 presents different strategies for choosing prediction residuals. Section 10.5 discusses the compression of the transmitted data. Section 10.6 summarizes this chapter.

10.2 Structure of a Remote 3D Visualization System by Image Transmission (RV-I)

Remote visualization of 3D models by image transission splits the standard way of viewing a 3D model by locally downloading and rendering it at the client (Fig. 10.2) in a client-server system. The key idea behind this class of remote visualization approaches is to split into two parts what a stan-

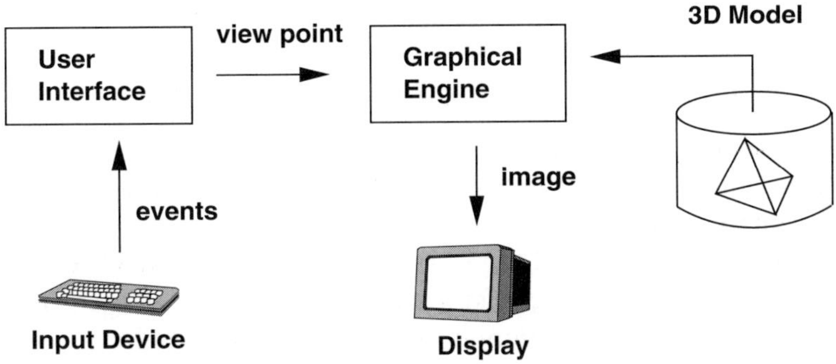

Fig. 10.2 Application structure (standard approach).

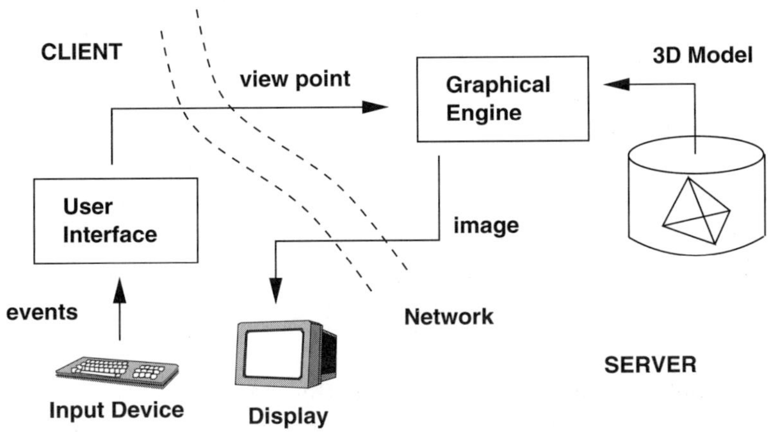

Fig. 10.3 Application structure (remote visualization).

dard 3D models browser does at client side by moving the rendering task (completely or partially) at server side (Fig. 10.3 shows a possible implementation). In such a remote visualization scheme the whole 3D model stored on the server should not be transmitted to the client. The server sends to the client only the rendered output eventually with associated depth information, a simplified version of the full model or a portion of it.

The server also includes the graphic engine, while the GUI remains at the client. In the simplest version of the scheme the user's requests are transmitted to the server over the network. At the server's side the graphic engine renders the required views and sends them back to the client as compressed images. Finally, the client (decompresses and) shows to the user the images received from the server.

This approach has the following potential advantages:

- The memory requirements of each image transmitted from server to client is much smaller than the full 3D model, especially if the images are suitably compressed.
- Visualization at client side can start just after the first view (a single compressed image) is received from the server. Instead, with the standard approach visualization at client's side starts after the whole 3D model description is downloaded, leading to unpredictable download times, since they depend on the 3D model's size.
- Channel capacity is evenly used.
- The client does not need strong computational resources or hardware 3D acceleration (it can be even a PDA or a mobile phone) since it does not have to render the views, but just decompress and display them. Furthermore, the visualization's fluidity is independent of the 3D model's size.
- The copyright control of the 3D models is fully ensured, since the end-user never receives the whole model, but its rendered views only.
- The data sent by the server can also contain depth informations to help the client in the prediction of the following views and reduce the amount of data to be transmitted (provided the client resources can afford the computation).

The simplest procedure to implement this concept, which we will refer to as Algorithm 0 for simplicity, is to have the server sending to the client the full views compressed by any standard image compression technique. It should be worth noting that even though the server has to initially send a sequence of images in order to support the user's visualization at the client side, video compression methods are not appropriate in this task for two reasons. The first reason is that video compression assumes that the image sequence is predefined, instead in the case of 3D model visualization the image sequence is defined by the user in real time. The second is that video compression methods assume a sequence of images with a fast frame rate and are not suited to inspect single frames at viewer's leisure, a possibility which must be considered in 3D model visualization. Therefore Algorithm 0 must be based on image rather then video compression methods.

An advantage of Algorithm 0 is that it requires minimal computational and memory resources at a client, and this may be a must for remote visualization on clients with very light resources (*e.g.* PDAs or mobile phones [Feißt and Christ (2004)]).

In general if the clients have some computation and memory resources, as typical of Internet visualization by way of personal computers, it is reasonable to assume that the client is capable of supporting non-standard decompression and visualization tasks which may reduce the bit-rate of the transmitted datastream. In principle the heavier work load at the client side the lighter the transmitted datastream can be.

Effective remote visualization systems based on the RV-I approach clearly require adequate resources at the server and adequate bandwidth, since the server must continually support the client visualization. Having a number of pre-computed views in compressed form at the server may be a helpful provision, which has to be supported by the client system. The number of simultaneous clients that a server can support within a given quality of service is an issue not treated in this chapter as it concerns networking, neverless it is very important for pratical purposes.

10.3 Prediction of the Views

The straightforward transmission of the rendered images considered in Section 10.2 does not exploit the redundancy between different views of the same model. To achieve this target it is necessary to use some geometry information in order to predict the new views.

10.3.1 *3D Warping*

Many approaches are based on 3D warping. This is an image-based rendering technique where the newly predicted view is obtained by reprojection of the z-buffer textured by previously transmitted images. Figure 10.4 shows point $\mathbf{X}_p$ on the prediction view P obtained as reprojection of the point $\mathbf{X}_r$ of the reference view R.

The general framework of a client/server visualization system based on 3D warping is shown in Fig. 10.5. The predicted views are compared with the actual rendering on the server and the residual difference is sent to the client that will use it to compensate its prediction. Clearly, the computational complexity of the prediction depends only on the resolution of the images and not on the model, making the system especially suitable for very complex meshes.

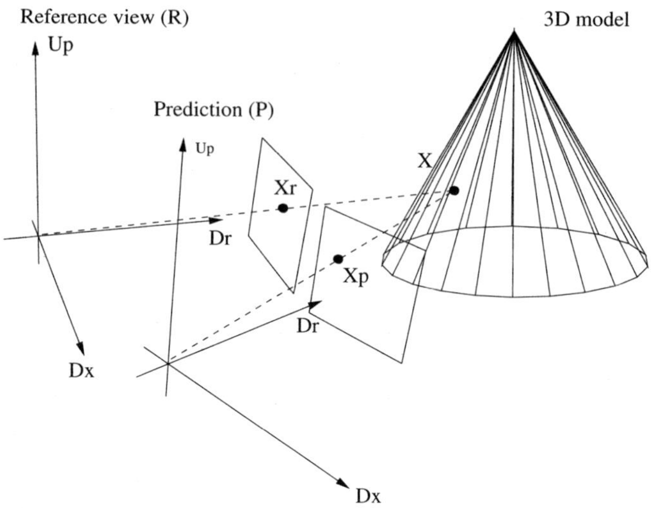

Fig. 10.4 3D warping.

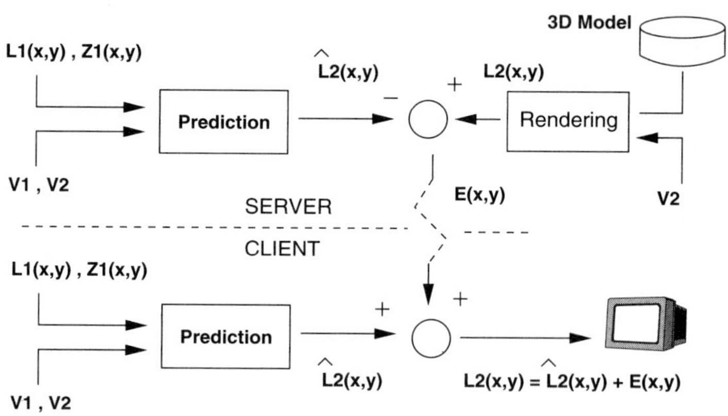

Fig. 10.5 IBR predictive compression scheme.

In order to formalize this concept, call $L_1(\mathbf{x}), \mathbf{x} \in Q_1 = [0, W_1] \times [0, H_1]$, the current view of the 3D model corresponding to position V_1 of the user's virtual camera. In the reference system of V_1 the 3D position of pixel $\mathbf{x} = [x, y]^T$ of $L_1(\mathbf{x})$, is $\mathbf{X} = [x, y, Z(x, y)]^T$ where $Z(x, y)$ is the z-buffer content at $\mathbf{x}$. Let $L_2(\mathbf{x}'), \mathbf{x}' \in Q_2 = [0, W_1] \times [0, H_1]$ denote the next view, associated to a user's virtual camera located at V_2. The position $\mathbf{X}'$ of $\mathbf{X}$ in the reference system V_2 is:

$$\mathbf{X}' = [x', y', Z(x', y')]^t = T(\mathbf{X}) = T(x, y, Z(x, y)) \tag{10.1}$$

where T is a suitable 3D projective transformation [Watt (2000)] that can be computed by simple matrix products in homogeneous coordinates (for details see [Segal and Akeley (1992)]).

Denote with $\widehat{L}_2(\mathbf{x}')$ the IBR prediction of $L_2(x')$, *i.e.*, the view with respect to V_2 built from $L_1(\mathbf{x})$ and $Z(\mathbf{x})$ via 3D warping. Neglecting the Z-coordinate in (10.1) one may obtain:

$$\mathbf{x}' = t(\mathbf{x}), \qquad x \in Q_1 \tag{10.2}$$

From $I_p = Q_2 \cap t(Q_1)$ and $I_n = Q_2 - I_p$, the relationship between $\widehat{L}_2$ and L_1 can be written as:

$$\widehat{L}_2(\mathbf{x}') = \begin{cases} L_1\left(t^{-1}(\mathbf{x}')\right) & \mathbf{x}' \in I_p \\ 0 & \mathbf{x}' \in I_n \end{cases} \tag{10.3}$$

The procedure to predict the next view $\widehat{L}_2(\mathbf{x}')$ by 3D warping can be summarized as follows:

(1) For every $(x, y) \in Q_1$, determine $\mathbf{X}^T = [x, y, Z(x, y)]$ and the corresponding homogeneous coordinates $\mathbf{X}_0^T = [x, y, Z(x, y), 1]$.
(2) Determine matrix T_g equivalent to the projective transformation T of (1) in homogeneous coordinates [Segal and Akeley (1992)] and compute $\mathbf{X}'_0 = T_g \mathbf{X}_0$.
(3) Determine $\mathbf{X}'^T = [X'_0/W'_0, Y'_0/W'_0, Z'_0/W'_0] = [x', y', Z(x', y')]$.
(4) If $(x', y') \in Q_2$ then $\widehat{L}_2(x', y') = L_1(x, y)$.

The reprojection gives an approximation of the required views, but within an intrinsic limitation. Namely, 3D warping is a procedure of forward mapping type [Wolberg (1990)] and so it does not define $\widehat{L}_2(\mathbf{x})$ on all the points of the new view. Let us call I_n the set of undefined points of Q_2 and for convenience set $\widehat{L}_2(\mathbf{x})$ equal to 0 on I_n. The unpredicted pixels can appear when parts of the 3D model, not visible from V_1, enter the scene which is seen from V_2; for example, because of a translation or when a zooming operation modifies the field of view. Furthermore, inside I_p the prediction could be wrong due to occlusion, different lighting conditions or quantization issues.

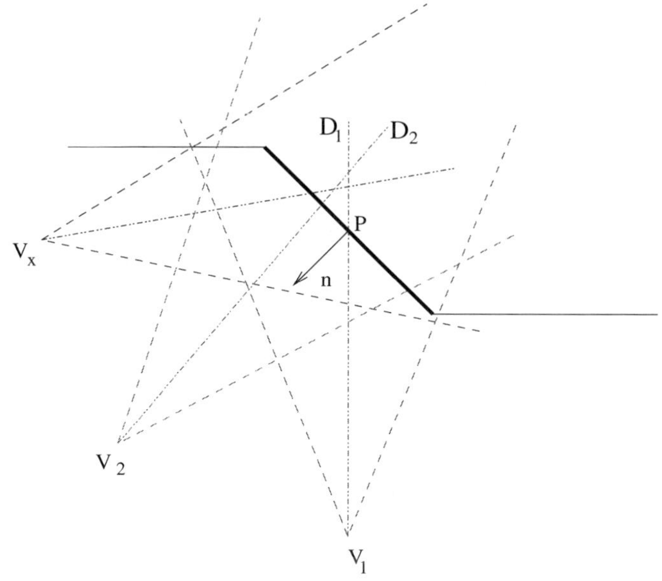

Fig. 10.6 Selecting pixels for multi-frame warping.

10.3.2 *3D Warping: Extensions*

Several extensions of the 3D warping scheme have been developed in order to overcome its drawbacks. A first extension of 3D warping is presented in [Mark *et al.* (1997)], where the warping of two different views is combined to predict the new frame. The selection of the source of every pixel of the predicted view is based on depth value comparison. The selected pixel corresponds to the closest point. In the case of pixels with the same depth, the selected pixel comes from the view with viewing direction more closely aligned with the surface normal at the point. Figure 10.6 shows a surface profile from the top and denotes with D_1 and D_2 the viewing directions of views V_1 and V_2, the two views which can be used to predict the new view V_x. The contribution for view V_x with respect to surface point **P** associated to normal n will come from view V_2, since direction D_2 is more closely aligned with n than D_1. In other words, the surface patch containing **P** is more densely sampled in view V_2 than in view V_1 where it appears more oblique than in V_2. The pixel selection strategy is functional to alleviate occlusion and quantization problems.

Another approach that exploits multi-frame prediction is presented in [Yoon and Neumann (2003)]. In this work, and in [Chang and Ger (2002)] Layered Depth Images (images taken from a single viewpoint but with multiple pixels along each line of sight [Shade *et al.* (1998)]) are used to handle the prediction artifacts due to occlusions.

In [Bao and Gourley (2004)], in order to speedup the computation of the novel view, the image is first decomposed by wavelet transform, then a quantization threshold is applied to the high frequency bands and finally only the non-zero coefficients are warped.

Other extensions aim to fill the holes in the predicted view due to zooming operations. The simplest solution is the pixel splatting in which every pixel in the destination image is mapped to all the pixels inside a square of a fixed size (usually from 1.1 to 1.5 pixels of side) centered on the warped pixel position. This solution is very fast but small size splats can still leave some holes open while larger splats can cause blocky images.

In [Mark *et al.* (1997)] the reference image is treated as a polygonal mesh and the warped mesh elements are filled as in 3D rendering. This system offers better performance than splatting at the price of more computations. Mark's PhD thesis [Mark (1999)] presents an interesting hole-filling algorithm.

10.3.3 *Model-Based Prediction*

A completely different approach, presented in [Levoy (1995)] and [Koller *et al.* (2004)], is to store a simplified or untextured version of the mesh on the client and to use its rendering for the view prediction. The server renders both the simplified and the complete model, subtracts the two renderings and sends the difference to the client, which adds it to the prediction in order to reconstruct the actual rendering (Fig. 10.7). ScanView is an application implementing this approach where the client renders in real time the simplified model and asks the server the rendering of the high quality mesh when the motion slows down or stops. The rationale for this provision is to exploit the limitation of visual perception with respect to image quality and resolution and to use high quality images only when most needed.

This solution avoids some of the prediction artifacts of 3D warping, but requires basic 3D rendering capabilities to be supported at the client.

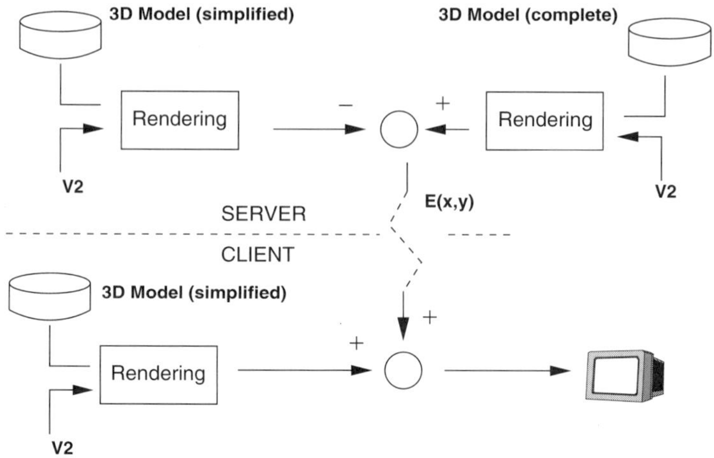

Fig. 10.7 Model based predictive compression scheme.

10.4 Residual Selection Strategies

The main issue of the predictive schemes is how to efficiently compress and transmit prediction errors. Since prediction errors become bigger when the predicted view moves farther from the starting view, it is common to periodically send a full view and the relative z-buffer in order to reset to zero the prediction error. Such a reset can be periodically made after a fixed number of new views or dynamically determined. A mechanism for the dynamic reset could be a comparison at the server between the compressed image size and the amount of data associated to the prediction residuals, and one may decide to send a new full view when such a ratio exceeds a fixed threshold.

Some possible residual selection strategies are presented next.

Send the error image

The first and simplest strategy is to use as residual the complete difference between the correct rendering and the prediction (Fig. 10.8). This way, it is possible to perfectly reconstruct the high quality rendering of the 3D model.

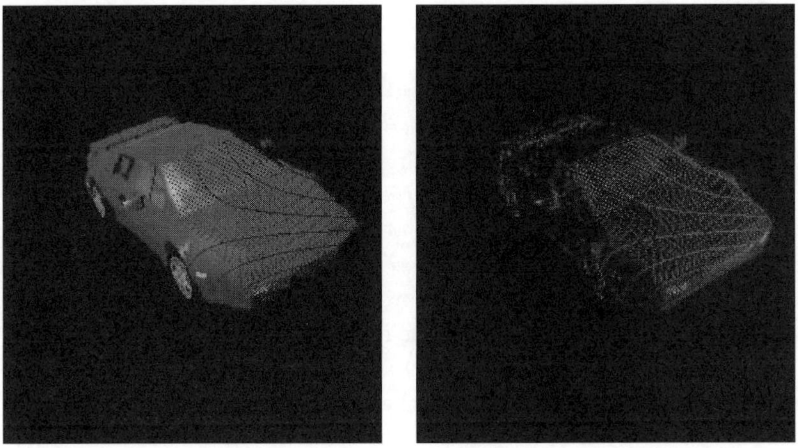

(a) (b)

Fig. 10.8 (a) prediction image and (b) error image.

Algorithm 1 is a first basic scheme of this principle, for remotely displaying p views $L_i(\mathbf{x})$, $i = 1, 2, \ldots, p$ of a 3D model:

Algorithm 1

(1) Send to the client both $L_1(\mathbf{x})$ and $Z_1(\mathbf{x})$ in compressed form;
(2) For $i = 2, 3, \ldots, p$
   (a) At both, server and client, compute:

$$\widehat{L}_i(\mathbf{x}) = \begin{cases} L_1\left(t^{-1}(\mathbf{x})\right) & \mathbf{x} \in I_{p_i} \\ 0 & \mathbf{x} \in I_{n_i} \end{cases} \tag{10.4}$$

   (b) At server side compute residual $E_i(\mathbf{x}) = L_i(\mathbf{x}) - \widehat{L}_i(\mathbf{x})$, compress it and send it to the client;
   (c) At client side decompress $E_i(x)$, compute $L_i(\mathbf{x}) = \widehat{L}_i(\mathbf{x}) + E_i(\mathbf{x})$ and display it.

Some aspects of this simple scheme deserve a comment;

Only the z-buffer $Z_1(\mathbf{x})$ relative to the first view is sent to the client and it is used for computing $\widehat{L}_i(\mathbf{x})$, $i = 2, 3, \ldots, p$ in (10.4). Sending the z-buffer for every view allows for better predictions, but it dramatically increases the amount of transmitted data. The difference between (10.4) and (10.3) is just the index of $\widehat{L}_i(\mathbf{x})$ which explicitly refers to the computation of the prediction of the next $i - th$ view.

The error image contains many isolated pixels (high frequency content). Since most of the classic transform coding tools (JPEG, JPEG2000, *etc.*) exploit the fact that images essentially exhibit low frequency content, their performance on this kind of data is rather poor.

Prediction based on 3D warping does not take into account color changes due to shifts of the 3D model with respect to the scene lights, inevitable when the viewpoint changes, therefore the size of the error image will be greater in the case of strong lights or reflective objects.

The error image is a color difference and so its bit-depth should be one bit greater than the color depth of the original images; for example in the case of standard 24 bit color images the error image will be 27 bit deep as it will use 9 bits per color channel.

Send the complement image

Unfortunately the compression of the data associated with the error images is a difficult task and it is necessary to look for other solutions in order to reduce the bandwidth requirements.

As exemplified in Fig. 10.9(a) the most visually conspicuous differences between predicted and actual view are the undefined values of $\widehat{L}_i(\mathbf{x})$, $x \in I_n$.

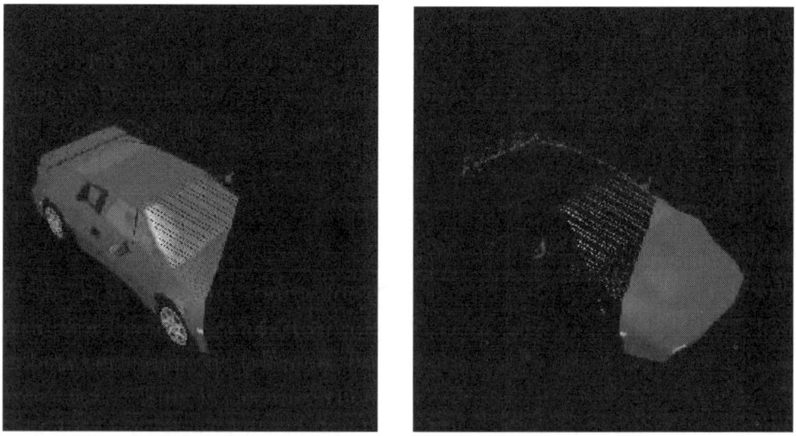

(a) (b)

Fig. 10.9 (a) prediction image and (b) complement image.

Let us introduce function:

$$\Psi_{I_{n_i}}(\mathbf{x}) = \begin{cases} 1 & if \quad \mathbf{x} \in I_{n_i} \\ 0 & otherwise \end{cases} \tag{10.5}$$

by which the unpredicted part of the image can be written as:

$$M_i(\mathbf{x}) = L_i(\mathbf{x})\Psi_{I_{n_i}}(\mathbf{x}) \tag{10.6}$$

This observation leads to a new predictive algorithm for remotely displaying 3D models, which uses as residual $M_i(\mathbf{x})$, hereafter also referred to as "complement image."

Algorithm 2

(1) Send to the client both $L_1(\mathbf{x})$ and $Z_1(\mathbf{x})$ in compressed form;
(2) For $i = 2, 3, \ldots, p$
   (a) At both, server and client, compute:

$$\widehat{L}_i(\mathbf{x}) = \begin{cases} L_1\left(t^{-1}(\mathbf{x})\right) & \mathbf{x} \in I_{p_i} \\ 0 & \mathbf{x} \in I_{n_i} \end{cases} \tag{10.7}$$

   (b) At server side compute $M_i(\mathbf{x})$ via (10.6), compress it and send it to the client;
   (c) At client side decompress $M_i(x)$, compute $\overline{L}_i(\mathbf{x}) = \widehat{L}_i(\mathbf{x}) + M_i(\mathbf{x})$ and display it.

Some comments are in order;

It is worth pointing out that while outside I_{n_i}, *i.e.*, on I_{p_i}, $M_i(\mathbf{x})$ is exactly equal to 0, $E_i(\mathbf{x})$ on I_{p_i} generally assumes small non-zero values. Therefore, the information to be transmitted in Algorithm 1 is generally much higher than that associated to $M_i(\mathbf{x})$ because of high frequency contributions.

As expected this second solution does not offer the same image quality as Algorithm 1, but the visual difference between $\widehat{L}_2(\mathbf{x}) + E(\mathbf{x})$ and $\widehat{L}_2(\mathbf{x}) + M(\mathbf{x})$ is typically acceptable.

The complement image cannot handle changes in the color of the pixels due to reflectances or lighting, therefore it is not suited to reflective objects.

One of the biggest issues with Algorithm 2 is that it assumes that the prediction is correct, *i.e.*, it ignores occlusions. Therefore, it does not know how to handle the case in which an object (or a part of an object) enters the scene and covers another one after changing the camera position; in this case the client will consider the pixel as predicted from the scene without the new object in it and visualize a wrong image.

Send pixels after Z-buffer comparison

The complement image approach gives good compression, but sometimes not a satisfactory image quality. Its biggest drawbacks is probably its intrinsic inability to handle occlusions. It can be observed that occlusions correspond to wrong z-buffer values. This suggests a third strategy in order to decide what to send as residual.

The first step is to select a suitable constant K and to define the function:

$$\Omega_{I_{n_i}}(\mathbf{x}) = \begin{cases} 1 & if \quad \mathbf{x} \in I_{n_i} \quad or \quad |\widehat{z}(\mathbf{x}) - z(\mathbf{x})| > K \\ 0 & otherwise \end{cases} \tag{10.8}$$

where $\widehat{z}(\mathbf{x})$ is the depth of pixel $\mathbf{x}$ in the predicted view and $z(\mathbf{x})$ its actual depth value (the comparison is done by the server). The residual can be written as:

$$N_i(\mathbf{x}) = L_i(\mathbf{x})\Omega_{I_{n_i}}(\mathbf{x}) \tag{10.9}$$

The new algorithm which will be called Algorithm 3 is reminiscent of Algorithm 2, where residual $M_i(\mathbf{x})$ is replaced by $N_i(\mathbf{x})$:

Algorithm 3

(1) Send to the client both $L_1(\mathbf{x})$ and $Z_1(\mathbf{x})$ in compressed form;
(2) For $i = 2, 3, \ldots, p$
   (a) At both, server and client, compute:

$$\widehat{L}_i(\mathbf{x}) = \begin{cases} L_1\left(t^{-1}(\mathbf{x})\right) & \mathbf{x} \in I_{p_i} \\ 0 & \mathbf{x} \in I_{n_i} \end{cases} \tag{10.10}$$

   (b) At server's side compute $N_i(\mathbf{x})$ via (10.9), compress it and send it to the client;
   (c) At client's side decompress $N_i(x)$, compute:

$$\overline{L}_i(\mathbf{x}) = \begin{cases} \widehat{L}_i(\mathbf{x}) & N_i(\mathbf{x}) = 0 \\ N_i(\mathbf{x}) & N_i(\mathbf{x}) \neq 0 \end{cases} \tag{10.11}$$

   and display it.

The idea behind this solution is to make a comparison between the predicted and the actual z-buffer at the server and to send only the pixels for which the depth error is bigger than a fixed value (or the unpredicted pixels).

A few comments are in order:

Since this strategy is a compromise between the error and the complement image strategies, it offers a reasonable image quality without sending all the pixels of the error image.

This strategy solves the occlusions problem but does not handle the color problems due to lighting. It does not perform well in case of reflective objects.

The transmitted data in this case includes high frequency content, but not as much as in the case of the error image.

Note that in case of correct prediction it is $\widehat{z}(\mathbf{x}) = z(\mathbf{x})$. Constant K in 10.8 makes this condition numerically robust. It is important to find a proper value for K. A large K leads to better image quality but it also increases the number of pixels to be transmitted. Too small a value could compromise the detection of the wrongly predicted pixels.

Send pixels after ray intersection test

In another approach by Yoon and Neumann [Yoon and Neumann (2000)] the pixels in the warped image are divided by an heuristic ray intersection test into three possible categories: definite hit, definite miss and possible hit. The ray intersection test algorithm proposed in [Yoon and Neumann (2000)] is the following:

Algorithm 4
(*Yoon and Neumann's intersection test* [*Yoon and Neumann* (*2000*)])

```
Intersection Test (viewray AB)
  projected_viewray A'B' = projectToImage(AB);
  Pixel p = first(A'B');
  Index i = index(p);
  While (p.depth < depthR(i) ) do
         prev_p = p
         p = next(A'B');
         // step 1 pixel in x or y direction
         // and add dz/(dx or dy)
```

```
i = index(p);
if(prev_p.depth - p.depth < threshold)
      return (definite hit, p);
else if (outside_image(p) &
            p.depth > max_depth_of_scene)
      return (definite miss, p);
else return (possible hit, p);
```

Clearly the pixels belonging to the definite hit group are properly predicted and the residual to be transmitted is formed by the pixels of the definite miss and possible hit groups.

Like in the previous case there is a threshold in the ray intersection test which can be adjusted in order to find a good trade-off between residual size and rendering accuracy.

10.5 Compression of the Transmitted Data

The data that need to be transmitted in a predictive scheme for remote visualization of 3D models can be divided into three main categories:

(1) Full images;
(2) Z-buffer information; and,
(3) Prediction compensation data.

The initial and the periodically reset views are standard images and can be compressed by any image compression standard. JPEG2000 [Taubman and Marcellin (2002)] is probably the best solution currently available for image compression and it is known to reduce the compressed data size by about 20% with respect to a JPEG compression of the same quality.

Even though sending only one Z-buffer out of p is way more efficient than sending p Z-buffers, in general it is desirable to also reduce the data associated with the depth buffer. Since the edges in the Z-buffer are fundamental for a correct reprojection, depth information needs to be compressed very carefully. Current video cards use 32 bit representations of the Z-buffer, therefore the Z-buffer is associated to a number of bit per pixel greater than that required by standard 24 bpp (16M colors) images. Classic LZ77 (zip) algorithm [Ziv and Lempel (1977)] is a good choice for lossless Z-buffer compression. Clearly a straightforward lossless compression of the Z-buffer is always feasible, but higher bandwidth savings call for lossy approaches

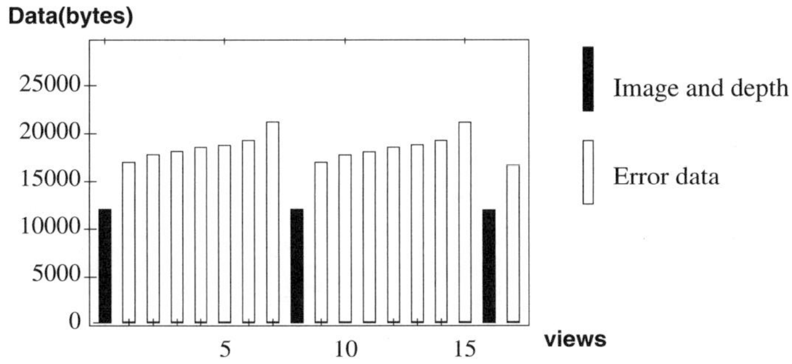

Fig. 10.10 Compressed error image (320 × 240 pixels).

such as down-sampling or Z-buffer quantization. The first solution may lead to inconsistencies between the views and their Z-buffers with distorted predictions not representative of the 3D model's geometry.

Better rendering results, at comparable memory savings, are obtained by quantizing the Z-buffer. However, the worse the approximation of $Z_i(\mathbf{x})$ is, the greater the information associated to the residual that needs to be transmitted at every frame. Since either $Z_i(\mathbf{x})$ and the residual need to be transmitted, it is not worth paying a data reduction in $Z_i(\mathbf{x})$ with extra data for the residual and a trade-off solution must be found. Experimental tests showed an 8-bit quantization $\overline{Z}_i(\mathbf{x})$ of the Z-buffer as the best trade-off.

A more sophisticated Z-buffer compression strategy based on the region of interest (ROI) feature of JPEG2000 and on a reshaping of the dynamic range of the depth is found in [Krishnamurthy *et al.* (2001)]. Other approaches are based on context modeling ([Bao *et al.* (2003)]) and on the representation of the depth map as a triangular mesh ([Chai *et al.* (2002)]).

At any rate the depth information typically represents only a small fraction of the whole datastream.

The compression of the residual remains the biggest issue. The bitstream associated with the error images compressed using JPEG is even bigger than the bitstream associated to the original JPEG compressed full images with a similar quality. The plot of Fig. 10.10 shows the residual of error images of size 320 × 240 compressed by JPEG. The black bars correspond to the data associated to the transmission of the full images plus the compressed Z-buffer. JPEG2000 offers better performance than JPEG with the error images, but the data size remains too big for an interactive browsing system. It is also important to note that error images are differences and so require an additional bit for the sign. Possible solutions are to use a

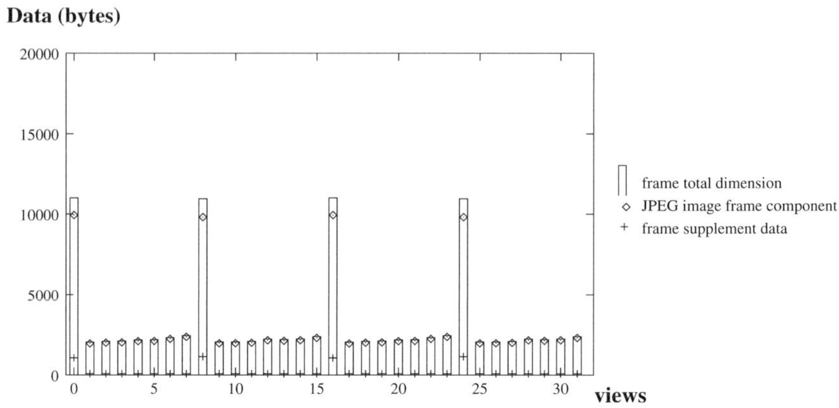

Fig. 10.11 Compressed complement image (320 × 240 pixels).

compression standard that supports higher bit-depths (such as JPEG2000) or to quantize the color components by removing the less significant bit as in [Levoy (1995)]. The high frequency content of the error image is very difficult to compress and alternative solutions as those in Section 10.4 are necessary.

The complement image can be compressed very efficiently using JPEG or JPEG2000, as the plot of Fig. 10.11 shows in this case.

Algorithm 3 reduces the data to be transmitted without compromising too much image quality. The plot of Fig. 10.12 (referring to a translation at 300 × 260) clearly shows the gain of Algorithm 3 with respect to full image transmission.

The problem of the scattered pixels can be addressed by sending a list of the pixels that need to be corrected and by packing them one after another in an array. In this way one also needs an additional array flagging wrong pixels positions, but its size is only 1 bit per pixel (a boolean that indicates if the prediction is correct). Such an array can also be compressed in a lossless way (LZ77).

The packed pixel array size is equal to the number of wrongly predicted pixels. Such a set of pixels should be much smaller than the complete image size. The reduced array size, combined with the absence of the high frequency content due to the pixel packing permits us to obtain a compact datastream even compressing the data simply with LZ77 coding.

In some residual selection schemes such as the ray intersection test of [Yoon and Neumann (2000)] the decoder can compute the wrong pixels list

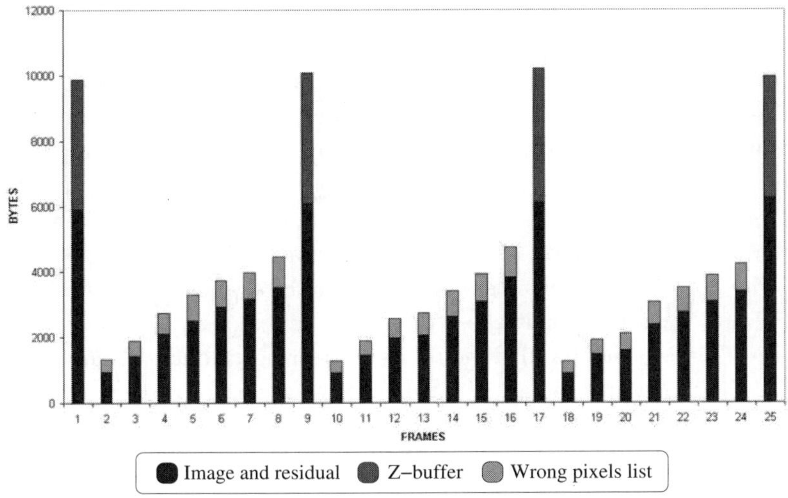

Fig. 10.12 Compressed complement image with depth comparison (300 × 260 pixels).

and so they can be sent without the additional array, thus allowing higher compression performances.

10.6 Summary

This chapter presents an alternative solution to the standard approach to the remote visualization of 3D models, namely an approach called RV-I where the server does not transmit the whole 3D model but essentially just the views requested by the client time after time.

This chapter reviewed the literature on this subject and analyzed the building blocks of this approach: prediction tools, residual selection and compression methods for the data to be transmitted. The literature indicates that 3D warping qualifies as a natural candidate for prediction. The use of a low-resolution model is also a sensible approach for clients with adequate computing power.

Several types of residual can be chosen as shown in Section 10.4 with the result that, as always in image compression, we find that also in the case of remote visualization of 3D models compression efficiency comes at a premium with respect to visual quality.

The compression of the various types of data to be transmitted within RV-I is finally considered. Further research is certainly needed to better exploit the information on the three dimensional structure of the scene in order to improve the overall performance of the compression system. Current research aims at blending the idea of prediction based on the low resolution model with prediction based on previous views.

It may be worth concluding by stressing both the conceptual and practical points of interest of RV-I. From the conceptual point of view RV-I holds the promises for consistent data-rate compressions provided one finds algorithmic ways to exploit the redundancy among views of the same 3D model. This is a new and difficult issue bearing strong similarities with the "missing view interpolation" problem encountered in image-based rendering. Such a connection lends itself to the use of IBR methods within predictive compression schemes for RV-I. Indeed quite a bit of literature in the field is inspired by this idea.

A second conceptually relevant aspect of RV-I is that it frames remote visualization of 3D models as a well posed transmission problem intrinsically immune to the limits of the standard approach based on the transmission of the full 3D model and its local visualization. This leads to important implications about the feasibility of RV-I. RV-I in principle is very robust with respect to client and network characteristics, in the sense that suitable versions of it can be supported by a wide range of network and terminals. More precisely RV-I may be the only practical solution for clients with limited resources which can only afford elementary decompression and display operations. RV-I can also straightforwardly adapt to network bandwidth by scaling the visualization window of the transmitted images.

These practical aspects together with the intrinsic copyright protection property of RV-I can make it a very valuable tool.

References

Bailey, M. and Michaels, C. (1997). VizWiz: a Java applet for interactive 3d scientific visualization on the web, in *Proceedings IEEE Visualization '97*, pp. 261–267.

Bao, P., Gourlay, D. and Li, Y. (2003). Context modeling based depth image compression for distributed virtual environment, in *Proceedings International Conference on Cyberworlds*, Vol. 00, p. 174.

Bao, P. and Gourley, D. (2004). Real-time rendering of 3d scenes using subband 3d warping, *IEEE Transactions on Multimedia* **6**, pp. 786–790.

Bernardini, R. and Cortelazzo, G. (2001). Accessing multi-user virtual worlds over ip, in *Proceedings Vision Modeling and Visualization 2001* (Stuttgart

(Germany)), pp. 407–413.

Bernardini, R., Cortelazzo, G. M. and Tormen, G. (2002). IBR-based compression for remote visualization, in *Proc. of 1st International Symposium on 3D Data Processing Visualization and Transmission (3DPVT2002)* (IEEE Press, Padova, Italy), pp. 513–519.

Chai, B. B., Sethuraman, S. and Sawhney, H. S. (2002). A depth map representation for real-time transmission and view-based rendering of a dynamic 3d scene, in *Proceedinngs First International Symposium on 3D Data Processing Visualization and Transmission* (Padova (Italy)), pp. 107–114.

Chang, C. and Ger, S. (2002). Enhancing 3d graphics on mobile devices by image-based rendering, in *Proceedings of IEEE Third Pacific-Rim Conference on Multimedia*, pp. 1105–1111.

Cortelazzo, G. and Zanuttigh, P. (2003). Predictive image compression for interactive remote visualization, in *Proceedings of the 3rd International Symposium on Image and Signal Processing and Analysis (ISPA2003)* (Rome), pp. 168–173.

Engel, K. and Ertl, T. (1999). Texture-based volume visualization for multiple users on the world wide web, in *Proceedings of the Eurographics Workshop* (Vienna, Austria), pp. 115–124.

Engel, K., Sommer, O., Ernst, C. and Ertl, T. (1999). Remote 3d visualization using image-streaming techniques, in *Proceedings of the International Symposium on Intelligent Multimedia and Distance Education.*

Engel, K., Sommer, O. and Ertl, T. (2000). A framework for interactive hardware accelerated remote 3D-visualization, in *Proc. VisSym Joint Eurographics-IEEE TCVG Symposium on visualization*, pp. 167–177.

Feißt, M. and Christ, A. (2004). Dynamically optimised 3d (virtual reality) data transmission for mobile devices, in *Proceedings 3DPVT 2004*, pp. 270–274.

Garland, M. and Heckbert, P. (1997). Surface simplification using quadric error metrics, in *Computer SIGGRAPH '97 Proceedings*, Vol. 31, pp. 209–216, URL `sherry.ifi.unizh.ch/garland97surface.html`.

Guskov, I., Sweldens, W. and Schröder, P. (1999). Multiresolution signal processing for meshes, *Computer Graphics Proceedings (SIGGRAPH 99)*, pp. 325–334.

Hoppe, H. (1996). Progressive meshes, *Computer Graphics* **30**, Annual Conference Series, pp. 99–108, URL `citeseer.csail.mit.edu/hoppe96progressive.html`.

Koller, D., Turitzin, M., Levoy, M., Tarini, M., Croccia, G., Cignoni, P. and Scopigno, R. (2004). Protected interactive 3d graphics via remote rendering, in *proc. SIGGRAPH 2004* (IEEE), pp. 695–703.

Krishnamurthy, R., Chai, B. B., Tao, H. and Sethuraman, S. (2001). Compression and transmission of depth maps for image-based rendering, in *Proceedings IEEE Int. Conf. on Image Processing (ICIP01)*, Vol. 3, pp. 828–831.

Levoy, M. (1995). Polygon-Assisted JPEG and MPEG compression of synthetic images, in *Proceedings of SIG-GRAPH Computer Graphics Proceedings, Annual Conference Series*, pp. 21–28.

Mark, W. R. (1999). *Post-Rendering 3D Image Warping: Visibility, Reconstruction, and Performance for Depth-Image Warping*, Ph.D. thesis, University of North Carolina.

Mark, W. R., McMillan, L. and Bishop, G. (1997). Post-rendering 3d warping, in *Proceedings of the 1997 symposium on Interactive 3D graphics*, pp. 7–ff.

Schroeder, W. J., Zarge, J. A. and Lorensen, W. E. (1992). Decimation of triangle meshes, *Computer Graphics (SIGGRAPH '92 Proc.)* **26**, 2, pp. 65–70.

Segal, M. and Akeley, K. (1992). *The OpenGL Graphics System: A Specification* (Addison-Wesley, Reading (MA)).

Shade, J., Gortler, S., wei He, L. and Szeliski, R. (1998). Layered depth images, in *Proceedings SIGGRAPH 98*, pp. 231–242.

Stegmaier, S., Diepstraten, J., Weiler, M. and Ertl, T. (2003). Widening the remote visualization bottleneck, in *Proceedings of ISPA '03.*

Taubman, D. S. and Marcellin, M. W. (2002). *JPEG2000 Image compression fundamentals, standards and practice* (Kluwer Academic Publisher, Cambridge, United Kingdom).

Tsoi, K. and Gröller, E. (2000). Adaptive visualization over the internet, TR-186-2-00-21.

Watt, A. (2000). *3D Computer Graphics* (Addison-Wesley, Reading (MA)).

Wolberg, G. (1990). *Digital Image Warping* (IEEE Computer Society Press, Los Alamitos (CA)).

Yoon, I. and Neumann, U. (2000). Web-based remote rendering with IBRAC (image-based acceleration and compression), in *Proceedings of EUROGRAPHICS 2000*, Vol. 19 (Blackell Publishers, Oxford (UK)).

Yoon, I. and Neumann, U. (2003). Image-assisted visualizations over network, *Journal of Electronic Imaging.*

Ziv, J. and Lempel, A. (1977). A universal algorithm for sequential data compression, *IEEE Transactions on Information Theory* **23**, 3, pp. 337–343.

Chapter 11

A Rate Distortion Theoretic Approach to Remote Visualization of 3D Models

N. Brusco, P. Zanuttigh, D. S. Taubman and G. M. Cortelazzo

11.1 Introduction

Remote visualization of 3D models is a new problem posing many challenging conceptual and practical questions. A basic issue addressed in some preliminary studies [Cheng and Basu (2004)] is the following: assuming one has a 3D model and may only use a fixed amount of data for it, how should he distribute the data between texture and geometry for the best rendering results? Current practical solutions for remote visualization of 3D models somehow resent the limited theoretical understanding of this issue. Indeed there exist essentially two approaches, both plagued by a considerable number of shortcomings which are worth recalling.

In the common approach to remote visualization of 3D models, which will be called for simplicity RV-CA, the server sends the 3D model geometry and its texture at the same time to the client. After transmission, the user at the client side has all the information needed in order to visualize the 3D environment and can freely navigate, even disconnecting from the server. Solution RV-CA, found in all commercial VRML browsers, suffers some notorious drawbacks. There is a latency in the visualization: since the 3D model must be completely transmitted before rendering at the client may begin, there is an unpredictable delay between the user request and the beginning of visualization. It does not take into account user interaction: all 3D data are sent, while the user might only want to navigate some parts of the 3D environment and ignore some others. The connection between server and client is badly used: after a burst of data sent at the beginning, the connection is never used again. The client resources are not taken into account: the model could be too large to be smoothly rendered by the client.

The dual approach, which consists in not transmitting the 3D model at all, but in keeping it at server side and transmitting only the views the user wants to inspect, has also been considered in the literature as reported in Chapter 10. This approach, which will be called RV-I for simplicity, turns remote visualization of 3D models into the transmission of views upon user's demand. Since subsequent views are closely related, one natural way to improve efficiency of system RV-I is to predict each new view from the views which have already been transmitted, forming the same prediction both at server and client so that only the prediction residual needs to be transmitted. Solution RV-I is interesting as, in principle, it can be free from the drawbacks of RV-CA. Indeed, the visualization at client side can begin right away, since all it takes is the transmission of the images prompted by the user (which can happen in real time, provided adequate bandwidth is available). Data transmission is completely based upon the user requests: no useless data are sent. The connection resources between client and server are evenly used. Approach RV-I can suit the computation and memory resources of any client since it just needs to visualize a sequence of images. Furthermore, copyright can be preserved, since the user never obtains the full 3D model but only images of it. However, the intrinsic limitations of RV-I are worth pointing out. In principle the sequence of views prompted by the user could be compressed at a much lower bit rate than a standard video-sequence. In practice how to exploit the fact that the views to be transmitted all come from the same 3D model is a difficult problem, barely explored yet. In the lack of effective solutions it is safe to allocate video-rates for the implementation of RV-I and this requires considerable bandwidth resources. In any case it remains rather difficult, if not impossible, to combine information from several similar yet different views in order to synthesize a new, high quality image at a subsequent time. Such a difficulty to reuse the received information to synthetize new views at a later time corresponds to a considerable overall waste of resources. Moreover, the predictive approach can only deliver approximate representation of each view requested by the user, no matter how close those views may be to each other. Finally, system RV-I is strongly conditioned by the network: if the bandwidth decreases, the quality of the remote rendering can only decrease. If connection went down, navigating would not be possible anymore. Indeed, the server must precisely replicate the steps performed by the client to render each new view from the previous ones.

Some hybrid solutions have been explorated in order to reduce the drawbacks of RV-CA and RV-I. In [Levoy (1995)] [Koller *et al.* (2004)] the server sends a low resolution version of the 3D model to the client which the client can autonomously display locally using a graphic engine. Such a low resolution rendering is essentially meant to be used for rapid navigation. As navigation slow-downs or stops, the transmitter sends the difference between the rendering of the high resolution model available at server side and the low resolution image produced by the client. The rationale behind this hybrid approach is that the details of a 3D model are hard to perceive during fast navigation.

What we present in this chapter can be regarded as a third approach for the remote visualization of 3D models, for simplicity called RV-RD, which rests upon a new rate distortion theoretical approach. It can also be regarded as an instrument for the experimental investigation of how to subdivide geometry and texture information within a predefined data quantity in order to achieve the best rendering results, indeed, as it will be seen, this operation is deeply connected to such a question and its answer.

System RV-RD satisfies the following requirements:

(1) Visualization at client side should start without delay, as soon as a limited amount of data is sent by the server.
(2) The transmitted data should be based upon the user's needs: no useless data should be sent.
(3) Data trasmission should be based on the available bandwidth, in order to avoid navigation delay.
(4) The server must have a policy to decide the kind of data most useful to send (just texture, just geometry or a suitable balance of both) and how to assign them given the available bandwidth.
(5) The connection between server and client should be used at its full capacity.
(6) The client must store the 3D information it receives, or part of it, according to its memory capacity.
(7) The client must have a policy to render the 3D model, using the available data in the best way it can.
(8) The client should be able to navigate at least some parts of the 3D environment, even if the connection with the server is down.

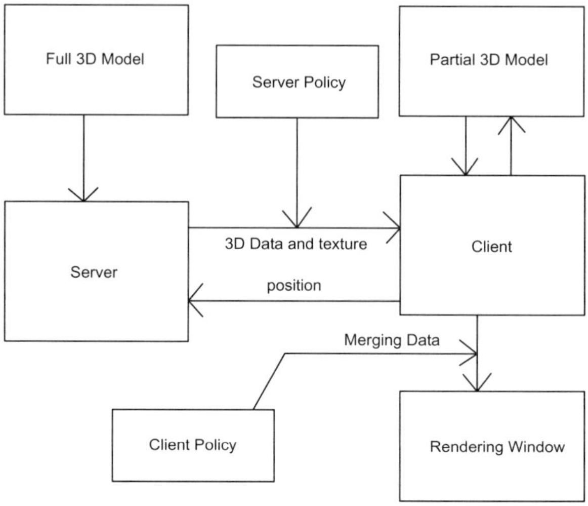

Fig. 11.1 The client-server paradigm.

The characteristics of system RV-RD are shown in Fig. 11.1. A server and a client are connected via a bandlimited channel. The server stores the full model, with high quality texture. At client side, the user interactively determines the particular view of interest, by communicating his or her position to the server. The server sends progressively compressed 3D data and texture, according to the user position and available bandwidth. The server never sends all its data (this would just happen if the bandwidth was infinite), but only the part that, according to the server policy, best fitting the user's needs and the available bandwidth. The client stores the 3D data and texture it receives from the server, according to its memory capacity. The available 3D data and texture are combined according to the client policy and the rendering engine provides the requested views.

In the RV-RD paradigm the client does not need to know the server policy and the server does not need to know the client policy. The client tries to use the available data the best way it can. The user can navigate in the 3D environment even if the connection between client and server is down, since the client will show only the data it has.

RV-RD avoids as much as possible the drawbacks of the two previously considered visualization paradigms and it may be worth noting that RV-CA and RV-I are special cases of RV-RD corresponding to different policies for client and server. If the server ignores the position of the client and sends all the model at the first request from the client, one obtains RV-CA where the full 3D model is transmitted at once. If the server does not send any 3D data, but just a sequence of rendered images according to the user's position, one obtains RV-I.

This chapter essentially describes the implementation of a smart client for system RV-RD which is the basic ingredient of a RV-RD system and the most critical for the rendering results. The next section dwelves into the difficulties of efficient RV-RD policies in light of the variety of user's behaviours and it establishes a conceptual connection between the plenoptic function and such policies. Section 3 introduces basic affine warping notation and concepts used at the client in order to render a view, under the assumption that the client, besides geometry, has received a single picture. The rendering is obtained by a suitable affine transformation approximating the actual projective transformation on each triangle of the mesh. Section 4 describes how to include warping within discrete wavelet transform (DWT) analysis and synthesis in order to exploit the availability of N transmitted views at a client side for rendering purposes. Section 5 defines the client policy which accounts for the distortion due to the limited quality of the texture and geometry data available at a client side. Section 6 describes a technique for the real-time computation of the distortion defined in Section 5. Section 7 presents some experimental results showing the practical effectiveness of the client policy. Section 8 draws the conclusions.

11.2 The Basic RV-RD Framework

In the RV-RD system we envisage a server and a client, connected via a bandlimited channel. Characteristics of the server, of the client and of the network are known. However, finding a good policy for the server and the client is not trivial. The main problem consists in the ignorance, both by the server and the client, of what the user interaction with the world will be like. In order to appreciate this, consider that the user can be expected to navigate between a variety of different views; however, we do not know beforehand which views will be of interest. We also do not know in advance how much time (transmission resources) the user will choose to devote to any particular view. At one extreme the user may keep focused on a single view for a considerable period of time, waiting until very high quality imagery has been recovered before moving on. In this case, the interactive retrieval problem is tantamount to that of interactive image browsing, which is most elegantly addressed by progressive transmission of a single scalably compressed image, formed at the server. One way to achieve this is to combine the JPIP interactive imaging protocol with a JPEG2000 compressed representation of the desired view [D.Taubman and R.Prandolini (2003)]. At the opposite extreme, the interactive user may select many different views in rapid succession, with the aim of understanding the scene geometry. This phase might itself be a precursor to later detailed inspection of some particular view of interest. All the intermediate cases between these two extremes should be considered during planning of the server and client policies. Close and accurate navigation in a 3D model should be allowed as well as an overall inspection. A slow navigation should be considered, as well as fast movements of the user's position.

In order to cope with all the possibilities, we assume that in a RV-RD system the server stores two types of data, forming the complete 3D environment:

(1) a collection of views of the scene $V^i_{original}$;
(2) the scene surface geometry, $G_{original}$.

As depicted in Fig. 11.2, the server delivers incremental contributions of these two types of data in the form of:

(1) scalably compressed images V^i of the scene, computed from the collection of views $V^i_{original}$;
(2) scalably compressed representation of the scene surface geometry G, obtained from the complete geometry $G_{original}$.

This provision is especially appropriate in view of the fact that the 3D environment is usually built from a collection of 3D views, merged together into a complete 3D model, and a collection of 2D images, which represent the texture of the environment. The 3D views may be obtained from the collection of 2D images or by other means. It is important to observe that while merging the 3D views usually leads to a more compact, complete and precise representation of reality, merging all the images taken from the scene might lead to loss of information. In fact, if the user looks at the 3D environment from a position where a photograph has been taken, sometimes the best choice might consist in serving the client directly with the scalably compressed representation of that photograph. If all the views were merged together, this could be not possible anymore. In Fig. 11.2, this means that the rendered view $V_{rendered}$ is identical to the corresponding image V^j.

Interestingly, though, this might not always be the best policy. If the

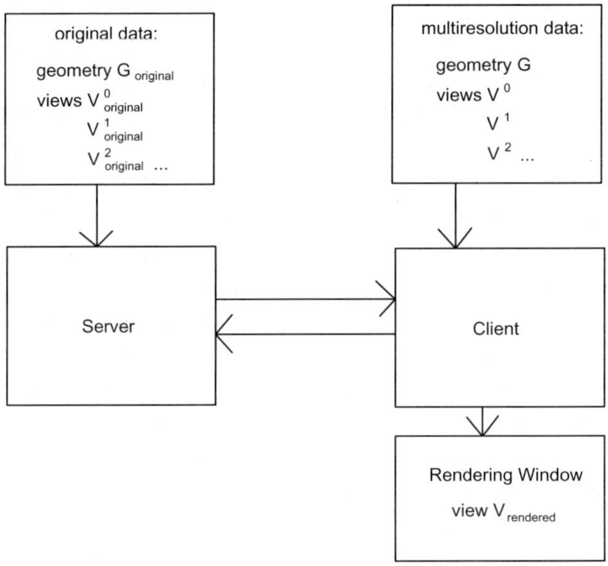

Fig. 11.2 Original and compressed data.

client has already received sufficient elements with sufficient quality from one or more nearby compressed view images, V^1, V^2, ..., it may be more efficient to send only the amount of geometric information required by the client to synthesize the requested view. In this case, the resulting bandwidth savings could be used to further augment the quality of these nearby original view images. It follows that even if the server has a large number of original view images, an efficient service policy would effectively sub-sample them based on the interactive user's navigation patterns. More generally, the server may choose to send some elements from V^i, while expecting the client to derive other aspects of the view from the previously delivered, but less closely aligned, original view images V^n. It is worth pointing out that the compressed server images V^i do not necessarily correspond to the new views rendered by the client.

With respect to geometry, there exist a vast amount of work about progressive compression of 3D (non textured) meshes [Garland and Heckbert (1997)] [Rusinkiewicz and Levoy (2000)] [Hoppe (1996)] [Guskov *et al.* (1999)] [Schroeder *et al.* (1992)] and there are many ways to implement this concept.

The server of RV-RD does not generate new views or compress differential imagery. Instead, within an optimal policy, it determines and sends appropriate elements from a fixed set of scalably compressed bit-streams, so as to provide its clients with the most appropriate data to render their desired views from. The framework RV-RD may thus be interpreted as fostering a greedy strategy for non-linear approximation of the plenoptic function [Zanuttigh *et al.* (2005)]. We will explain this concept. The server, with geometry G and views V^i, stores a representation of the plenoptic function. The plenoptic function must be approximated in order to be sent through the network and this is done through a greedy strategy, which means that the best immediate, or local, solution must be found.

We would expect that a good strategy considers both view sub-sampling and rate-distortion criteria. The fact that efficient service policies can be expected to automatically sub-sample the existing content, contrasts the proposed approach with the previously mentioned predictive approach RV-I, where imagery is delivered for every view requested by the user.

A fundamental question an implementation of RV-RD system must reply is how the client should combine information from available original view images into a new view of interest, using the available description of the surface geometry. Such a possibility is instrumental to reuse the transmitted information and to avoid the waste of resources intrinsic of predictive system RV-I. The rest of this chapter describes a possible solution.

11.3 Rendering from a Single View by Affine Warping

This section describes how the client can combine information from available 3D and texture data into a new view of interest. Here we assume that the client has already received the surface geometry G and one single image V^i from the server at a certain resolution, according to the server policy. We assume a triangular mesh representation for surface geometry G.

Wanted view V^* corresponds to the user's request. View V^* is rendered by a projection matrix P^*. Namely, matrix P^* projects nodes $\mathbf{X_i}$ of G from the 3D space onto the 2D points $\mathbf{J_i}$, of the domain of V^*, as shown in Fig. 11.3, according to the following relationship in homogeneous coordinates [Hartley and Zisserman (2000)]:

$$\begin{bmatrix} w\mathbf{J_i} \\ w \end{bmatrix} = P^* \begin{bmatrix} \mathbf{X_i} \\ 1 \end{bmatrix} \tag{11.1}$$

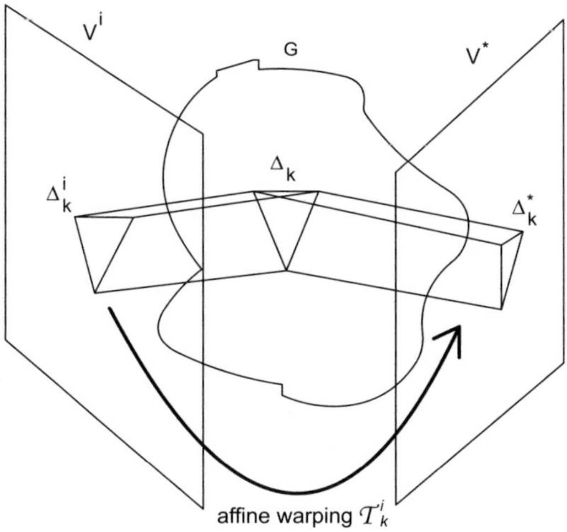

Fig. 11.3 Rendering V^* from geometry G and view V_i.

The structure of P^* is:

$$P^* = \begin{bmatrix} f_x & s & c_x \\ 0 & f_y & c_y \\ 0 & 0 & 1 \end{bmatrix} \begin{bmatrix} R^T & t \end{bmatrix} \tag{11.2}$$

where R and t are the rotation matrix and translation vector of the user reference system, with respect to the world reference system. Entries f_x, f_y, c_x, c_y and s are the intrinsic parameters of the virtual camera used by the client in order to render the world to the user.

We assume that V^i was taken by a pre-calibrated camera with projection matrix P^i. Let Δ_k^* and Δ_k^i denote the triangular patches obtained by projecting the same triangle Δ_k of 3D mesh G on V^* by P^* and on V^i by P^i (Fig. 11.3). Let us denote as $V^*(\Delta_k^*)$ and as $V^i(\Delta_k^i)$ the portions of image V^* and V^i supported by Δ_k^* and Δ_k^i respectively.

$$\left(V^i\left(\Delta\right)\right)[\mathbf{n}] = \begin{cases} V^i[\mathbf{n}] & \mathbf{n} \in \Delta \\ 0 & \mathbf{n} \notin \Delta \end{cases}$$

where $\mathbf{n} = [n_1, n_2]$ is a sample in the image.

Of course some of the projected triangles may be hidden in one image, but not in the other. If Δ_k^* is hidden, then Δ_k^i is not involved in rendering, while if Δ_k^i is hidden, Δ_k^* is a "hole" in V^*, *i.e.* an area which cannot be rendered from V^i.

Apart from the holes, each exposed triangle Δ_k^* is rendered by an affine warping: $\mathcal{T}_k^i$ is the mapping on image V^i which takes Δ_k^i to Δ_k^*. The resulting portion of image is $(\mathcal{T}_k^i V^i)(\Delta_k^*)$.

The wanted view V^* is rendered as the sum of all the triangular image patches produced by operators $\mathcal{T}_k^i$ delivering the result of each triangular patch Δ_k^*. We denote as $\mathcal{T}^i$ such a global operator, *i.e.*:

$$V^* = \mathcal{T}^i V^i = \sum_k (\mathcal{T}_k^i V^i)(\Delta_k^*) \tag{11.3}$$

Note that while the triangle vertices are correctly transformed with respect to projective transformation P^* by the affine warping, such a transformation only approximates the action of P^* in their interior, which is an homography between triangles. However, this error can be rendered arbitrarily small by reducing the size of the surface mesh elements. Affine warping is preferable to projective warping since it is supported by most graphic engines and it is faster. Algorithms for fast warping of images are well known in computer graphics [Foley *et al.* (1995)].

11.4 Rendering from Multiple Views by DWT Analysis, Warping and DWT Synthesis

In the general case, the client has available many images $V^i, i = 1 \ldots N$ previously sent by the server. Assume that V^i were taken by pre-calibrated cameras, each one with projection matrix $P^i, i = 1 \ldots N$. One way to combine information from multiple original view images, $V^0, V^1, \ldots$, is to simply average the results obtained by mapping each of them onto the desired view, *i.e.*,

$$V^* = \frac{1}{N} \sum_{i=0}^{N-1} \mathcal{T}^i V^i \tag{11.4}$$

Unfortunately, any imperfection in the surface geometry description produces misalignment amongst the separate renderings $\mathcal{T}^i V^i$, so that averaging tends to blur high frequency spatial features. Also, the simple average shows no preference for one possible rendering over another. Indeed some view may be less noisy or closer than the others to the wanted view, therefore it would be sensible to give a higher weight to its contribution. Figures 11.4(a) and 11.4(b) show two objects, a Santa Claus and a log. Figures 11.5(a) and 11.5(b) show the effects of rendering a view by averaging two images ($N = 2$) for the Santa Claus and for the log.

(a) (b)

Fig. 11.4 The objects: (a) Santa Claus; (b) The log.

(a) (b)

Fig. 11.5 Rendering by averaging: (a) Santa Claus; (b) The log.

An alternative strategy is to select a single most appropriate original view image from which to render each triangle. We refer to this as stitching: in $(\mathcal{T}_k^{i_k} V^{i_k,k})\,(\Delta_k^*)$, i_k is the "best stitching source" for the kth triangle. The rendered image becomes:

$$V^* = \sum_k (\mathcal{T}_k^{i_k} V^{i_k})(\Delta_k^*) \tag{11.5}$$

The problem, of course, is identifying the best stitching source for each Δ_k^*. Although stitching avoids the blurring problem, it tends to produce visible discontinuities at the boundaries between adjacent triangles which are rendered from different original source views. This is because the surface geometry will inevitably contain modeling errors, and the considered rendering process does not account for illumination-dependent shading effects. This artifact due to stitching can be seen in Fig. 11.6, and it is rather evident on the leg of the model.

Fig. 11.6 Rendering from two views by stitching not in the DWT domain.

To hide these artifacts, and also to open the door to resolution-dependent stitching algorithms, we prefer to form V^* in the discrete wavelet transform or DWT domain [Taubman and Marcellin (2002)]. The process is shown in Fig. 11.7. Each possible rendering is generated through warping of each image V^i, which gives $(\mathcal{T}^i V^i), i = 1 \ldots N$. This process corresponds to the one described in Section 11.3. Each possible rendering is subjected to DWT analysis. This produces a collection of subbands: we call $\mathbf{b} \equiv (\theta, d)$ a generic subband, where $\theta \in \{0, 1, 2, 3\}$ stands for {LL,HL,LH,HH} and $d \in \{1, 2, \ldots, D\}$ is the level of wavelet decomposition, where D is the number of DWT levels ("depth" in the tree), see Fig. 11.8.

Stitching is carried out within the individual subbands to produce subbands $\mathbf{b}$ of V^*, as shown in Fig. 11.7. Each triangular portion $V_{\mathbf{b}}^*(\Delta_k^*)$ of each subband $\mathbf{b}$ of the destination image V^* is chosen by a suitable policy among the DWT decompositions of $(\mathcal{T}_k^i V^i), i = 1 \ldots N$ relative to the same subband.

At the end, V^* is recovered by DWT synthesis. Experimental evidence for the benefits of the DWT-based stitching is provided in Section 11.7. The policy used for the stiching strategy is explained in the next section.

In order to formalize the procedure for rendering from multiple views let us introduce some notation.

Let $\mathcal{A}_{\mathbf{b}}$ denote the subband analysis operator: it is a sequence of filtering and downsampling operators [Taubman and Marcellin (2002)], which transform an image $V[\mathbf{n}]$ in the matrix of coefficients $V_{\mathbf{b}}[\mathbf{n}]$ at subband $\mathbf{b}$,

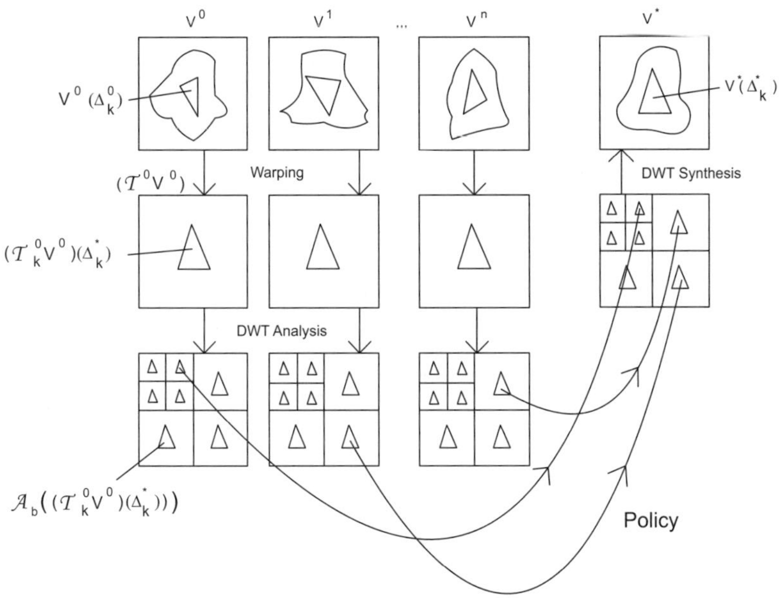

Fig. 11.7 Stitching in DWT domain.

as shown in Fig. 11.8(a):

$$V_{\mathbf{b}}^{i} = \mathcal{A}_{\mathbf{b}}\left(V^{i}\right) \equiv V_{\mathbf{b}}^{i}[\mathbf{n}] = \left(\mathcal{A}_{\mathbf{b}}\left(V^{i}\right)\right)[\mathbf{n}]$$

Let $\mathbf{S_b}$ denote the subband synthesis operator: it is a sequence of up-sampling and filtering operators, which brings the contribution of a matrix of wavelet coefficients $V_{\mathbf{b}}[\mathbf{n}]$ at subband $\mathbf{b}$ to image $V[\mathbf{n}]$, as shown in Fig. 11.8(b):

$$V^{i} = \sum_{\mathbf{b}} \mathcal{S}_{\mathbf{b}}\left(V_{\mathbf{b}}^{i}\right) \tag{11.6}$$

Image V^* is obtained through synthesis from all the coefficients $V_{\mathbf{b}}^*$ at subbands $\mathbf{b}$:

$$V^{*} = \sum_{\mathbf{b}} \mathcal{S}_{\mathbf{b}}(V_{\mathbf{b}}^{*}) \tag{11.7}$$

The coefficients of each subband can also be seen as sum of the coefficients with support Δ_k^* at subbands $\mathbf{b}$, which can be written as:

$$V^{*} = \sum_{\mathbf{b}} \mathcal{S}_{\mathbf{b}}\left(\sum_{k}(V_{\mathbf{b}}^{*}(\Delta_{k}^{*}))\right) \tag{11.8}$$

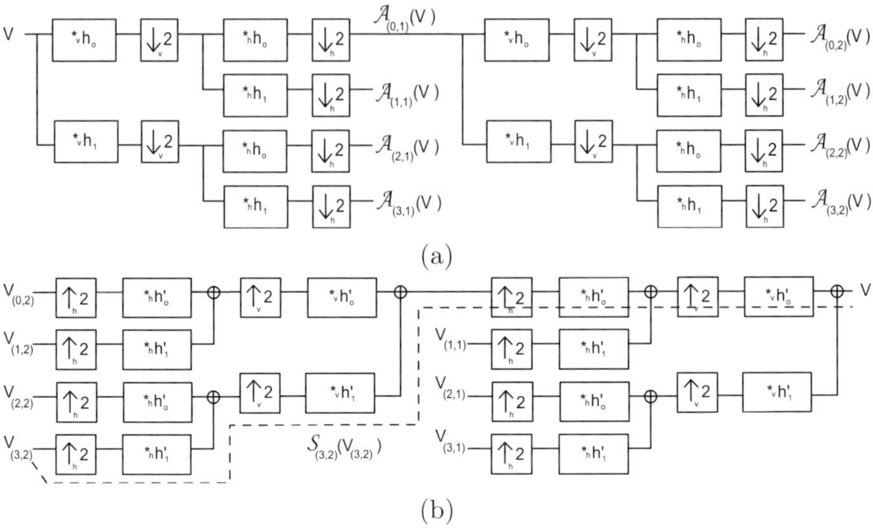

Fig. 11.8 (a) analysis operators $\mathcal{A}_{\mathbf{b}}$; (b) synthesis operators $\mathbf{S}_{\mathbf{b}}$ (the contribution of $\mathbf{b} = (3, 2)$ is shown as a dotted line).

11.5 The Client Policy

In expression (11.8) each portion of coefficients $V^*_{\mathbf{b}}(\Delta^*_k)$ in subband $\mathbf{b}$ comes from one of the warped triangle coefficients $(\mathcal{T}^i_k V^i)(\Delta^*_k)$, $i = 1 \ldots N$, in the subband $\mathbf{b}$, *i.e.*,

$$V^*_{\mathbf{b}}\left(\Delta^*_k\right) = \left[\left(\mathcal{A}_{\mathbf{b}} \circ \mathcal{T}^{i_{\mathbf{b},k}}\right)\left(V^{i_{\mathbf{b},k}}\right)\right]\left(\Delta^*_k\right) \qquad (11.9)$$

where $i_{\mathbf{b},k}$ identifies the selected source image, $V^{i_{\mathbf{b},k}}$, for triangle Δ_k in subband $\mathbf{b}$. We call this the stitching source. We must determine a policy for choosing the "best" stitching source $i_{\mathbf{b},k}$. Such a source depends on the subband $\mathbf{b}$ and the triangle index k.

When selecting one source instead of another, the client suffers a certain error bringing various types of distortion in the rendered views which must be minimized. The strategy for defining policy function $i_{\mathbf{b},k}$ is the minimization of such an error, which will be formally expressed in this section.

There are three sources of error. The first source of error, which will be called quantization error for simplicity, is the quality of images that are sent by the server: the server usually sends data in a progressive fashion (as JPIP) and at a certain time the client owns images of a certain quality, usually different from the full quality of the pictures available at the server side.

A second error source is the warping process, which is bound to introduce some distortion. Such a distortion is correlated with the viewing geometry, indeed a patch of the model which is seen well from the user could be present in the original images from a very acute angle. This means that warping will expand the patch in a relevant way and high frequencies could be missing. The distortion must combine affine approximation and viewing geometry. For example, let us assume that two photos have been sent by the server to the client: the first image has a very high quality and the second one a low quality. In the same geometric conditions, the best quality picture will be used to create the final picture, in the way described in previous section. However, it could happen that a certain patch, seen by the user, is best described, in low and high frequencies, by a lower quality picture which is more parallel to the viewer.

The third source of error is due to geometric modeling: the geometry G_{server} available at the server side is not exactly identical to the real scene. Errors in calibration, acquisition and reconstruction may be present. Furthermore the geometry G_{client} available at the client side in general is a simplified or compressed version of the geometry G_{server}, and this introduces a quantization error.

We assume that the original view images were compressed in the DWT domain (*e.g.*, using JPEG2000). The full quality images at the server side and their compressed versions (sent by the server), represented by Expression 11.6, available at client side are different because of quantization. This difference is an error image e^i. We call $\mathbf{b}'$ a subband of V^i, and $\mathbf{b}$ a subband of the destination image V^*, made by warped contributions. We call B the complete set of subbands $\mathbf{b}$, and B' the complete set of subband $\mathbf{b}'$. A quantization error is associated to each matrix of coefficients $V^i_{\mathbf{b}'}(\Delta^i_k)$ in the subband $\mathbf{b}'$ of V^i falling within the scope of triangle Δ^i_k and is called $e^i_{\mathbf{b}',k}(\Delta^i_k)$.

In order to understand how the quantization error intrinsic to the limited quality images (11.6) affects the final rendered view V^*, consider the error propagation chain due to the DWT with the aid of Fig. 11.9.

At client side, because of the warping and of the subsequent analysis, the limited image quality error propagates down to the warped triangles $(\mathcal{T}^i_k V^i)(\Delta^*_k)$ in all subbands. Such triangles are selected as the coefficients of 11.9 of V^* at subband $\mathbf{b}$, V^* is obtained through synthesis (11.8) and it is affected by the errors as shown in Fig. 11.9. Once the stitching source

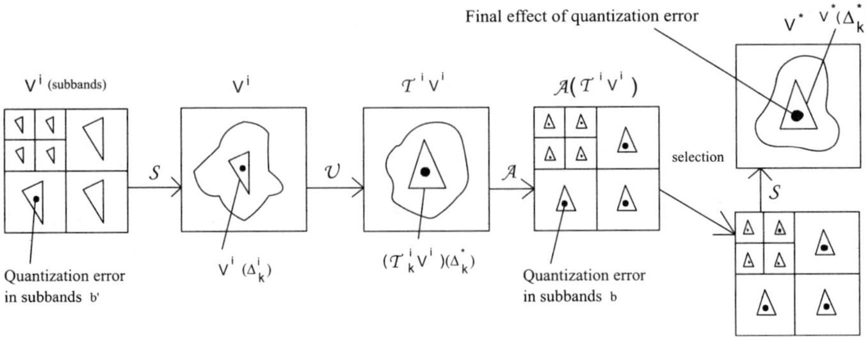

Fig. 11.9 Quantization error.

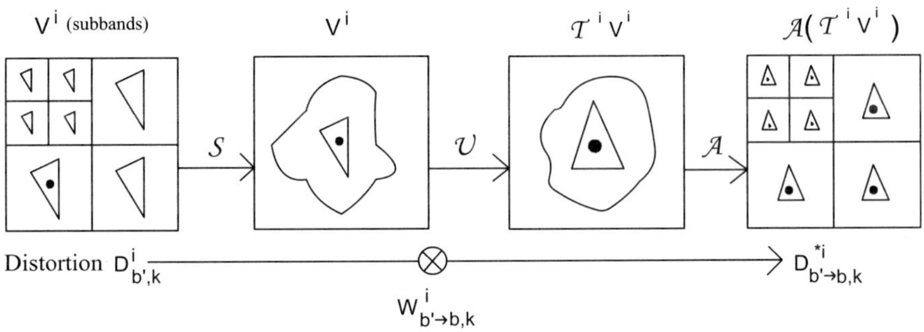

Fig. 11.10 Propagation of the quantization error.

$i_{\mathbf{b},k}$ has been selected, we know that error $e^{i_{\mathbf{b},k}}_{\mathbf{b}',k}(\Delta^{i_{\mathbf{b},k}}_k)$, due each to subband $\mathbf{b}'$, affects image $V^{i_{\mathbf{b},k}}$ through synthesis, which gives the error:

$$e^{i_{\mathbf{b},k}} = \sum_{\mathbf{b}' \in B'} \mathcal{S}_{\mathbf{b}'} \left(\sum_k e^{i_{\mathbf{b},k}}_{\mathbf{b}'}(\Delta^{i_{\mathbf{b},k}}_k) \right) \tag{11.10}$$

Error $e^{i_{\mathbf{b},k}}$ propagates in the subband $\mathbf{b}$ of the warped image, as shown in Fig. 11.10, and brings to V^* the error:

$$e^*_{\mathbf{b}} = \left[\left(\mathcal{A}_{\mathbf{b}} \circ \mathcal{T}^{i_{\mathbf{b},k}} \right) \left(e^{i_{\mathbf{b},k}} \right) \right] (\Delta^*_k) \tag{11.11}$$

If we analyze the contribution of only one source triangle Δ^i_k and only one source subband $\mathbf{b}'$ on a destination subband $\mathbf{b}'$, we can write:

$$e^{*i_{\mathbf{b},k}}_{\mathbf{b}'\to\mathbf{b},k} = \left[\left(\mathcal{A}_{\mathbf{b}} \circ \mathcal{T}^{i_{\mathbf{b},k}} \right) \left(\mathcal{S}_{\mathbf{b}'} e^{i_{\mathbf{b},k}}_{\mathbf{b}'} \right) \right] (\Delta^*_k) \tag{11.12}$$

A useful parameter to evaluate the error propagation is the mean square error of the error image, which we call distortion. The distortion of error $e_{\mathbf{b}'}^{i_{\mathbf{b},k}}\left(\Delta_k^{i_{\mathbf{b},k}}\right)$ is:

$$D_{\mathbf{b}',k}^{i_{\mathbf{b},k}} = ||e_{\mathbf{b}'}^{*i_{\mathbf{b},k}}(\Delta_k^{i_{\mathbf{b},k}})||^2 \tag{11.13}$$

The correlated distortion at the $\mathbf{b}$ subband in V^* is:

$$D_{\mathbf{b}'\to\mathbf{b},k}^{*i_{\mathbf{b},k}} = ||e_{\mathbf{b}'\to\mathbf{b},k}^{*i_{\mathbf{b},k}}||^2 \tag{11.14}$$

Parameter $D_{\mathbf{b}'\to\mathbf{b},k}^{*i_{\mathbf{b},k}}$ only accounts for the error contribution from the $\mathbf{b}'$ subband of $V^{i_{\mathbf{b},k}}$ to the $\mathbf{b}$ subband of V^*.

The distortion at the $\mathbf{b}$ subband of V^* due to the limited quality of the images available at client side, warping and DWT analysis and synthesis can be approximated as:

$$D_{\mathbf{b},k}^{*} = \sum_{\mathbf{b}'\in B'} D_{\mathbf{b}'\to\mathbf{b},k}^{*i_{\mathbf{b},k}} \tag{11.15}$$

The distortion of one triangle is:

$$D_k^* = \sum_{\mathbf{b}\in B} D_{\mathbf{b},k}^* \tag{11.16}$$

The complete distortion of the final image V^* is:

$$D^* = \sum_k D_k^* \tag{11.17}$$

The best stitching source $i_{\mathbf{b},k}$ for each triangle Δ_k is the one for which $D_{\mathbf{b},k}^*$ is smallest. Note that the best stitching source could potentially differ from subband to subband. We can now write the policy function as:

$$i_{\mathbf{b},k} = argmin(D_{\mathbf{b},k}^*) \tag{11.18}$$

11.6 How to Compute the Distortion Contribution?

In an environment where the user must be able to navigate in real-time it is not possible for each error associated to each triangle Δ_k and for each source V_i, to compute synthesis, warping, analysis and to get the terms of distortion (11.30) in real-time. Moreover, the client does not know the original images and the actual geometry in order to compute the difference between them and the images it has available. Such differences are indeed available only at the server side. At the client one may estimate the needed information and compute the differences on the basis of such estimates. The estimation methods of [Taubman and Secker (2003)] can be used in this task. This section will describe a practical method for computing distortion (11.30) in real-time. For simplicity, let us begin with the computation of just the quantization error (11.15), ignoring the second and third term of (11.30).

Basic distortion term (11.14) can be evaluated as the product of the previously introduced quantization errors $D^{i_{\mathbf{b}},k}_{\mathbf{b}',k}$ of 11.13 by suitable weights which can be stored in a look-up table (see Fig. 11.10), namely,

$$D^{*i_{\mathbf{b}},k}_{\mathbf{b}'\to\mathbf{b},k} = W^{i_{\mathbf{b}},k}_{\mathbf{b}'\to\mathbf{b},k} D^{i_{\mathbf{b}},k}_{\mathbf{b}',k} \tag{11.19}$$

This formula is correct if we assume uncorrelated quantization errors, or orthogonal basis vectors, as is the case of the DWT basis vectors. This formula is an approximation, because we assign all of the incurred distortion to Δ^i_k ignoring the fact that the error signal is smeared out by the overlapping DWT basis vectors. Hence, from (11.19) Equation (11.15) can be rewritten as:

$$D^*_{\mathbf{b},k} = \sum_{\mathbf{b}'\in B'} W^{i_{\mathbf{b}},k}_{\mathbf{b}'\to\mathbf{b},k} D^{i_{\mathbf{b}},k}_{\mathbf{b}',k} \tag{11.20}$$

By comparing (11.20) with (11.15) one notices than $W^{i_{\mathbf{b}},k}_{\mathbf{b}'\to\mathbf{b},k}$ must account for the effects of synthesis, warping and analysis.

11.6.1 *Effects of the Affine Warping*

Let us first describe how to consider the effects of the affine warping. An affine transformation is a composition of translation, rotation, scaling and shear. The actual results of analysis and synthesis slightly depend on the position of the error in the image. Since we are only interested in an approximation, in this context the translation contribution can be ignored.

Therefore, we will consider affine transformations mapping (x_1, y_1) to (x_2, y_2) according to the following expression:

$$\begin{bmatrix} x_2 \\ y_2 \end{bmatrix} = \begin{bmatrix} \cos(\alpha) & -\sin(\alpha) \\ \sin(\alpha) & \cos(\alpha) \end{bmatrix} \begin{bmatrix} 1 & s \\ 0 & 1 \end{bmatrix} \begin{bmatrix} c_1 & 0 \\ 0 & c_2 \end{bmatrix} \begin{bmatrix} x_1 \\ y_1 \end{bmatrix} \tag{11.21}$$

where α is the angle of the 2D rotation; s is the shear factor and c_1 and c_2 the scaling factors.

First, we quantize the possible affine transformations, in order to have a small number of possible warping operators. Angle α can be linearly quantized as:

$\alpha_i = 2\pi * i/N_\alpha$, with $i = 0 \dots N_\alpha - 1$.

Shear s usually is very close to zero because the same triangle, from different points of view is rotated and scaled but not stretched, since the parameters of the user's camera do not change. Shear s is quantized in a cubic way as:

$s = K_s * (2i/N_s - 1)^3$, with K_s constant value and $i = 0 \dots N_s$.

Scaling factors c_1 and c_2 are frequently equal to one, since usually most surface triangles are parallel to the viewer. Therefore, it makes sense to sample c_1 and c_2 more densely near one.

$c_1 = K_1 * (2i_1/N_1 - 1)^3 + 1$, with K_1 constant value and $i_1 = 0 \dots N_1$,

$c_2 = K_2 * (2i_2/N_2 - 1)^3 + 1$, with K_2 constant value and $i_2 = 0 \dots N_2$.

Values $W^{i_{\mathbf{b}},k}_{\mathbf{b}' \to \mathbf{b},k}$ are computed for each possible quantization of the affine transformation $\mathcal{T}^i_k$. The quantized values can be denoted as $W(\mathbf{b}, \mathbf{b}', \alpha, s, c_1, c_2)$ for each possible source subband $\mathbf{b}'$, destination subband $\mathbf{b}$ and affine warping parameters.

The size of the look-up table depends on the above parameters N_α, N_s, N_1, N_2 and the number of subbands, as explained in the next section. It was experimentally verified that with $N_\alpha = N_s = N_1 = N_2 = 10$, and with $D = 6$ subband levels, the approximation is quite good and the table is not too large (around 30 Mbytes).

11.6.2 *Effects of Analysis and Synthesis*

In order to evaluate the effects of analysis and synthesis together with warping, consider an impulse $e^i_{\mathbf{b}',k}$, *i.e.*, a difference image with a value 1 placed at the center and compute synthesis $\mathcal{S}_{\mathbf{b}'}$, warping with s, c_1, c_2 and analysis $\mathcal{A}_{\mathbf{b}}$ in order to get $W(\mathbf{b}, \mathbf{b}', \alpha, s, c_1, c_2)$.

Figure 11.11(a) shows a 16×16 example of $e^i_{\mathbf{b}',k}$ with a single sample at the center of subband $\mathbf{b}' = (0, 4)$. After synthesis a blob appears in the form of the 256×256 image of Fig. 11.11(b). Figure 11.11(c) shows the result of warping by an affine transformation. The result of the analysis in the subband $\mathbf{b} = (0, 4)$, the squared value of which gives $W(\mathbf{b}, \mathbf{b}', \alpha, s, c_1, c_2)$, is shown by the 16×16 image of Fig. 11.11(d).

There is a point worth noting. The position of the sample affects the result of analysis and synthesis in DWT. An impulse error placed at the center of the subband approximates only an error at the origin, but errors can be positioned anywhere in the original image. More sensible values

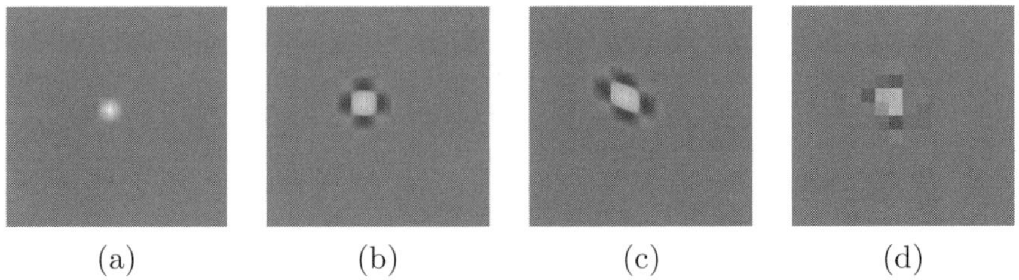

Fig. 11.11 Computation of $D_{jd \to hm, \alpha, s, c_1, c_2}$: (a) impulsive error in subband $d = 4$, $j = 1$, (b) result of synthesis, (c) result of warping, (d) result of analysis in subband $h = 4, m = 1$.

of W are obtained if one places the impulse errors in a certain number of positions around the center and then averages the results.

This procedure gives satisfactory results because analysis and synthesis are linear operators and error image $e^i_{\mathbf{b}',k}$ is the sum of scaled impulse contributions. Experiments showed that the weights $W(\mathbf{b}, \mathbf{b}', \alpha, s, c_1, c_2)$ obtained by this procedure approximate very well the actual values of $D^{*i_{\mathbf{b},k}}_{\mathbf{b}' \to \mathbf{b},k}$ given by (11.19).

11.6.3 *Effects of Extra-Band Energy*

Operator $\mathcal{T}^i_k$ stretches the portion of image V^i within triangle Δ^i_k by ratio $|\Delta^*_k| \,/\, |\Delta^i_k|$ between the areas of warped and original triangles. ($|\Delta_k|$ denotes the area of triangle Δ_k) and amplifies the image energy roughly by the same amount. Assuming an orthonormal transform, we can say that given unitary distortion $D^i_{\mathbf{b}',k} = ||e^i_{\mathbf{b}',k}||^2 = 1$, the contribution of the error from subband $\mathbf{b}'$ to the warped image $\mathcal{T}^i_k V^i$ is:

$$||\mathcal{T}^i_k \mathcal{S}_{\mathbf{b}'}(e^i_{\mathbf{b}',k})||^2 = W^i_{\mathbf{b}' \to \mathbf{b},k} = |\Delta^*_k| \,/\, |\Delta^i_k| \tag{11.22}$$

The energy is preserved in all the subbands by DWT analysis. Incidentally, the 9/7 biorthogonal wavelet transform used for our experiments is very nearly orthonormal, subject to appropriate normalization of the subband samples. Therefore, if $(\mathcal{T}^i_k V^i)$ is decomposed in subbands the total energy in each subband stays the same, and,

$$\sum_{\mathbf{b}'} W^i_{\mathbf{b}' \to \mathbf{b},k} = ||\mathcal{T}^{\mathbf{b},k}_k(\mathcal{S}_{\mathbf{b}'}(e^i_{\mathbf{b}',k}))||^2 = |\Delta^*_k| \,/\, |\Delta^i_k| \tag{11.23}$$

From (11.19) we see that distortion $D^i_{\mathbf{b}',k}$ is scaled by $W^i_{\mathbf{b}' \to \mathbf{b},k}$ in order to obtain $D^{*i}_{\mathbf{b}'\to\mathbf{b},k}$, hence:

$$\begin{aligned} D^*_k &= \sum_{\mathbf{b}'\in B';\mathbf{b}\in B} D^{*i}_{\mathbf{b}'\to\mathbf{b},k} \\ &= \sum_{\mathbf{b}'\in B';\mathbf{b}\in B} (W^i_{\mathbf{b}'\to\mathbf{b},k} D^i_{\mathbf{b}',k}) \\ &= \sum_{\mathbf{b}'\in B'} D^i_{\mathbf{b}',k} \sum_{\mathbf{b}'\in B';\mathbf{b}\in B} W^i_{\mathbf{b}'\to\mathbf{b},k} \\ &= |\Delta^*_k| \,/\, |\Delta^i_k| \sum_{\mathbf{b}'\in B'} D^i_{\mathbf{b}',k} \end{aligned} \tag{11.24}$$

The above expression apparently suggests that the total distortion in the warped triangle (left hand side) is roughly independent from the affine operator $\mathcal{T}^i_n$, since the total distortion in the source triangles $\sum_{\mathbf{b}\in B} D^i_{\mathbf{b},k}$ should be nearly proportional to their areas $|\Delta^i_k|$. However, this is not the case for two reasons. Firstly, $\mathcal{T}^i_k$ must be a bandlimited warping operator, so that $||\mathcal{T}^i_k(\mathcal{S}_{\mathbf{b}'}(e^i_{\mathbf{b}',k}))||^2 = |\Delta^*_k| \,/\, |\Delta^i_k| \cdot F\left(||\mathcal{T}^i_k(\mathcal{S}_{\mathbf{b}'}(e^i_{\mathbf{b}',k}))||^2\right)$, where $F\left(||\mathcal{T}^i_k(\mathcal{S}_{\mathbf{b}'}(e^i_{\mathbf{b}',k}))||^2\right)$ is the fraction of the energy of $||\mathcal{T}^i_k(\mathcal{S}_{\mathbf{b}'}(e^i_{\mathbf{b}',k}))||^2$ within the Nyquist frequency. Secondly, expansive operators $\mathcal{T}^i_k$ cannot predict the highest frequency details of V^* at all. Both effects can be taken into account by extending the sums in equation (11.20) to include subbands from a set of hypothetical resolutions above those of the original images.

Figure 11.12(a) indicates that if an affine transformation shrinks a triangle, most of the energy comes from the lower subbands. Usually the energy from the higher level subbands of V^i is lost, since their contribution does not appear in the final image V^*. The picture is different in Fig. 11.12(b) showing an affine transformation expanding a triangle. It can be seen that the energy which should be transferred to higher levels of V^* is missing, since the corresponding subbands of V^i do not exist. This must be taken into account when computing the total distortion of Equation (11.20) together with the dual fact of the energy going to non-existing subbands in case of shrinking, since it does not appear in the final rendered view V^*.

This problem can be solved adding extra-band energy in the source image: the set of subbands of V^i becomes $B'' = B' \cup \mathbf{b}_{EB}$ with an extra level $\mathbf{b}_{EB}$ added. In this extra-band we have the source distortions $D^i_{\mathbf{b}_{EB},k}$, which we estimate by projecting each source image V^i onto the other in turn and taking the maximum of the energy produced by such projections.

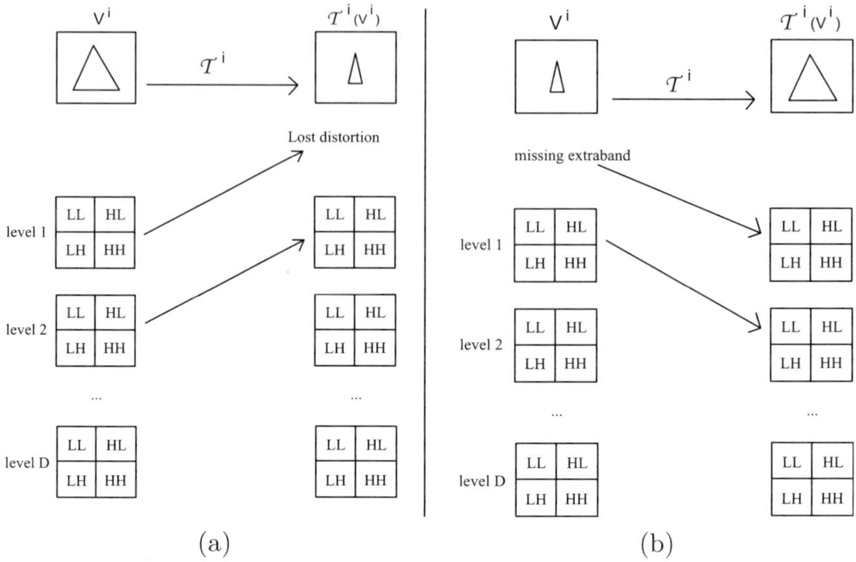

Fig. 11.12 Effects of (a) Shrinking (b) Expansion.

This in practice means that we consider the energy of the source image with more detail. Indeed, it is not necessary to know the real energy of the details which were present in the real 3D model at higher resolution, since they will never appear if no image with such details is available. However, if the details exist in one of the images, they must be taken into account.

Equation (11.20) with the extra-band contribution accounted for by $\mathbf{b}_{EB}$ becomes:

$$D^*_{\mathbf{b},k} = \sum_{\mathbf{b}' \in B''} W^{i_{\mathbf{b},k}}_{\mathbf{b}' \to \mathbf{b},k} D^{i_{\mathbf{b},k}}_{\mathbf{b}',k} \tag{11.25}$$

The extra contribution on the right hand side of Equation (11.25), shown in Fig. 11.12(b), grows with $|(\Delta^*_k)| \,/\, \left|\Delta^{i_{\mathbf{b},k}}_k\right|$. Instead, the target distortions of hypothetical subbands, as shown in Fig. 11.12(a), represent an unconsidered contribution to the left hand side of equation (11.25), which grows with $\left|\Delta^{i_{\mathbf{b},k}}_k\right| \,/\, |(\Delta^*_k)|$. As a result, we expect to find that the best stitching source $i_{\mathbf{b},k}$ is the one for which $\mathcal{T}^{i_{\mathbf{b},k}}_k$ is most contractive, all other things being equal. Of course, this usually does not happen: at a certain time, images can be present at different resolutions and this strongly affects the decision.

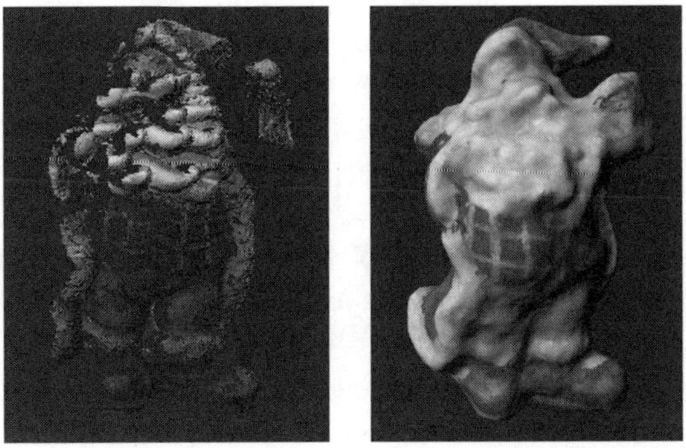

(a) (b)

Fig. 11.13 Santa Claus from a 3D model obtained by: (a) range-camera (b) 3D passive reconstruction from a set of photographs.

11.6.4 *Effects of Geometry*

The error on V^* due to wrong or approximate geometry is considered in this section.

The reliability of the 3D geometry depends on different causes. First of all, the accuracy of the acquisition and 3D modeling tools affects reliability. For example, range-cameras can scan objects with a precision of a few tenths of a micron, while passive 3D reconstruction methods can be affected by errors of millimeters. Figure 11.13 shows two rendered views of Santa Claus; the one in Fig. 11.13(a) comes from a 3D model obtained by a range-camera and is much more precise than the view in Fig. 11.13(b), coming from a 3D model obtained by a passive method based on a set of photographs (see Chapter 12).

A second source of error comes from quantization and transmission of multi-resolution 3D meshes from server to client: the model at the client side is not the same as the original 3D model available at the server. Furthermore, if geometry and texture are acquired by different instruments (*e.g.* a range camera for the former and a photocamera for the latter) possible calibration errors between the two instruments can produce misalignments between 3D data and texture.

All these sources contribute a geometric error: uncertainty in the surface geometry translates into uncertainty in the parameters of the transformations $\mathcal{T}_k^i$, more specifically affected by a translational uncertainty, which has been studied in [Taubman and Secker (2003)]. Its effect may be modeled by augmenting each term $D^*_{\mathbf{b},k}$ in Equation (11.15) by a second contribution of the form:

$$D^*_{\mathbf{b},k} = \sum_{\mathbf{b}' \in B'} W^{*i_{\mathbf{b},k}}_{\mathbf{b}' \to \mathbf{b},k} \left(D^{*i_{\mathbf{b},k}}_{\mathbf{b}',k} + \left[g_k^{i_{\mathbf{b},k}} \left| \omega_{\mathbf{b}'} \right|^2 \right] E^{i_{\mathbf{b},k}}_{\mathbf{b}'} (\Delta_k^{i_{\mathbf{b},k}}) \right) \tag{11.26}$$

which is function on the subband $\mathbf{b}'$ from which the texture is taken, the triangle Δ_k^* and the view V^i. Most specifically g_k^i accounts for the influence on the geometry error of the actual shape of Δ_k^* over V^*; $\omega_{\mathbf{b}'}$ is "represen-tative" of the spatial frequencies belonging to subband $\mathbf{b}'$ and expresses the influence of geometric error over such subband; $E^{i_{\mathbf{b},k}}_{\mathbf{b}'}(\Delta_k^{i_{\mathbf{b},k}})$ is the energy of subband $\mathbf{b}'$ inside triangle Δ_k^i.

If we knew the power spectrum in the subband, *i.e.*, how the energy density were distributed over the subband $\mathbf{b}'$, it would be logical to choose $\omega_{\mathbf{b}'}$, for example, as the maximum point of the centroid of the power spectrum. As we only know the energy of the subband (*i.e.*, the integral of the power spectrum over the subband itself) we can simply take $\omega_{\mathbf{b}'}$ as the middle of the subband, according to:

$$\omega_{\mathbf{b}'} = \begin{cases} (\pi/2^d, \pi/2^d) & \text{when } \theta = 0 \\ ((\pi * 2)/2^d, \pi/2^d) & \text{when } \theta = 1 \\ (\pi/2^d, (\pi * 2)/2^d) & \text{when } \theta = 2 \\ ((\pi * 2)/2^d, (\pi * 2)/2^d) & \text{when } \theta = 3 \end{cases} \tag{11.27}$$

A more rigourous approach would fit a model to the power spectrum, and can be found in [Taubman and Secker (2003)].

For the computation of g_k^i one should consider how the wrong position of the mesh nodes (which are vertexes of the mesh triangles) of geometry G_{client} available at server side, *i.e.*, an error in the 3D space, translates to an error on the 2D space of image V^*. This error corresponds to the error associated with each triangle Δ_k of G_{client}, and can be computed as the distance from the baricenter of Δ_k and the surface G_{server} (which is supposed to be the correct geometry of the object). That error is a vector $\mathbf{e_k}$. It can be projected over V^i and can be projected over V^i: it becomes $\mathbf{e^i_k} = (\mathbf{e^i_{k}}_x, \mathbf{e^i_{k}}_y)$, as shown in Fig. 11.14.

When a view V^* is rendered from V^i, the error of view V^i could be cancelled by the error of view V^*. For example, if $V^i \equiv V^*$, error in reprojection of V^i cannot be distinguished since V^* is taken from the same point of view (see Fig. 11.15). Thus, error can be approximated as:

$$g_k^i = \sqrt{||(\mathbf{e^i_{k}}_x - \mathbf{e^*_{k}}_x)||^2 + ||(\mathbf{e^i_{k}}_y - \mathbf{e^*_{k}}_y)||^2} \tag{11.28}$$

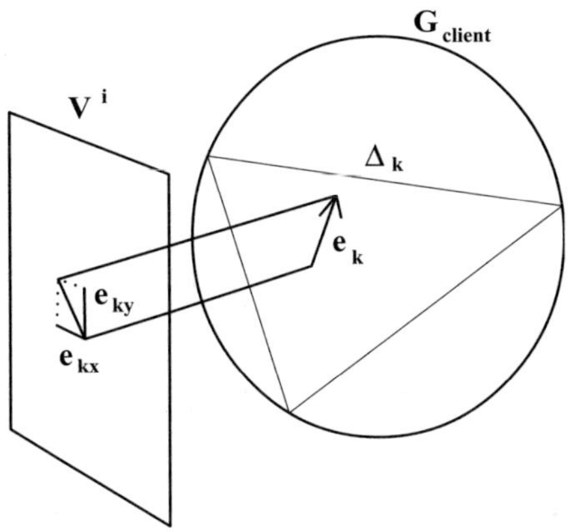

Fig. 11.14 Geometric error $\mathbf{e}_k$ on V^i.

Error along the z axis (along the line of sight of the camera) does not appear here, since its contribution is included if it corresponds to an error along $(\mathbf{e}^*_{\mathbf{k}x}, \mathbf{e}^*_{\mathbf{k}y})$.

This way of evaluating g^i_k suffers some drawbacks. First, it assumes that G_{server} is the real surface of the object, ignoring the fact that G_{server} may be affected by modeling errors. Also, it assumes that g^i_k is computed for each triangle and each new view V^*, which is a very time-consuming task. Furthermore, since g^i_k should be sent for each triangle (because the client does not know G_{server}), the network bit-rate is increased.

Rather than computing g^i_k for each triangle Δ^*_k at server side, one may consider estimating the global contribution of geometric errors g^i_k, which we denote as σ^2_G at the server side and send it to the client. The value of σ^2_G can be estimated by a priori considerations coming from the precision of G_{client} due to the precision of the acquisition and modelling instruments used to obtain it: for instance, if one uses a range camera with resolution characterized by a given σ, for example $\sigma = 100\mu$, one could simply approximate σ^2_G with σ^2. Once σ^2_G is received by the client it could be used to compute an approximate value g^i_k which depends on the requested view V^* and on V^i.

As shown in Fig. 11.15, as a simplification, if we assume that an error equally affects both x and y axes on images, the maximum geometric error happens when the lines of sight of V^* and V^i are orthogonal: that is the case when errors do not cancel each other. If they are parallel, the requested

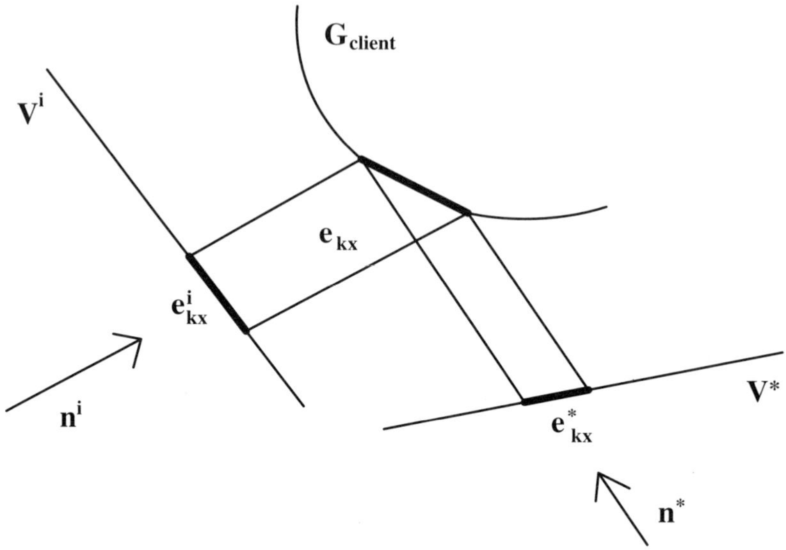

Fig. 11.15 Geometric error $\mathbf{e}_k$ on V^i and V^*.

view V^* is almost equal to V^i and the geometric error would not affect rendering significantly.

Note that the only characteristic of Δ_k affecting the norm of vector $(\mathbf{e}^*_{\mathbf{k}x}, \mathbf{e}^*_{\mathbf{k}y})$, which enters Equation 11.28, is the distance of Δ_k from V^*, since in the projective transformation the size of the projection is inversely proportional to the distance from the object. Therefore, to avoid computation of g^i_k for each triangle, for surfaces of limited depth one could consider an average 3D model depth Δ' and approximate all the g^i_k as:

$$g^i_k = g^i = \frac{\langle \mathbf{n}^i, \mathbf{n}^* \rangle k \sigma^2_G}{d(\Delta', V^*)} \tag{11.29}$$

where $d(\Delta', V^*)$ is the distance between Δ' and V^*; $\mathbf{n}^i$ the line of sight of V^i and $\mathbf{n}^*$ the line of sight of V^*; and k is a constant value.

Approximation (11.29) is certainly inadequate when the surface depth is large or in general when some portions of the scene are very close and others very far from V^*. When this is not the case, parts of the 3D model can be grouped together, and a Δ' is associated to each group.

Note also that our surface model does not account for the illumination-dependent effects of shading and reflection, which are more relevant when

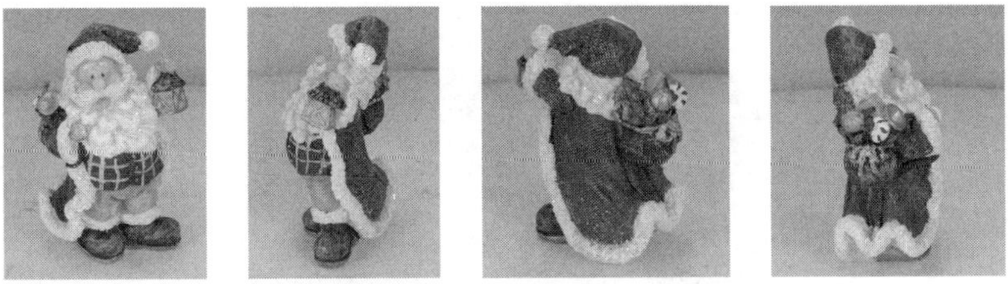

Fig. 11.16 Santa Claus: pictures $V^i, i = 0 \ldots 3$.

the rendered view V^* is far from original views V^i. We can expect a second distortion contribution which grows with the deviation between the orientation of views V^* and V^i. Ignoring specularity, we expect this distortion term to be proportional to the signal power, suggesting the following augmented overall error:

$$D^*_{\mathbf{b},k} = \sum_{\mathbf{b}' \in B'} W^{*i_{\mathbf{b},k}}_{\mathbf{b}' \to \mathbf{b},k} \left(D^{*i_{\mathbf{b},k}}_{\mathbf{b}',k} + \left[g^{i_{\mathbf{b},k}}_k \left| \omega_{\mathbf{b}'} \right|^2 + g(\langle \mathbf{n}^{i_{\mathbf{b},k}}, \mathbf{n}^* \rangle) \right] E^{i_{\mathbf{b},k}}_{\mathbf{b}'} (\Delta^{i_{\mathbf{b},k}}_k) \right) \tag{11.30}$$

where $\mathbf{n}^i$ and $\mathbf{n}^*$ are the surface normals to V^i and V^* respectively, and in the absence of careful modeling, $g(x)$ is set to $\gamma \tan\left(\cos^{-1} x\right)$, where γ determines the value we place on illumination fidelity.

Expression (11.30) explicitly formalizes the impact on V^* of the various sources of error: limited image quality at client side, geometric inaccuracies at client side and illumination, warping within DWT analysis and synthesis.

11.7 Experimental Results

This section presents some experimental results about the performance of the RV-RD system.

Figure 11.16 shows four original images $V^i, i = 0, \ldots, 3$ of an object (Santa Claus), taken 90 degrees apart. Assume that the four images are sent to the client together with geometry information G, given by the 1000 triangles mesh as shown in Fig. 11.17 and that a new image V^* is requested. Figure 11.18(a) shows the result of stitching without DWT as described in Section 11.4, while the other pictures of Fig. 11.18 show the results of stitching by DWT according to policy function f_{choice} based on distortion expressions (11.25) and (11.30) respectively.

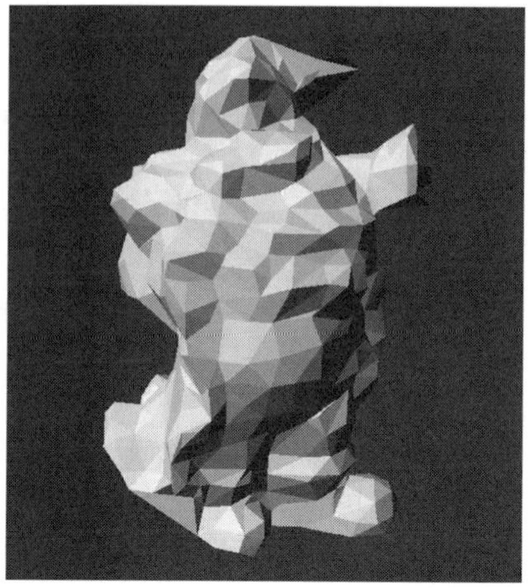

Fig. 11.17 Santa Claus: geometric information G.

In order to interpret the results it may be useful to recall that in the case of distortion (11.25), if the images available at the client have all the same (good) quality, the stitching source is the one for which each triangle is more parallel to the viewer, *i.e.*, the triangle with greatest ratio $\left|\Delta_k^i\right| / \left|\mathcal{T}_k^i(\Delta_k)\right|$. The chosen triangles in this case are shown in Fig. 11.18(b): different colors indicate different sources V^i. Figure 11.18(c) shows the results of wavelet fusion with $D = 3$. If f_{choice} is based upon distortion expression (11.30) the stitching sources are shown in Fig. 11.18(d) and the wavelet fusion with $D = 3$ in Fig. 11.18(e). Some details (like the internal part of the left hand) cannot be reproduced since they are missing from the set of images V^i. Figure 11.18(f) shows a photograph taken from the same position as V^*. Such a picture of course was not included in the set $V^i, i = 0, 1, 2, 3$.

The rendered views of Fig. 11.18 show that rendering according to a stitching policy based on (11.25), Fig. 11.18(c), gives better results than stitching without DWT, Fig. 11.18(a). As expected a policy based on (11.30) which considers also geometry errors, Fig. 11.18(e), performs better than (11.25) and gives results close to real photographs. It is also worth noting that the triangles selections corresponding to (11.25) and (11.30) are rather different.

Consider also the case in which only three of the images of Fig. 11.16 are available at the client with similar good quality, and one, shown in Fig. 11.19(a), at low quality. The results of stitching according to (11.30)

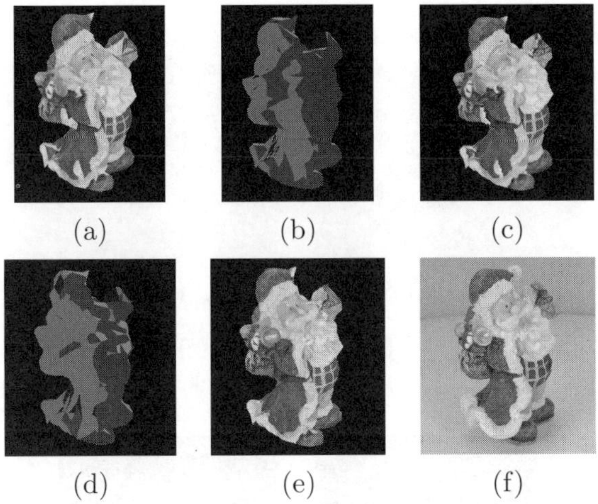

Fig. 11.18 Santa Claus from images with the same quality (a) with stitching without DWT; (b) stitching source and (c) stitching based on DWT and distortion (11.25); (d) stitching source and (e) stitching based on DWT and distortion (11.30); (f) a photograph taken from the rendering position.

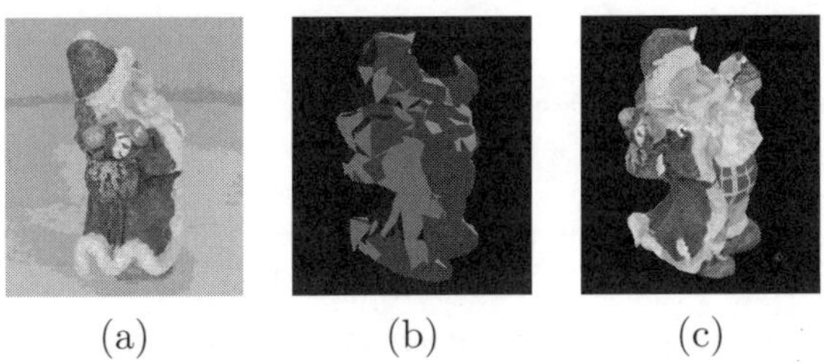

Fig. 11.19 Santa Claus from images with different quality (a) the low quality image; stitching based on DWT and distortion (11.30): (b) selected triangles; (c) rendered view.

are shown in Fig. 11.19, namely the triangles selection according to (11.30) is shown in Fig. 11.19(b) and the result of the wavelet fusion with $D = 3$ is shown in Fig. 11.19(c). Such results should be compared with those of Fig. 11.18(d) and Fig. 11.18(e), respectively. The triangle selection of Fig. 11.19(b) shows an increase in the number of green and blue triangles with respect to Fig. 11.18(d). Purple triangles are chosen when no other source is available or when the image Fig. 11.19(a) is still the best source, in spite of its quality. The quality of the rendering of Fig. 11.19(c) is lower than that of Fig. 11.18(e), but is still of good quality.

(a) (b)

Fig. 11.20 (a) V^1 (good quality); (b) V^2 (poor quality).

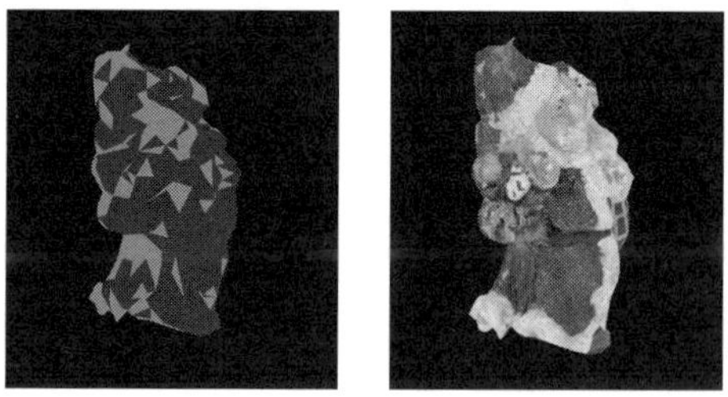

(a) (b)

Fig. 11.21 Stitching from V^1 and V^2: (a) selected triangles; (b) rendered view V^*.

The impact of image quality on the choice of the triangles is more evident if the points of view of V^i are close, since in this case the orientations of the triangles with respect to V^* are rather similar and there is a large number of triangles essentially offering the same information. Triangle selection in this case can exploit image quality. Let us assume that the client has available the two images V^1 and V^2 as shown in Fig. 11.20, of which V^2 has a much lower quality than V^1.

Figure 11.21(a) and Fig. 11.21(b) show the choice of triangles according to (11.30) and the rendered view view V^* (between V^1 and V^2, a little closer to V^2) with $D = 3$. Clearly the majority of the triangles is selected from V^1 (the dark green ones at the right), since it is the best quality view. Some parts were selected from the low quality view: probably the right cheek of Santa Claus comes from V^1 because it is a rather homogeneous region with a small distortion value with respect to the original view.

Finally assume that the client, after some delay, besides V^1 has available a new view $V^{2'}$ shown in Fig. 11.22(a), of quality higher than that of V^2 and

(a) (b) (c)

Fig. 11.22 Stitching from V^1 and $V^{2'}$: (a) $V^{2'}$; (b) selected triangles; (c) rendered view V^*.

comparable with that of V^1. In this case (11.30) leads to an f_{choice} giving the triangle selection and the rendered view V^* shown in Fig. 11.22(b) and Fig. 11.22(c) respectively. As expected, distortion (11.30) in this case takes a large number of triangles from $V^{2'}$ and less triangles from V^1 than in the previous case.

11.8 Summary

This chapter introduced a new framework for the remote visualization of 3D models, for convenience called RV-RD, where the geometry and texture information available at server side is incrementally delivered to the client according to a server policy and the client has its own policy for using the available information for best rendering results. It is important to note that the server and client policies are assumed to be independently optimal, *i.e.*, the server does not need to know what the client does in order to decide what to send; and the client, independently of what the server does, uses at best the information it has available.

The contribution of this chapter besides the overall RV-RD scenario is the presentation of a client policy based on a distortion measure accounting for the possible limited quality of the images and the possible errors in the geometry available at the client. The proposed client policy rests on strong theoretical considerations and the experimental performance confirms the expectations.

It may be worth observing that the client policy is the reasonable starting point for the implementation of an RV-RD system, since this is what directly controls the visualization quality. The implementation of a RV-RD system requires an effective server policy which can be supported by any reasonable scheme for transmitting the information available at the server.

Our current research explores server policy with the fundamental issues related to how the server should distribute available transmission resources amongst the various original view images and geometry informations needed by the client to render a new view. Included in this question is whether the server should transmit elements from an entirely new original view image, which is more closely aligned with the requested view, rather than refining nearby original view images of which the client already has a low resolution version. It is appropriate to relate such issues to more general considerations concerning sampling and quantization of the plenoptic function to which they are deeply connected.

As pointed out in the introduction, the RV-RD system approach offers a new intriguing conceptual environment for addressing basic fundamental questions about the visual impact of geometry and texture as well as practical solutions enabling the remote visualization of 3D models.

References

Cheng, I. and Basu, A. (2004). Reliability and judging fatigue reduction in 3d perceptual quality, in *The 3rd International Symposium on 3DPVT* (IEEE).

D. Taubman and R. Prandolini (2003). Architecture, philosophy and performance of JPIP: internet protocol standard for JPEG 2000, in *Int. Symp. Visual Comm. and Image Proc.*, Vol. 5150 (IEEE), pp. 649–663.

Foley, J. D., van Dam, A., Feiner, S. K. and Hughes, J. F. (1995). *Computer Graphics Principles and Practice* (Addison-Wesley).

Garland, M. and Heckbert, P. (1997). Surface simplification using quadric error metrics, URL `sherry.ifi.unizh.ch/garland97surface.html`.

Guskov, I., Sweldens, W. and Schröder, P. (1999). Multiresolution signal processing for meshes, *Computer Graphics Proceedings (SIGGRAPH 99)*, pp. 325–334.

Hartley, R. and Zisserman, A. (2000). *Multiple View Geometry in Computer Vision* (Cambridge University Press, Cambridge, United Kingdom).

Hoppe, H. (1996). Progressive meshes, *Computer Graphics* **30**, Annual Conference Series, pp. 99–108, URL `citeseer.csail.mit.edu/hoppe96progressive.html`.

Koller, D., Turitzin, M., Levoy, M., Tarini, M., Croccia, G., Cignoni, P. and Scopigno, R. (2004). Protected interactive 3d graphics via remote renderin, in *proc. SIGGRAPH 2004* (IEEE).

Levoy, M. (1995). Polygon-Assisted JPEG and MPEG compression of synthetic images, in *Proceedings of SIG-GRAPH Computer Graphics Proceedings, Annual Conference Series*, pp. 21–28.

Rusinkiewicz, S. and Levoy, M. (2000). QSplat: A multiresolution point rendering system for large meshes, in K. Akeley (ed.), *Siggraph 2000, Computer Graphics Proceedings* (ACM Press/ACM SIGGRAPH/ Addison Wesley Longman), pp. 343–352, URL `citeseer.csail.mit.edu/rusinkiewicz00qsplat.html`.

Schroeder, W. J., Zarge, J. A. and Lorensen, W. E. (1992). Decimation of triangle meshes, *Computer Graphics (SIGGRAPH '92 Proc.)* **26**, 2, pp. 65–70.

Taubman, D. and Secker, A. (2003). Highly scalable video compression with scalable motion coding, *Proceedings of International Conference on Image Processing* **3**, 3, pp. 273–276 v.2.

Taubman, D. S. and Marcellin, M. W. (2002). *JPEG2000 Image compression fundamentals, standards and practice* (Kluwer Academic Publisher, Cambridge, United Kingdom).

Zanuttigh, P., Brusco, N., Taubman, D. and Cortelazzo, G. (2005). Greedy nonlinear optimization of the plenoptic function for interactive transmission of 3d scenes, *International Conference of Image Processing ICIP2005, Genova.*

Chapter 12

3D Content Creation by Passive Optical Methods

L. Ballan, N. Brusco and G. M. Cortelazzo

12.1 Introduction

The possibility of obtaining 3D models, *i.e.*, mathematical descriptions of real objects or scenes has paved the way to a wide range of new and exciting applications in fields such as virtual simulation, human-computer interaction (HCI), scientific visualization, cultural heritage documentation, medicine, industrial prototyping, reverse engineering, entertainment (movies and video games), web-based commerce and marketing, just to name a few.

The construction of the 3D model of a real object or scene by optical sensors, also referred to as *3D modeling pipeline*, essentially consists of four steps: 1) data acquisition, 2) calibration, 3) reconstruction, and 4) model editing. Any optical sensing device used to collect data can only capture the surface front side and not what is occluded by it. Therefore, a full model must be built from a number of images covering the entire object (data acquisition). In order to perform 3D reconstruction, the camera's parameters must be estimated by a procedure called calibration. Such information can also be obtained from the acquired images if they represent some common regions (by a procedure which is typically called self-calibration). Reconstruction is then performed and the resulting model is stored in an efficient description such as polygonal meshes, implicit surfaces, depth maps or volumetric descriptions. In practical situations, reconstruction may lead to models with some imperfections; thus, a further repairing step is recommend (model editing) [Davis *et al.* (2002); Levoy *et al.* (2000)].

Optical 3D reconstruction methods can be classified into passive or active methods based on the type of sensors used in the acquisition process. Passive sensing refers to the measurement of the visible radiation which is already present in the scene; active sensing refers instead, to the projection of structured light patterns into the scene to scan. Active sensing facilitates the computation of 3D structure by intrinsically solving the correspondence problem which is one of the major issues with some passive techniques. For a detailed description of the operations of the 3D modeling pipeline by active sensing see [Rushmeier and Bernardini (2002); Rioux *et al.* (2000)]. In general, active techniques such as those based on laser scanning tend to be more expensive and slower than their passive counterparts. However, the best active methods generally produce more accurate 3D reconstructions than those obtained by any passive technique.

Passive optical methods, as previously mentioned, do not need auxiliary light sources. In this case, the light reflected by the surface of the object comes from natural sources, that is, sources whose characteristics are generally unknown and in most cases, not controllable by the acquisition process. Furthermore, passive methods do not interact in any way with the observed object, not even with irradiation. Passive reconstruction, in principle, can use any kind of pictures, *i.e.*, it does not need pictures taken for 3D reconstruction purposes (even holiday photographs could be used). Passive methods are more robust than their active counterparts, can capture a wider range of objects, can be obtained by inexpensive hardware (such as a simple digital camera) and are characterized by fast acquisition times. Such features are the reason for the attention they received and they continue to receive. Their drawbacks concern accuracy and computational costs. Indeed, passive reconstruction algorithms are complex and time-consuming. Moreover, since their acquisition scenarios are often far from the ideal conditions, noise level is typically much higher than that of active methods which tend to guarantee optimal conditions.

Passive optical methods are classified by the types of visual cues used for 3D reconstruction. For this reasons, they are also called *"Shape from X"* (SfX) techniques, where X stands for the cue or the cues used to infer shape. Methods which deal with one single type of visual cue are called monomodal whereas methods jointly exploiting information of different types are called multimodal. The simultaneous use of different cues, in principle, is clearly more powerful than the use of a single one; however, this poses the challenge of how to synergistically fuse different information avoiding mutual conflicts.

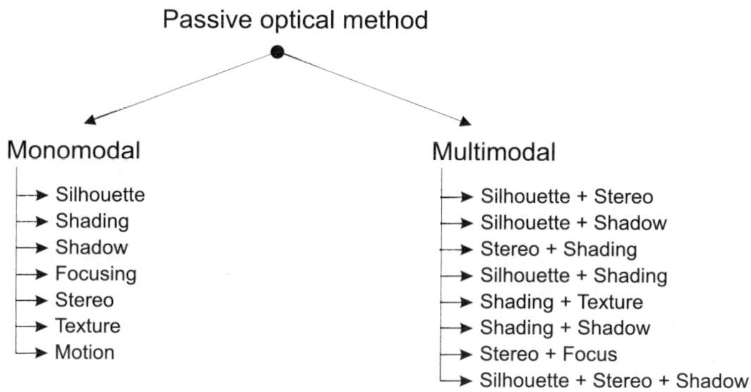

Fig. 12.1 Overview of existing passive optical methods.

Figure 12.1 proposes a taxonomy of the passive optical methods. Typical information used for reconstruction are:

- Silhouette or apparent contour;
- Shading;
- Shadow;
- Focusing;
- Pictures differences, *i.e.*, stereo information;
- Texture;
- Motion;

This chapter reviews 3D reconstruction by passive optical methods. This is not an easy task in light of the broad scope of the topic. The spirit we adopted is to give a conceptual outline of the field, referring the reader to the literature for details. We also reserve special attention to recent methods. Section 12.2 introduces basic concepts and terminology about the image formation process. Section 12.3 reviews major monomodal methods: shape from silhouette, shape from shading, shape from shadows, shape from focus/defocus and shape from stereo. In Section 12.4 we introduce a framework for multimodal methods, focusing on the deformable model technique. Finally, Section 12.5 draws the conclusions.

12.2 Basic Notation and Calibrated Images

A calibrated image is an image for which all the parameters of the camera used to take it are known. Formally, a calibrated image is an ordered pair

(I, ζ) where I is an image and ζ is an image formation function $\Re^3 \rightarrow \Re^2$ that maps the points from the physical 3D world to the image plane. An image is a function from a rectangular subset of $\Re^2$ representing the image space coordinates to an interval of $\Re$ representing the image intensity values. In this section, the image formation process is approximated using the ideal pinhole camera model (see Fig. 12.2) with lens distortion. This means that neither the effects due to finite aperture nor other types of lens aberrations are considered. In this case, ζ can be expressed as the combination of two functions, namely

$$\zeta = \phi \circ V \tag{12.1}$$

where $\phi : \Re^2 \rightarrow \Re^2$ is a nonlinear bijection representing the camera lens distortion and V is a function $\Re^3 \rightarrow \Re^2$, called *view*, incorporating both the pinhole model and the camera point of view information. Function V is a combination of two further functions, *i.e.*, $V = \pi \circ T$. Function π is the pinhole perspective projection[1] simply defined as $\pi(x, y, z) = \left(\frac{x}{z}, \frac{y}{z}\right)$ for all point $P = (x, y, z)$ in $\Re^3$ with $z > 0$. Function $T : \Re^3 \rightarrow \Re^3$ is an affine bijective transformation which performs 3D coordinates transformation from the world space to the camera space. Let us note that, given a calibrated image (I, ζ), one can always find its non-distorted version $(I \circ \phi, V)$ by estimating camera lens distortion parameters ϕ from image I. This is a classical inverse problem for which a vast literature is available. Popular methods are due to [Tsai (1987)] which estimates ϕ using known calibration patterns and to [Prescott and McLean (1997)] which use the knowledge that the image represents straight lines of the scene.

Projective Geometry is a powerful framework for describing the image formation process, not adopted in this chapter for reasons of simplicity. Interested readers are referred to [Hartley and Zisserman (2000)] for an excellent introduction.

By definition, transformation T can be written as

$$T(P) = M \cdot P + O \tag{12.2}$$

where M is an invertible 3×3 matrix and $O, P \in \Re^3$. Furthermore, M and O form to the so-called projection matrix K, a 3×4 matrix defined as follows

$$K = \begin{bmatrix} M & O \end{bmatrix} \tag{12.3}$$

[1]This model was first proposed by Brunelleschi at the beginning of the 15th century.

Projection matrix K is related to the physical model of the ideal pinhole camera and can be decomposed according to the following scheme

$$K = I \times \begin{bmatrix} 1 & 0 & 0 & 0 \\ 0 & 1 & 0 & 0 \\ 0 & 0 & 1 & 0 \end{bmatrix} \times E \tag{12.4}$$

where I is the intrinsic matrix, depending on the so-called intrinsic parameters only due to the camera internal characteristics, and E is the extrinsic matrix, depending on the so-called extrinsic parameters only due to the camera position and orientation in the space. Namely, matrix I is defined as follows

$$I = \begin{bmatrix} \dfrac{f}{p_x} & \dfrac{(\tan\alpha)f}{p_y} & c_x \\ 0 & \dfrac{f}{p_y} & c_y \\ 0 & 0 & 1 \end{bmatrix} \tag{12.5}$$

where f (expressed in millimeters) is the camera focal length, that is the distance between the sensor surface (also known as retinal plane or image plane) and pinhole C (also known as center of projection); p_x, p_y respectively are the width and the height in millimeters of a single pixel on the retinal plane; α is the skew angle, measuring how much the image axes x and y are away from orthogonality; $c = (c_x, c_y, 1)$ is the principal point of the camera, *i.e.*, the point at which the optical axis intersects the retinal plane. We recall that the optical axis is the line, orthogonal to the retinal plane, passing through the center of projection C. Another useful parameter is the camera field-of-view along the y axis defined as

$$FOV_y = 2\mathrm{arctan}\left(\frac{p_y\, N_y}{2f}\right) \tag{12.6}$$

where N_y is the vertical resolution of the sensor. Figure 12.2(above) shows the ideal pinhole camera. Rays of light pass through the pinhole and form an inverted image of the object on the sensor plane. Figure 12.2(below) shows an equivalent pinhole model where the image plane is placed in front of the center of projection obtaining a non-inverted image.

Matrix E is defined as

$$E = \begin{bmatrix} R & t^T \\ 0 & 1 \end{bmatrix} \tag{12.7}$$

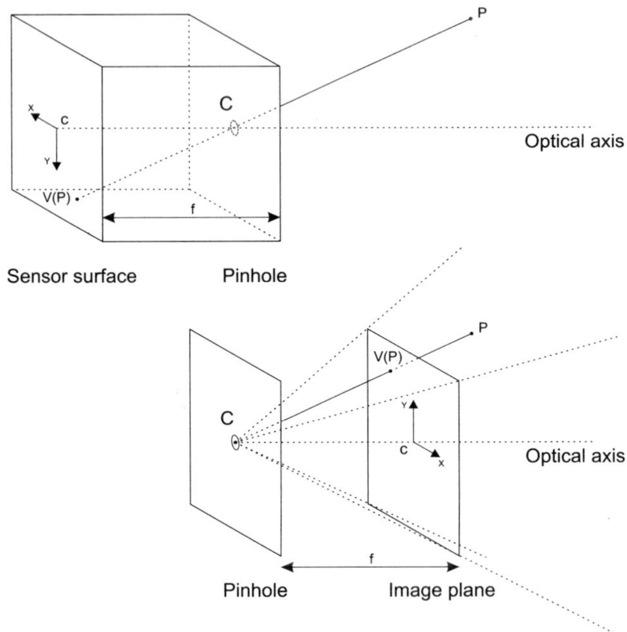

Fig. 12.2 Ideal pinhole camera (above) and its equivalent model (below) where the image plane is placed in front of the center of projection.

where R is 3×3 rotation matrix and t is a vector belonging to $\Re^3$. For example, given a camera with center of projection C, optical axis D and *up-vector* U (that is the y axis of the camera reference system), the relative extrinsic matrix is:

$$E = \begin{bmatrix} B^{-1} & -B^{-1}C^T \\ 0 & 1 \end{bmatrix} \tag{12.8}$$

where:

$$B = \left[(U \times D)^T \;\; U^T \;\; D^T \right] \tag{12.9}$$

The center of projection $C = (X_c, Y_c, Z_c)$ can be obtained from the columns of projection matrix $K = \left[k1\ k2\ k3\ k4 \right]$ as follows

$$X_c = \frac{\det\left(\left[k2\ k3\ k4\right]\right)}{Q} \tag{12.10}$$

$$Y_c = -\frac{\det\left(\left[k1\ k3\ k4\right]\right)}{Q} \tag{12.11}$$

$$Z_c = \frac{\det\left(\left[k1\ k2\ k4\right]\right)}{Q} \tag{12.12}$$

where:

$$Q = -\det\left(\left[k1\ k2\ k3\right]\right) \tag{12.13}$$

In order to extract 3D information from a set of images, the related view functions must be estimated for each image of this set. This can be done in two ways: conventional calibration or self-calibration. The first approach uses pictures imaging a known target object such as a planar checkerboard. In this case, function V can be estimated by solving an over-constrained linear system [Hartley and Zisserman (2000)]. Self-calibration instead, computes the view functions associated to a set of un-calibrated images without any information about the scene or any object in it. These methods, see for instance [Mendoca and Cipolla (1999)], essentially extract relevant features from two or more images then, find the matching between them and finally, proceed like conventional calibration methods.

12.3 Monomodal Methods

This section introduces the most common monomodal methods namely, the methods using silhouette, shading, shadow, focus and stereo as 3D reconstruction information. Texture and motion are excluded from this analysis, however the interested reader is referred to [Forsyth (2002)] and [Jebara *et al.* (1999)] for an example of these two techniques.

12.3.1 *Silhouette*

Algorithms which reconstruct 3D objects using only silhouette information extracted from a set of images are called *"Shape from Silhouette"* methods. They were first proposed in [Baumgart (1974)] and afterwards formalized in [Laurentini (1994)], where the concept of *visual hull* was first introduced.

All these methods must face the problem of extracting silhouette information from the set of images. In other words, in each picture, they must identify the points belonging to the object to be acquired with respect to the background. This problem does not have a general solution as it strongly depends on the scene characteristics. The most common approaches to this task are chroma keying (*e.g.*, blue screen matting [Chuang *et al.* (2001)]), background subtraction [Piccardi (2004)], clustering [Potmesil (1990)] and

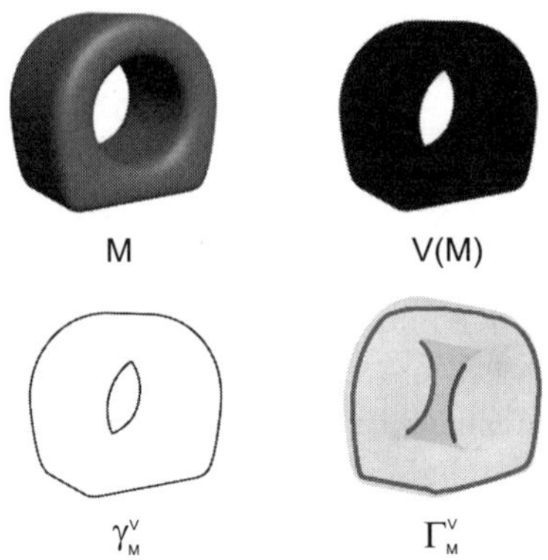

Fig. 12.3 M is a 3D object. $V(M)$ represents the silhouette of M, γ_M^V its apparent contour and Γ_M^V its 3D contour. In the figure, Γ_M^V is slightly rotated with respect to the point of view of the other three pictures in order to evidence that Γ_M^V is a set of not necessarily closed 3D curves.

many other segmentation techniques. For a comprehensive account see [Lucchese and Mitra (2001)]. However, silhouette information is affected by two types of error. The first one is the quantization error due to image resolution and it is directly proportional to the camera-object distance z as

$$\varepsilon_x = \frac{p_x}{2f} z, \quad \varepsilon_y = \frac{p_y}{2f} z \tag{12.14}$$

The second one depends on the specific silhouette extraction method and its amount is usually confined within ± 1 pixel.

In order to recall the concept of visual hull, some definitions related to the notion of contour may be useful. Given a view V and a closed surface M in $\Re^3$, let us denote by $V(M)$ the projection (or the *silhouette*) of M on the image plane of V, *i.e.*, the shape of M viewed by V, and by

$$\gamma_M^V = \partial V(M) \tag{12.15}$$

the *apparent contour* of M viewed by V, and by

$$\Gamma_M^V = V^{-1}\left(\gamma_M^V\right) \tag{12.16}$$

the *3D contour* of M viewed by V.

By definition $V(M)$ is a set of points in $\Re^2$ and its boundary γ_M^V is a set of curves in $\Re^2$ which do not intersect each other. As we can easily see with the aid of Fig. 12.3, neither $V(M)$ nor γ_M^V are generally regular.

Indeed, it is likely that they have some singularities. On the contrary, Γ_M^V is a set of not necessarily closed curves in $\Re^3$, with points belonging to M.

Shape from silhouette methods use $V(M)$ as source of information. However, there exists a class of methods, called *"Shape from Contour"* [Cipolla and P.Giblin (2000)], that use the apparent contour γ_M^V instead of $V(M)$ in order to infer shape.

The concept of *visual hull* [Laurentini (1994)] is a fundamental definition for the shape from silhouette methods.

Definition 12.1. Given a set of views $R = (V_1, \ldots, V_n)$ and a closed surface M in $\Re^3$, the visual hull of M with respect to R, denoted as $vh(M, R)$, is the set of points of $\Re^3$ such that $P \in vh(M, R)$ if and only if for every view $V_i \in R$, the half-line starting from the center of projection of V_i and passing through P, contains at least one point of M.

In other words, the visual hull of a surface M related to a set of views R is the set of all points in the 3D space which are classified as belonging to the object for every view $V_i \in R$. Laurentini proved that the boundary of the visual hull $\partial vh(M, R)$ is the best approximation of M that can be obtained using only silhouette information coming from the projections of M in each view of R. Some implications of this result follow:

- the visual hull always includes the original surface, *i.e.*, $M \subseteq vh(M, R)$, or in other words, the visual hull is an upper-bound of the original object;
- $\partial vh(M, R)$ and M have the same projections in R, in other words for every $V \in R$, we have:

$$V(M) = V(\partial vh(M, R)) \tag{12.17}$$

- If $R_1 \subseteq R_2$ then $vh(M, R_2) \subseteq vh(M, R_1)$
- $vh(M, R) = \bigcap_{V \in R} vh(M, \{V\})$

The last property suggests a method for computing the visual hull as the intersection of the visual cones $vh(M, \{V\})$ generated by M for every view $V \in R$ (see Fig. 12.4). A visual cone $vh(M, \{V\})$ is formed by all the half-lines starting from the center of projection of V and intersecting the projection of M on the image plane of V.

All shape from silhouette methods are based on the above principle. They can be classified by the way the visual hull is internally represented, namely by voxels or by polyhedra. The former class, called *"Volume Carving"* algorithms [Potmesil (1987)], was the first to be proposed. The idea

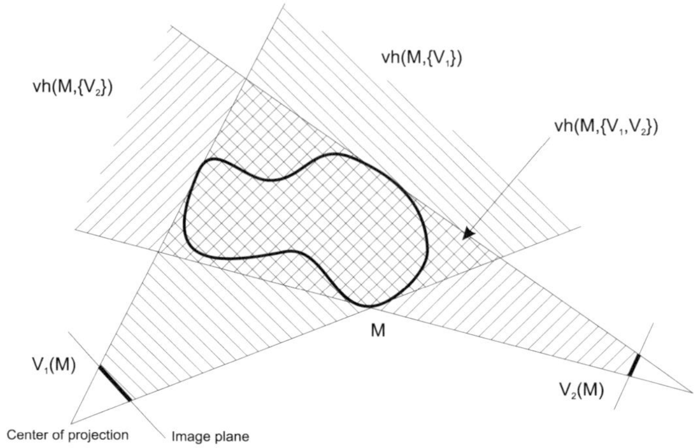

Fig. 12.4 Computation of the visual hull as intersection of the visual cones generated by V_1 and V_2.

behind it is to divide space into cubic elements of various sizes, called *voxels*, in order to store volume information of the reconstructed object. The latter class of algorithms, recently formulated in [Matusik *et al.* (2001)], represents the boundary of the reconstructed visual hull by polygonal meshes. They are proposed for real-time applications aimed at acquiring, transmitting and rendering dynamic geometry. Indeed, polyhedral visual hull can be rapidly computed and rendered using the projective texture mapping feature of modern graphics cards [Li *et al.* (2003)]. Besides, polyhedral representations give exact estimations of the visual hulls avoiding the quantization and the aliasing artifacts typical of the voxel approach. However, voxel representations are preferred when the result of shape from silhouette is used as first approximation to be refined by other reconstruction algorithms such as shadow carving (see Section 12.3.3) and some multimodal methods (see Section 12.4).

For this reason the remaining of this section focuses on the volume carving algorithms. In this case, the 3D space is divided into voxels which can bear three types of relationship with respect to the visual hull: "belong", "partially belong" or "not belong". In order to verify such characteristics one must check if a voxel completely belongs to every visual cone[2]. In this case the voxel belongs to the visual hull of M. Otherwise, if the voxel is

[2]Observe that, since voxels are cubes, one can determine whether all their points belong to a visual cone only by checking the eight vertices of the cube.

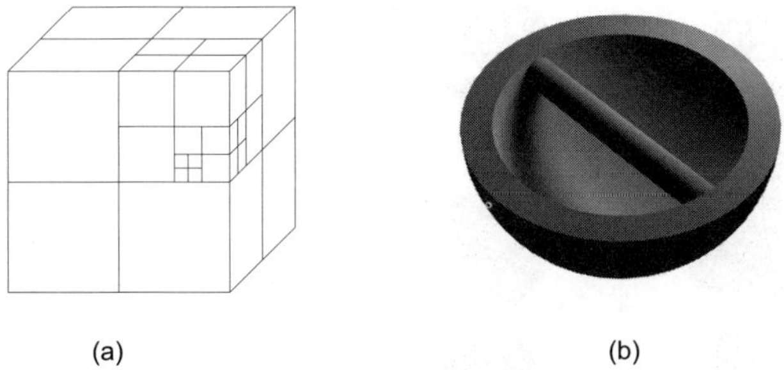

Fig. 12.5 (a) Space subdivision by an octree. (b) Example of surface M for which its external visual hull has genus lower than the genus of M. The visual hull cannot completely describe the topology of this surface.

completely outside at least one visual cone, then it does not belong to the visual hull. In any other case, the voxel partially belongs and one must further subdivide it and repeat the check with respect to its sub-voxels until the desired resolution is reached.

Data structures like *octrees* [de Berg *et al.* (1999)] allow for a fast space subdivision and reduce the memory requirements. An octree is a tree where each internal node has 8 children. Every node j is associated with a cube B such that the set of the cubes associated to each child of j is an equipartition of B. The root of the tree represents the whole space under analysis, which is divided into 8 cubes of equal size as shown in Fig. 12.5(a). Each of these cubes can be again subdivided into 8 further cubes or alternatively be a leaf of the tree. The possibility of arbitrarily stopping the subdivision is the key characteristic of octrees. In fact, octrees can optimize memory requirements since they allow to describe volumes by a multi-resolution grid where detailed regions are described at resolutions higher than those in uniform regions.

Finally, in order to find a polygonal mesh representation of the boundary of the estimated volume, one may resort to the *"marching cubes"* algorithm [Cline and Lorensen (1987)]. Figure 12.6 shows an example of a model obtained by a volume carving algorithm.

Let us observe that given the set of all possible views whose centers of projection are outside the convex hull of M, the relative visual hull, called $vh_{\infty}(M)$, is in general not equal to M. In fact, $vh_{\infty}(M)$ cannot describe the concave regions of M which are not visible from viewpoints outside the convex hull of M. As a consequence, in general, the visual hull cannot completely capture the topology of a surface. $vh_{\infty}(M)$ is called the external

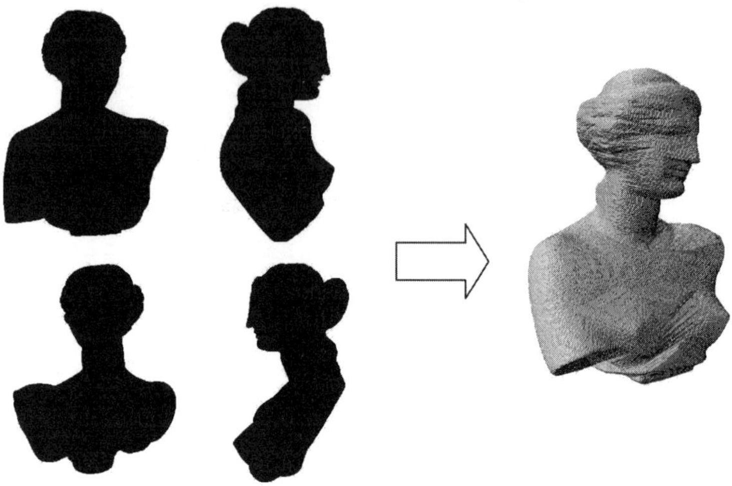

Fig. 12.6 Model obtained by volume carving algorithm.

visual hull and it is a subset of the convex hull of M. Figure 12.5(b) shows an object for which its external visual hull has genus lower than that of the original surface.

In conclusion, shape from silhouette algorithms are fast and robust but can only reconstruct a small set of objects, *i.e.*, those objects the visual hulls of which, related to the available views, are similar to their surfaces.

12.3.2 *Shading*

Shading information is used in both photometric stereo and shape from shading algorithms. The former operates with a series of pictures of the object taken under different lighting conditions. The latter instead, recovers the surface shape from the brightness of a single picture.

Both methods rest on approximations of the reflectance characteristics of the object to be reconstructed, that are the relationships between incoming illumination to a point on the surface and the light reflected by it. For this reason, it may be useful to recall some radiometric definitions.

Light power is the amount of light energy per unit time, measured in Watt $[W]$. The *outgoing radiance* at surface point P in the direction $\omega_o = (\theta_o, \phi_o)$ (where θ_o and ϕ_o are the two angles defining direction ω_o) is the light power per unit area perpendicular to ω_o emitted at P in the unit solid angle of direction ω_o. Such a radiance is denoted as $L_o(P, \omega_o)$ where the subscript o denotes that it is an outgoing radiance. It is measured in $[W][m]^{-2}[sr]^{-1}$, where *Steradian* [sr] is the unit of solid angle. On the other hand, the *incoming radiance* $L_i(P, \omega_i)$ at surface point P in direction $\omega_i = (\theta_i, \phi_i)$ is the incident light power at P per unit area perpendicular to ω_i in the unit solid angle of direction ω_i. Note that, if the surface normal at P forms an angle β with respect to direction ω_i, the infinitesimal area dA centered at P seen from the direction ω_i is $dA\cos(\beta)$. Therefore, the incoming light power per unit area contributed to P by the light sources through the infinitesimal solid angle $d\omega$ of direction ω_i, is $L_i(P, \omega_i)\cos(\beta)\,d\omega$. This quantity is called *incident irradiance* at surface point P in the direction ω_i and it is measured in $[W][m]^{-2}$.

The *bidirectional reflectance distribution function* (BRDF) was introduced in [Nicodemus (1970)] as a unified notation of reflectance in terms of incident and reflected beam geometry. It is defined as the ratio between the outgoing radiance at surface point P in the direction ω_o and the incident irradiance at P in the direction ω_i, *i.e.*,

$$f_r(P, \omega_o, \omega_i) = \frac{L_o(P, \omega_o)}{L_i(P, \omega_i)\cos(\beta)\,d\omega} \tag{12.18}$$

and it is measured in $[sr]^{-1}$.

The actual BRDF of an object is usually a very complex function and it is difficult to estimate in practical situations, therefore a number of approximations are used instead. For example, *Lambertian* (or ideal diffuse) surfaces, *i.e.*, surfaces that reflect light equally in all directions, lead to a strong simplification namely, they have a constant BRDF

$$f_r(P, \omega_o, \omega_i) = \rho(P) \tag{12.19}$$

where ρ is called the *albedo* or the diffuse reflectance of the object. Models for partially specular surfaces were developed by Torrance-Sparrow [Torrance and Sparrow (1967)], Phong [Phong (1975)] and Blinn [Blinn (1977)]. The last two models are widely used in computer graphics.

The algorithms described in this section consider only Lambertian surfaces and local shading models; thus, neither specularity nor interreflections are considered. However, state of the art of photometric stereo and shape from shading algorithms make use of more general BRDF models such as the simplified Torrance-Sparrow model used in [Healey and Binford (1988)].

Some definitions used in both types of algorithms are in order. Let M be the unknown surface in $\Re^3$ and let $I(x, y)$ be the image intensity seen by a view V. If the surface point $P \in M$ is visible from the viewpoint V then $I(V(P))$ is its brightness. Clearly, $I(V(P))$ is proportional to the outgoing radiance leaving P in direction of the center of projection of V. Therefore, for Lambertian objects illuminated by a single point light source, one can write

$$L_o(P, \omega_o) = \rho(P) L_i(P, \omega_i) \cos(\beta) \tag{12.20}$$

thus,

$$I(V(P)) = \rho(P) l(P) L(P) \cdot N(P) \tag{12.21}$$

where $l(P)$ and $L(P)$ are respectively, intensity and direction of the incident light at P, $\rho(P)$ is the surface albedo at P and $N(P)$ is the surface normal.

12.3.2.1 *Photometric Stereo*

Photometric stereo was first introduced in [Woodham (1980)]. Given a set of calibrated images $(I_1, V), \ldots, (I_n, V)$ taken from the same point of view V but under different lightings $L_1, \ldots, L_n$, one can estimate surface normal $N(P)$ for every visible point of M. Let

$$\mathbf{I}(x, y) = [I_1(x, y), \ldots, I_n(x, y)] \tag{12.22}$$

be the vector of all measured brightness at image point $(x, y) = V(P)$, for any visible point P of M, and let

$$\mathbf{L}(x, y) = \begin{bmatrix} l_1(P) L_1(P) \\ \vdots \\ l_n(P) L_n(P) \end{bmatrix} \tag{12.23}$$

be the matrix of all light directions and intensities incident at P. From Equation (12.21), one may write

$$\mathbf{I}^T(x, y) = \rho(P) \mathbf{L}(x, y) \times N^T(P) \tag{12.24}$$

which is a linear system of n equations in the three unknowns $\rho(P) N(P)$ [3]. Equation (12.24) has a unique solution when $n > 3$ and it can be solved using least square methods.

---

[3] $\rho(P) N(P)$ has only three degrees of freedom because $N(P)$ is assumed to be normalized.

Once the values of $\rho(P)\,N(P)$ are available for each visible point P, one can extract the surface albedo and the normal at P using $\rho(P) = \|\rho(P)\,N(P)\|$ and $N(P) = \rho(P)\,N(P) / \|\rho(P)\,N(P)\|$ respectively. Retrieving shape from normals is trivial under the assumption that the view V performs an orthographic projection. Indeed, let us represent M by a Monge patch description, *i.e.*,

$$M = \{(x, y, z(x, y)) \mid \forall (x, y)\} \tag{12.25}$$

where $z(x, y)$ is the surface depth at (x, y). Consequently, the surface normal at $P = V^{-1}(x, y) = (x, y, z(x, y))$ is

$$N(P) = \frac{(\partial z_x, \partial z_y, -1)}{\sqrt{1 + \partial z_x^2 + \partial z_y^2}} \tag{12.26}$$

where $(\partial z_x, \partial z_y)$ are the partial derivatives of $z(x, y)$ with respect to x and y. $(\partial z_x, \partial z_y)$ can be recovered from $N(P) = (N_x(P), N_y(P), N_z(P))$ using the following

$$(\partial z_x, \partial z_y)(P) = \left(-\frac{N_x(P)}{N_z(P)}, -\frac{N_y(P)}{N_z(P)}\right) \tag{12.27}$$

Surface M can be finally reconstructed by integrating a one-form:

$$z(x, y) = z(x_0, y_0) + \int_\gamma (\partial z_x dx + \partial z_y dy) \tag{12.28}$$

where γ is a planar curve starting at (x_0, y_0) and ending at (x, y). $(x_0, y_0, z(x_0, y_0))$ is a generic surface point of known height $z(x_0, y_0)$. Clearly, if $z(x_0, y_0)$ is unknown, the result will be the actual surface up to some constant depth error.

Unfortunately, errors in surface normal measurements can propagate along the curve γ generating unreliable solutions. For this reason, [Vega (1991)] suggests an alternative height recovery method based on local information only. The more general case where V performs a perspective projection is treated in [Tankus and Kiryati (2005)].

12.3.2.2 *Shape from Shading*

Shape from shading algorithm operates only on a single image I, therefore for each image point $(x, y) = V(P)$, we have one equation in three unknowns

$$I(x, y) = \rho(P)\,l(P)\,L(P) \cdot N(P) \tag{12.29}$$

which cannot be solved without imposing additional constraints.

The first attempt to solve Equation (12.29) was done by Horn in his PhD thesis [Horn (1970)]. Since then, many other solution approaches were developed typically classified into: minimization approaches, propagation approaches, local approaches and linear approaches. For an extensive description of all these methods the reader is referred to [Zhang *et al.* (1999)].

In this chapter we only introduce the minimization approach suggested in [Ikeuchi and Horn (1981)]. Ikeuchi and Horn reformulated the solution of Equation (12.29) as the minimization of a cost functional ξ defined as

$$\xi(M) = Bc\,(M) + \lambda \cdot Sc\,(M) \tag{12.30}$$

where $Bc\,(M)$ is the brightness constraint and $Sc\,(M)$ is the smoothness constraint. The former measures the the total brightness error of the reconstructed image compared with the input image, namely

$$Bc\,(M) = \int\int \left(I\,(x,y) - \overline{I}\,(x,y)\right)^2 dxdy \tag{12.31}$$

where $I\,(x,y)$ is the input image and $\overline{I}\,(x,y)$ is the image related to the estimated surface M.

Cost functional $Sc\,(M)$ penalizes non-smooth surfaces, reducing the degrees of freedom of Equation (12.29). It is defined as

$$Sc\,(M) = \int\int \left(\left\| \frac{\partial N}{\partial x}\,(x,y) \right\|^2 + \left\| \frac{\partial N}{\partial y}\,(x,y) \right\|^2 \right) dxdy \tag{12.32}$$

Constant λ controls surface smoothness.

In this formulation, $\rho\,(P)$ is assumed to be known for all $P \in M$ thus, one can add another constraint which imposes normals to be unit. This is what Brooks and Horn did in 1985. The new term was named unit normal constraint and it was defined as follows

$$\int\int \left(1 - \|N\,(x,y)\|^2\right) dxdy \tag{12.33}$$

The numerical solution is typical achieved using gradient descent algorithms on the Euler-Lagrange equation related to Equation (12.30) (see Section 12.4.1 for additional information).

12.3.2.3 *Estimating the Light Source Properties*

It can be proven that both photometric stereo and shape from shading become ill-posed problems if light direction, intensity and surface albedo are unknown. This means that a solution may not be unique and it strongly

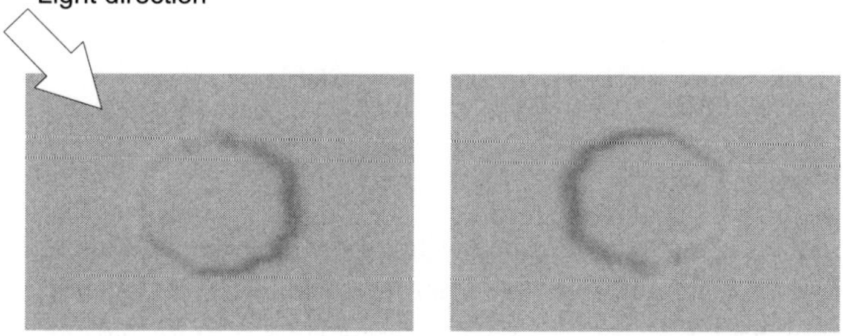

Fig. 12.7 An example of the concave/convex ambiguity: it seems that this two images represent two different objects, a concave and a convex one. Nevertheless, the first image is a rotated version of the second one.

depends on these three parameters[4]. The so-called concave/convex ambiguity, occurring when light orientation is unknown, is a clear example of this ill-posed characteristic. The concave/convex ambiguity refers to the fact that, the same image seems to describe two different objects, one concave and the other convex as shown in Fig. 12.7.

More generally, [Belhumeur *et al.* (1997)] showed that a surface $(x, y, z(x, y))$ is indistinguishable from its *"generalized bas-relief"* (GBR) transformation, defined as

$$\overline{z}(x, y) = \lambda z(x, y) + \mu x + \nu y \tag{12.34}$$

if its albedo and the light properties are unknown. More precisely for all possible values of λ, μ and ν there exists an albedo $\overline{\rho}(x, y)$ and a light $\overline{L}$ such that the brightness image related to the depth map $\overline{z}$ is equal to the one related to z. Moreover, Belhumeur *et al.* showed that even if self-shadow information is used in addition to shading, the two surfaces $\overline{z}$ and z remain indistinguishable.

Two interesting methods to estimate light direction are due to [Koenderink and Pont (2003)] and [Vogiatzis *et al.* (2005a)]. The former recovers the azimuthal angle of the light sources from a single image using texture information. The limit of this approach is the assumption that the textured surface has to be an isotropic gaussian random rough surface with constant albedo.

Instead, [Vogiatzis *et al.* (2005a)] use the brightness values of the contour points of the imaged object in order to estimate light direction by

[4]If we suppose Lambertian surfaces, $\rho(P)$ an $l(P)$ can be grouped together thus, we have only three degrees of freedom.

Equation (12.21). Indeed in such points, surface normals can be retrieved knowing that they are perpendicular to the viewing ray connecting these points to the center of projection of the camera.

12.3.3 *Shadows*

Scene shadows bear a lot of information about the shape of the existing objects. They can give information when no other sources do, indeed shadow regions represent the absence of any other type of information. Methods which exploit this particular visual cue are called either *"Shape form Shadows"* or *"Shape from Darkness"*. They first appear in [Shafer and Kanade (1983)] where shadows were used to relate the orientations of two surfaces. Subsequent works on shadows generally used either the shape of the object casting the shadow in order to constrain the shape of the object being shadowed or vice versa. Indeed, one can infer the shape of an unknown object from the shadows casted on it by a known one. This is the same principle used in structured light projectors with the only difference that the methods based on shadow information use shadow patterns instead of light patterns. The interested reader is sent to [Bouguet and Perona (1999)] for the description of a low cost scanner based on this principle. On the contrary, if an unknown object casts shadows on a known one, for simplicity, let it be a plane, one can use an appropriately modified shape from silhouette method in order to reconstruct its shape. This approach is proposed in [Leibe *et al.* (2000)] in order to avoid segmentation problems implicit in shape from silhouettes methods.

However, in general, shape from darkness methods deal only with the shadow that an object casts on itself, the so-called *self-shadow*. In this case, both the object that casts the shadow and the object being shadowed are unknown as they are all parts of the same unknown surface. Nevertheless, self-shadow can reveal a lot of information. Indeed, let us observe the situation depicted in Fig. 12.8(a) where p_1 is first shadow boundary points and p_2 is the last one. Knowing their coordinates, one can obtain an upper bound for the shadowed region, *i.e.*, the line η. In other words, a point in such a region cannot be above line η, otherwise it would be a lighted point. Furthermore, all lighted points at the right of p_1 must be above η otherwise they would be shadowed. Thus, η is also a lower bound for the lighted points. Obviously, same results can be obtained if one knows the coordinates of the light source and the coordinates of one of the points p_1 or p_2.

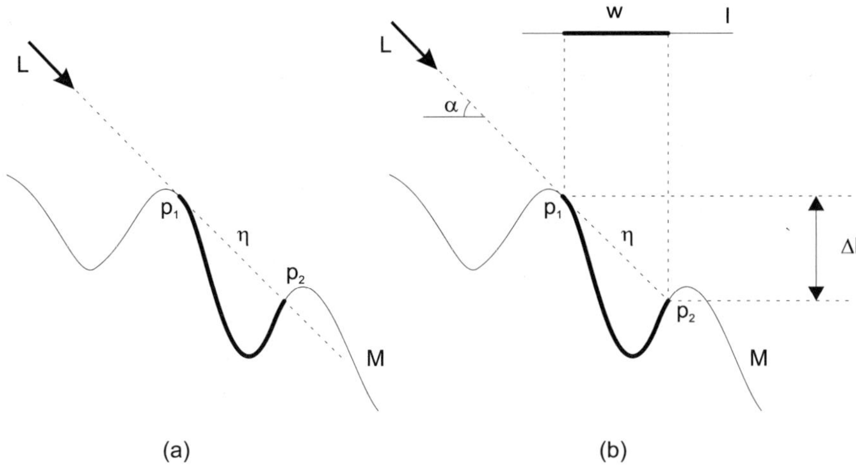

Fig. 12.8 Shadowed surfaces: (a) the coordinates of p_1 and p_2 are assumed to be known; (b) α and w are known.

Figure 12.8(b) shows a situation similar to the previous one but, in this case, it is assumed that the coordinates of p_1 and p_2 are unknown. Moreover, it is supposed that the camera performs an orthographic projection of the scene and that the light source casts parallel rays of known direction α. This can be obtained by placing both the camera and the light source far away from the scene. The measured shadow width w can be used to estimate the relative height between p_1 and p_2 using the following

$$\Delta h = w \tan(\alpha) \tag{12.35}$$

Moreover, if one assumes that the unknown surface M admits a tangent plane in p_1, such a plane must be parallel to η.

From the above considerations, using multiple images taken with different light source positions, one can estimate the unknown surface by constraining a model (*e.g.* a spline) to fit all the extracted information about relative heights and tangent planes (see [Hatzitheodour and Kender (1988)]).

Furthermore, combining equations of type (12.35) together with the linear inequality constraints related to the various η, one can obtain a set of upper/lower bounds and equations which can be solved by *Linear Programming* algorithms as in [Yang (1996)] or by iterative relaxation methods like in [Daum and Dudek (1998)].

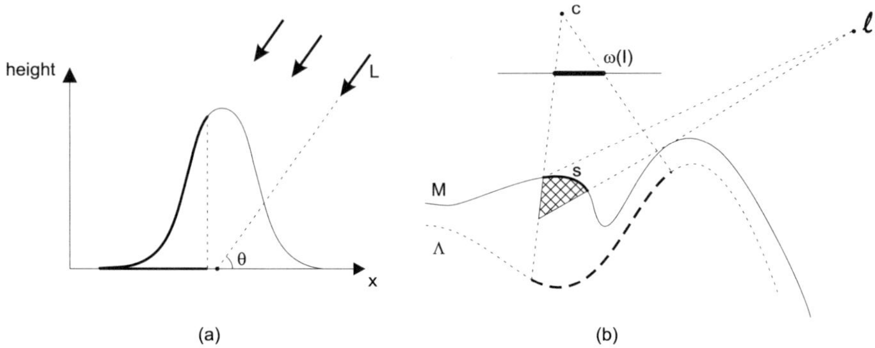

Fig. 12.9 (a) Surface to be reconstructed using the shadowgram technique. (b) Conservative shadow carving.

[Smith and Kender (1986)] introduced the concept of *shadowgram*. Let us suppose the situation depicted in Fig. 12.9(a) where θ is the angle between the x-axis and the light rays. A shadowgram is a binary function $f(x, \theta)$ recording, for each value of θ, a 0 (black) value at the x coordinates of the shadow points and a 1 (white) value at the x coordinates of the lighted points. Therefore, a shadowgram typically looks like two irregular black stripes of variable thickness. Smith and Kender demonstrate that the real surface can be reconstructed from the curves representing the discontinuities of the shadowgram $f(x, \theta)$, *i.e.*, the edges of the dark stripes.

The definition of self-shadow consistency follows. Let us assume first that the scene is only illuminated by a point light source positioned at ℓ. Given an object M, the self-shadow generated on M by the light ℓ is the set of all the points on its surface not visible from ℓ. Let $\Theta(M, \ell)$ denote this set. In other words, a generic point P belongs to $\Theta(M, \ell)$ if and only if the segment joining P and ℓ intersects M in at least one point different from P. Therefore, given a calibrated image (I, V), the shadow region generated by ℓ on M and viewed by V is the set of the V-projections of all the points of $\Theta(M, \ell)$ visible from V. Let $\Omega(M, \ell, V)$ denotes this set; then, formally it is

$$\Omega(M, \ell, V) = V(\Theta(M, \ell) \cap \Pi(M, V)) \tag{12.36}$$

where $\Pi(M, V)$ is the set of all the points of M visible from V. Now, given the image I and the estimated shadow regions on I, call them $\omega(I)$, one can say that M is self-shadow consistent with image I if and only if $\omega(I) \subseteq \Omega(M, \ell, V)$. In other words, it is consistent if V does not see shadow points which are not theoretically generated by M. The contrary is not required, since, as we will describe below in this section, in practical situations, only subsets of $\omega(I)$ can be accurately estimated. In this way, the consistent condition is relaxed making consistent surfaces which are not. However, for correctness, one could also estimate $\overline{\omega(I)}$, *i.e.* the complement of $\omega(I)$, and define that consistency holds when also $\overline{\omega(I)} \subseteq \overline{\Omega(M, \ell, V)}$ holds. Extension to multiple lights is trivial; since, given the set of active lights $(\ell_1, \ldots, \ell_k)$ one can define

$$\Omega(M, L, V) = \bigcup_{\forall \ell_j} \Omega(M, \ell_j, V) \tag{12.37}$$

Besides, consistency for multiple views holds if only if it holds for each singular view. Finally, given an unknown surface Λ and a set of images taken under different lighting conditions, one can build the maximal surface[5] consistent with the extracted shadow information. Let $\Psi(\Lambda)$ denotes this surface, then it is obvious that it contains the actual surface Λ, since Λ is consistent with shadow information.

In [Savarese *et al.* (2007)] a carving approach is proposed to the problem of finding $\Psi(\Lambda)$. The algorithm, called *"Shadow Carving"*, computes first a coarse estimate of the surface using volume carving then it incrementally carves the model removing inconsistencies with self-shadow information. It is known, from Section 12.3.1 that volume carving computes a volume which certainly contains the original object. The subsequent carving based on shadow cue is performed in a conservative way, *i.e.*, in such a way that the carved model will always contain the actual surface Λ.

Given the situation shown in Fig. 12.9(b) where Λ is the actual surface and M is its current estimates. Let (I, V) be a calibrated image, c the center of projection of V and $\omega(I)$ the shadow region on I generated by the light source ℓ. Let us call inconsistent shadow region s, the set of all surface points which are visible from both c and ℓ and such that they project in $\omega(I)$. Savarese *et al.* proved that the cross-hatched area in Fig. 12.9(b) can be removed from M in a conservative way, *i.e.*, obtaining a new estimate that still contains the actual surface Λ.

The major problem of all these algorithms is how to decide whether a surface point P lies on a shadow region or not. This is not a trivial task since it is difficult to distinguish low reflectance points from points in actual shadow regions. The camera only measures radiance coming from some point of the scene. Thus, low radiance measured in a particular direction

[5] A maximal surface for a property Q is the surface which satisfied Q and contains every other surfaces that satisfied Q. In order to avoid degeneration, the maximal surface is typically upper bounded.

can be due to a low reflectance (dark textured) point as well as to insufficient illumination. Moreover, insufficient illumination may be due to light sources too far from the object or to an actual shadow region. In the latter case, one must ensure that the shadow is generated by the object itself and not by other objects in the scene. Using only a single image, there is no way to distinguish between these four cases. Furthermore, even if a shadow region is detected, it difficult to accurately extract its boundaries, because shadows, in general, vanish gradually on the surface. Unfortunately, shadow detection plays an important role in reconstruction since small errors can lead to a totally incorrect reconstruction.

[Savarese *et al.* (2001)] propose a conservative shadow detection method, *i.e.*, a technique which classifies a point as shadow only when it is certain that it is a shadow. The inverse condition is not required so that there can be shadow points classified as non-shadow. Obviously, the more shadow points are detected the more accurate is the reconstruction result. First of all, one must fix a threshold δ which separates light points from dark points. A point P of the surface is *"detectable"* if and only if in at least one picture it appears lighter than δ, otherwise it is *"undetectable"*. This provision ensures that P is not a low reflectance point, but unfortunately, it excludes many points not lighted by the actual light sources. For every image, a point is a shadow point if and only if it is *"detectable"* and it is darker than the threshold δ.

It is finally worth observing that, like shading information, also shadow is subject to the rules of the GBR [Kriegman and Belhumeur (2001)]. Therefore, even if the exact position of the light source is not known, one can reconstruct the observed surface up to a GBR transformation.

12.3.4 *Focus/Defocus*

There are two techniques to infer depth from a set of defocused images, called *"Shape from Focus"* (SfF) and *"Shape from Defocus"* (SfD). The first one, SfF, acquires a large number of images with small focal settings differences. On the other hand, the second one, SfD, needs only few differently focused images, typically two or three, in order to estimate depth information. In both cases, defocused images are obtained by varying settings like the camera or the lens focal length, the aperture radius or the distance between the object to be acquired and the camera. Afterwards, depth is estimated by comparing the blurriness of different regions in the acquired images.

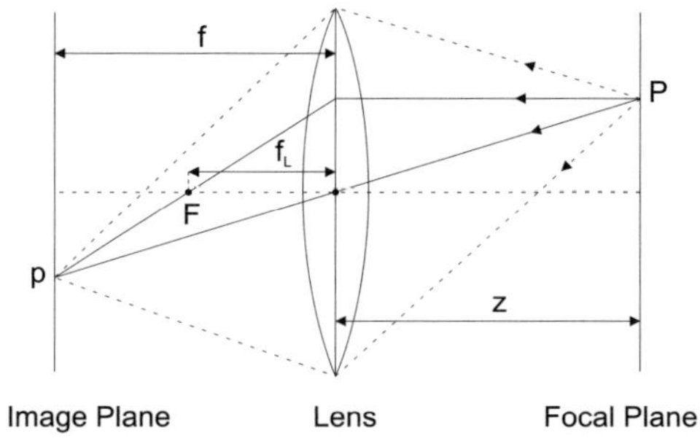

Fig. 12.10 Camera with lens: all the light rays coming from a point P in the focal plane are projected into a single point p in the image plane.

Both methods are based on the assumption that a defocused image is obtained by convolving the focused one with a kernel h_ϕ^s, called *point spread function* (PSF), that depends on the camera optic ϕ as well as on the scene shape s. Such an assumption comes from the observation that, since pinhole cameras with an infinitesimal aperture are not feasible, each point of the image plane is not illuminated by a single light ray but by a cone of light rays subtending a finite solid angle. Consequently, these points appear blurry. This effect can be reduced by a proper use of lenses. Indeed, it is well known that in this case, there exists a plane Π, called the *focal plane*, parallel to the retinal plane, the points of which are all in focus, or in other words, each point of Π projects into a single point of the image plane. The situation is shown in Fig. 12.10, where z is the distance between Π and the center of the lens (the equivalent of the center of projection), f_L is the focal length of the lens and f is the camera focal length defined in Section 12.2. These quantities are related by the *thin lens equation*

$$\frac{1}{z} + \frac{1}{f} = \frac{1}{f_L} \tag{12.38}$$

Figure 12.10 shows that all light rays coming from a point P in the focal plane are projected into a single point p in the image plane. Consequently, an object is perfectly imaged only if it lies exactly on Π, otherwise, it appears blurred. As shown in Fig. 12.11, all the rays coming from a point P'' outside the focal plane are projected to a circular region Θ on the image plane.

The image of P'' can be modeled as the integral of the ideal image, where P'' is correctly imaged, weighted by a function (the PSF) which generates

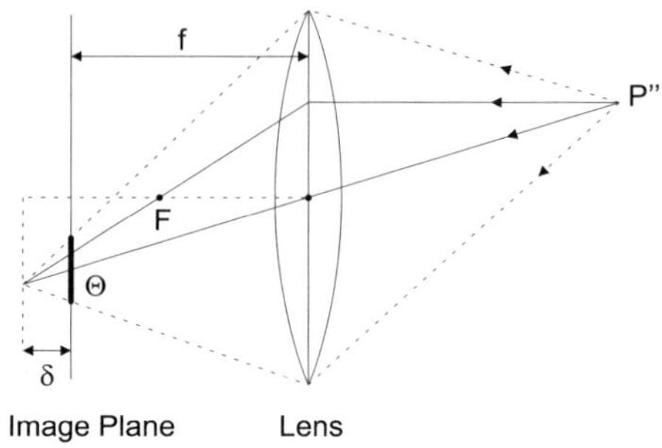

Fig. 12.11 All the light rays coming from a point P'' outside the focal plane are projected to a circular region Θ on the image plane.

the blur effect. Therefore, the relationship between the actual image $\overline{I}$ and the ideal image where all the scene points are correctly imaged I is given by

$$\overline{I}(p) = \int h^s_\phi(p,q)\, I(q)\, dq \tag{12.39}$$

If the surface to be acquired is parallel to the focal plane then the PSF can be assumed to be shift invariant, *i.e.*, $h^s_\phi(p,q) = h^s_\phi(p-q)$ and Equation (12.39) can be rewritten as a convolution

$$\overline{I}(p) = \int h^s_\phi(p-q)\, I(q)\, dq = \left(h^s_\phi * I\right)(p) \tag{12.40}$$

As a first approximation, the blur intensity depends on the radius r of Θ, also known as the blurring radius, which is proportional to the distance δ between the actual image plane and an ideal one where P would be correctly imaged (see Fig. 12.11). More precisely,

$$r = \frac{\delta R}{f} \tag{12.41}$$

where R is the radius of the lens.

As mentioned above, both SfF and SfD estimate depth from Equation (12.40). Namely, SfF identifies the regions of the input images where h^s_ϕ has not been applied, *i.e.*, the in-focus regions. Since h^s_ϕ is a low pass filter, a defocused region appears poor of high spatial frequency. Furthermore, if the surface to be acquired has high spatial frequency content, *i.e.*, for instance it is a rough surface, a focused region can be recognized by analyzing its local Fourier transform.

The typical approach is to filter each input image $\overline{I}$ with a high pass FIR with impulse response ω and to evaluate the level of blur $v(p)$ of each point p as

$$v(p) = \int_{A_\varepsilon(p)} \left(\omega * \overline{I}\right)(q)\, dq \tag{12.42}$$

where $A_\varepsilon(p)$ is a neighborhood of p. Once these values are computed for a set of images $\left(\overline{I_1}, \ldots, \overline{I_n}\right)$, shape can be inferred by the following algorithm:

- Let $v_i(p)$ be the level of blur of the point p of image $\overline{I_i}$.
- Let z_i be the depth of the focus plane related to $\overline{I_i}$.
- For each point p, find j such that $j = \arg\max\{v_j(p)\}$ (*i.e.*, find the image $\overline{I_j}$ with the sharpest representation of p).
- assign to p depth z_j.

For a more precise reconstruction using gaussian interpolation the reader is referred to [Nayar and Nakagawa (1994)].

SfD methods instead, try to invert directly Equation (12.40). The difficulty lies in the fact that neither h^s_ϕ nor I are known. Thus, *blind deconvolution* techniques are used in this task. Given a set of blurred images $\left(\overline{I_1}, \ldots, \overline{I_n}\right)$, from Equation (12.40), one can write

$$\begin{aligned} \overline{I_1} &= h^s_{\phi_1} * I \\ &\vdots \\ \overline{I_n} &= h^s_{\phi_n} * I \end{aligned} \tag{12.43}$$

where ϕ_i is the optical setting used for image $\overline{I_i}$. Many strategies were developed to solve the above ill-posed problem. Classical approaches can be found in [Chaudhuri and Rajagopalan (1999)]. Effective variational and optimization approaches are due to [Jin and Favaro (2002)] and [Favaro and Soatto (2005)] respectively. In particular, in [Favaro *et al.* (2003)] shape is estimated by inferring the diffusion coefficient of a heat equation.

These methods are widely used in optical microscopy because microscopes have narrow depth of field; therefore, it is easy to obtain pictures containing both blurry and sharp regions.

12.3.5 *Picture Differences: Stereo Methods*

Algorithms which exploit the differences between two or more pictures of a scene are called *"stereo-matching algorithms"* [Marr and Poggio (1979)].

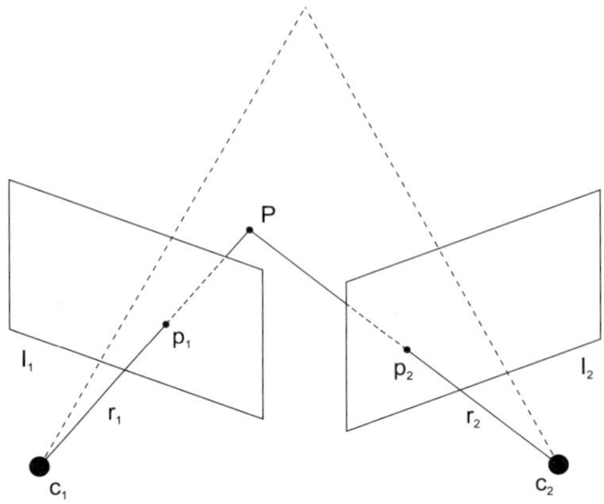

Fig. 12.12 From a pair of matched points p_1 and p_2, the 3D coordinates of point P can be computed by triangulation.

They are based on the same process used by human vision system to perceive depth, called *stereopsis*. For this reason, this particular depth cue is typically called stereo information.

In stereo methods, 3D reconstruction is accomplished in two main steps, the first addressing the so-called correspondences (or matching) problem and the second addressing the so-called reconstruction problem. The former recognizes if two or more points belonging to different images are the projection of the same point P of the 3D scene. The latter uses these correspondences in order to estimate the exact position of P in the 3D space.

Reconstruction task is achieved by triangulation. For example, let p_1 and p_2 be a pair of matched points in two different images I_1 and I_2 respectively. Thus, the real point P which they refer to, belongs to both the optical rays r_1 and r_2 related to p_1 and p_2 respectively. The situation is schematically depicted in Fig. 12.12. Therefore, P must lie at the intersection of r_1 and r_2. In practice, r_1 and r_2 may not intersect due to a imperfect camera calibration or to image discretization errors. The associated depth estimation problem in projective geometry is a linear overconstrained system with three unknowns and four independent equations which can be solved by least squared methods. Details can be found in any computer vision book, for instance in [Hartley and Zisserman (2000)].

Stereo methods were widely used in many applications; hence, various versions of these algorithms were developed in order to cope with different types of practical challenges. Recent comparisons of existing stereo matching techniques can be found in [Scharstein and Szeliski (2002)] and in [Seitz *et al.* (2006)]. A classification of these techniques is not easy because of the number of characteristics to take into account. In the following, stereo methods will be presented according to a basic taxonomy distinguishing them with respect to baselines lengths, number of input images and type of correspondences used. A baseline is a segment connecting the centers of projection of a pair of cameras. Stereo methods which operate with long baselines are called *wide baseline stereo* methods, otherwise they are called *small baseline stereo* methods. Matching problem is different in these two situations. For example, perspective deformations effects can be ignored in the small baseline case but not in the wide baselines case.

Algorithms which use two, three and $n > 3$ images as input are called respectively *binocular stereo*, *trifocal stereo* and *multi-view stereo*. The use of multiple cameras simplifies the reconstruction task reducing errors in the 3D coordinates estimation; moreover, in many situations it eliminates matching ambiguities. In fact, one can use a third camera to check if an hypothetical match is correct or not.

Binocular stereo stores matching information in a map, called *disparity map*, which associates each pixel of the first input image with the matched pixel of the second input image as follows

$$p_2 = p_1 + d\,(p_1) \tag{12.44}$$

where p_1 and p_2 are the coordinates of the two matched pixels and d is the disparity map.

In a multi-view stereo algorithm the matching and reconstruction tasks are mixed together. Therefore, a disparity map is typically replaced by a complex internal scene representation, such as, a volumetric or a level-sets [Faugeras and Keriven (1998)] representation. In particular, using a volumetric representation, reconstruction is achieved by techniques like voxel coloring [Seitz and Dyer (2000)], space carving [Kutulakos and Seitz (2000)] and max-flow [Roy and Cox (1998); Vogiatzis *et al.* (2005b)]. Space carving applies the above mentioned carving paradigm. In this case, voxels are carved out if they do not project consistently into the set of input images. Therefore, starting from an initial estimate of the surface which includes the actual one, the algorithm finds the maximal surface, called *Photo Hull*, photo-consistent with all the input images. Instead, voxel coloring operates in a single pass through the entire volume of the scene, computing for each voxel a likelihood ratio used to determine whether this voxel belongs to the scene or not.

With respect to the type of correspondences used, an important family of algorithms, called *features based stereo* (FBS), concerns the methods which use image features as stereo information. A feature is a high level data structure that captures some information locally stored in an image. The most used features are edges and corners, but in the literature one can find many other higher order primitives such as regions [Cohen *et al.* (1989)] or topological fingerprints [Fleck (1992)]. It is important to note that a feature in the image space does not always correspond to a real feature in the 3D scene.

Restricting matching problem to a small set of *a priori* fixed features has two big advantages. First of all, features are not affected by photometric variations because they are simple geometrical primitives. Furthermore, since the correspondence search space is highly reduced, the matching task is speeded up. Unfortunately, any feature space gives a discrete description of the scene; thus, reconstruction results in a sparse set of 3D points.

Methods which perform matching between two or more points comparing the regions around them are called *area based stereo* (ABS) methods. These techniques are based on the assumption that given two or more views of the same scene, the image regions surrounding corresponding points look similar. This can be justified by the fact that since corresponding points are the projection of the same point P, their surrounding regions are the projection of the same piece of surface around point P. Therefore, what ABS methods do is to perform matching using only the local reflectance properties of the objects to be acquired.

A formal explanation requires some definitions. Let P be a point of surface M and denote by $A_\epsilon(P) \subset M$ the surface neighborhood of P with radius ϵ. Let (I_1, V_1) and (I_2, V_2) be two calibrated images, assume that P is visible on both images and let $(p_1, p_2) = (V_1(P), V_2(P))$ be a valid correspondence. Therefore, $V_1(A_\epsilon(P))$ and $V_2(A_\epsilon(P))$ are the projection of $A_\epsilon(P)$ on the image space of I_1 and I_2 respectively. Suppose that the cameras are placed in such a way that the shapes of the image regions $V_1(A_\epsilon(P))$ and $V_2(A_\epsilon(P))$ look similar, *i.e.*, they are subject to a limited projective distortion. This can be achieved by a pair of parallel cameras with equal up-vectors (see Section 12.2) and small baseline/depth ratio. In other words, the surface to be acquired has to be far away from the point of views or/and the camera baseline has to be small. Assume that surface M, in $A_\epsilon(P)$, behaves as a pure Lambertian surface. Therefore, the radiance leaving $A_\epsilon(P)$ is independent of the viewpoint. Consequently, the image intensities acquired by the viewpoints V_1 and V_2 in $V_1(A_\epsilon(P))$ and

$V_2(A_\epsilon(P))$ must be equal, up to different camera optical settings (such as focusing, exposure or white balance). More formally, let

$$\begin{aligned} n_1(p_1) &= I_1|_{V_1(A_\epsilon(P))} \\ n_2(p_2) &= I_2|_{V_2(A_\epsilon(P))} \end{aligned} \tag{12.45}$$

be the image intensities around the corresponding points p_1 and p_2, *i.e.*, the restrictions of the images I_1 and I_2 to respectively $V_1(A_\epsilon(P))$ and $V_2(A_\epsilon(P))$. Since $V_1(A_\epsilon(P))$ and $V_2(A_\epsilon(P))$ can be supposed to be equal, images $n_1(p_1)$ and $n_2(p_2)$ are defined in the same domain up to different discretization of the image space. Therefore, one can make a one to one intensities comparison between $n_1(p_1)$ and $n_2(p_2)$ using simple similarity measures such as for example, *Sum of Squared Differences* (SSD), *Sum of Absolute Differences* (SAD) or *Intensity Correlation Distance* (ICD), respectively defined as:

$$\begin{aligned} SSD(p_1,p_2) &= \|n_1(p_1) - n_2(p_2)\|_2 \\ SAD(p_1,p_2) &= \|n_1(p_1) - n_2(p_2)\|_1 \\ ICD(p_1,p_2) &= \langle n_1(p_1), n_2(p_2)\rangle \end{aligned} \tag{12.46}$$

where $\|\cdot\|_1$, $\|\cdot\|_2$ and $\langle\cdot,\cdot\rangle$ are respectively the one-norm, the two-norm and the dot-product in function space. In order to make the above measures invariant to camera settings such as white balance and exposure, $n_1(p_1)$ and $n_2(p_2)$ should be replaced by their normalized versions $\overline{n_1}(p_1)$ and $\overline{n_2}(p_2)$, where

$$\overline{n}(p) = \frac{n(p) - \mu}{\sigma} \tag{12.47}$$

with μ the sample mean of $n(p)$ and σ^2 its sample variance.

If the above assumptions were satisfied, one could choose an arbitrary shape for image region $V_1(A_\epsilon(P))$ and $V_2(A_\epsilon(P))$ and compare them by one of the "metrics" of Equation (12.46). Usually, square or rectangular shaped windows are preferred since they simplify the computation. Window size plays a crucial role in matching problem. Indeed, small windows are unable to solve matching ambiguities, while large windows make no longer valid the assumption of limited perspective distortion.

In synthesis, given a metric $D(\cdot,\cdot)$, the matching problem is reduced to finding all correspondences (p_1,p_2) such that $D(p_1,p_2)$ is less than a given threshold. Matching task is time expensive since it has to compare each pixel of each image with all the pixels of the other images. However,

Fig. 12.13 Left and right images of a stereo pair: ℓ is the epipolar line associated to p_1.

the knowledge of the calibration parameters can help to restrict the correspondence search space. Indeed, given a scene point P and its projection p_1 on the image I_1, then P certainly belongs to the optical ray r_1 related to p_1 as depicted in Fig. 12.12. Ray r_1 starts from the center of projection c_1 of the image I_1 and passes through p_1 in the image plane of I_1. Therefore, if p_2 is the projection of P on the second image I_2, then p_2 must belong to the projection of ray r_1 on I_2, *i.e.*, it must belong to the half-line $\ell = V_2(r_1)$ called the epipolar line associated to p_1 (see Fig. 12.13). As a consequence, the correspondence search space related to point p_1 is reduced from a two-dimensional search domain to a one-dimensional one.

In order to improve speed in binocular stereo one may replace the two input images I_1 and I_2 with their rectified versions, *i.e.*, the two equivalent pictures obtained with cameras positioned in such a way to have a common image plane parallel to the baseline and equal up-vectors. Such a process, known as *rectification*, is achieved by projecting the original images I_1 and I_2 into the new image plane. For a comprehensive tutorial on image rectification the reader is referred to [Fusiello *et al.* (1997)]. The main characteristic of a rectified image is that its epipolar lines are either all horizontal or all vertical, thus, the search for the correspondences can be performed only along rows or columns. In this case, disparity in Equation (12.44) can be rewritten as

$$x_2 = x_1 + d(x_1, y_1), \qquad y_2 = y_1 \tag{12.48}$$

where $p_1 = (x_1, y_1)$ and $p_2 = (x_2, y_2)$. Consequently, the matching problem is reduced to the following maximization problem

$$d(x_1, y_1) = -x_1 + \arg\max\{D((x_1, y_1), (x_2, y_1)) \mid \forall x_2 \in [1, N_X]\} \tag{12.49}$$

where $D(\cdot, \cdot)$ is a generic similarity metric and N_X is the image width.

Sometimes rectification is used also in multi-view stereo systems with appropriate adjustments.

The physics of the image formation process imposes that each image point has at most one corresponding point in each other image. Therefore, an ambiguity occurs when the solution of the maximization Problem (12.49) is not unique. Such an ambiguity can be solved by adding constraints to the problem, such as surface continuity, disparity bounds or disparity ordering constraint which the scene to be acquired may respect or not. The first type of constraints is obvious while the second says that $d(x_1, y_1)$ must be less than a given threshold for all possible values of (x_1, y_1). The third imposes that the ordering along the epipolar lines must be preserved. This last one allows one to use *dynamic programming* approaches to the matching problem as in [Meerbergen *et al.* (2002)].

Computation can be further speeded up if it is organized in a pyramidal structure. In this case, each image is partitioned into different resolution layers (*e.g.* a Gaussian or a Laplacian pyramid) and the 3D reconstruction is performed at each resolution. At the first iteration, the algorithm runs at the lowest resolution layer creating a first coarse estimate of the surface. At the subsequent stages, the correspondence search interval is restricted using information extracted at the previous layer so that the search is considerably simplified. A detailed account of this method can be found in [Menard and Brandle (1995)].

Unfortunately, the pure Lambertian assumption for the surface reflectance is too strict for general purpose, indeed objects with constant BRDF are rather rare while surfaces with some kind of specularity are much more common. Therefore, since the radiance reflected by a surface point P changes as a function of the point of view, image intensities $n_1(p_1)$ and $n_2(p_2)$ can be quite different. A typical example is the highlight on a specular surface which moves as the point of view moves. In order to face this problem, one can estimate the object radiance together with its shape as in [Jin *et al.* (2003)]. Another solution is proposed in [Yang *et al.* (2003)] which describes a similarity measure invariant with respect to the specularity effects.

Another difficulty in the matching task is due to the fact that it is not always possible to have $V_1(A_\epsilon(P))$ and $V_2(A_\epsilon(P))$ within limited projective distortions. Indeed, in general, they are only related by a projective transformation; thus, their shapes can differ in scale, orientation and so on. Sometimes rectification may help to reduce projective distortions. Several techniques were developed to avoid this problem. It is worth recalling the level set method proposed in [Faugeras and Keriven (1998)] which uses the current geometry estimate to infer shape and size of the matching windows $V_1(A_\epsilon(P))$ and $V_2(A_\epsilon(P))$. This method iteratively refines the model geometry and performs the match with the estimated windows.

12.4 Multimodal Methods

As previously mentioned, multimodal methods reconstruct the shape of an object from more than just one type of information. Since some methods work well in some situations but fail in others, the basic idea of multimodal methods is to integrate information not supplied by one method with that provided by the others. These methods hold the promise of reconstructing a wide range of objects, avoiding the restrictions characterizing individual monomodal methods. Furthermore, the possibility of measuring the same information in different ways allows us to reduce errors typical of specific methods. In short, the characteristics that make these methods superior to monomodal methods, are their robustness and the possibility of acquiring wider ranges of objects.

Unfortunately, the use of more types of information increases algorithmic and time complexity. Indeed, multimodal methods often need a computationally expensive final stage that fuses together all the data extracted and processed in the previous stages. In the literature there exist several ways to combine these data and the specific algorithms depend on the type of data to be fused. For example, [Vogiatzis *et al.* (2006)] proposes a method that combines silhouette and shading information. In particular silhouettes are employed to recover camera motion and to construct the visual hull. This is then used to recover the light source position and finally, the surface is estimated by a photometric stereo algorithm. In [White and Forsyth (2006)] a method is described that combines texture and shading cues. More precisely, this latter information is used to solve surface estimation ambiguities of the shape from texture algorithm.

However, most techniques combine multiple cues by classical paradigms like carving or optimization. In particular, as we mentioned before, the carving approach leads to a maximal surface consistent with all the extracted information and certainly including the actual surface. The idea behind multimodal methods based on carving, is to carve all voxels inconsistent with at least one type of information. *"Shadow carving"* and *"Space carving"* are examples of this approach combining respectively shadow and silhouette information and stereo and silhouette information.

On the other hand, the optimization paradigm minimizes a cost functional that takes into account of all the various types of information, delivering as solution a surface fitting the extracted data as much as possible. More formally:

Problem 12.1. *Given* Ω *the set of all closed surfaces in* $\Re^3$*, i.e., the set of all the possible surfaces that can be reconstructed, and* $(\alpha_1, \alpha_2, \ldots, \alpha_j)$ *a j-tuple, where* α_i *is information of type i extracted from the input images, the multimodal fusion problem consists in finding* M *such that*

$$M = \arg\min \{\xi(M) \mid \forall M \in \Omega\} \tag{12.50}$$

where $\xi : \Omega \to \Re$ *is the cost functional*

$$\xi(M) = \kappa_{int} \cdot \xi_{int}(M) + \sum_i \kappa_i \cdot \xi_i(M, \alpha_i) \tag{12.51}$$

with ξ_{int} *a cost functional that penalizes non-smooth surfaces and* $\xi_i(\cdot, \alpha_i)$ *functionals that penalize surfaces inconsistent with information* α_i*;* κ_{int} *and* $\kappa_1, \ldots, \kappa_j$ *are constants a priori fixed.*

Consequently, the solution surface M will be as smooth as possible and consistent with as many data as possible. Constants κ_{int} and $\kappa_1, \ldots, \kappa_j$ balance the impact of the various types of information and the smoothness requirement.

Typically ξ_{int} is related to the mean or to the Gaussian curvature of the surface. For example, it can be defined as

$$\xi_{int} = \int_M \overline{\kappa} ds \tag{12.52}$$

where $\overline{\kappa}$ is the mean curvature.

Functionals $\xi_i(\cdot, \alpha_i)$ instead, depend on the type of information to which they are related. The literature reports many of such functionals accounting for a great variety of visual cues. An interesting functional which penalizes surfaces far from a generic cloud of points Σ is defined as

$$\xi_{cloud}(M) = \left(\int_M d_\Sigma(P)^k ds\right)^{\frac{1}{k}} \tag{12.53}$$

where $d_\Sigma(P)$ is the minimum distance between point $P \in M$ and the points of set Σ (see Fig. 12.14). Therefore, Equation (12.53) can be used as one of the ξ_i, in order to penalize surfaces inconsistent with information extracted, for example, by the stereo-matching algorithm.

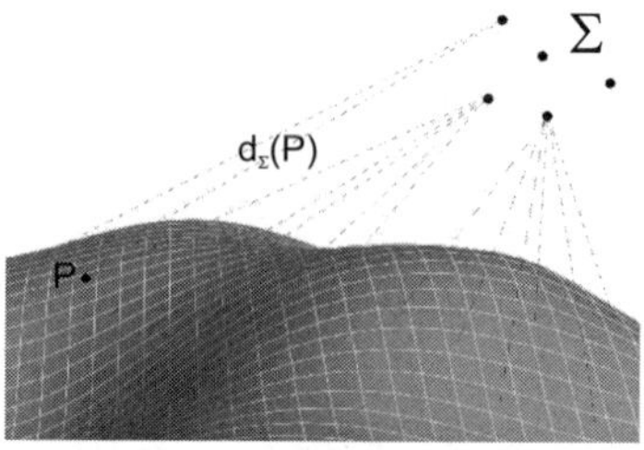

Fig. 12.14 In order to evaluate Equation (12.53), one must measure the distance between Σ and each infinitesimal part of the surface.

Let us observe that Equation (12.53) accounts for the contribution $d_\Sigma(P)$ of the distance between each $P \in M$ and Σ. Therefore, a surface through empty regions of Σ is bound to have a high value of ξ_{cloud}. Consequently, the solution will be a surface that avoids those regions. This is not always desirable because the empty regions of Σ may be due to actual holes in the object or to failures of the stereo matching algorithm (*e.g.* in case of dark or poor texture areas).

Several works in the literature address the multimodal fusion problem by an optimization approach. [Wohler (2004)] uses both shading and shadow information to reconstruct the lunar surface. [Fua and Leclerc (1995)] fuse together stereo and shading. [Gheta *et al.* (2006)] use stereo and focus information. [Esteban and Schmitt (2004); Matsuyama *et al.* (2004); Sinha and Pollefeys (2005)] fuse stereo and silhouette. [Ballan and Cortelazzo (2006)] combine silhouette, stereo and shadow information.

Problem (12.1) can be solved in several ways, but, the current trends are the *max-flow/min-cut* and the *deformable models* techniques. Max-flow/min-cut techniques transform the fusion problem into a graph problem where the optimal surface is obtained as the minimum cut solution of a weighted graph. For a recent account see [Sinha and Pollefeys (2005)]. Instead, deformable models techniques [Kass *et al.* (1987); Osher and Fedkiw (2003)] solve Problem (12.1) by a gradient descent algorithm on the Euler-Lagrange equation obtained from functional ξ as described in the next section.

12.4.1 *Deformable Models*

A *deformable model* is a manifold deforming itself under forces of various nature. Typically, but not always, these forces make the surface minimize an *a priori* fixed functional. These forces are classified as internals or externals. The former are generated by the model itself and usually have an elastic nature while the latter depend on the specific problem to solve.

Deformable models appeared for the first time in [Kass *et al.* (1987)] within the definition of *snake* or *active contour*. A snake is a parametric curve $x(s)$ in the two-dimensional image space that deforms itself maintaining its smoothness and converging to the boundary of a represented object in the image. It is associated to a functional similar to the one of Equation (12.51) with

$$\xi_{int}(x) = \frac{1}{2}\int_0^1 \left[\alpha \left|x'(s)\right|^2 + \beta \left|x''(s)\right|^2\right] ds \tag{12.54}$$

$$\xi_1(x) = -\int_0^1 \left|\nabla[G_\sigma * I](x(s))\right|^2 ds \tag{12.55}$$

where $I(x, y)$ is the image intensity function and $G_\sigma(x, y)$ the zero mean bi-dimensional gaussian function with standard deviation σ. Note that, in this case, the manifold M of Equation (12.51) is replaced by the snake, $x(s)$, which is a specific parameterization of M.

Since their introduction, deformable models were used in many computer vision tasks, such as: edge-detection, shape modeling [Terzopoulos and Fleischer (1988); McInerney and Terzopoulos (1995)], segmentation [Leymarie and Levine (1993); Durikovic *et al.* (1995)] and motion tracking [Leymarie and Levine (1993); Terzopoulos and Szeliski (1992)]. Actually, in the literature there exist two types of deformable models: the *parametric* (or classical) one [Kass *et al.* (1987); Terzopoulos and Fleischer (1988); Cohen (1991)] and the *geometric* one [Caselles *et al.* (1993, 1995); Osher and Fedkiw (2003)]. The former are the direct evolution of snakes, while the latter are characterized by the fact that their surface evolution only depends on the geometrical properties of the model.

Geometrical framework is based on the level set methods. In this case, the model M is a surface in $\Re^3$, for which there exists a regular function $\psi : \Re^3 \to \Re$ and a constant $c \in \Re$ such that

$$M = \left\{x \in \Re^3 \mid \psi(x) = c\right\} = LevelSet^{\psi}(c) \tag{12.56}$$

In other words, M is the section of level c of a function $\Re^3 \to \Re$ (see Fig. 12.15). Besides, the forces are applied to ψ and not directly to M and only when convergence is reached, M is computed. Thus, both ψ and M

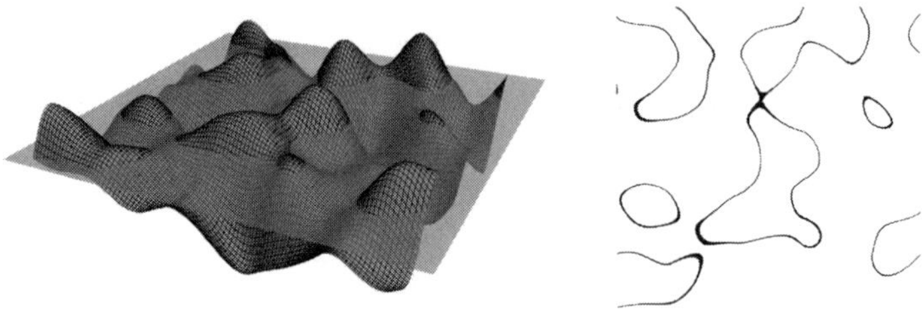

Fig. 12.15 Left: representation of $LevelSet^{\psi}(c)$ where $\psi : \Re^2 \rightarrow \Re$. Right: the result of the operation.

evolve over time according to the partial differential equation

$$\begin{cases} \psi(0) = \psi_0 \\ \dfrac{\partial \psi}{\partial t}(t) = F(\psi(t)) \end{cases} \tag{12.57}$$

where $\psi(t)$ is the function ψ at time t, ψ_0 is its initial state and $F(\psi(t))$ is the force applied to ψ at time t. Hence, since this method operates only on ψ, surface M can dynamically change its topology. Roughly speaking, M can change its number of holes. For example, the reader could imagine to move upwards and downwards the plane of Fig. 12.15, as the plane moves one obtains sections of ψ with a different number of connected components. Dynamic topology is the key feature that makes the geometrical framework a more powerful tool than the parametric one. The interested reader is sent to [Osher and Sethian (1988)] for further details.

The remainder of this section is focused on classical deformable model techniques. In this case, in order to solve the minimum problem researchers propose a standard variational approach based on the use of a gradient descent on the Euler-Lagrange equation obtained from functional ξ, which we explain by way of the following example.

Let s be a specific parameterization of M, *i.e.*, s is a function from an open subset $A \subset \Re^2$ to $\Re^3$, and consider the functional

$$\xi(s) = \kappa_{int} \cdot \xi_{int} + \kappa_{cloud} \cdot \int_A d_{\Sigma}(s(u,v))dudv \tag{12.58}$$

where d_{Σ} is the same as in Equation (12.53) and

$$\xi_{int} = \int_A \left\| \frac{\partial s}{\partial u} \right\|^2 + \left\| \frac{\partial s}{\partial v} \right\|^2 dudv + \int_A \left\| \frac{\partial^2 s}{\partial u^2} \right\|^2 + \left\| \frac{\partial^2 s}{\partial v^2} \right\|^2 + 2 \left\| \frac{\partial^2 s}{\partial v \partial u} \right\|^2 dudv \tag{12.59}$$

where the first term penalizes non-isometric parameterizations of M and the second term is equal to the total curvature of M if s is an isometry, thus penalizing non-smooth surfaces.

The related Euler-Lagrange equation [Fox (1987)] is:

$$-\nabla^2 s\left(u,v\right)+\nabla^4 s\left(u,v\right)-F_{cloud}\left(s\left(u,v\right)\right)=0 \tag{12.60}$$

where $\nabla^2 s$, $\nabla^4 s$ are respectively the laplacian and the bi-laplacian of s and $F_{cloud}:\Re^3\to\Re^3$ is a field that associates to each point P in the space a unit vector pointing to the point of Σ nearest to P.

The problem of finding M which minimizes ξ has been turned into the problem of finding s, a parameterization of M, which satisfies Equation (12.60). Therefore, the solution can be computed by a gradient descent algorithm on the following problem

$$\arg\min\left\{\left\|-\nabla^2 s\left(u,v\right)+\nabla^4 s\left(u,v\right)-F_{cloud}\left(s\left(u,v\right)\right)\right\|,\forall s\right\} \tag{12.61}$$

Consequently, this algorithm can be interpreted as the deformation of a parametric surface s subject to two forces defined as follows

$$F_{int}=\nabla^2 s-\nabla^4 s \tag{12.62}$$

$$F_{ext}=F_{cloud} \tag{12.63}$$

Let $s(t)$ be the model s at time t, therefore the evolution is described by the following partial differential equation

$$\begin{cases} s\left(0\right)=s_0 \\ \dfrac{\partial s}{\partial t}\left(t\right)=\beta\cdot\left(F_{int}+F_{ext}\right) \end{cases} \tag{12.64}$$

where s_0 is the initial surface and β determines the evolution speed. In order to find a numerical solution of Equation (12.64), one can use forward Euler and apply the forces to all the vertices of the mesh. The discrete versions of ∇^2 and ∇^4 on a triangular mesh can be computed using the umbrella $\widetilde{\Delta}$ and the squared umbrella $\widetilde{\Delta}^2$ operators respectively [Esteban and Schmitt (2004)].

The advantages and the drawbacks of geometric and parametric deformable models can be summarized as follows. Geometric models have dynamic topology but are not easy to control. Their computation is typically slower than that of parametric models. On the other hand, parametric models have a fixed topology and suffer local minima problems in proximity of concavities. Their computation is faster and by a suitable parameters choice one can also control the parametric characteristics of the final mesh.

12.4.2 *Application Examples*

Multimodal methods, in principle, can use any combination of the visual cues previously seen. Clearly, some combinations can be more effective and manageable than others. This section reviews two multimodal techniques recently proposed in the literature.

A method that combines silhouette and stereo information using classical deformable models is described in [Matsuyama *et al.* (2004); Esteban and Schmitt (2004)]. A first estimate s_0 of M is found by volume carving. Starting from s_0, the model evolves subject to three types of forces:

$$\frac{\partial s}{\partial t}(t) = \beta \cdot (F_{int} + F_{stereo} + F_{sil}) \tag{12.65}$$

where F_{int} is defined as above, F_{stereo} enforces stereo consistency and F_{sil} silhouette information.

In order to avoid local minima problems, [Esteban and Schmitt (2004)] define F_{stereo} as the *gradient vector flow* (GVF) [Xu and Prince (1998)] of Σ, that is a vector field solution of a diffusion equation.

Let $P_1, \ldots, P_m$ be the projections (silhouettes) of the real surface Λ viewed by $V_1, \ldots, V_m$ respectively and M be the mesh that currently approximates Λ. Let v be a vertex of mesh M, $F_{sil}(v)$ in [Esteban and Schmitt (2004)] is defined as

$$F_{sil}(v) = \alpha(v) \cdot d_{vh}(v) \cdot N(v) \tag{12.66}$$

where $N(v)$ is the surface normal in v, d_{vh} is the signed distance between the visual hull and the projection of vertex v, defined as

$$d_{vh}(v) = \min_j d(V_j(v), P_j) \tag{12.67}$$

where $d(V_j(v), P_j)$ is the signed distance between $V_j(v)$ and P_j, *i.e.*, it is positive if v belongs to the visual hull and negative otherwise. $\alpha(v)$ is defined as

$$\alpha(v) = \begin{cases} 1 & if \quad d_{vh}(v) \leq 0 \\ \dfrac{1}{(1 + d(V_c(v), V_c(M)))^k} & if \quad d_{vh}(v) > 0 \end{cases} \tag{12.68}$$

where $c = \arg\min_j d(V_j(v), P_j)$ and $V_c(M)$ is the projection of M viewed by V_c. This means that if v is outside the visual hull, $F_{sil}(v)$ is equal to $d_{vh}(v) \cdot N(v)$. Instead, if v is inside the visual hull, $\alpha(v)$ controls the transition of v from a contour point where $d(V_c(v), V_c(M)) = 0$ to a concave point where $d(V_c(v), V_c(M)) > 0$. In this way, F_{sil} reduces its

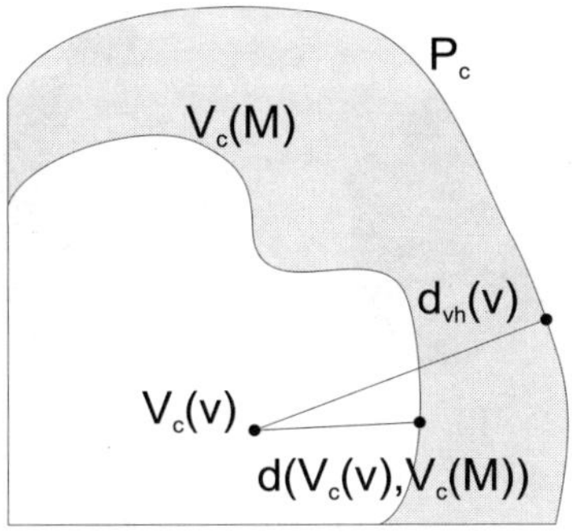

Fig. 12.16 Distances involved in F_{sil} computation.

intensity as much as v is inside the visual hull and parameter k controls the decreasing factor. Figure 12.16 exemplifies the situation.

As we can see in Fig. 12.17(a) and in Fig. 12.17(b), silhouette information cannot describe model concavities which cannot be seen from the acquisition viewpoints, while stereo based methods fail in low variance regions and contours. Silhouette and stereo fusion Fig. 12.17(c) makes a better reconstruction of the original surface correcting errors and integrating information missing in each monomodal reconstruction. The final mesh turns out to be smooth and rather uniformly sampled.

An algorithm which combines stereo, silhouette and shadow information using the deformable model framework is proposed in [Ballan and Cortelazzo (2006)]. In particular F_{shadow}, *i.e.*, the force related to shadow information, is defined in a way that minimizes the inconsistency with shadow information. In fact, like in the carving approach, the inconsistent surface portions (for example, portion s in Fig. 12.9(b)) are pushed inside the surface. More formally,

$$F_{shadow}(v) = -i(v) \cdot N(v) \tag{12.69}$$

where $N(v)$ is the outer normal to the surface in v and $i(v)$ is a scalar function equal to 1 if the vertex v is inconsistent with shadow information, and equal to 0 otherwise.

Shadow information can improve the reconstruction obtained from just stereo and silhouette information; indeed, it can describe the shape of the concavities where stereo and silhouette information are missing.

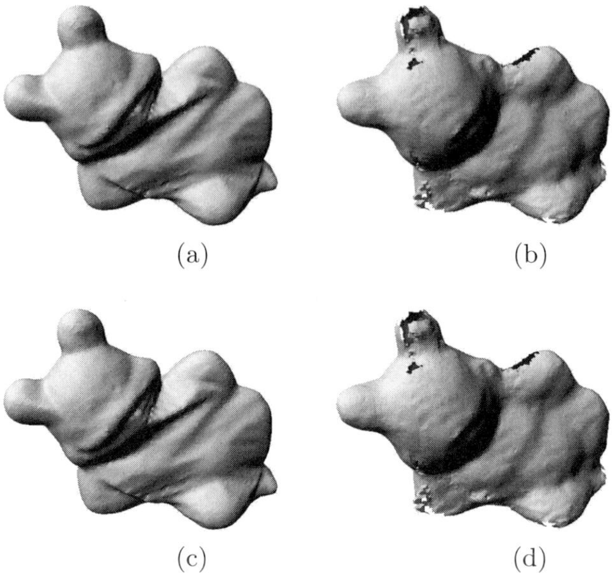

Fig. 12.17 Multimodal vs monomodal methods: (a) smoothed model obtained by volume carving; (b) model obtained by fusing together different partial models obtained by stereo matching; (c) model obtained by silhouette and stereo fusion; (d) model obtained by texturing model c.

12.5 Summary

This chapter presented an overview of passive optical 3D reconstruction methods as a tool for creating content. The main reason for the great attention that passive methods received in the literature probably rest in their acquisition speed (without intruding into the scene in any way, not even by just radiating energy) and in their inexpensive acquisition equipment (as simple as a digital camera). The counterpart of such a simplicity is the complication that the reconstruction algorithms may have. However, algorithmic complexity, when needed, can be effectively handled by parallel computation or special hardware such as GPUs. In this context it may be worth recalling that passive methods are also employed for real time reconstructions of dynamic scenes, in applications such as interactive television, *3DTV* and *free-viewpoint video* [Matsuyama *et al.* (2004); Hilton and Starck (2004); Magnor (2005)].

While early research about passive methods concentrated in the discovery and exploration of the various types of visual cues available from images, the current research trend, instead, aims to blend together several types of information in order to overcome the limitations of monomodal reconstruction. This operation at present uses carving or optimization approaches for synergistically fusing the various information sources. Detailed examples of how to combine different visual cues were presented in Section 12.4. Multimodal passive methods, as expected, are more robust than monomodal methods with respect to errors and scene characteristics.

References

Ballan, L. and Cortelazzo, G. M. (2006). Multimodal 3d shape recovery from texture, silhouette and shadow information, *International Symposium on 3D Data Processing, Visualization and Transmission (3DPVT)*.

Baumgart, B. G. (1974). Geometric modelling for computer vision, *PhD thesis, Standford University*.

Belhumeur, P., Kriegman, D. and Yuille, A. (1997). The bas-relief ambiguity, *Proceedings of IEEE International Conference on Computer Vision*, pp. 1060–1066.

Blinn, J. (1977). Models of light reflection for computer synthesized pictures, *SIGGRAPH*, pp. 192–198.

Bouguet, J.-Y. and Perona, P. (1999). 3D photography using shadows in dual-space geometry, *International Journal of Computer Vision* **35**, 2, pp. 129–149.

Brooks, M. and Horn, B. (1985). Shape and source from shading, *Proceedings of the International Joint Conference on Artificial Intelligence, Los Angeles*, pp. 932–936.

Caselles, V., Catte, F., Coll, T. and Dibos, F. (1993). A geometric model for active contours, *Numerische Mathematik* **66**, 1, pp. 1–31.

Caselles, V., Kimmel, R. and Sapiro, G. (1995). Geodesic active contours, *Proceedings 5th International Conference Computer Vision*, pp. 694–699.

Chaudhuri, S. and Rajagopalan, A. N. (1999). *Depth from Defocus: a real aperture imaging approach* (Springer verlag).

Chuang, Y., Curless, B., Salesin, D. and Szeliski, R. (2001). A bayesian approach to digital matting, *Proceedings of IEEE Conference on Computer Vision and Pattern Recognition* **2**, pp. 264–271.

Cipolla, R. and P. Giblin (2000). *Visual Motion of Curves and Surfaces* (Cambridge University Press).

Cline, H. and Lorensen, W. (1987). Marching cubes: a high resolution 3D surface construction algorithm, *Computer Graphics* **21**, 4, pp. 163–168.

Cohen, L., Vinet, L., Sander, P. and Gagalowicz, A. (1989). Hierarchical region based stereo matching, *Proceedings of IEEE Conference on Computer Vision and Pattern Recognition*, pp. 416–421.

Cohen, L. D. (1991). On active contour models and balloons, *CVGIP: Image Understand* **53**, pp. 211–218.

Daum, M. and Dudek, G. (1998). Out of the dark: Using shadows to reconstruct 3D surfaces, *Proceedings Asian Conference on Computer Vision, Hong Kong, China*, pp. 72–79.

Davis, J., Marschner, S., Garr, M. and Levoy, M. (2002). Filling holes in complex surfaces using volumetric diffusion, *International Symposium on 3D Data Processing, Visualization and Transmission (3DPVT)*, pp. 428–438.

de Berg, M., Kreveld, M. V., Overmars, M. and Shwarzkopf, O. (1999). *Computational Geometry* (Springer).

Durikovic, R., Kaneda, K. and Yamashita, H. (1995). Dynamic contour: A texture approach and contour operations, *Visual Computing* **11**, pp. 277–289.

Esteban, C. H. and Schmitt, F. (2004). Silhouette and stereo fusion for 3D object modeling, *Computer Vision and Image Understanding* **96**, 3, pp. 367–392.

Faugeras, O. and Keriven, R. (1998). Variational principles, surface evolution, PDE's, level set methods and the stereo problem, *IEEE Transactions on Image Processing* **7**, 3, pp. 336–344.

Favaro, P., Osher, S., Soatto, S. and Vese, L. (2003). 3d shape from anisotropic diffusion, *Conference on Computer Vision and Pattern Recognition* **1**, pp. 179–186.

Favaro, P. and Soatto, S. (2005). A geometric approach to shape from defocus, *IEEE Transactions on Pattern Analysis and Machine Intelligence* **27**, 3, pp. 406–417.

Fleck, M. M. (1992). A topological stereo matcher, *International Journal of Computer Vision* **6**, 3, pp. 197–226.

Forsyth, D. A. (2002). Shape from texture without boundaries, *Proceedings of European Conference on Computer Vision*, pp. 225–239.

Fox, C. (1987). *An Introduction to the Calculus of Variations* (Dover Publications).

Fua, P. and Leclerc, Y. G. (1995). Object-centered surface reconstruction: combining multi-image stereo shading, *The International Journal of Computer Vision* **16**, 1, pp. 35–56.

Fusiello, A., Trucco, E. and Verri, A. (1997). Rectification with unconstrained stereo geometry, *Proceedings of the British Machine Vision Conference*, pp. 400–409.

Gheta, I., Frese, C. and Heizmann, M. (2006). Fusion of combined stereo and focus series for depth estimation, *Workshop Multiple Sensor Data Fusion, Dresden.*

Hartley, R. and Zisserman, A. (2000). *Multiple View Geometry in Computer Vision* (Cambridge university press).

Hatzitheodour, M. and Kender, M. (1988). An optimal algorithm for the derivation of shape from shadows, *Proceedings of Computer Society Conference on Computer Vision and Pattern Recognition*, pp. 486–491.

Healey, G. and Binford, T. O. (1988). Local shape from specularity, *Computer Vision, Graphics and Image Processing*, pp. 62–86.

Hilton, A. and Starck, J. (2004). Multiple view reconstruction of people, *International Symposium on 3D Data Processing, Visualization and Transmission (3DPVT)*, pp. 357–364.

Horn, B. K. P. (1970). Shape from shading: A method for obtaining the shape of a smooth opaque object from one view, *PhD thesis, MIT*.

Ikeuchi, K. and Horn, B. (1981). Numerical shape from shading and occluding boundaries, *Artificial Intelligence* **17**, pp. 141–184.

Jebara, T., Azarbayejani, A. and Pentland, A. (1999). 3D structure from 2D motion, *IEEE Signal Processing Magazine* **16**, 3, pp. 66–84.

Jin, H. and Favaro, P. (2002). A variational approach to shape from defocus, *Proceedings of the European Conference on Computer Vision, Part II*, pp. 18–30.

Jin, H., Soatto, S. and Yezzi, A. (2003). Multi-view stereo beyond Lambert, *Proceedings of IEEE Conference on Computer Vision and Pattern Recognition*, pp. 171–178.

Kass, M., Witkin, A. and Terzopoulos, D. (1987). Snakes: Active contour models, *International Journal of Computer Vision* **1**, pp. 321–331.

Koenderink, J. J. and Pont, S. C. (2003). Irradiation direction from texture, *Journal of the Optical Society of America* **20**, 10, pp. 1875–1882.

Kriegman, D. J. and Belhumeur, P. N. (2001). What shadows reveal about object structure, *Journal of the Optical Society of America* **18**, 8, pp. 1804–1813.

Kutulakos, K. N. and Seitz, S. M. (2000). A theory of shape by space carving, *International Journal of Computer Vision* **38**, 3, pp. 197–216.

Laurentini, A. (1994). The visual hull concept for silhouette based image understanding, *IEEE Transactions on Pattern Analysis and Machine Intelligence* **16**, 2, pp. 150–162.

Leibe, B., Starner, T., Ribarsky, W., Wartell, Z., Krum, D., Weeks, J., Singletary, B. and Hodges, L. (2000). Toward spontaneous interaction with the perceptive workbench, *IEEE Computer Graphics and Applications* **20**, 6, pp. 54–65.

Levoy, M., Pulli, K., Curless, B., Rusinkiewicz, R., Koller, D., Pereira, L., Ginzton, M., Anderson, S., Davis, J., Ginsberg, J., Shade, J. and Fulk, D. (2000). The digital michelangelo project: 3D scanning of large statues, *Proceedings of SIGGRAPH Computer Graphics*, pp. 131–144.

Leymarie, F. and Levine, M. D. (1993). Tracking deformable objects in the plane using an active contour model, *IEEE Transactions Pattern Analysis and Machine Intelligence* **15**, pp. 617–634.

Li, M., Magnor, M. and Seidel, H. (2003). Hardware-accelerated visual hull reconstruction and rendering, *Proceedings of Graphics Interface*, pp. 65–72.

Lucchese, L. and Mitra, S. K. (2001). Color image segmentation: A state of the art survey, *Proceedings of the Indian National Science Academy* **67**, 2, pp. 207–221.

Magnor, M. A. (2005). *Video-Based Rendering* (AK Peters, Ltd.).

Marr, D. and Poggio, T. (1979). A computational theory of human stereo vision, *Proceedings Royal Society of London* **204**, pp. 301–328.

Matsuyama, T., Wu, X., Takai, T. and Nobuhara, S. (2004). Real-time 3D shape reconstruction, dynamic 3D mesh deformation, and high fidelity visualiziation for 3D video, *Computer Vision and Image Understanding* **96**, 3, pp. 393–434.

Matusik, W., Buehler, C. and McMillan, L. (2001). Polyhedral visual hulls for real-time rendering, *Proceedings of 12th Eurographics Workshop on Rendering*, pp. 116–126.

McInerney, T. and Terzopoulos, D. (1995). A dynamic finite element surface model for segmentation and tracking in multidimensional medical images with application to cardiac 4d image analysis, *Comput. Med. Imag. Graph.* **19**, pp. 69–83.

Meerbergen, G. V., Vergauwen, M., Pollefeys, M. and Van Gool, L. (2002). A hierarchical symmetric stereo algorithm using dynamic programming, *International Journal of Computer Vision* **47**, pp. 275–285.

Menard, C. and Brandle, N. (1995). Hierarchical area-based stereo algorithm for 3D acquisition, *Proceedings International Workshop on Stereoscopic and Three Dimensional Imaging, Greece*, pp. 195–201.

Mendoca, P. and Cipolla, R. (1999). A simple technique for self-calibration, *Proceedings of IEEE Conference on Computer Vision and Pattern Recognition* **1**, pp. 500–505.

Nayar, S. K. and Nakagawa, Y. (1994). Shape from focus, *IEEE Transactions on Pattern Analysis and Machine Intelligence* **16**, 8, pp. 824–831.

Nicodemus, F. (1970). Reflectance nomenclature and directional reflectance and emissivity, *Applied Optics* **9**, pp. 1474–1475.

Osher, S. and Fedkiw, R. (2003). *Level Set Methods and Dynamic Implicit Surfaces*, *Applied Mathematical Sciences*, Vol. 153 (Springer).

Osher, S. and Sethian, J. A. (1988). Fronts propagating with curvature-dependent speed: Algorithms based on Hamilton-Jacobi formulations, *Journal of Computational Physics* **79**, pp. 12–49.

Phong, B. T. (1975). Illumination for computer generated images, *Communications of the ACM* **18**, 6, pp. 311–317.

Piccardi, M. (2004). Background subtraction techniques: a review, *Proceedings of IEEE International Conference on Systems, Man and Cybernetics* **4**, pp. 3099–3104.

Potmesil, M. (1987). Generating octree models of 3D objects from their silhouettes in a sequence of images, *Computer Vision, Graphics and Image Processing* **40**, pp. 1–29.

Potmesil, M. (1990). *Introduction to statistical pattern recognition* (Academic press).

Prescott, B. and McLean, G. (1997). Line-based correction of radial lens distortion, *Graphical Models and Image Processing* **59**, 1, pp. 39–47.

Rioux, M., Blais, F., Beraldin, A., Godin, G., Blulanger, P. and Greenspan, M. (2000). Beyond range sensing: XYZ-RGB digitizing and modeling, *Proceedings of the 2000 IEEE International Conference on Robotics and Automation, San Francisco, CA*, pp. 111–115.

Roy, S. and Cox, I. J. (1998). A maximum-flow formulation of the n-camera stereo correspondence problem, *Proceedings of IEEE International Conference on*

Computer Vision, pp. 492–502.

Rushmeier, H. and Bernardini, F. (2002). The 3D model acquisition pipeline, *Computer Graphics Forum* **2**, 2, pp. 149–172.

Savarese, S., Andreetto, M., Rushmeier, H., Bernardini, F. and Perona, P. (2007). 3D reconstruction by shadow carving: Theory and practical evaluation, *International Journal of Computer Vision* **71**, 3, pp. 305–336.

Savarese, S., Rushmeier, H. E., Bernardini, F. and Perona, P. (2001). Shadow carving, *ICCV*, pp. 190–197.

Scharstein, D. and Szeliski, R. (2002). A taxonomy and evaluation of dense two-frame stereo correspondence algorithms, *International Journal of Computer Vision* **47**, 1, pp. 7–42.

Seitz, S., Curless, B., Diebel, J., Scharstein, D. and Szeliski, R. (2006). A comparison and evaluation of multi-view stereo reconstruction algorithms, *Proceedings of IEEE Conference on Computer Vision and Pattern Recognition* **1**, pp. 519–528.

Seitz, S. and Dyer, C. (2000). Photorealistic scene reconstruction by voxel coloring, *International Journal of Computer Vision* **38**, 3, pp. 197–216.

Shafer, S. and Kanade, T. (1983). Using shadows in finding surface orientations, *Computer Vision, Graphics and Image Processing* **22**, 1, pp. 145–176.

Sinha, S. and Pollefeys, M. (2005). Multi-view reconstruction using photo-consistency and exact silhouette constraints: A maximum-flow formulation, *Proceedings of IEEE International Conference on Computer Vision* **1**, pp. 349–356.

Smith, E. and Kender, J. (1986). Shape from darkness: Deriving surface information from dynamic shadows, *In AIII*, pp. 664–669.

Tankus, A. and Kiryati, N. (2005). Photometric stereo under perspective projection, *Proceedings of IEEE International Conference of Computer Vision*, pp. 611–616.

Terzopoulos, D. and Fleischer, K. (1988). Deformable models, *Visual Computing* **4**, pp. 306–331.

Terzopoulos, D. and Szeliski, R. (1992). Tracking with kalman snakes, in A. Blake and A. Yuille (eds.), *Active Vision* (Eds. Cambridge, MA, MIT Press), pp. 3–20.

Torrance, K. E. and Sparrow, E. M. (1967). Theory for off-specular reflection from roughened surfaces, *Journal of Optical Society of America* **57**, pp. 1105–1114.

Tsai, R. Y. (1987). A versatile camera calibration technique for high-accuracy 3D machine vision metrology using off-the-shelf tv cameras and lenses, *IEEE Journal of Robotics and Automation* **3**, 5, pp. 323–344.

Vega, O. (1991). Default shape theory: with applications to the recovery of shape and light source from shading, *Master's thesis, University of Saskatchewan, Computational Sciecne Department*, pp. 1474–1475.

Vogiatzis, G., Favaro, P. and Cipolla, R. (2005a). Using frontier points to recover shape, reflectance and illumination, *Proceedings of IEEE International Conference on Computer Vision*, pp. 228–235.

Vogiatzis, G., Hernández, C. and Cipolla, R. (2006). Reconstruction in the round using photometric normals and silhouettes, *Proceedings IEEE Conference on Computer Vision and Pattern Recognition*, pp. 1847–1854.

Vogiatzis, G., Torr, P. and Cipolla, R. (2005b). Multi-view stereo via volumetric graph-cuts, *Proceedings of IEEE Conference on Computer Vision and Pattern Recognition*, pp. 391–398.

White, R. and Forsyth, D. A. (2006). Combining cues: Shape from shading and texture, *Conference on Computer Vision and Pattern Recognition* **2**, pp. 1809–1816.

Wohler, C. (2004). 3d surface reconstruction by self-consistent fusion of shading and shadow features, *Proceedings of 17th International Conference on Pattern Recognition* **2**, pp. 204–207.

Woodham, R. J. (1980). Photometric method for determining surface orientation from multiple images, *Optical Engineering* **19**, 1, pp. 139–144.

Xu, C. and Prince, J. L. (1998). Snakes, shapes, and gradient vector flow, *IEEE Transactions on Image Processing*, pp. 359–369.

Yang, D. K.-M. (1996). Shape from darkness under error, *Ph.D. thesis, Columbia University.*

Yang, R., Pollefeys, M. and Welch, G. (2003). Dealing with textureless regions and specular highlights — a progressive space carving scheme using a novel photo-consistency measure, *Proceedings of the 9th International Conference on Computer Vision*, pp. 576–584.

Zhang, R., Tsai, P., Cryer, J. and Shah, M. (1999). Shape from shading: A survey, *IEEE Transactions on Pattern Analysis and Machine Intelligence* **21**, 8, pp. 690–706.

Chapter 13

3D Visualization and Progressive Compression of Photorealistic Panoramic Backgrounds

P. Zanuttigh, G. M. Cortelazzo and L. MacDonald

13.1 Introduction

The idea of bypassing the difficulties of 3D modeling and rendering and obtaining photorealistic environmental descriptions by real images or videos has been used extensively in video games as reported in [Chen (1995)] and the references therein. Precursors of such an approach, using the so-called branching movies, can be found in [Lippman (1980); Ripley (1989); Miller *et al.* (1992)]. Panoramic images of various types rendered from synthetic environments made their appearance in computer graphics around the concept of "environment map" [Blinn and Newell (1976); Greene (1986)]. Cylindrical panoramas have a long tradition in analog photography [Malde (1983)]. The work of [Chen (1995)] is milestone in the field of panoramic images since it combined all the above into a commercial product called QuickTimeVR which was very successful and which was the first of a series of many authoring tools for panoramic images. Thanks to these products panoramic images became a very popular mean for representing complex real environments, *i.e.*, for obtaining "environment maps" to use in virtual tours of buildings, cities, in heritage sites, and similar and gained the attention of the computer graphics and image processing communities which devoted considerable conceptual speculation to panoramic imagery and possible extensions.

More specifically, panoramic images in computer graphics were seen as a special case of the more general idea of rendering novel views from a suitable collections of images (concept called image-based rendering) rather than from 3D models (concept called model-based rendering). Image-based rendering attracted a lot of attention because of its potential of bypassing the difficulties of both 3D modeling real objects and of rendering photorealistic scene illuminations [Chen and Williams (1993); McMillan and Bishop (1995); Gortler *et al.* (1996); Levoy and Hanrahan (1996); Kang (1997)].

Panoramic images appeared in the image processing and computer vision literature as a special instance of the more general problem of "image mosaicing", *i.e.*, the composition of images covering portions of a scene into a larger image representing the scene. In the technical literature the issue of mosaicing is considered together with the automatic estimation of planar projective transformations. Indeed, it is well known that, if the scene geometry is planar or if the camera nodal point is held fixed while taking the images, the images are related by 2D projective transformations characterized by 8 parameters (typically called homographies in the computer vision literature). In this respect the general issue of automatically estimating projective transformations from images, bears strong ties with the issue of automatic image mosaicing and of automatic construction of panoramic images [Mann and Picard (1994); Szeliski (1994); Irani *et al.* (1995); Chen (1995); McMillan and Bishop (1995); Szeliski (1996); Cortelazzo and Lucchese (1999); Shum and Szeliski (2000)]. Although panoramic images in principle can be supported by any type of surface [Shum and Szeliski (2000)], the surface interiors used in practice are cylinders, spheres and cubes. This chapter will concentrate on cylindrical panoramas which are the most popular ones, owing to the ease of their image capture. Indeed cylindrical panoramas can be built from a series of photographs taken with a camera on a leveled tripod (the images must be taken holding the camera nodal point fixed).

The construction of a cylindrical panorama or 'stitching' within this framework requires the solution of two basic problems: the automatic estimation of the projective transformation between adjacent pairs of images from their overlap; and the redistribution of the registration error between the whole series of images in order to compensate for error propagation and to make the last image to perfectly fit onto the first one. The second issue is relevant especially for high resolution imagery [Szeliski and Shum (1997); Kang and Weiss (1997); Hasler *et al.* (1999); Shum and Szeliski (2000)]. It is fair to say that the theoretical problems and solutions behind stitching are well understood (for a comprehensive account see [Shum and Szeliski (2000)]). Nevertheless, fully automatic stitching with high quality results, in practice is rather hard. Current commercial products typically combine automatic passes with manual adjustments. Geometrical stitching artifacts may easily go unnoticed if a small version the panoramic images is shown. This is typically the case of the panoramic images currently used on the Internet in order to avoid transmission delays. However, large panoramas require proper stitching.

Another practically relevant issue which must be overcome in the stitching process concerns the photometric imbalances between adjacent images due to non-uniform illumination and vignetting. Such colorimetric border artifacts can be overcome in many ways. A simple solution called "feathering" in [Shum and Szeliski (2000)] consists of blending the colors according to convex weights proportional to the distance of the pixels from the image border. More complex multi-resolution blending algorithms can be found in [Burt and Adelson (1983); Hsu and Wu (1996)]. The issue of stitching images within prescribed colorimetric tolerances has not received much attention yet.

It may be worth mentioning that panoramic images can also be obtained by special optics such as fisheye lenses [Xiong and Turkowski (1997)] and pyramidal or parabolic mirrors, capable of directly conveying to the optics 360 degrees field of views [Nayar (1997)].

These last solutions have the advantage of waiving from stitching. All of them have the drawback of not exploiting the full camera resolution and some of them are the election choice in current omnidirectional robotics applications [Benosman and Kang (2001); Omn (2003)].

Panoramic images, analog or digital, can also be obtained by dedicated hardware, *i.e.*, cameras typically equipped with a shutter of linear rather than circular shape and therefore called "slit cameras", rotating by a step-motor around the vertical axis.

Slit cameras are an excellent tool for making cylindrical panoramas, their drawback, beside cost, is that the image capture may be slow in presence of limited illumination.

While the construction of panoramic images indisputably received a fair amount of attention in the technical literature, the issue of local or remote visualization of panoramic images did not receive comparable consideration.

The original paradigm [Chen (1995)] of visualizing panoramic images essentially by a procedure dual to stitching (*i.e.*, by sectioning the panorama into a number of slices, converting the slice selected by the user from cylindrical to Cartesian coordinate and displaying it) was generally adopted since, either in academic prototypes or in commercial products. Minor conceptual variations concerned programming languages (*e.g.*, the use of Java) or the compression of panoramic images by schemes such as JPEG or IPIX, in order to improve transmission's efficiency.

In light of the rendering performance of graphic cards and of their current diffusion it seems sensible to explore visualization solutions for panoramic images which can take advantage of their presence. Exploiting graphic cards for various tasks is a growing trend also in computer vision [Yang and Pollefeys (2003)]. It is also fair to say that such an approach would have made little sense from the practical viewpoint at the time [Chen (1995)] appeared in the middle 1990s, considering the limited capabilities and diffusion of the graphic cards of the time. In the subsequent sections we will present a visualization scheme for panoramic images which treats them as 3D objects, in accord with the early approach of the environment maps of the computer vision literature [Blinn and Newell (1976); Greene (1986)], enabling therefore the use of graphic hardware.

Another important issue is the remote visualization of large panoramic images. Recently several image zooming applications based on the use of video-servers have appeared. Within this scheme a very high-resolution image resides in the server. When a user, at client side, selects an image portion of any size, the graphic interface sends the server its position and size. The server computes in real time the required image and sends it back to the client. In this way image zooming becomes a video-on-demand operation relying on a dedicated server, an approach conceptually close to the one presented in Chapter 10 for the remote visualization of 3D models. A positive aspect of this solution is the continuous range of high quality enlargements it can give (provided that the server can perform complex interpolation algorithms in real-time). A first disadvantage is that a dedicated server is required, *i.e.*, a server must be purchased, maintained in operation 24 hours a day, 7 days a week, its computation/memory resources must be adequate to serve the expected number of clients, when a peak of demand occurs the quality of service will be degraded, *etc.* A second disadvantage currently exhibited by the commercial products based on this technology is that they only support small size visualization windows. Small size windows make it hard locating the details within the whole scene. Image-zooming based on dedicated video-servers can also be implemented within viewers of panoramic images.

This chapter discusses an alternate solution for the remote visualization of panoramic images which rests on the use of current progressive compression standards. This solution is conceptually closer in spirit to the one presented in Chapter 11 for the remote visualization of 3D models. Practical experimentation shows that such an approach allows to remotely display and zoom panoramic images in large visualization windows in a very effective way. It is well known that JPEG2000 is intrinsically more efficient than JPEG and that it is scalable in image resolution and quality. Therefore, not only it can speed up the transmission of panoramic data with respect to JPEG, but, perhaps most importantly, it allows for a size vs. quality scalable delivery without data retransmission as would be the case with JPEG. There are, of course, many ways of incorporating progressive compression within a viewer of panoramic images. We will present a solution that is demonstrated to be very effective within our visualization scheme.

Section 2 reviews the basics of panoramic image construction and visualization. Section 3 describes the structure of the 3D viewer specialized for the visualization of panoramas. Section 4 describes the progressive compression of panoramic images by way of features of the JPEG2000 standard. Section 5 provides a summary.

13.2 Basic Characteristics of Panoramic Images

Panoramic images offer a compact representation of what is possible to see looking in almost every direction from a fixed viewpoint. The key idea is that, unless the viewpoint changes, it is not possible to see the difference between a still scene surrounding the viewer and the interior of a closed shape textured with the same scene. The most common shapes used for panoramic images are cylinders, spheres and cubes.

Cylindrical panoramas

Fig. 13.1 Cylindrical panoramic image.

Cylindrical panoramas (Fig. 13.1) are the most common approach. In these images the scene is projected on the interior of a cylinder with axis through the center of projection and parallel to the imaging plane.

The construction of a cylindrical panorama starts by taking a suitable set of photos (usually 20) from a fixed nodal point (called the center of projection of the panorama). Usually the camera is placed on a tripod and rotates horizontally by a fixed amount until it returns to the starting position. The acquired photos are then projected onto the cylinder surface and merged together. The merging procedure (stitching) is performed by ad-hoc softwares usually based on correlation methods. The idea is to find the maximum of the correlation between adjacent pairs of images in order to estimate the projective transformation between them. It is also necessary to redistribute the registration error between the whole series of images in order to compensate for error propagation and to make the last image perfectly fit onto the first one. In the literature it is possible to find many works on stitching and related issues [Shum and Szeliski (2000); Szeliski and Shum (1997); Kang and Weiss (1997); Hasler *et al.* (1999)].

Fig. 13.2 Sample set of photos (5 out of 20) and corresponding cylindrical panorama.

To develop the cylindrical warping procedure let us place the projection center on the origin of the reference system and call r the radius of the cylinder and f the focal length of the camera (the image plane is orthogonal to the Z axis and has its origin at $(0,0,f)$).

The projection (x_p, y_p) of the point $P = (X, Y, Z)$ on a planar image can be easily found by triangle similarity (see Fig. 13.3):

$$\begin{cases} x_p = f\,\dfrac{X}{Z} \\[2ex] y_p = f\,\dfrac{Y}{Z} \end{cases} \tag{13.1}$$

The projection (x, y) of the same point $P = (X, Y, Z)$ on a cylindrical surface of radius $r = \sqrt{f^2 + l^2}$ and axis coinciding with the Y axis can be obtained by observing that $\tan\theta = \dfrac{X}{Z}$ and $x = \theta \cdot r$ and is given by the equation:

$$\begin{cases} x = r \ \tan^{-1}\left(\dfrac{X}{Z}\right) \\ \\ y = r \ \dfrac{Y}{\sqrt{X^2 + Z^2}} \end{cases} \tag{13.2}$$

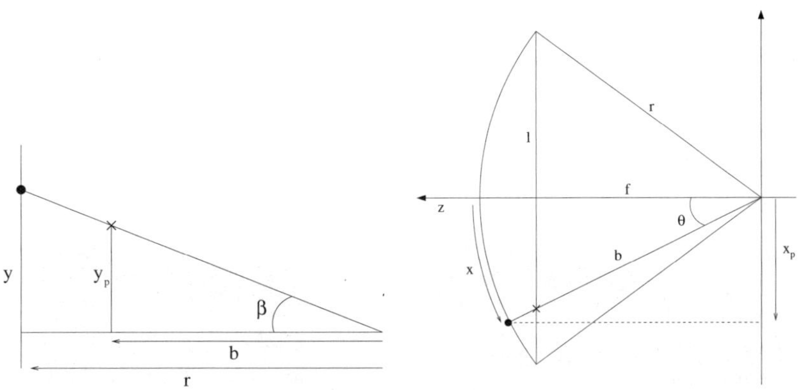

Fig. 13.3 Projection of a point on planar and cylindrical surfaces: a)side view b)top view.

The relationships between (x, y) and (x_p, y_p) are fundamental to cylindrical panoramic imaging. The fusion of the acquired photos into a cylindrical image (stitching procedure) requires mapping regular images formed on a plane onto a cylindrical surface and then merging them together. Panorama visualization requires instead remapping into planar surfaces images positioned on cylindrical surfaces. By comparing the first equations of (13.1) and (13.2) and by eliminating from them term $\dfrac{X}{Z}$ it can be easily seen that:

$$x_p = f \ \tan\theta = f \ \tan\left(\frac{x}{r}\right) \tag{13.3}$$

Figure 13.3(b) shows that since $b = f \ \cos\theta$, the relationship $\dfrac{y_p}{b} = \dfrac{y}{f}$ can be written as:

$$y_p = y\ \frac{f}{r}\ \frac{1}{\cos\left(\dfrac{x}{r}\right)} \tag{13.4}$$

From (13.3) and (13.4) one obtains:

$$\begin{cases} x = r\ \arctan\left(\dfrac{x_p}{f}\right) \\ \\ y = y_p\ \dfrac{r}{f} \cos\left(\dfrac{x}{r}\right) \end{cases} \tag{13.5}$$

The computation of (13.5) requires first evaluating the expression concerning coordinates x and x_p.

It is worth observing that when images projected on a cylindrical surface are displayed on a planar surface (such as a monitor or a paper sheet) horizontal lines exhibit a characteristic distortion as shown in Fig. 13.4.

(a) (b)

Fig. 13.4 (a) An example image and (b) its projection on a cylindrical surface.

Other panoramic projections

Other projection types can overcome cylindrical projection limitations.

Spherical projection allows a complete 360° field of view on the horizontal and vertical axes and a uniform sampling in every direction. It also requires more complex warping computations for the rendering and ad-hoc acquisition equipment and procedure.

Cubic panoramas, present also in the last version of the QuickTime VR product, allow for a complete look-around but are much faster to render than spherical panoramas due to the planar cube surfaces. In this approach the sampling is not uniform as with spheres but the 6 faces of the cube offer a straightforward solution for the storage of the image.

The proposed viewer uses a prism as projection surface. It is a trade-off between cylindrical and cubic panoramas that allows simple acquisition through the various cylindrical panorama authoring tools and fast visualization.

13.3 Visualization of Panoramic Images

Visualization by image warping

Commercial panorama viewers, such as Apple's QuickTime VR, perform the rendering of cylindrical panoramas simply by reprojecting pixel by pixel the section of panorama currently observed onto a planar surface following Equations (13.3) and (13.4). Usually image warping is combined with some filtering techniques (*e.g.* bilinear filtering) to improve image quality. This approach is quite simple to implement but requires more computations per pixel than the 3D based approaches and cannot exploit 3D hardware acceleration.

Visualization by specialized graphic engines

In this section we consider that the shape where the panorama is projected on is considered as a 3D object with the panorama as its texture (Fig. 13.5). The rendering of the panoramic image is performed as a standard 3D rendering, thus exploiting hardware acceleration of current 3D video cards. To fully exploit the graphic card in a web-based environment the viewer can be developed in the form of a Java Applet which uses the additional JAVA 3D API (see Appendix A) to access the three dimensional hardware acceleration.

The viewer is based on a standard 3D graphic engine modified for the specific task of panoramic image visualization. Navigation freedom must be reduced in order to respect the panoramic image limitations. The first constraint is that while true three-dimensional objects can be observed from any point of view, panoramic images can only be observed from a fixed viewpoint. The viewer allows observation only from the center of projection and the permitted movements are rotations and zooming only. On the horizontal axis it is possible to look at every direction, but the vertical field of view is limited by the height of the cylinder on which the panorama

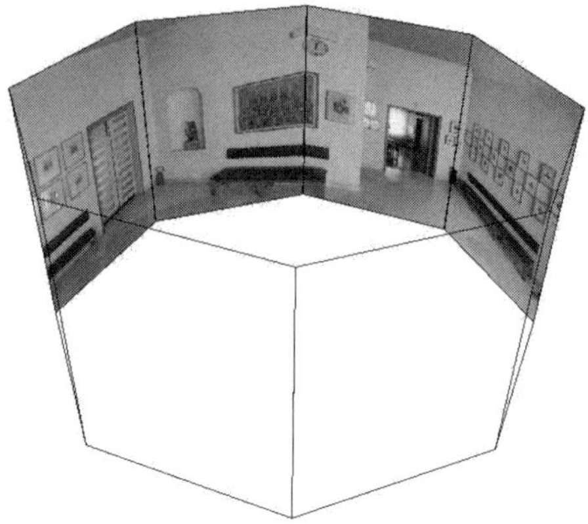

Fig. 13.5 Regular prism with a panorama as texture.

is projected. The zooming features must be performed by modifying the field of view, since, as previously mentioned, the point of view is fixed. However, the perceptual result approximates rather nicely the moving closer or farther of the actual view-point.

To fully exploit the 3D hardware acceleration the cylinder is approximated by a prism with a regular polygonal basis, as shown in Fig. 13.6. The choice of the prism is due to the fact that planar surfaces are simpler to render by standard 3D graphics and texture mapping techniques. The base of the prism is inscribed in the circular base of the cylinder. Clearly, the higher the number of sides (N) of a polygon the better the similarity between the prism and cylinder is. It is worth recalling that the perimeter of a regular N sided polygon inscribed in a circle of radius r is:

$$P = 2\ N\ r \sin\left(\frac{\pi}{N}\right) \tag{13.6}$$

This formula gives the width of an image obtained by mapping a panoramic image supported by a cylinder onto an N sided prism inscribed in it.

The original panoramic image height H will need to be adjusted to have maximum height h_M given by $h_M = H\ \dfrac{P}{2\pi r} = \dfrac{HN}{\pi}\ \sin\left(\dfrac{\pi}{N}\right)$ in order to keep its original proportions. Furthermore, since the distance from the cylinder of the points on each prism's side varies from zero (for the points on the prism's edges which are tangent to the cylinder) to a maximum of $r - a$ (for the points exactly at the middle of each prism's side), the height of the image mapped on the prism varies from the maximum value h_M to

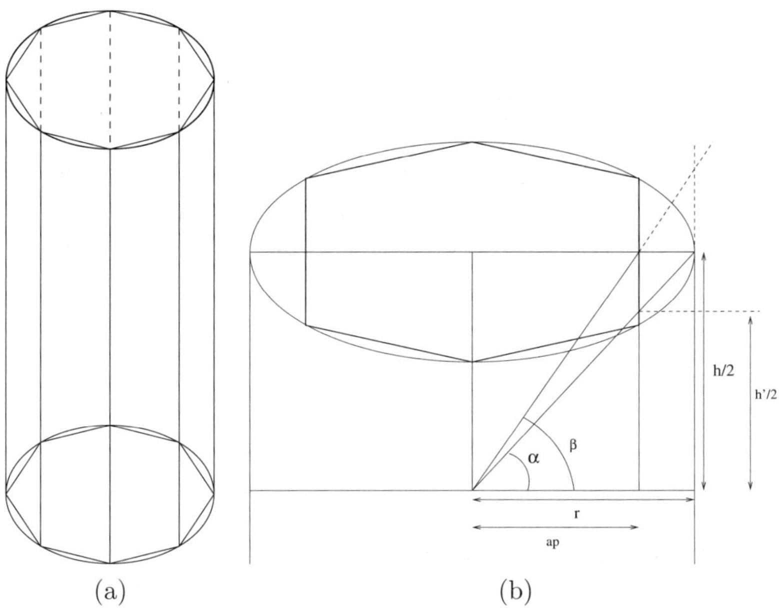

Fig. 13.6 Approximation of a cylinder by a prism (a) general view; (b) detail.

the minimum value h_m given by:

$$h_m = h_M \frac{a}{r} = \frac{HN}{\pi} \sin\left(\frac{\pi}{N}\right) \cos\left(\frac{\pi}{N}\right) \tag{13.7}$$

A small section of the panorama, corresponding to the difference $h_M - h_m$ is lost in the conversion, but its size quickly decrease as N grows. For example, with N equal to 16 one can see more than 98% of the original panorama.

Figure 13.7 shows a panoramic image mapped onto a cylinder and on two prisms, one with 6 (Fig. 13.7(b)) and the other with 20 (Fig. 13.7(c)) sides. The mapping on the prism of 20 sides of Fig. 13.7(c) is very close to the cylindrical panorama of Fig. 13.7(a) showing that it is possbile to have a very good approximation when there are enough sides.

The shape of the prism limits the vertical viewing angle allowed to image sections of size h_m in order to prevent the user from looking outside the panorama. It is possible to include also the textured top and bottom basis of the prism to allow a complete look-around, but this would considerably complicate the acquisition and stitching of the panorama and it will not be considered.

(a)

(b)

(c)

Fig. 13.7 Section of a panoramic image mapped (a) on a cylinder (b) on a prism (N = 6) (c) on a prism (N = 20).

More specifically, if β is the vertical viewing angle of the visualization window, assumed to be centered at angle α as shown in Fig. 13.8, the graphic engine must ensure that:

$$\alpha + \frac{\beta}{2} \leq \tan^{-1}\left(\frac{h_m}{2}\right) \tag{13.8}$$

It is worth recalling that the vertical angle constraints affect also the maximum horizontal viewing angle φ, which must satisfy:

$$\varphi \leq \frac{V_w}{V_h} \tan^{-1}\left(\frac{h_m}{2}\right) \tag{13.9}$$

where V_w and V_h denote the visualization window width and height respectively.

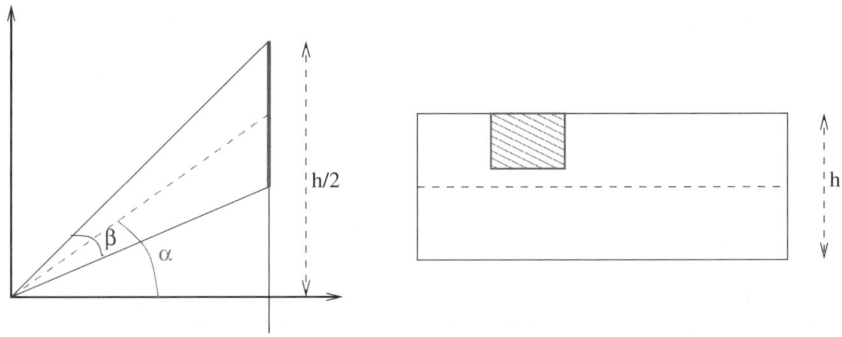

Fig. 13.8 Vertical viewing angle constraints.

The cylindrical panoramic image is first projected on the cylinder and then split into a suitable set of sub-images (usually one for each side of the prism). This is due to the fact that most OpenGL or DirectX graphic cards cannot handle single textures exceeding 2048 × 2048 pixels and high resolution panoramas can easily override this limitation. The sub-images should have a small overlapping section to ensure correct filtering on the edges of the prism.

13.4 Progressive Compression of Panoramic Images

High resolution panoramic images can easily require tens of megabytes and become quite difficult to handle in their entirety. Specially in the case of a web-based viewer, the memory requirements can be prohibitive and the complete download of the image, even if it is compressed, can be too long for slow connections like 56k modems.

A practical way of coping with these limitations is by partitioning the panoramic texture into a suitable number of sub-regions. The simplest and more natural sub-division is given by a regular grid that divides the panorama into a set of rectangular regions (Fig. 13.9). The number and size of the regions depends on the image size.

The spatial sub-division alone cannot guarantee an efficient navigation of the panorama. When the user looks at the whole panorama a smaller resolution version of the image is enough to fill the screen, high resolution information is necessary only when zooming operation is performed, but in this case only a small section of the panorama is visible. This observation suggests to integrate the tiling sub-division into a multi-resolution scheme. A possible solution is to use a base resolution level, which will be loaded completely at startup and some high resolution levels divided into small tiles, that will be loaded when an enlargement in the corresponding region is performed. In the sequel we will refer to an example application we implemented with two high resolution levels, each one at twice the resolution (double width and height, corresponding to four times the previous area) of the previous level, which we will call zoom 2X and zoom 4X. The choice of doubling the resolution at each step is due to the behavior of the wavelet transform of JPEG2000 that will be used to compress these data.

Fig. 13.9 Example of sub-division of a panorama.

The idea is to include in the graphic engine a static texture area which contains the images relative to the base resolution level, and one dynamic texture area for each high resolution level in which the compressed image decoder will place the high resolution texture of the section under observation after a zoom operation. After an enlargement a suitable set of high resolution tiles is downloaded and decoded and the resulting image is applied as texture to the corresponding section of the cylinder (the 3D model of the cylinder is divided with the same grid used for the panorama, see Fig. 13.10).

In our example application the first high resolution tier is supported by a dynamic texture area whose size corresponds to 9 basic sub-regions arranged in a 3×3 square region. For example, using base resolution tiles of 128×128, the high resolution texture is made of nine 256×256 sections arranged in a 768×768 texture. When the user's enlargement exceeds twice the resolution of the basic level, the graphic engine loads in the dynamic area reserved to zoom 2X the double resolution textures of the sub-region

Table 13.1 Examples of texture partitioning for panoramic images.

	Texture sub-division (rows-columns)	Basic resolution	Zoom 2X	Zoom 4X
Exhibition in Cividale	3–18	2304 × 384	4608 × 768	9216 × 1536
Country house	3–14	1792 × 384	3584 × 768	7168 × 1536
Royal Albert Hall	3–18	2304 × 384	4608 × 768	—
Urban scene	4–24	3072 × 512	6144 × 1024	—

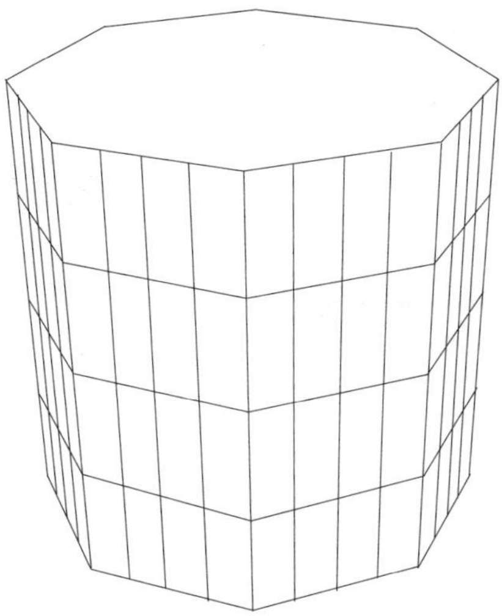

Fig. 13.10 Prism with tiling sub-division.

under observation and of the 8 tiles surrounding it, and applies them as texture to the corresponding section of the prism (see Fig. 13.11). If the user moves and exits from the zoomed region a new high resolution texture is built (the viewer also includes a caching system that stores compressed data relative to previously zoomed tiles).

The same procedure is used for the second tier. The dynamic texture area covers 4 tiles arranged in a 2×2 block at four times the base resolution. In the previous example this corresponds to four 512×512 tiles in a 1024×1024 texture. The selected tiles correspond to the observed one and the three surrounding tiles closer to the central point, *i.e.*, if the central point is in the bottom right, the right, bottom and diagonal bottom-right tiles are decoded (see Fig. 13.11). As in the previous case the new texture replaces the high resolution tier 1 and is used in the rendering of the prism.

Resolutions in-between zoom levels are handled by interpolation. The texture interpolation filter is a feature of the graphic engine supported by the hardware of the graphic card. This provision at high resolution allows real time rendering much faster than the one made available by 2D warping-based cylindrical viewers.

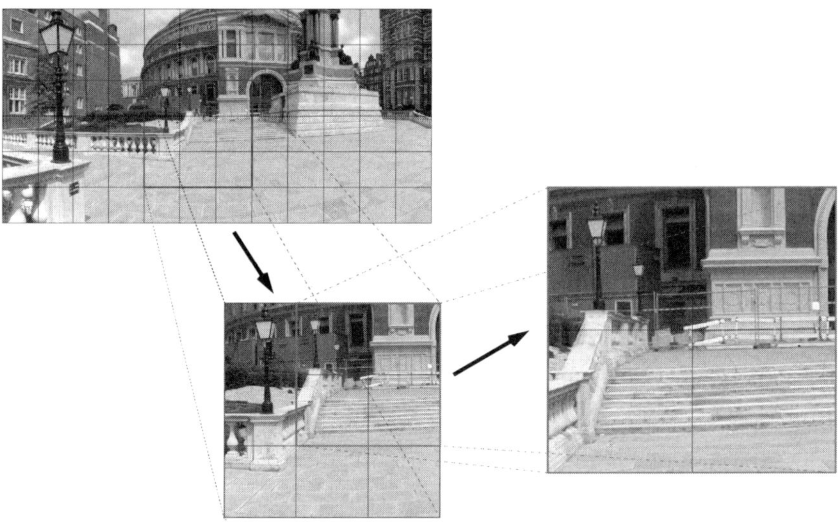

Fig. 13.11 Multi-resolution zoom.

In order to effectively implement this scheme in practice one needs a compression algorithm capable of handling multi-resolution images. An example of a compression standard that includes multi-resolution features is JPEG2000 [Boliek (1996); Taubman and Marcellin (2001)] introduced by the Joint Photographic Expert Group in December 2000. A first recognized characteristic of JPEG2000 is a typical compression improvement over a JPEG image of comparable quality by at least 13% (and up to 20%). Another important feature is its scalability with respect to both image res-

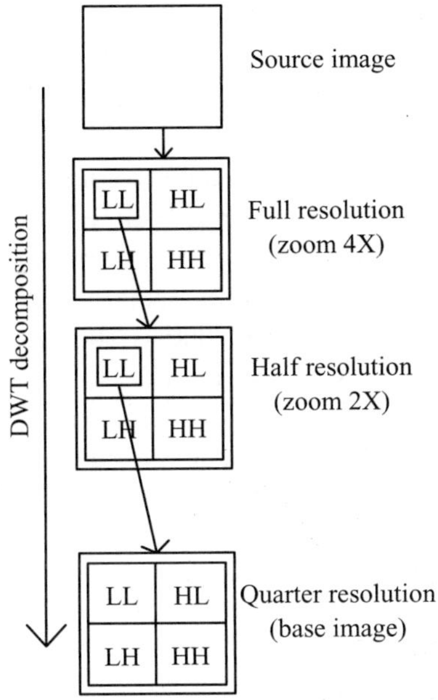

Fig. 13.12 Multi-resolution wavelet decomposition.

olution and image quality. This means that it is possible to decode an image at different resolutions and visual qualities from suitable subsets of the same code-stream.

The multi-resolution scheme previously described fits perfectly inside the JPEG2000 compression system: the wavelet transform used by JPEG2000 performs a subband decomposition that gives a compact multi-resolution representation of the image. At every filtering step the Discrete Wavelet Transform (DWT) decomposes the image into four separate subbands typically denoted as LL, HL, LH and HH, as shown in Fig. 13.12, where letters "L" (low) and "H" (high) denotes the type of their frequency content in the horizontal and vertical directions. For example "LL" indicates that the subband contains the low horizontal and vertical frequency content of the image considered, "HL" that the subband contains the high vertical and low horizontal frequency content, *etc.* A recursive iteration on the LL band permits us to obtain a pyramidal decomposition of the image in several resolution levels each one with half the resolution of the previous one. Usually JPEG2000 compression use a five level wavelet decomposition, and some of them can be used for the different zoom levels of the panorama. Unfortunately, this approach introduces the obvious limitation that each resolution level must have double width and height with respect to the previous one. The wavelet filter takes as input the wavelet coefficients of the low resolution image and the high frequency subbands of the new resolution levels and returns the high resolution image. In this way, a higher resolution image does not require the decoding of a whole new image and the redundancy between different resolution versions of the same image can be exploited.

Another useful feature of JPEG2000 is the sub-division of the codestream into small subsections corresponding to different spatial regions of the image at a certain resolution level. Each of these packets of data, called precinct, contains the coefficient of the wavelet transform relative to the corresponding region at a specified resolution level and can be used to double the resolution in that region. The precinct dimension is variable but must be a power of 2, in our implementation it matches the tiling previously described.

In the proposed application the base resolution is loaded completely at startup while the high resolution data is split into many small blocks corresponding to the precincts. When the user performs an enlargement, the precincts corresponding to the observed region (matching the 3×3 blocks of texture) are downloaded and sent to the decoder that generates the high resolution texture. The second high resolution tier works exactly as the first, but the 2×2 blocks are decoded directly from the first high resolution level data and the new coefficients. The base resolution is not used in this process and the decoding can start only after the first tier is available. The viewer also includes a caching system that records previously downloaded precincts to be used in case of enlargement in sections close to previous zooms: all the transmitted tiles once downloaded are stored in the cache in compressed form, when the user's navigation prompts a zooming request, the graphic engine first of all checks whether the requested precincts are already in the cache. If so, they are decompressed at run-time and placed in the proper dynamic texture area; otherwise the graphic engine requests their transmission from the server. The tiles in compressed form do not require large amount of RAM, their size is at most a few Mbytes (the size of the whole image compressed in JPEG2000).

The last feature of JPEG2000 used in the remote visualization of panoramas is the scalability with respect to the image quality. In JPEG2000 the coefficient quantization is also performed in a progressive way, the compressed coefficient data is organized into "quality layers", so-called because

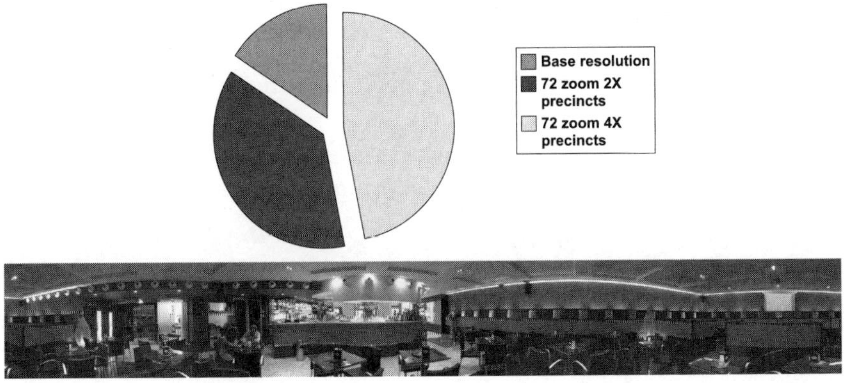

Fig. 13.13 Panorama compression: percentage of data pertaining to basic resolution, first and second zoom levels.

each of them is associated to a visual quality level. The more quality layers are jointly used for the coefficients the better the image quality will be. In our example application a low quality version of the image is first transmitted and the visual quality is subsequently improved in one or more steps by the transmission of further packets of data.

To exemplify the whole system let us consider the panoramic image of Fig. 13.13. The original panorama is a 12288x1536 pixels image that occupies about 56 Mbyte in uncompressed form and around 2 Mbyte when compressed by JPEG2000 with reasonable quality. The download of the whole image can require a long time on slow channels and the whole uncompressed image data is quite big for a Java Applet. The pie chart of Fig. 13.13 shows the percentage sub-division of the 2 Mbytes of data. The base resolution (3072×384 pixels and 330 Kbytes of compressed data) is transmitted and decoded completely at startup using the quality layer feature for progressive download and decoding. The availability of the complete image at low resolution allows a quick exploration of the complete scene. The next resolution level (6144×768 and 773 Kbytes) is divided by a regular grid in 72 precincts each one 256×256 pixels wide and stored as a standalone file. Other 72 precincts of 512×512 pixels (summing to 982 Kbyte of data) contain the coefficients of the last level of the subband transform corresponding to the full resolution image.

When the zoom factor overcomes a threshold, the precincts relative to the zoomed region are downloaded and used to generate the high resolution texture that is applied to the prism model. In this way, every enlargement operation requires only a small amount of data (in the example the average zoom 2X precinct size is 10 Kb and at most 9 of them are downloaded in a single zoom operation) and the complete high resolution image is never stored in the memory.

Some data about examples of compressed partitioned panoramic images of various sizes are presented in the following tables.

Table 13.2. Examples of compressed partitioned panoramas.

	Panorama's dimension	Uncompressed RGB 24 bit/pixel (Mbyte)	JPEG2000 compressed (Kbyte)
Bar	12288 × 1536	56	2124
Country house	7168 × 1536	33	1244
Urban scene	6144 × 1024	19	614
Royal Albert Hall	4608 × 768	11	346

	Basic resolution basic quality (kbyte)	Basic resolution improved quality (kbyte)	Zoom level 1 total memory (kbyte)	Zoom level 1 single tile (kbyte)	Zoom level 2 total memory (kbyte)	Zoom level 2 single tile (kbyte)
Bar	73	265	753	10,5	982	13,6
Country house	77	159	338	8	635	15,1
Urban scene	62	230	323	3,4	—	—
Royal Albert Hall	36	110	201	3,7	—	—

13.5 Summary

Panoramic images are currently a very common tool for virtual walk-through of real places. This chapter presents an innovative scheme for their remote visualization with several conceptual and practical points of interest.

A major characteristic of the proposed visualization scheme is that it does not consider cylindrical panoramas as warped 2D images as typically assumed by current viewers, but as 3D objects, namely as interiors of textured cylinders (with axis coinciding with the panorama capture axis). Even though this is a substantial novelty in the field of panoramic visualization, it should be noted that it recovers the conceptual position of the environmental maps, an idea that appeared in the computer graphics literature of the early 80's [Blinn and Newell (1976); Greene (1986)].

Such an approach allows us to frame the visualization of cylindrical panoramas as a rendering issue to be dealt with by a dedicated graphic engine. The graphic engine must indeed satisfy the constraints required by the inspection of a panoramic image, notably, it can only allow for horizontal panning (and a limited vertical rotation) around one central viewpoint. This fact has several implementation implications, as explained in Section 3, such as zooming-in (out) must be dealt as a viewing angle reduction (or enlargement) and not as motions of the viewing position closer (or further) to the textured cylinder.

Treating panoramic images as 3D objects and deploying a graphic engine for their visualization gives the ability of exploiting graphic cards for visualizing panoramas. Graphic cards, rather powerful and ubiquitous in current computers, enable large window size visualization and zooming of panoramic images at quality clearly superior to that of merely software supported visualization. Graphic cards can indeed implement effective real-time linear and non-linear texture processing operations not possible with software implementations.

Another important novelty of the proposed visualization scheme is that it incorporates progressive compression based on JPEG2000 in order to effectively handle the remote visualization of panoramas.

The performance of the proposed scheme for visualizing panoramas is demonstrated by a prototype (http://lttm.dei.unipd.it/vitra-final) implemented within VITRA's project. The current viewer's implementation is in Java 3D, which is an extension of Java enabled to access graphic accelerators (standard Java cannot use graphic cards). Java 3D has the portability features typical of Java, but it requires an addition to the libraries of the standard Java virtual machine. For an overview of Java 3D see Appendix A.

As the standard scheme for panorama visualization based on image warping from cylindrical to Cartesian coordinate has been implemented in many versions with different languages and various compression algorithms, one can envision a similar activity also for the panorama visualization method presented in this chapter.

In this connection, implementation tests certainly worth considering are represented by GL4Java and by Shout3D which are specialized graphic libraries in Java language giving access to graphic hardware facilities. More performing implementation of the viewer can be obtained by plug-ins tailored to specific system characteristics.

It is also worth recalling that the structures of JPEG2000 and in general of current progressive compression algorithms offer many possibilities of integration within remote viewers of panoramic images in order to support zooming and visualization window enlargements. There is relatively little research in this area at this time and further investigation will certainly be beneficial.

As a final remark it is worth observing that visualizing panoramic images as 3D objects is a perspective which makes their use as photorealistic backgrounds for games more convenient, in the spirit of the "movie maps" encountered in the early video-game literature. The possibility of effectively visualizing panoramas remotely allows for their use in on-line games as well. The connection between panoramic imagery and games is clearly an exciting direction of investigation.

Acknowledgment

We would like to acknowledge EC project *VITRA* which supported in part this work.

References

(2003). *Omnivis 2003: Workshop on Omnidirectional Vision and Camera* (IEEE, Madison, Wisconsin).

Benosman, R. and Kang, S. B. (eds.) (2001). *Panoramic Vision: Sensors, Theory and Applications* (Springer-Verlag).

Blinn, J. F. and Newell, M. E. (1976). Texture and reflection in computer generated images, *Communications of the ACM* **19**, 10, pp. 542–547.

Boliek, M. (1996). New work item proposal: JPEG2000 image coding system, Tech. Rep. N390, ISO/IEC JTC1/SC29/WG1.

Burt, P. J. and Adelson, E. H. (1983). A multiresolution spline with application to image mosaics, *ACM Transactions on Graphics* **2**, 4, pp. 217–236.

Chen, S. and Williams, L. (1993). View interpolation for image synthesis, in *Computer Graphics (SIGGRAPH'93)*, pp. 279–288.

Chen, S. E. (1995). Quicktime VR, an image-based approach to virtual environment navigation, in *Computer Graphics (SIGGRAPH'95)*, pp. 29–38.

Cortelazzo, G. M. and Lucchese, L. (1999). A new method of image mosaicking and its application to cultural heritage representation, *Computer Graphics Forum* **18**, 3, pp. C265–275.

Gortler, S. J., Grzeszczuk, R., Szeliski, R. and Cohen, M. F. (1996). The lumigraph, in *Computer Graphics Proceedings, Annual Conference Series, Proc. SIGGRAPH'96*, pp. 43–54, new Orleans, ACM SIGGRAPH.

Greene, N. (1986). Environment mapping and other applications of world projections, *Computer Graphics and Applications* **6**, 11, pp. 21–29.

Hasler, D., Sbaiz, L., Ayer, S. and M., V. (1999). From local to global parameter estimation in panoramic photographic reconstruction, in *Proc. of IEEE International Conference on Image Processing*, pp. 113–117.

Hsu, C.-T. and Wu, J.-L. (1996). Multiresolution mosaic, in *Proc. of ICIP'96*, Vol. 3 (Switzerland), pp. 743–746.

Irani, M., Anandan, P. and Hsu, S. (1995). Mosaic based representations of video sequences and their applications, in *Fifth International Conference on Computer Vision (ICCV'95)* (Cambridge, Massachusetts), pp. 606–611.

Kang, S. B. (1997). A survey of image-based rendering techniques, Tech. Rep. 97/4, Digital Equipment Corporation, Cambridge Research Lab.

Kang, S. B. and Weiss, R. (1997). Characterization of errors in compositing panoramic images, in *IEEE Computer Society Conference on Computer Vision and Pattern Recognition (CVPR'97)* (San Juan, Puerto Rico), pp. 103–109.

Levoy, M. and Hanrahan, P. (1996). Light field rendering, in *Computer Graphics Proceedings, Annual Conference Series, Proc. SIGGRAPH'96*, pp. 31–42, new Orleans, ACM SIGGRAPH.

Lippman, A. (1980). Movie maps: An application of the optical videodisc to computer graphics, in *Computer Graphics(Proc. SIGGRAPH'80)*, pp. 32–43.

Malde, H. E. (1983). Panoramic Photographs, *American Scientist* **71**, 2, pp. 132–140.

Mann, S. and Picard, R. W. (1994). Virtual bellows: constructing high-quality images from video, in *First IEEE International Conference on Image Processing (ICIP'94)* (Austin, Texas), pp. 363–367.

McMillan, L. and Bishop, G. (1995). Plenoptic modeling: an image based rendering system, in *Computer Graphics (SIGGRAPH'95)*, pp. 39–46.

Miller, G., Hoffert, E., Chen, S. E., Patterson, E., Blackketter, D., Rubin, S., Applin, S. A., Yim, D. and Hanan, J. (1992). The virtual museum:

Interactive 3d navigation of a multimedia database. the journal of visualization and computer animation, *The Journal of Visualization and Animation* **3**, pp. 183–197.

Nayar, S. (1997). Catadioptric omnidirectional camera, in *IEEE Computer Society Conference on Computer Vision and Pattern Recognition (CVPR'97)* (San Juan, Puerto Rico), pp. 482–488.

Ripley, G. D. (1989). Dvi a digital multimedia technology, *Commun. ACM* **32**, 7, pp. 811–822.

Shum, H.-Y. and Szeliski, R. (2000). System and experiment paper: Construction of panoramic image mosaics with global and local alignment, *International Journal of Computer Vision* **36**, 2, pp. 101–130.

Szeliski, R. (1994). Image mosaicing for tele-reality applications. in *IEEE Workshop on Applications of Computer Vision (WACV'94)* (IEEE Computer Society, Sarasota, Florida), pp. 44–53.

Szeliski, R. (1996). Video mosaics for virtual environments, *IEEE Computer Graphics and Applications* **16**, 2, pp. 22–30.

Szeliski, R. and Shum, H.-Y. (1997). Creating full view panoramic image mosaics and texture-mapped models, in *Computer Graphics (SIGGRAPH'97)*, pp. 251–258.

Taubman, D. and Marcellin, M. (2001). *JPEG2000: Image compression fundamentals, standards and practice* (Kluwer Academic Publishers, Boston).

Xiong, Y. and Turkowski, K. (1997). Creating image-based VR using a self-calibrating fisheye lens, in *IEEE Computer Society Conference on Computer Vision and Pattern Recognition (CVPR'97)* (San Juan, Puerto Rico), pp. 237–243.

Yang, R. and Pollefeys, M. (2003). Multi-resolution real-time stereo on commodity graphics hardware, in *IEEE Computer Society Conference on Computer Vision and Pattern Recognition (CVPR'03)* (IEEE Computer Society, Madison, Wisconsin), pp. I211–217.

Chapter 14

A 3D Game — Castles

G. Xiao, Z. Cai, L. Ying and A. Basu

14.1 Introduction

In this chapter we will design a simple online game called "Castles" that allows two players to build structures in a 3D space and claim territory in the space. The person with the most space at the end of the game wins. In the game, there are two main rules. One is checking enclosure. The smaller region (SR) occupied by Player A will be taken over by Player B if Player B can create a larger region (LR) that entirely encloses SR. At the end of the game, the person with larger overall territory wins. Another rule is collapse detection. Constructions must follow the laws of gravity; to simplify this problem we only test whether a newly added piece can rest on an existing structure without toppling over. We use Java3D to implement the game. Java3D is convenient to implement 3D online graphics applications as it can be executed on any computer and operating system.

14.2 Game Design

Figure 14.1 shows the user-interface of the game. The game follows the rules below:

1. Units of the building blocks (rocks) are of fixed size.
2. The 3D space and size of the rocks are scalable.
3. Structures must follow the normal laws of gravity, which should be clearly specified and justified; *e.g.*, no floating rocks in the sky, no tower of Pisa leaning at an angle of 60 degree, and so on.
4. Ownership of a Structure: A smaller structure (SM) created by Player A will be taken over by Player B, if Player B can create a larger structure (SL) that predominantly encloses SM.

In this game, two players can build blocks in a three-dimensional space and claim territory in the space. The person who occupies more regions in the end wins. The blocks used by the players can consist of all kinds of objects with different sizes and structures. When the structures are specified, they should follow the laws of gravity. Otherwise, the buildings will collapse. Initially, the whole space is blank, which means it does not belong to either player. If any player occupies a region with some structures, then the region belongs to that player.

At the beginning of this game, users need to set up the game type. There are two types of this game, the first is called "single collapse," in which we only consider whether or not the new block added follows gravitational rules. If this block follows the normal laws of gravity, the structure of castle do not need to change. Otherwise the new block will collapse. For this type of game, adding a new block does not affect any other block. The other type of game is called "multiple collision." In this type, adding a new block may affect other blocks that occupy nearby space.

Fig. 14.1 User interface of multiplayer game.

Player A starts by moving a block first. Blocks with different sizes and structures are randomly introduced from the top; which a player can move, rotate and position in a desired location. The 3D space is made up of cubes covering a $8 \times 8 \times 16$ space. Each cube is implemented as an object of class Transformgroup. The size of the space can be changed at any time. When a player moves a block to some position, we only need to change the properties of the corresponding object representing that position, and test if some blocks are enclosed by others or if gravitational laws are violated. Figure 14.2 shows the whole algorithm of our game.

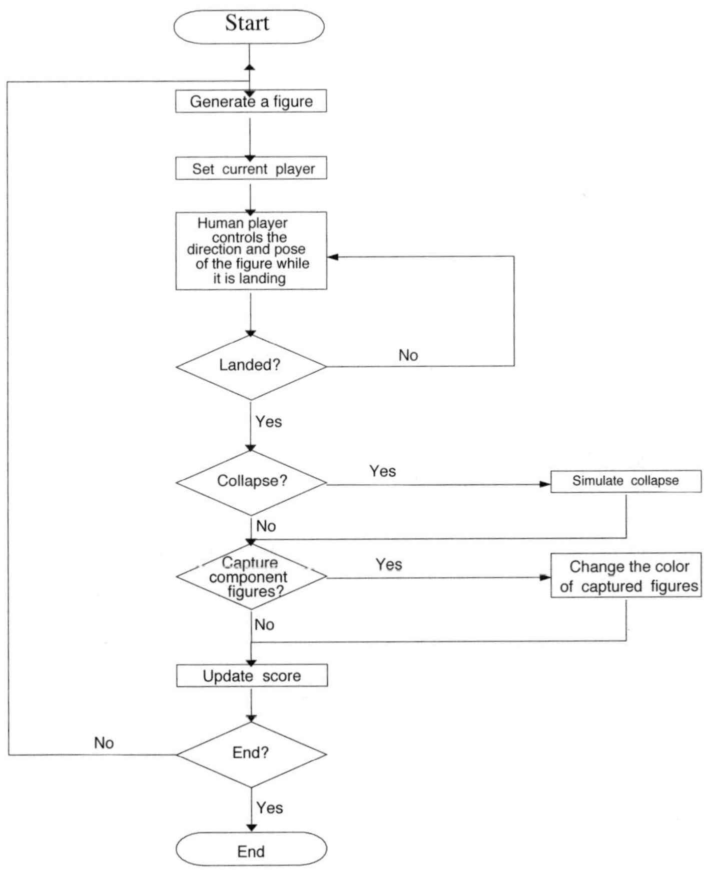

Fig. 14.2 Flow chart of the implementation.

14.3 Implementation Details

The game is implemented following the Java 3D API, an application programming interface which can be used for designing three-dimensional graphics applications and 3D applets. The programmer constructs for creating and manipulating 3D geometric objects. These geometric objects reside in a virtual universe, which is then rendered. The API is designed with the flexibility to create precise virtual universes of a wide variety of sizes, from astronomical to subatomic. Java 3D follows Java's "write once, run anywhere" benefit to developers of 3D graphics applications. We can look java 3D as part of Java Media suite of APIs. It supports multiple platforms, such as windows, Linux, supports multiple display environments, such as Direct3D, OpenGL, QuickDraw3D, and XGL, and also supports multiple input models. The program using by Java 3D API have access to the entire set of Java classes and it integrates well with the Internet. Java 3D is a network centric, scene graph-based API. It provides three benefits for end-users: application portability, hardware independence and performance scalability.

There are two key algorithms in the implementation, one for checking enclosure, the other for collapse detection and handling. Details on these two algorithms are given below.

Algorithm for Checking Enclosure

To determine if a region is enclosed, we check the six directions (top, bottom, left, right, front, back) of this region. When checking whether a region is enclosed, some information are needed, such as the positions need to be checked and the owner of each position. Then the recursive method is used to check in all the six directions.

Algorithm for Collapse Detection and Handling

Implementing collapse is a challenging part in this program. There are two subtasks for collapse task. First, we should know which object(s) is (are) currently unstable. Then, for the unstable objects, the collapse needs to be simulated. Followings are some of the steps in dealing with the collapse problem.

- Collapse Detection

We present a recursive algorithm to solve this problem:

1. Set up an unstable object set, denoted by **F**, put the currently active object into F.

2. Calculate the centre of gravity (on XY plane, denoted as **x** and **y**) for the objects in F and find out the lowest Z coordinate (denoted as **z**) of those objects in **F**.

3. Check the position **(x, y, z-1)**.

IF objects besides **F** are stable Return **F**

ELSE put all the neighbors of **F** into **F** and go to Step 2.

- Collapse Simulation

The task is to simulate the collapse of the objects in **F**. We not only need to consider the collision among the unstable objects and the stable objects, but also among the unstable objects. We first implement a simple version of this task. We assume that only the active object is unstable, if an unstable object exists (we call this collapse "Single Collapse"). Our solution for Single Collapse is based on two parameters: the centre of gravity of active object and the supporting point.

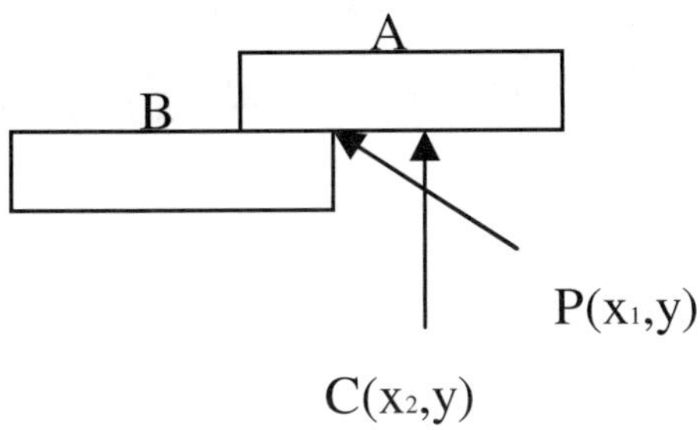

Fig. 14.3 Detecting single collapse.

In Fig. 14.3, A is the active object and B is a stable object. P is the supporting point for A, and C is the centre of gravity for A. Suppose that P and C have the same coordinate on the Y-axis. The reasonable collapse for A is to let A rotate around the line passing through P clockwise. This gives an example of our algorithm for simulating Single Collapse.

However, in many cases, A and B may collapse together; a situation called "Multiple Collapse." Our solution for multiple collapse only considers the collision among unstable objects and stable ones. Our solution is based on extending Single Collapse. Following the order from bottom to top for unstable objects, we consider each and check their collision with *stable objects*.

For the Multiple Collapse example in Fig. 14.4, suppose A and B are unstable objects, and C and D together is a stable object. We consider

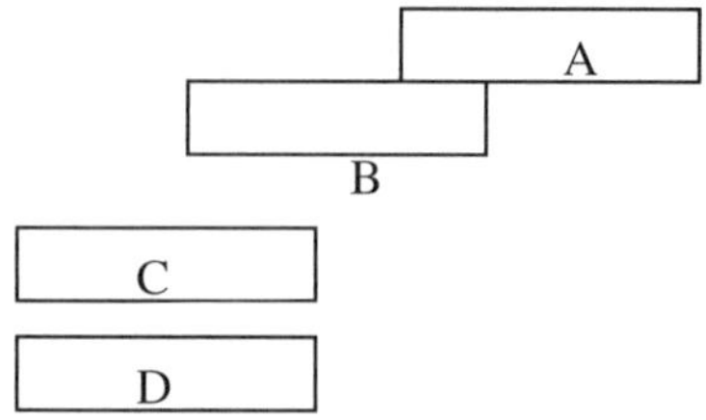

Fig. 14.4 Detecting multiple collapse.

Fig. 14.5 Stages of the game.

unstable objects following a bottom-to-top order: B, A. We consider the bottom to top order because the unstable objects at the bottom could have no legal move; which affects the number of legal moves for the higher unstable object. For the above example, if B has no legal move, B becomes a stable object and we will take this into account when looking for legal moves for A.

Index of Classes

In order to make the code clearer, classes index and descriptions are given below.

Castle

The main program which builds the basic JAVA 3D environment (*e.g.*, SimpleUniverse, background, sound *etc.*) and the user interface(*e.g.* menu, button, *etc.*).

Field

Field means the Castle's building site. It is a predefined grid cube.

Block

Blocks are the basic construction units which occupy Field.

Important members:

Mplayer

Which player currently owns a block.

mEnalbed

The flag indicates if the space of a block is occupied or not.

mgroup

The Figure ID of a block.

Important methods:

Block (int player, int group)

construction methods, initializing color, texture, owner, *etc.*

Void setEnabled (boolean enalbed, int group, int player)

Assign (or take away) a block to (from) a player, identifying it with Figure ID at the same time.

Figure

Figures consist of Blocks. There are two types of figures: active figures and still figures. After a figure is generated, it becomes an active figure. This figure can fall down toward the ground at a certain speed. The current human player manipulates the figure's position, pose and landing speed before the active figure lands on the bottom of the field or any still figure. After landing, the active figure becomes a still one and cannot be operated by the player. The color of a still figure could be changed if this figure is surrounded by opponent's figures.

Important members:

mgroup

figure ID

mplayer

owner ID

Important methods:

void createFigure(int type)

generate a figure from the figure type library.

boolean touchDownCheck(Field field)

checks whether one part of the figure collides with an enabled field position.

public boolean outOfFieldCheck(Field field)

checks if at least one Block of the Figure is outside the Field.

public void doStep(float fStepDef)

translates the Figure in unit steps in z-direction.

public void translate(int iX, int iY)

translates the figure in x or y direction.

public void rotate(int iAxis, int iDirection)

rotates the figure, without checking for touchdown or out-of-field position.

TetrisScene

Scenegraph root class for this Game. Most game features, including surrounding and collapse algorithms, are implemented here.

Important members:

MFigure

current active figure

Mfigures

the still figure's information (*e.g.* blocks' positions, owner *etc.*).

MneighborTable

the neighborhood table for each figure, used for surrounding and collapse algorithm.

CollapseFigures

the figures which are going to collapse: a hashMap.

Important methods:

public void newFigure()

creates new Figure at the top of the field, centered in xy direction.

public void removeFigure()

remove the current Figure from the (live) scenegraph.

public void startGame()

adds the step behavior to the scenegraph tree and adds a new Figure to start the action.

public void pauseGame()

pause the game.

public void continueGame()

continue the game.

public void gameOver()

end the game.

public synchronized void downStep(float fStep)

main even handling function. Every certain time, this function will be invoked and choose different actions(algorithms) based on current situation.

public synchronized void updateNeighborTable(int group, Vector block-Positions) update the neighbor table for figures when the position changed.

public synchronized Set checkCollapse()

check if collapse happens, if so, return the corresponding figures.

private synchronized boolean dealCollapse()

handle collapse.

public synchronized Set checkCollapse()

check if collapse happens, if so, return the coresponding figures.

public synchronized boolean translateFigure(int iX, int iY)

translates the Figure *if possible*.

public synchronized boolean rotateFigure(int iAxis, int iDirection)

rotates the figure *if possible*.

Chapter 15

A Networked Version of Castles

D. Lien, M. McElhinney, L. Ying and A. Basu

15.1 Introduction

More and more, gaming is becoming popular not only with stand-alone computer and game systems, but with multi-player, online versions as well. In this chapter we discuss implementation for a very large number of players in an online game with a game server.

We also include mouse and keyboard interface interaction, texturing, randomly generated terrain mapping, and text communication between players. We will describe the design and architecture of the underlying game and network structure as well as the interesting algorithms and design patterns used.

15.2 Game Design and User Manual

The basic idea of the game is that two players compete on building a castle with the same available blocks. To build a castle, the requirement is exactly the same as for building houses in the real world. The criterion of winning is the total area that could be used for living. As a result, we could build several floors to increase the available area. The typical procedure of playing this game is illustrated by Fig. 15.1. A detailed user manual is given in the Appendix.

15.3 Implementation Details

Major 3D Objects

The major objects of the game are the 3D playing board and the block for building castle. Following are the major properties of two of the objects, which are commented.

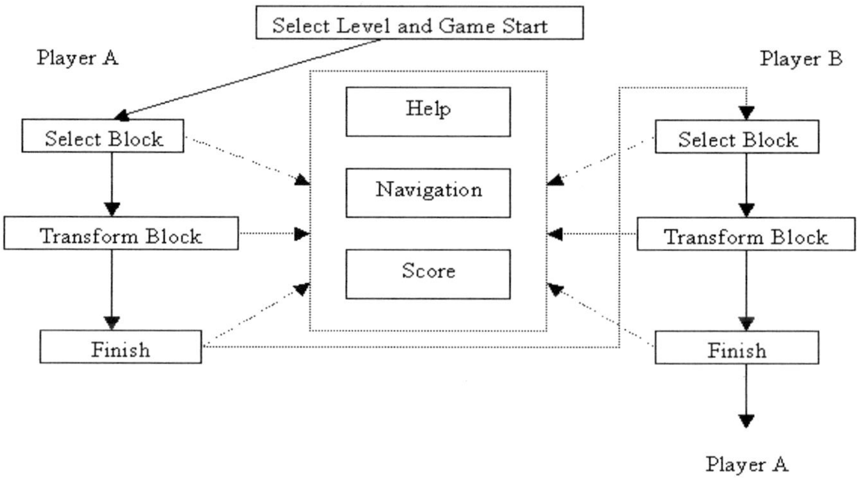

Fig. 15.1 A typical procedure of playing the game.

```
public class Board extends Group {
    /********* Major Data ******/
    // the size of 3D play board
    int m_nSize;
    // the matrix of 3D board
    // '0' means available
    // '1' means occupied by A
    // '2' means occupied by B
    public int M[][][];
    // the blocks that have been settled in the play board
    public Vector A, B;
    // score
    public int m_nScoreA = 0, m_nScoreB = 0;
    ...
```

```
}
public class Block extends BranchGroup {
    /********* Major Data *******/
    // the number of cells
    public int m_nCellNum = 0;
    // the cells' coordinate according to the reference cell (0, 0, 0)
    public Point3d C[];
    // the coordinate of reference cell in the play board
    public Vector3d m_vecRef = new Vector3d(0, 0, 0);
    // rotation
    public float m_fRotateX = 0, m_fRotateY = 0, m_fRotateZ = 0;
    ...
}
```

Key Algorithms and Server Architecture

The multiplayer functionality relies on the fact that there is a centralized server running in a known location. For our purposes, we ran the server on a hard-coded machine. However, this could be changed by simply modifying the constant src.network. NetworkConstants. SERVER_ADDRESS to the desired server.

During execution, the server waits for incoming connections from clients, and processes requests and commands from them. These commands and requests come in the form of message segments which are written by the client using a ServerMessageWriter, and read by the server using a Game-ClientReader. When receiving an initial connection, a socket is created for that connection, and further processing only occurs by receiving a Network-Constants.LOGIN or NetworkConstants. REGISTER_USER message. If the former is received, the database of usernames and passwords is queried and login succeeds only if the username and passwords match. In the latter case, login occurs and a new user is created only if the username does not already exist in the database. Passwords are stored in whatever form they are transmitted to the server.

After login is completed, information on other clients is dispatched to the new user complete with IP address and port number on which they are listening. Additionally, the updated client list along with the newly added user is sent to all other clients. In this way, every client has the information of every other client so that they may challenge them to a game, or see whether they are presently in a game and unavailable.

Finally, when a client closes their connection, the server drops this client and notifies all connected clients with the updated client list.

Networked Client Architecture

The CastleGame client application is set up to be in one of three modes or states. In the first mode (Fig. 15.2), the user has the option of playing a networked game, a local game, or seeing some documentation.

Fig. 15.2 Selecting game mode.

Once the network option is selected, the user is asked to login or register a new user as shown in Fig. 15.3.

If login is successful, players reach a server screen which displays their statistics, a list of all available players, and a top ten score list. This screen looks like the one shown in Figure 15.4:

At this point, the client creates a ClientConnectThread which waits for

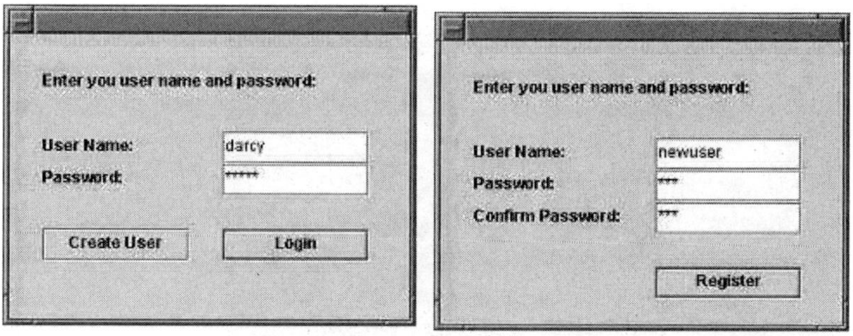

Fig. 15.3 Login screen.

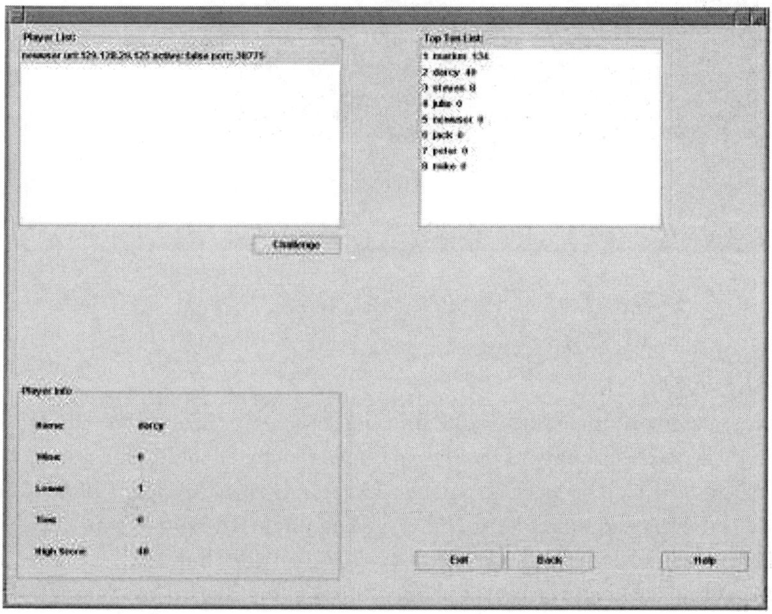

Fig. 15.4 Player list screen.

challenges from other clients on the first available port. The client's IP address and listening port are broadcast to all other clients by the centralized server. Once a client-client connection is made, either by challenging another player or by being challenged, the actual gameplay begins. The gameplay mode can be seen in Fig. 15.5.

This implementation can be found in: src/client/CastleGame.java.

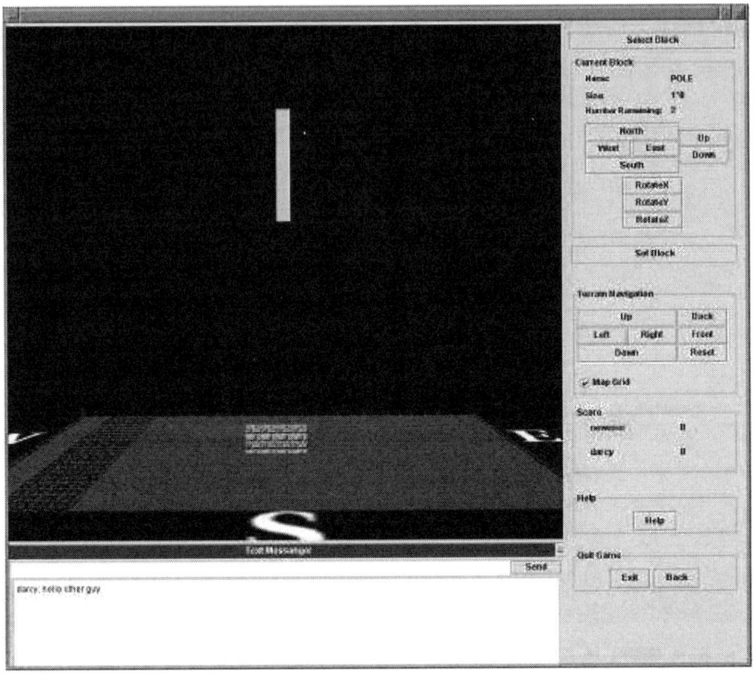

Fig. 15.5 Main screen.

Scoring Algorithm

The scoring algorithm for the game is created to calculate the enclosed space of the user's blocks. The algorithm works by checking for any enclosed spaces created by the user and their blocks. Scores are then based on the size of the enclosed space and the level the enclosed space is at.

The scoring algorithm is a recursive algorithm that first searches for a location that is taken up by the user. The scoring algorithm then checks all possible paths from the block to see if the path returns back to the block from another direction from where it started searching, hence creating an enclosed space.

To keep track of the path used to check for an enclosed space, two vectors are used. One vector keeps track of the spaces where the search algorithm has been and the other vector keeps track of the spaces that make up the good path.

When the algorithm moves to a new location, the location is added to both vectors. However, when the algorithm runs into a dead end, the space is removed from the good path vector but still kept track of in the regular vector. The algorithm then goes to the last good space, which is the previous space in the good path vector, and continues its search. If there are no good paths remaining, then the search algorithm returns with a value of 3 or less since that is the minimum amount of space that cannot make up an enclosed space. Otherwise, the algorithm returns the number of blocks making up the enclosed space.

When an enclosed space is found, a point is given for each block that makes up the enclosed space and the point is multiplied by the height of the y-axis it is on. Only blocks that make up the enclosed space are counted and the blocks that may be attached to the enclosed space but do not make up the enclosed space are ignored.

Consider the following example:

000000000000
011111100000
001000100000
001000100000
001111111000
000000000000

In this example, there are 17 blocks involved in the enclosed space. However, only 14 blocks make up the enclosed space. Therefore the user will get 14 points multiplied by the height at which the enclosed space occurs. Therefore, if the enclosed space is at level one then the user will get 14 points. If the enclosed space is at level one and level two then the user will get $14 \times 1 + 14 \times 2 = 42$ points.

The algorithm encourages the users to build their castles as high as possible while attempting to maximize their enclosed space. The functionality for the scoring algorithm can be seen in *src.client.Board.java* in the *calScore* and *calEnclosedSpace* functions.

15.3.1 *Password Encryption*

A big problem with networked games is the security risk associated with transmitting sensitive information across the network. It is possible for people to monitor what is being sent back and forth. As a result, information that needs to remain private should be encrypted in one way or another. In our case, the only information that is sensitive enough to need encryption is the sending of passwords from the client to the server. To implement security measures, we used a 160 bit SHA-1 (Secure Hash Algorithm 1) one-way encryption algorithm that converts an input string of characters into a unique message digest. It is referred to as "one-way" because one cannot figure out what data is produced given a message digest. This is also a collision-free mechanism that guarantees that no two different values will produce the same digest.

Upon entering the password in the PasswordDialog (PasswordDialog.java) we use the SHA-1 encryption to create an encrypted password. It is this encrypted password that is then transmitted over the network to the server and stored in the database. In this way, even if someone was to intercept the password, they could not actually enter it into any dialog to gain access to the user account, nor could they reverse engineer the encrypted password to discover the actual password.

SHA-1 encryption is slower than some other encryption algorithms, such as MD5 but is more resistant to brute force attacks. If security is even more important than we have perceived it, we could make use of SHA- 256 or SHA-384, which are longer message digest and even more resistant to brute force "cracking" attempts. These algorithms can be found in:

src/util/PasswordService.java
src/util/PasswordDialog.java
SHA-1 Password encryption,
http://www.evolt.org/article/Password_encryption_rationale_and_Java_example/18/60122/

High-Scores Database

To add persistence to the Game Server, and incentive for players to continue to play the game, we made use of a database to maintain information about player's win-loss-tie record, as well as their high scores from previous games. Any time a game is finished, the player that initially made the challenge reports to the server the names and scores of the two players that just played. The server updates the player's high scores if their new score is greater than their old one, and updates the win-loss-tie statistics based on the score. This new high score information is then disseminated to all the other online clients, and the individual players whose win-loss-tie record was modified are updated.

This functionality can be found in:
src.server.ServerDb.java
src.server.GameServer.java
src.client.CastleGame.java

Text Messenger

Many online games encourage and offer interaction methods other than just straight game-play. Most offer some method to talk to each other over the network using either text or voice. We followed suit and integrated a text-messaging unit into the lower portion of the networked version of the game allowing users to send text comments back and forth while playing. A screenshot is shown below:

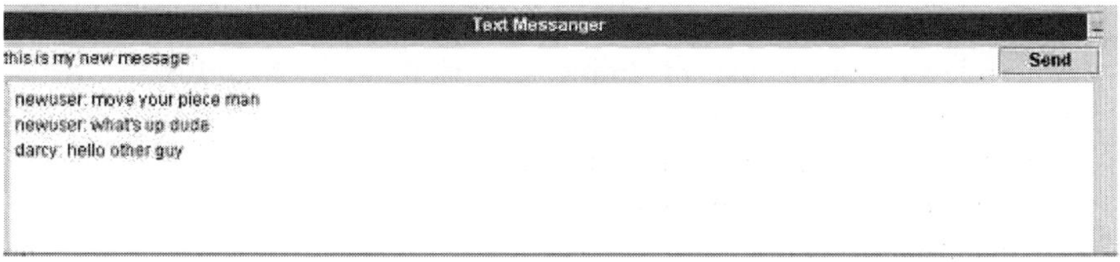

If this option is not useful for a particular user, they have the option of minimizing it using the minimize button in the top right corner of the panel to collapse the panel vertically and reduce the overall size of the application frame. Text messages are sent through the client-client socket using a ClientMessageWriter and read using a ClientMessageReader. Both classes make use of functions in the IOStreamFunctions class that encode and decode strings into specially formatted byte streams.

This functionality can be found in:
src.util.TextMessageViewer.java
src.util.ShrinkyPanel.java
src.network.ClientMessageWriter.java
src.network.ClientMessageReader.java
src.network.ClientMessageListener.java
src.network.IOStreamFunctions.java

Reader-Listener Design Pattern

Once a client-to-client communication link is created a communication protocol is set up to retrieve data from an input stream, and dispatch it to listening objects. As events are read in from the input stream by the ClientMessageReader, they are sorted by type and dispatched to any and all objects that implement the ClientMessageListener interface and have registered as listeners for client messages. A set of Listeners is maintained in the ClientMessageReader which is iterated through when a message is to be dispatched. All a Listener must do is implement a response to the message and fill in the contents of the interface method. For example, both the TextMessageViewer and the CastleGame implement the ClientMessageListener interface, and are listeners to the ClientMessageListener that handles communication between clients in a game. When any message is read by the MessageReader, it dispatches the event to both the TextMessageViewer and the CastleGame objects.

The same pattern of Reader-Listener dispatch is used by the ServerMessageReader-ServerMessageListener as well as the GameClientReaderGameClientListener sets of classes.

The relevant classes for this implementation can be found in:
src.network.ClientMessageReader.java
src.network.ClientMessageListener.java
src.util.TextMessageViewer.java
src.client.CastleGame.java

Terrain Texturing and Mapping

The terrain texturing and mapping are used not only to make the visual component of CastleGame more appealing but also to make it more challenging. Not only are there currently three different types of landscapes but there is also a water element. Areas that contain water are not allowed to be directly built-on, but one can build above them. There are also navigational textures (north, south, east, and west) to help one move their pieces, with the red grid being removable.

The terrain texturing and mapping is created randomly each time a new game is started. For the local version of the game, the texture and mapping are randomly chosen and set for the user. The game board is then created using these random values to decide what textures are used and in the case of water, and where they are placed.

For the network game, terrain texture and mapping is done only by the accepting player and the textures and mapping values are passed by to the challenging player via the client-to-client socket. Both players' board will now load with the same texture and mapping values.

The terrain landscape texture is first chosen using a random number between 0 and 9 in CastleGame. If the random number is between 0 and 3 then the texture will be grass, if it is between 4 and 7 then it will be sand, and if it is above 7 then it will be the moon. The water texture and its placement on the map are then decided. The values are then sent to Board which creates the game board using them.

The relevant classes for this implementation can be found in:
src.client.CastleGame.java
src.client.Board.java
src.client.Map.java
src.client.Letters.java

The red grid was changed to be its own separate element, that way it could be removed or added back without affecting the terrain or blocks. The grid is now created in CastleGame.java using Grid.java and set to its own branch group which is then added to the main branch group in CastleGame.

The relevant classes for this implementation can be found in:
src.client.CastleGame.java
src.client.Grid.java

Verify Gravity

One key algorithm of the game is to verify the legality of placement of blocks, following rules of gravity. Following is the major code implementing this algorithm, which is documented and self-explanatory.

```
public boolean isSupportLegal(RectBlock blk, int nWho) {
    boolean ret = false;
    ...
    // if touch the ground
    if (lowestY <= -m_nSize) {
        // create a new pile
        BlockPile newPile = new BlockPile(nWho); // The pile of blocks,
        //which pile up
        newPile.add(blk);
        vecPiles.add(newPile);
        ret = true;
    }
    // else, check further whether gravity is legal
    if (ret == false) {
        ret = checkSupportPile(vecPiles, blk);
    }
    return ret;
}
private boolean checkSupportPile(Vector vecPiles, RectBlock blk) {
    boolean suc = false;
    Vector supportPiles = getSupportPiles(vecPiles, blk);
    BlockPile mergePile = new BlockPile(supportPiles);
    if (mergePile.size() != 0 && mergePile.isPileGravityLegal(blk) == true) {
        // merge support piles
        for (int j = 0; j < supportPiles.size(); j++) {
```

```
            BlockPile supportPile = (BlockPile) supportPiles.get(j);
            for (int i = 0; i < vecPiles.size(); i++) {
                if ( (BlockPile) vecPiles.get(i) == supportPile) {
                    vecPiles.remove(i);
                }
            }
        }
        mergePile.add(blk);
        vecPiles.add(mergePile);
        suc = true;
    }
    else {
        suc = false;
    }
    return suc;
}
public boolean isPileGravityLegal(RectBlock blkPlused) {
    boolean bRet = true;
    Point3d newGravity = calGravity(blkPlused);
    // compute the rectanle of ground cell
    calGroundCellsRect();
    // if (x, z) the gravity is in the rectangle of ground cells, it won't fall down
    // NOTICE: this is a simplified algorithm
    if (m_rectGroundCells.contains(newGravity.x, newGravity.z)
    //whole gravity
    &&
    m_rectGroundCells.contains(blkPlused.m_ptGravity.x + // block gravity
    blkPlused.m_vecRef.x,
    blkPlused.m_ptGravity.z +
    blkPlused.m_vecRef.z)) {
        bRet = true;
    }
    else {
        bRet = false;
    }
    return bRet;
}
```

15.4 Summary and Future Work

We implemented a highly interactive multiplayer game through the use of many established and emerging multimedia techniques and concepts. A framework for online games of these types was discussed. By pushing the actual game play down to the clients, rather than having to communicate via only the server, we made the game more manageable on a much larger scale. The framework is not limited to this game and can be expanded upon for other games in the future.

15.5 Appendix: User Manual

Running CastleGame Client Application

To start CastleGame:

1. Go to the main CastleGame directory
2. Enter the command on the command line

   > make runclient

The game should now compile and run. Once the server is running, one should see the opening CastleGame screen.

Running CastleGame Server

To connect to the network, the server must be running. If the server is not running, one can start it by running the following commands on a specified machine (The hard-coded part 'ua56.cs.ualberta.ca' should be modified to ones specific machine name at src.client.CastleGame.java and src.server.GameServer.java):

1. Go to main CastleGame directory
2. Enter the command on the command line.

   >make runserver

The server should now compile and start.

Starting CastleGame Local Version

The local game allows two players to play against each other using only one application of CastleGame and on the same machine.

To play a local game:

1. Start the CastleGame application.
2. Click on the *Local* button (see Fig. 15.2).

The game should now load up and be ready to play.

Starting CastleGame Network Version

The network game allows you to log on to the server and challenge other users using a separate application and on a separate machine. The network version also keeps track of players' wins, losses, ties, and high score. There is also a top-ten list displayed for the current scores of registered users.

Players can then log on to the server using their own user name and password. Or, if they do not have an account, players can create a new account.

To start a network game:

1. Start the CastleGame application.
2. Click on the *Network* button (see Fig. 15.2).
3. If the server is currently running, then user will be prompted to enter user name and password. If the server is not running, then user will be informed that it is currently not started (To start the server, please see *Running CastleGame Server*).
4. If a user name and password is available, then those can be entered in the *Login screen* (Fig. 15.3, left). Otherwise, one can create an account by clicking *Create User*, entering new user name and password and clicking *Register* (Fig. 15.3, right).
5. User will then be taken to the network server screen, and can start a network game by challenging another player (see *Challenging Players*).

Challenging Players

Players can challenge other players by:

1. Selecting the player one wants to challenge by clicking on them in the Challengers list.
2. Clicking on *Challenge*
3. The other player can now accept or decline the challenge by clicking on the *Yes* or *NO* button in the Challenge Request prompt below.

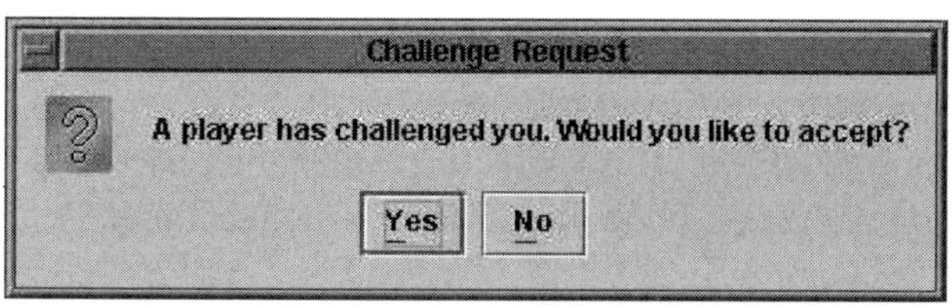

Once a challenge has been accepted, the game will load between the two players.

Playing CastleGame

Game play in CastleGame is turn based with the accepting player going first (local version will have Player 1 always starting first, see Fig. 15.5).

Selecting Ones Blocks

On a turn, a block is automatically provided. However, one can change the block by clicking the *Select Block* button (Fig. 15.5) until one gets the block (s)he desires. Note that a player has a limited number of blocks (s)he can use during the game, so players must eventually use all of their blocks.

Moving or Rotating Blocks

One can move your blocks north, south, east, and west around the board to wherever one wants to place them. To move blocks, a player can use either the navigational control panel to the right of the screen (Fig. 15.5) or the keyboard.

One can also rotate pieces along the x-axis, y-axis, and z-axis so suit needs for placing them. Like moving blocks, one can use either the navigational control panel on the right of the screen or the keyboard.

Here are the navigational control panel buttons and their keyboard equivalents.

- Rotate your piece along x-axis: RotateX button / X button
- Rotate your piece along y-axis: RotateY button / Y button
- Rotate your piece along z-axis: RotateZ button / Z arrow
- Move your piece Up: UP Button / Page Up
- Move your piece Down: DOWN button / Page Down
- Move your piece North: NORTH button / up arrow
- Move your piece South: SOUTH button / down arrow
- Move your piece West: WEST button / left arrow
- Move your piece East: East button / right arrow

Rotating and Zooming in on Map

To assist in placing blocks, CastleGame supports the ability to rotate or zoom in and out on the map. Rotating and zooming in and out on the map can be done using either the navigational terrain panel buttons (Fig. 15.5) or the mouse.

Here are the navigational terrain panel buttons and the mouse commands.

- Rotate the board right: Right button / Right click and drag right
- Rotate the board left: Left button / Right click and drag left
- Move the board up: Up button / Left click and drag up
- Move the board down: Down button / Left click and drag down
- Zoom in on board: Front Button / hold control, right click, and drag down

• Zoom out on board: Back Button / hold control, right click, and drag up

Turning Off Map Grid

Some people may find the grid on the board to be not useful or even irritating. To remove it, simply uncheck the checkbox *Map Grid* (Fig. 15.5) in the control panel on the right of the game board. To turn the grid back on simply check the checkbox *Map Grid* (Fig. 15.5) in the control panel on the right of the game board.

Sending a Text Message

This option is only available for the network CastleGame. Text messaging is a great way to converse during a game.

To send a text message:

1. Type in your text message in the text box just below the game board.
2. Click the *send* button.
3. The message should now appear in the text message board for both players, as shown below.

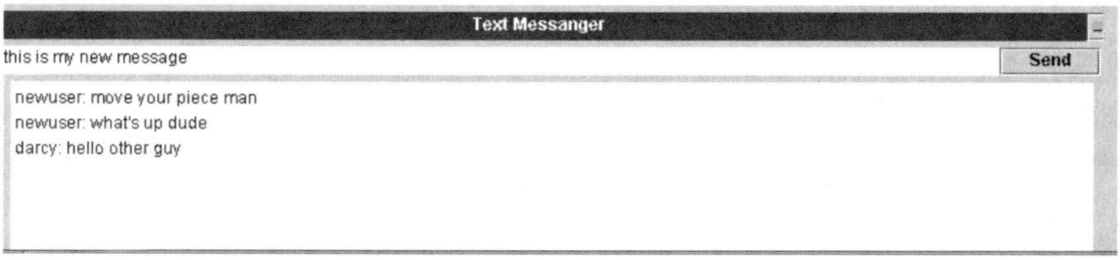

Minimizing or Maximizing the Text Message Area

One can also maximize or minimize the text message area of the screen. To do this, click on the minimize button to the right of the text box. The text messenger box should now not appear in the GUI.

To make the text message box reappear, click on the enlarge icon to the right of the now minimized text messenger. The text messenger will now appear back in the GUI.

Help Menu

CastleGame also contains a help menu, shown below, that is accessible throughout the entire application. To open the help menu, click on the

Help button on either the opening screen, the game screen, or the network screen. A help menu will now appear supporting a variety of information about the game and how to play it.

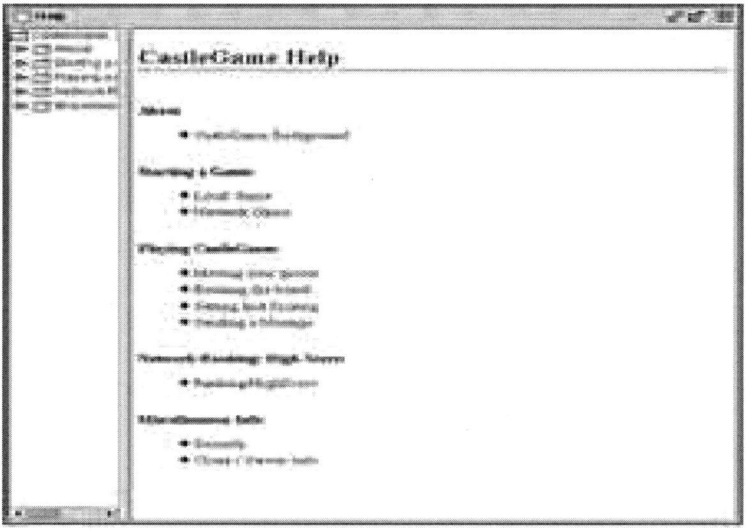

Chapter 16

A Networked Multiplayer Java3D Game — Siege

E. Benner, J. Kostek, L. Ying and A. Basu

16.1 Introduction

In this chapter, we design and implement a networked multiplayer game — siege using Java3D. Many 3D game technologies by Java and Java3D, such as loading 3D model OBJ files, constructing terrain, networking, and collision detection, are involved. By studying the source code of the game, one can learn to use most of Java3D programming skills to implement a practical networked 3D game.

16.2 Game Design and User Manual

Game Objective

The idea behind Siege is to protect your tower from attacks by other players while at the same time using your own siege weapons to destroy others' towers. Siege is based on a 1983 board game called Crossbows and Catapults by Base Toys.

16.3 User Manual

The game of Siege can be started by typing "java NetLogin." This will start the network screen (Fig. 16.1). In Microsoft Windows, this can be done by double clicking the "Siege.bat" file. Once the network screen is started it can be used to host or join a game of Siege.

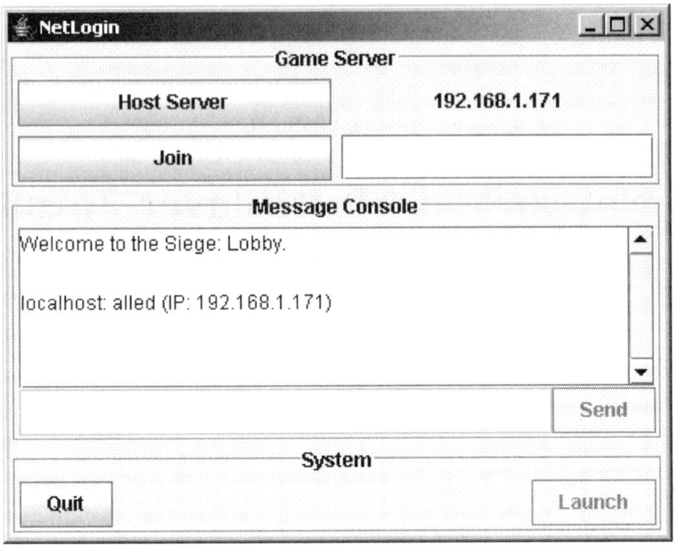

Fig. 16.1 Initial network screen.

Hosting a game of Siege is done by simply clicking the "Host Server" button and selecting the user name the host will use in the game. Joining a game is similar, but requires that the user input the IP or the name of the host they wish to join. Once these data are entered the user can join the game indicated by the address by clicking join and selecting a name the user wishes to use in the game. To start the game as a client, click ready; or as a host, click the launch button after all users are ready. Once a game has two or more players, they may "chat" from this window by typing their message in the dialogue box at the bottom of the window and clicking the send button.

Building Castles

In this section of the game, we discuss how players can build their castles (Fig. 16.2). The building strategy should be focused on protecting the player's own tower. The castle is built on a 10×10 grid and must be completed within one minute. The player moves objects on the grid by clicking the left mouse button and dragging. Dragging upward moves an object backward and dragging downward moves the object forwards. Dragging left moves an object left on the grid, and dragging right moves the object right on the grid. The view can be rotated any time during

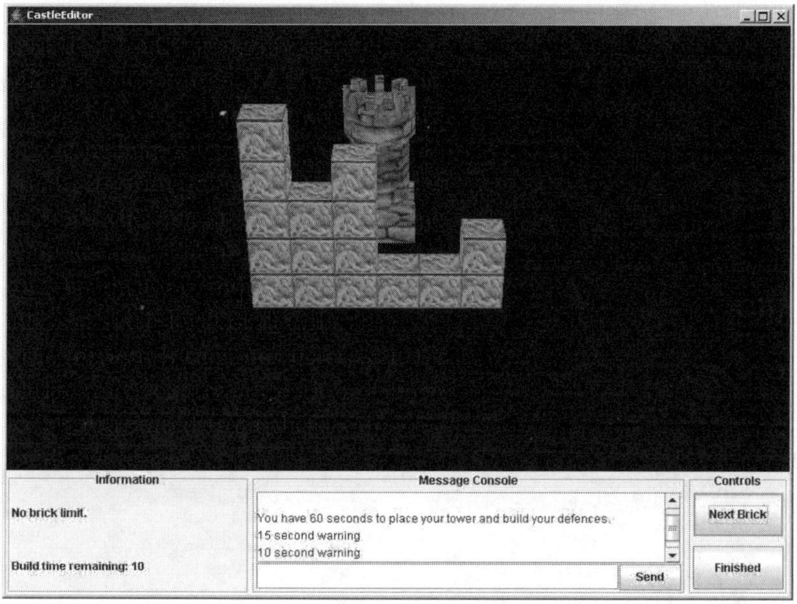

Fig. 16.2 Building castles.

building by clicking the right mouse button and dragging. The controls are automatically updated to suit the viewing angle (*i.e.*, an upward drag always moves back on the grid). Players can also chat inside the castle editor by typing text into the dialogue at the bottom of the screen and typing send.

To build a castle a user must first choose the position of his or her tower. The tower's starting position is at the center of the grid; however, it may be moved by clicking and dragging the left mouse to a desired position. Once the user has placed the tower it may not be moved again. It is important to note that the starting view looks at the front of the castle.

Once the tower is placed in its final location, bricks may be laid to protect it. The user may lay as many bricks as possible within the one-minute time limit. Bricks can be created by clicking the Add Brick button or by clicking the middle mouse button. Once a brick is added it can be moved to its final location by clicking and dragging the left mouse. The next brick will always be added on top of the last brick placed. Once a brick is laid it cannot be moved later.

If a player completes building their castle before the one-minute time limit is reached they may click ready to indicate to the server that they are finished. If other players have not yet completed their castles, the player will need to wait for them before continuing. When all other players have also completed building their castles, the game will begin.

Playing Siege

Figure 16.3 shows the screenshot of the main game screen. Siege will place all castles opposite to one another and two siege weapons beside each castle. Once the positions of all the players have been determined, the game begins. Players can change their views by right clicking and dragging at any time.

Fig. 16.3 Screenshot of main game screen.

Siege Weapons

Each player is provided with two siege weapons. The weapons share common controls. The arrow keys move the weapons. The left and right arrows rotate the weapon. The up and down arrow move it forward and backward. To fire a weapon the player must press and hold the space bar. The weapon powers up while the space bar is depressed. This can be observed by the animation of the weapon being fired on screen. Once the shot has sufficient power, it can be fired by releasing the space bar. If a shot goes over the target, the power needs to be reduced. If a shot does not make it to the target the power needs to be increased. Both weapons take 6 seconds to reload.

The first of the two weapons is the Trebuche. The Trebuche uses a giant counter weight to fire its projectile. A shot from the Trebuche is fired as a lob, possibly at great distances. Although this weapon is harder to aim, it can inflict higher damage on opponent towers. It can also avoid enemy defenses by landing right on top of its target. The Trebuche is selected by pressing 1.

The other weapon is the Hammer. This weapon fires by smashing its projectile into enemy walls with a gigantic hammer. This weapon can rip clean through walls by firing low and hard. This weapon is easy to aim but cannot clear brick walls, it must break right through them. The Hammer is selected by pressing 2.

Winning a Game

To win a game a player must destroy his or her opponents' towers while preserving their own. Once a player's tower is destroyed, the player is removed from the active game and may only continue as an observer. Each tower can sustain several blows before it is destroyed. The owner of the last tower is declared the winner.

16.4 Technologies, Algorithms and Data Structures

Wave Front OBJ Files

The models used in Siege are in Wave Front OBJ format. The animation of these objects is done in real time. These models for the weapons are built in parts and assembled into a game. Following is the main code of loading an OBJ file in JAVA3D (in Hammer.java).

```
private Scene scene; //The Model subtree
private ObjectFile hammerBody; //The body model
hammerBody = new ObjectFile();
hammerBody.setFlags (ObjectFile.RESIZE |
ObjectFile.TRIANGULATE | ObjectFile.STRIPIFY);
scene = hammerBody.load(new String("data/hammerBody.obj"));
```

Terrain

The terrain in Siege follows a Quad Tree data structure providing a number of levels of detail. The terrain is built recursively from an 8-bit grey scale bitmap (height map) and a 24-bit environment map (texture map). The heights are calculated from the bitmap where white represents terrain of higher altitude and black indicates terrain of low altitude. Shades of grey represent heights in between. Since the height map is 8-bit, the terrain can represent 256 different height levels. The terrain used in the game is constructed from a $256 \times 256 \times 8$ height map and provides 8 levels of detail. The game by default uses only the sixth level of detail.

The weapon models fully adapt to the terrain as they move across it by sampling four height values in the positive and negative direction of both the X and Z-axes. The models are tilted and rotated from these values to suit to conditions of the terrain as they drive over it.

Collision Detection

Collision detection in Siege was implemented using hierarchical bounding volumes to improve efficiency. To avoid a large number of unneeded calculations, collisions were considered on the following basis. Collisions were detected only for fired projectiles. Collision detection first only detects collisions with other players' grids. Once a projectile has been verified to be inside a player's grid is it tested against all bricks inside that grid. This avoids the cost of calculating collisions with all bricks, and for all players, for each projectile.

The collisions are detected using bounding volumes. Collision with the individual bricks is computed using a bounding sphere, and collision with the tower is derived with a bounding cylinder.

Networking

Networking in the Siege game is supported using a Client/Server architecture. The server manages all the information and keeps all clients consistent.

Networking in Siege is kept to a minimal level. Bytes are used for most information passed across the network. Initialization is performed by transferring only a starting position and a direction vector. The physical simulations are then computed independently on each client to avoid constant coordinate updates. Collision detection is performed only on the server to ensure consistency and fairness across the network.

16.5 Appendix: Source Code Description

	File Name	Descriptions
GUI		
	NetLogin.java	Responsible for initalizing network services by allowing the player the option of either hosting a server or joining an existing server as a client. This class also provides the needed GUI for player chat and launch synchronization. • The main entry of the game.
	CastleEditor.java	The interface of building castle
	SiegeGame.java	The main game interface
Networking		
	Client.java	Responsible for communication with the server. This class contains all the network communication code for the client side.
	Server.java	Server is responsible for opening a socket and listening for client connections. Every time a client connects to the server, a ClientConnection object is created to manage communication with the client. Server is also the central class for synchronizing player states and network communication between all clients.
	ClientConnection.java	Responsible for communication with the client. This class contains all the network communication code for the server side and acts as an intermediate layer between the Server and Client objects.

	File Name	Descriptions
Game Status		
	Player.java	Manages player states for all clients connected to the server including the server itself. Contains the player's id, name, weapons (trebuche & hammer), their projectile ammunition, as well as the castle structure and the tower's health.
3D Elements		
	Castle.java	Represents a player's castle. Built on a 10×10 grid. Composed of a series of Bricks and one Tower object. The tower and brick location is relative to the center of the grid in the Castle Editor, and is absolute once a real-time game has started.
	Tower.java	Represents the tower portion of the castle. Used for the geometry only in the real time game. The coordinates are only used for placement in the Castle Editor.
	Brick.java	Brick.
	BrickShape.java	Represents the geometry of a brick.
	Terrain.java	Uses a Quad Tree data structure to represent terrain using Java3D. 8-bit black and white Bitmaps are used for height information (height maps). Supports up to 8 different Levels of Detail for a $256 \times 256 \times 8$ Bitmap.
	Hammer.java	The class for the Hammer weapon that performs animation and rendering services.

	File Name	Descriptions
	Trebuche.java	The class for the Trebuche weapon that performs animation and rendering services.
	Projectile.java	The class for projectile.
Class Interface		
	Weapon.java	A simple interface for the different weapons. Implemented by Hammer.-java and Trebuche.java.
	Communication.java	A simple interface for the two different network sides, to permit generic treatment of the communication protocols. Implemented by Client.java and Server.java.
	Console.java	Simple interface for printing console messages. Implemented by NetLogin, CastleEditor and the real-time class of the game.
Misc		
	Bitmap.java	A 8-bit Grayscale Bitmap Image.
	QuadTree.java	A Quad Tree Data Structure. Each node of the tree, that is not a root, has four children.
	QuadNode.java	A node on a Quad Tree. If a Quad Node is not a leaf node it has four children.
	GameCanvas.java	The specified Canvas3D class extending Canvas3D.
	DefaultConsole.java	Simply uses System.out to print messages to standard output.

Chapter 17

Collaborative Online 3D Editing

I. Cheng, M. Bates and A. Basu

17.1 Introduction and Related Work

Fig. 17.1 (from left to right) Zoomage3D scanning device, a 1 ft tall nut-cracker toy and a 18,720 polygon mesh of the toy.

In this chapter we describe software that multiple users can use over the Internet to collaboratively and simultaneously edit 3D objects. 3D editing can be useful for correcting inaccurately scanned vertices, such as with a 3D scanner that can be used to create texture and mesh (Fig. 17.1). Collaborative 3D editing can also be used by digital artists and graphic designers to interactively create new 3D content starting with existing models.

There are other collaborative 3D products but they are designed for different applications. CoCreate's OneSpace [CoCreate (2002)] is a software package that provides a way to have online meetings that discuss a 3D object. This software includes meeting management features like meeting planning, and automatic generation of meeting reports. It does allow editing of the object being discussed. However, the OneSpace meeting is not web based. SolidWorks' "eDrawings" [SolidWorks (2002a)], and "SolidWorks Viewer" [SolidWorks (2006b)] are 3d viewers, and do not allow manipulation of the shape of the object. "3D Instant Website" [SolidWorks (2006a)] creates a website to display a particular object, the generated site has the standard 3D display tools (zoom, rotate, *etc.*), but again does not allow editing of the object. The Pointshop 3D software [Zwicker *et al.* (2002)] proposes a set of point based surface editing tools; however, this work cannot be used in an online collaborative environment. In contrast, the Zoomage Online Collaborative Editor (ZOCE) is a small web based applet that not only allows a client to view a 3D object, but also allows multiple clients to simultaneously edit the same 3D object via a Java applet. While [CoCreate (2002)] and SolidWorks [SolidWorks (2002b)] use AutoCAD type objects, ZOCE maintains range data captured from actual objects; preserving both realistic geometric and texture information on an object.

17.2 Description of the System

In order to allow flexibility, either texture maps or mesh representations can be edited at a client site. To assist the choosing of a direction in which to move a vertex, an Edit Bar is available. This bar is pivoted at the selected vertex, and can be rotated around this vertex. To change the location of a vertex a user simply orients the bar to the desired position then clicks on the bar at a location where the vertex needs to be moved to.

Figures 17.2 and 17.3 show different stages of the editing process. Clients can choose either a texture or mesh view. Modified data is instantaneously updated at the server. Other clients can see the revised model within seconds. At present, we maintain a central data repository and allow an unlimited number of clients to edit an object simultaneously. 3D objects of standard formats can be added to the central database.

17.3 Summary

The preliminary implementation allows only a single vertex to be edited by a user at any instant of time. In the next stage we will allow the user to define a local region that can be collectively modified by the editing process. Region based editing will require the identification of faces that need to be

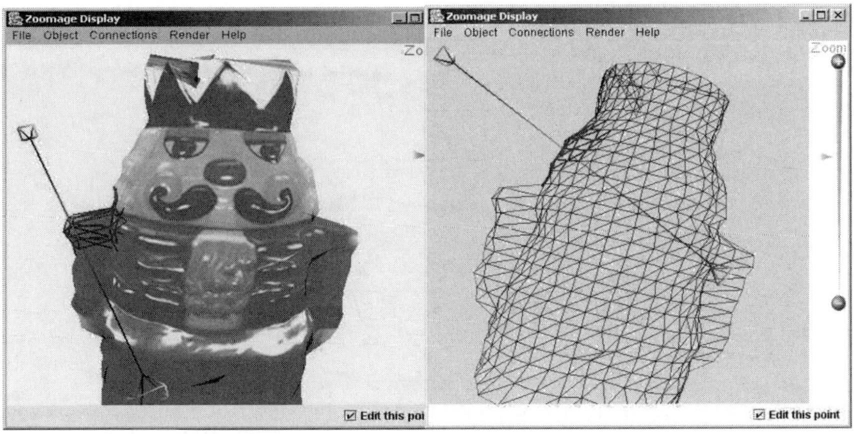

Fig. 17.2 Start of editing: Client 1 (left) wants to modify shoulder, while Client 2 (right) wants to modify head.

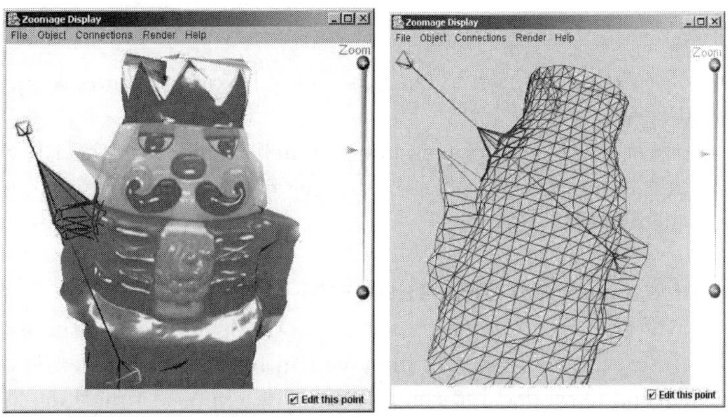

Fig. 17.3 Modifications on client sites during the editing process. Note that changes made at one site are reflected at all sites.

"locked" during modification (Fig. 17.4); an issue we are currently working on.

17.4 Using RMI for Collaborative 3D Editing

RMI can be used to create a system where multiple users can simultaneously modify the same object from distributed locations. Each user can edit the

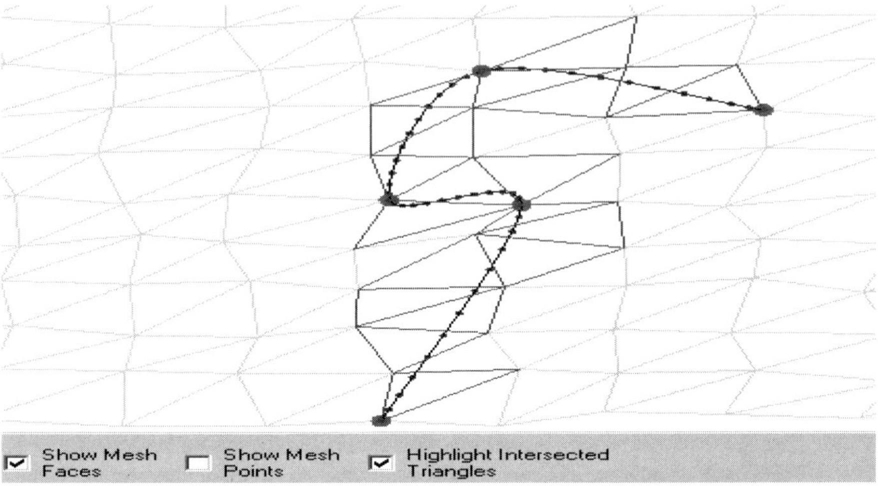

Fig. 17.4 Faces identified as intersecting a spline curve being used for smoothing boundaries of a 3D scan.

geometry of a 3D object, while changes made by other users are applied in almost real-time.

The purpose of this chapter is not to teach Remote Method Invocation (RMI), rather it describes a possible strategy to implementing a collaborative editor using RMI.

Review of Remote Method Invocation (RMI)

The server program exposes a set of methods. These methods are defined in an interface that extends the java.rmi.Remote interface. The clients can then use the extended interface to call the exposed functions.

Once the server is running, communications from the client to the server is as simple as calling a method on an object. Following is a detailed example.

Interface:

```
public interface RMI_Interface extends java.rmi.Remote {
  void setNumber(int n) throws java.rmi.RemoteException;
  int getNumberSquared() throws java.rmi.RemoteException;
}
```

Server:

```
import java.rmi.*;
import java.rmi.server.*;
public class RMI_Server extends UnicastRemoteObject implements
    RMI_Interface{
    private int number_from_client = 0;
    public void setNumber(int num) throws RemoteException{
        number_from_client = num;
    }
    public int getNumberSquared() throws RemoteException{
        return number_from_client * number_from_client;
    }
    public RMI_Server() throws RemoteException{
        try {
            // Bind this object instance to the name "theServer"
            Naming.rebind("//localhost/theServer", this);
            System.out.println("Server bound in registry");
        } catch (Exception e) {
            System.out.println("RMI_Server error");
        }
    }
    public static void main(String[] args) {
        try{
            new RMI_Server();
        } catch(Exception e){
            // exception
            System.out.println("ERROR "+ e.getMessage());
        }
    }
}
```

Client:

```
public class Client{
    public static void main(String[] args) {
        String rmiPath = "//localhost/theServer";
        try {
            RMI_Interface server
            =(RMI_Interface)java.rmi.Naming.lookup(rmiPath);
            try{
                server.setNumber(5);
                int sq_num = server.getNumberSquared();
                /* sq_num now equals 25 */
```

```
            System.out.println("Number Squared: "+sq_num);
        } catch (java.rmi.RemoteException e){
            // error communicating with the remote host
            System.out.println("RemoteException "+ e.getMessage());
        }
    } catch (Exception ex){
        // handle exception
        System.out.println("Exception "+ ex.getMessage());
    }
  }
}
```

To compile and run the above example the following commands are needed:

Compile java source javac *.java
RMI compile rmic RMI_Server
Run the RMI registry rmiregistry
Run the server java RMI_Server
Run the client java Client

RMI and Collaborative 3D Editing

RMI is easy to setup and use, but since only the server is exposing methods, all communication must be initiated by the client programs. This means when geometry data is changed by one client the other clients cannot be automatically notified of the change by the server. The clients will not know of the change until they specifically ask the server, this in turn means each client must poll the server and ask for updates on a regular basis. For this application a polling interval of 5 seconds was chosen as a balance between server load and usability.

All data transferred between client and server must be serializable, including the texture information, 3d object data, and update information.

The client and server have certain responsibilities. Besides user interaction, the client's responsibilities are focused on initiating data exchanges with the server. The Server's responsibilities are more focused on maintaining the current state of information.

Client Responsibilities

- Retrieve list of available 3D objects from server
- Retrieve user specified 3D objects from the server

- Ask server for updated object information
- Inform server when user changes the object

Server Responsibilities

- Maintain the following lists
  - List of clients currently connected
  - For each object, a list of the clients viewing / modifying it
  - Know the current state of each client via a queue of updates still to be applied for each client
- Provide a list of available objects to the clients
- Provide objects to clients when requested
- Provide updates to the clients

Let's first look at the client program, and its client-server communications, the program execution follows this flow chart:

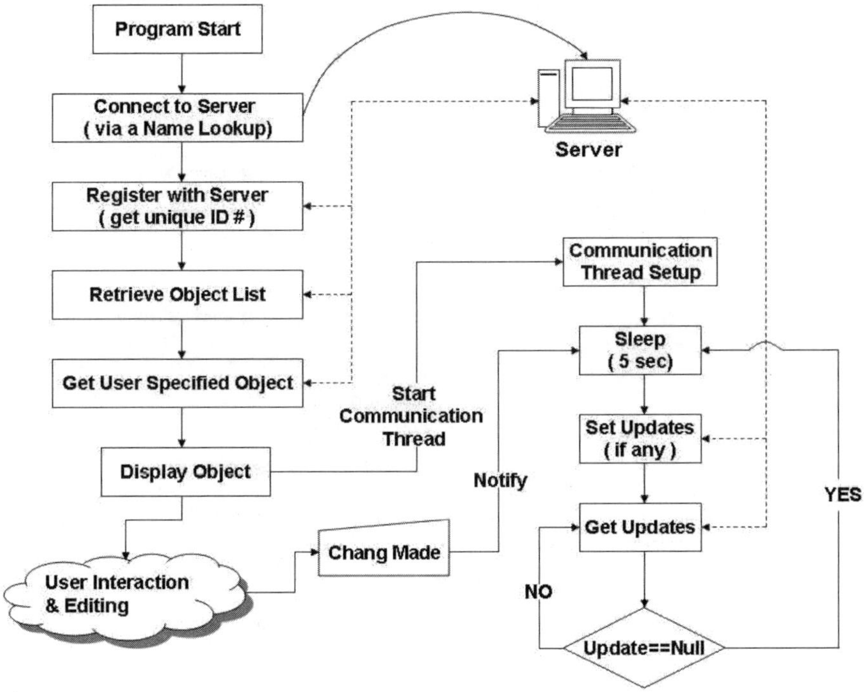

After initialization the server on the other hand only has 2 states, service client, and wait for client communication. But handling the server's responsibility is more complicated. The server has the following class structure:

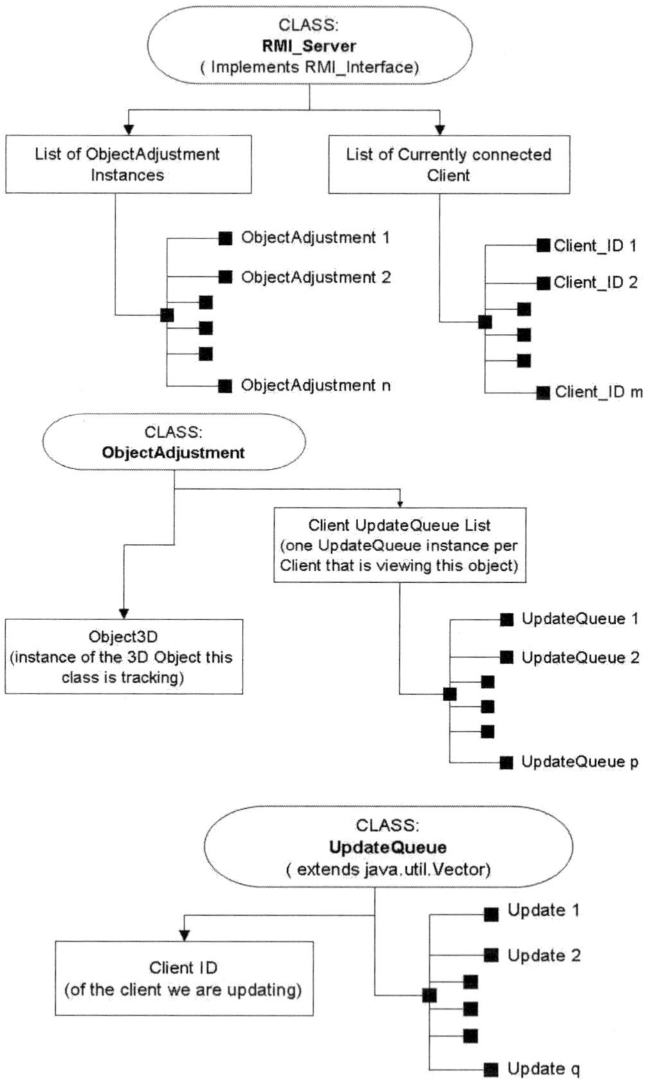

Each instance of the ObjectAdjustment contains the 3D object it will be handling. It also has a hash table with an UpdateQueue for each of the clients that are currently editing this object. The rmi_Server passes all update sets and requests directly to the ObjectAdjustment instance that is responsible for the affected object. When a client sends an update, the ObjectAdjustment applies the adjustment to the object, and then adds the update object to the UpdateQueue for each of the other clients currently viewing this object. When a client requests an update, the first item from the queue is returned to the client. The client will then call back for another update, this repeats until no more updates are available and null is returned. For more information, see the code listings at the end of this chapter.

Other Information:

The Server in this example is not multi-threaded; this means while the server is dealing with one client, all others must wait.

Since multiple clients could be modifying the same 3D point at the same time, a process of locking a point before modifying it should be provided.

Code Listings:

Not all of the code is listed here, only parts that are relative to the RMI communications discussed in this chapter are listed.

Interface:

RMI_Interface.java

```
// define the functions that are to be available remotely
import java.rmi.RemoteException;
public interface RMI_Interface extends java.rmi.Remote {
    // A client wants to register and be added to the client list.
    // return the client ID if the registration was successful
    String registerClient(java.net.InetAddress ip)
                        throws RemoteException;
    //A client wants to unregister and be removed to the client list.
    void unregisterClient(String ID) throws RemoteException;
    //A client wants the list of available objects
    String[] getObjectList() throws RemoteException;
    // A client wants an object returned to them
    Object3D getObject(String client, String filename)
                        throws RemoteException;
    // A client is done with the object they have been editing,
    // and needs to be removed from that object update list.
```

```
    void finishedWithObject(String client, int objectID)
                        throws RemoteException;
    // A client wants to update the object they are working on,
    // so let them
    void setUpdate(UpdateItem update, String client, int objectID)
                        throws RemoteException;
    // A client wants to get an update for the object
    // they are working on
    UpdateItem getUpdate(String client, int objectID)
                        throws RemoteException;
}
```

Client Classes:

Client.java

```
public class Client{
    // majority of Client code here is not relevant to the chapter.
    ...
    // this is the RMI object, that allows us to call remote methods
    public RMI_Interface rmi = null;
    // this is the key for this client.
    public String rmiKey = null;
    // Given a host this will attempt to setup the RMI object,
    // to allow remote function calls
    public boolean setupRMI(String host){
        String rmiPath = "//"+host+"/RMIServer";
        try{
            // get our IP address (so we can tell the server)
            java.net.InetAddress localaddr =
                java.net.InetAddress.getLocalHost();
            // get a reference to the server
            rmi = (RMI_Interface)java.rmi.Naming.lookup(rmiPath);
            // call the register method on the server
            rmiKey = rmi.registerClient(localaddr);
            if (rmiKey == null) return false;
            // Connected... enable GUI
            ...
            return true;
        }catch (Exception e){
            // exception connecting to the host.
        }
        return false;
    }
    // We are done with this server... unregister and finish
```

```
    public void removeRMI(){
        try{
            if(rmi != null){
                rmi.unregisterClient(rmiKey);
                rmi = null;
            }
        }catch (Exception e){
            // error unregistering
        }
        // Disconnected... disable GUI
        ...
    }
    // open file from the server
    private void openFromServer(){
        try{
            // get filelist from server
            String list[] = rmi.getObjectList();
            // display list
            if (list == null){
                // The server does not have any objects available
                return;
            }
            // get selection
            String selected = (String)JOptionPane.showInputDialog(
                null,
                "Choose an object to load:",
                "Select object",
                JOptionPane.INFORMATION_MESSAGE,
                null,list, list[0]);
            if (selected == null) return;
            // get object from the server
            Object3D o3d = rmi.getObject(rmiKey,selected);
            if (o3d != null) {o3d.setPath(null);}
            //create new thread
            Communication comm = new Communication(rmiKey, rmi, o3d);
            // the comm thread is started by the scene class after
            // the object is displayed.
            // display object
            scene3d.changeObject(o3d, comm);
        }catch(java.rmi.RemoteException ex){
            // An error occured trying to exchange
            // information with the server
        }
    }
}
```

Communication.java

```
// Provide an interface between a remotely loaded object and
// the server to track changes
public class Communication extends java.lang.Thread {
    // the rmi interface with the server
    RMI_Interface rmi = null;
    // a reference to the object that is being edited
    Object3D object = null;
    // a representation of a change made
    UpdateItem update = null;
    // the id of the object (assigned by the server)
    int objectID = -1;
    // The unique identifier of this client
    String rmiKey = null;
    // should this thread exit
    boolean done = false;
    // how long the thread should sleep between checking for updates
    long sleepTime = 5000;
    // the time the last update was checked
    long lastUpdateCheck = 0;
    // Create a new comm thread
    public Communication(String rmiKey,
                RMI_Interface rmi,
                Object3D o3d)
            throws java.lang.IllegalArgumentException{
        this.rmi = rmi;
        this.rmiKey = rmiKey;
        if(o3d == null) throw new
            IllegalArgumentException("null object");
        object = o3d;
        if(o3d.objectID == -1) throw new
            IllegalArgumentException("Bad object ID");
        objectID = o3d.objectID;
    }
    // cleanup, before finishing with the remote object
    public void cleanUp(){
        // we are finished with this object.
        object.finished();
        object = null;
        try{
            rmi.finishedWithObject(rmiKey, objectID);
        }catch (Exception e){}
    }
    // checks for updates periodically and sends updates to the server.
    public void run() {
```

```
    this.lastUpdateCheck = System.currentTimeMillis();
    while(!done) {
        try{
            synchronized(this){
            this.wait(sleepTime);
            }
        }catch (Exception e){
            //EXCEPTION
        }
        if(!done){
            setUpdate();
            getUpdate();
        }
    }
}
// Tries to retrieve an update from the server, then makes
// the necessary changes to the local object if needed
public void getUpdate(){
    // dont do premature updates
    long now = System.currentTimeMillis();
    long time = now - this.lastUpdateCheck;
    if(time < sleepTime) return;
    this.lastUpdateCheck = now;
    // check if an update needs to be sent first
    if (update != null) setUpdate();
    try{
        // check if there is an update available
        update = rmi.getUpdate(rmiKey, objectID);
        while ((update != null) && (!done)){
            // got an update... make the changes
            object.updateGeometry(update);
            // check if there is another update available
            update = rmi.getUpdate(rmiKey, objectID);
        }
    }catch (java.rmi.RemoteException e){
        // communitation error
    }
}
// if this user has made a change to the object
// we need to tell the server
public synchronized void setUpdate(){
    // if there is nothing to set, then go back
    if (update == null) return;
    try{
        // we have and update, send it to the server.
```

```
            rmi.setUpdate(update, rmiKey, objectID);
            // set... delete the update
            update = null;
        }catch (java.rmi.RemoteException e){
            // communitation error
        }
    }
}
```

Server Classes:

RMI_Server.java

```
// This class provides the implimentation of thr RMI interface.
// This is the class that is run to start the server
import java.rmi.RemoteException;
import java.rmi.RMISecurityManager;
import java.rmi.server.UnicastRemoteObject;
import java.rmi.Naming;
import javax.swing.*;
public class RMI_Server extends UnicastRemoteObject
            implements RMI_Interface{
    //——— PRIVATE DATA AND METHODS ————-
    // the address of this host
    static String thisHost = "localhost";
    // the list of available files
    private JComboBox availableFilesList = null;
    // the curent number of registered clients
    private int numClients = 0;
    // A hashtable of all the currently registered clients
    private Hashtable clients = null;
    // A vector to hold the objects (via an ObjectAdjustments)
    private Vector objectAdj = null;
    // finished... remove this server from the naming lookup
    public void unbindAndExit(){
        try {
            Naming.unbind("//"+thisHost+"/RMIServer");
        }catch (Exception e){}
        availableFilesList = null;
        clients = null;
        objectAdj = null;
    }
    // Initialize this server.
    public RMI_Server(String[] fileList) throws RemoteException {
        clients = new Hashtable();
        objectAdj = new Vector();
```

```
    try {
        // Bind this server instance to the name "RMIServer"
        Naming.rebind("//"+thisHost+"/RMIServer", this);
        // RMI Server bound in registry
        for(int j=0;
            ((fileList != null)&&(j < fileList.length));
            j++){
            openFile(fileList[j]);
        }
    } catch (Exception e) {
        //RMI_Server error
    }
}
// Other private methods not listed
//...
//———————— PUBLIC METHODS ————————
// A client wants to register and be added to the client list.
public String registerClient(java.net.InetAddress ip)
                    throws RemoteException {
    String time = ""+System.currentTimeMillis();
    //("#register request from: "+ip + "at time: "+time)
    boolean inTable = clients.contains(time);
    if (inTable){
        // the client has already registered
        return null;
    }
    else{
        // the client is not yet in the list.. add it
        clients.put(time,ip);
        numClients++;
    }
    // return the time as the client unique ID
    return time;
}
// A client wants to unregister and be removed to the client list.
public void unregisterClient(String ID) throws RemoteException {
    boolean inTable = clients.containsKey(ID);
    if (inTable){
        // the client is registered
        clients.remove(ID);
        numClients–;
    }
}
//A client wants the list of available objects
public String[] getObjectList() throws RemoteException{
```

```
    int numItems = this.availableFilesList.getItemCount();
    if (numItems == 0) return null;
    String str[] = new String[numItems];
    for(int i= 0; i< numItems; i++){
        str[i] = (String)this.availableFilesList.getItemAt(i);
    }
    return str;
}
// A client wants an object returned to them
public Object3D getObject(String clientID, String name)
            throws RemoteException{
    int numItems = this.availableFilesList.getItemCount();
    if (numItems == 0) return null;
    // find the appropriate item in the list of available objects
    for(int i= 0; i< numItems; i++){
        if(name.equals((String)
            this.availableFilesList.getItemAt(i))){
            // return the appropriate object
            ObjectAdjustments oa =
                (ObjectAdjustments) this.objectAdj.get(i);
            Object3D o3d = oa.addClient(clientID);
            return o3d;
        }
    }
    return null;
}
// A client is done with the object they have been editing,
// and needs to be removed from that object update list.
public void finishedWithObject(String client, int objectID)
            throws RemoteException{
    ((ObjectAdjustments)this.objectAdj.get(objectID)).
                removeClient(client);
}
// A client wants to update the object they are working on,
// so let them
public void setUpdate(UpdateItem update,
            String client,
            int objectID) throws RemoteException{
    // tell the object adjustments about the update.
    ObjectAdjustments oa =
        (ObjectAdjustments)objectAdj.elementAt(objectID);
    oa.addUpdate(client, update);
}
// A client wants to get an update for the object they
// are working on... so let them
```

```
    public UpdateItem getUpdate(String client, int objectID)
                throws RemoteException{
        // tell the object adjustments about the update.
        ObjectAdjustments oa =
            (ObjectAdjustments)objectAdj.elementAt(objectID);
        return oa.getUpdate(client);
    }
}
```

ObjectAdjustments.java

```
//- Contains an object for users to make changes to
//- Maintains a list of all the clients editing this object
//- Every time an update is made this class
// updates each client's queue
import java.util.*;
public class ObjectAdjustments {
    // The object for users to edit
    Object3D object = null;
    // the queues for each clients
    Hashtable clientQueues = null;
    // Initialize the client Queue and set the object
    public ObjectAdjustments(Object3D o3d) {
        this.object = o3d;
        this.clientQueues = new Hashtable();
    }
    // A client wishes to participate in editing this object,
    // return the object to them.
    public Object3D addClient(String client){
        UpdateQueue q = new UpdateQueue(client);
        this.clientQueues.put(client,q);
        return object;
    }
    // A client wishes to no longer participate in editing this object
    public void removeClient(String client){
        UpdateQueue q = (UpdateQueue) this.clientQueues.remove(client);
        q = null;
    }
    // A client wishes to update this object
    public void addUpdate(String client, UpdateItem item){
        if (!item.valid()) return;
        object.updateGeometry(item);
        // go through all the elements, add the update to all
        // but the one that sent the message.
        Enumeration e = this.clientQueues.keys();
```

```
        for( ;e.hasMoreElements(); ){
            String key = (String)e.nextElement();
            if(! key.equals(client)){
                ((UpdateQueue)this.clientQueues.get(key)).add(item);
            }
        }
    }
    // A client wants an update if one is available
    public UpdateItem getUpdate(String client){
        UpdateQueue q = (UpdateQueue)this.clientQueues.get(client);
        return q.getUpdate();
    }
}
```

UpdateQueue.java

```
// Maintains a queue of updates for a specific client
public class UpdateQueue extends java.util.Vector{
    // the id of the client for which this queue belongs to
    String client = null;
    // Initialize this queue
    public UpdateQueue(String client) {
        super();
        this.client = client;
    }
    // An update has been made, we must add it to the queue
    public boolean add(UpdateItem item){
        if(!item.valid()) return false;
        // update the queue
        this.add((Object)item);
        return true;
    }
    // An update has been requested, if one is available, then send it.
    public UpdateItem getUpdate(){
        if (this.elementCount == 0) return null;
        // get the update from the list
        return (UpdateItem)this.remove(0);
    }
}
```

Common to Client & Server:

Other than UpdateItem, Object3D (not listed) should also be serializable, and common both to the client and server, since it will be shared via RMI.

UpdateItem.java

```
// represents a change made to an object, can be easily transmitted
// to and from a remote server.
import java.io.*;
public class UpdateItem implements Serializable {
    // The index of the specific point that was changed
    int point = -1;
    // the vertex's new location
    float newLoc[] = null;
    // Creates a new update
    public UpdateItem(int changedPoint, float verts[], int offset) {
        point = changedPoint;
        newLoc = new float[3];
        for(int i = 0; i<3; i++){
            newLoc[i] = verts[i+offset];
        }
    }
    // returns the point of this update
    public int getMinorUpdatePoint(){
        if(fullUpdate()) return -1;
        return point;
    }
    // returns the point position for this update
    public float[] getUpdateValue(){
        return this.newLoc;
    }
}
```

References

CoCreate (2002). Onespace, URL `www.cocreate.com`.

SolidWorks (2002a). edrawings — 2D CAD and 3D CAD viewer and publisher, URL `solidworks.com/edrawings`.

SolidWorks (2002b). Solidworks, URL `www.solidworks.com`.

SolidWorks (2006a). 3D instant website, `solidworks.com/3dinstantwebsite`.

SolidWorks (2006b). Solidworks viewer, URL `www.solidworks.com/swdocs`.

Zwicker, M., Pauly, M., Knoll, O. and Gross, M. (2002). Pointshop 3D, in *SIGGRAPH*, pp. 322–329.